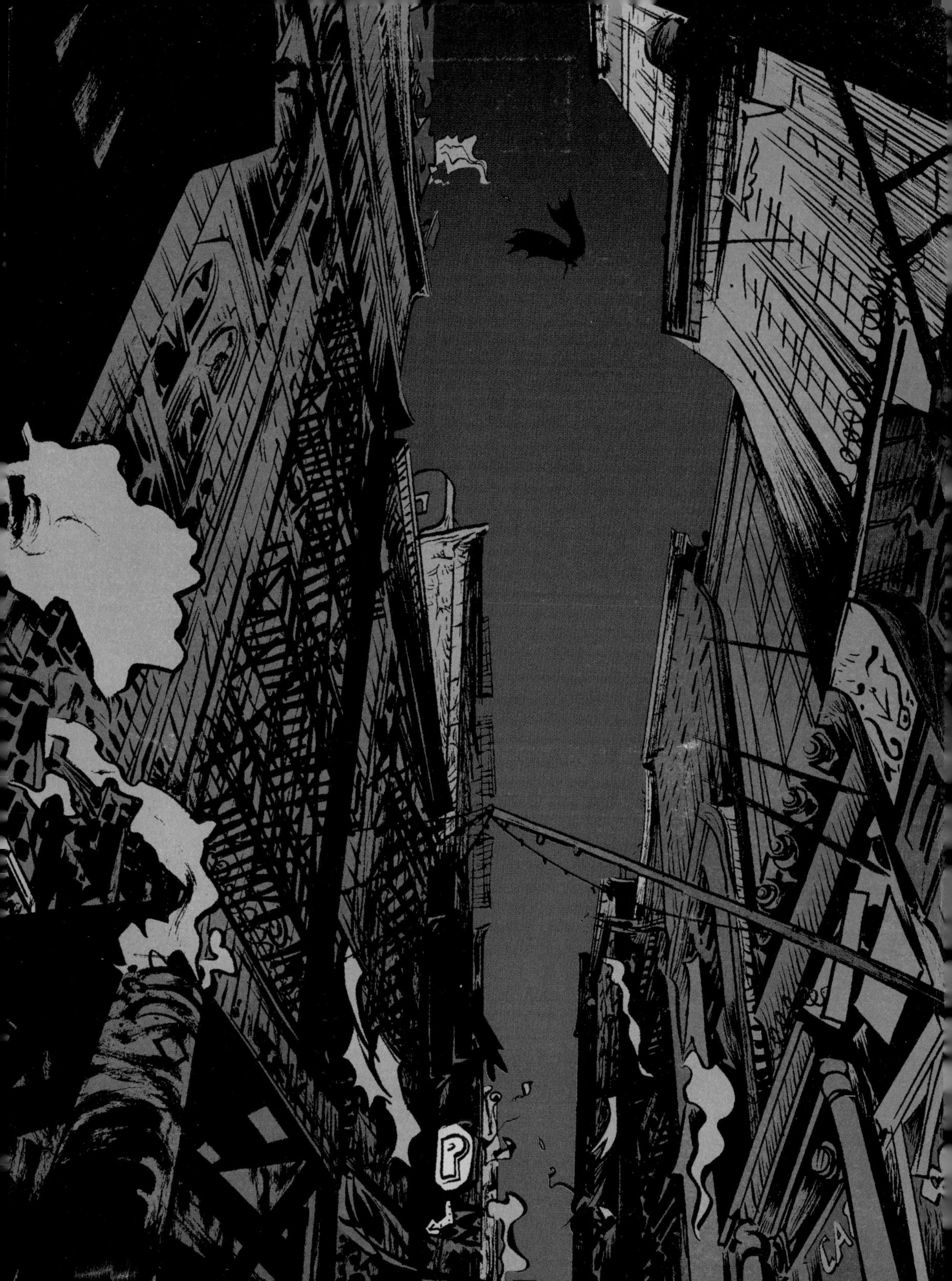

BATMAN: YEAR 100

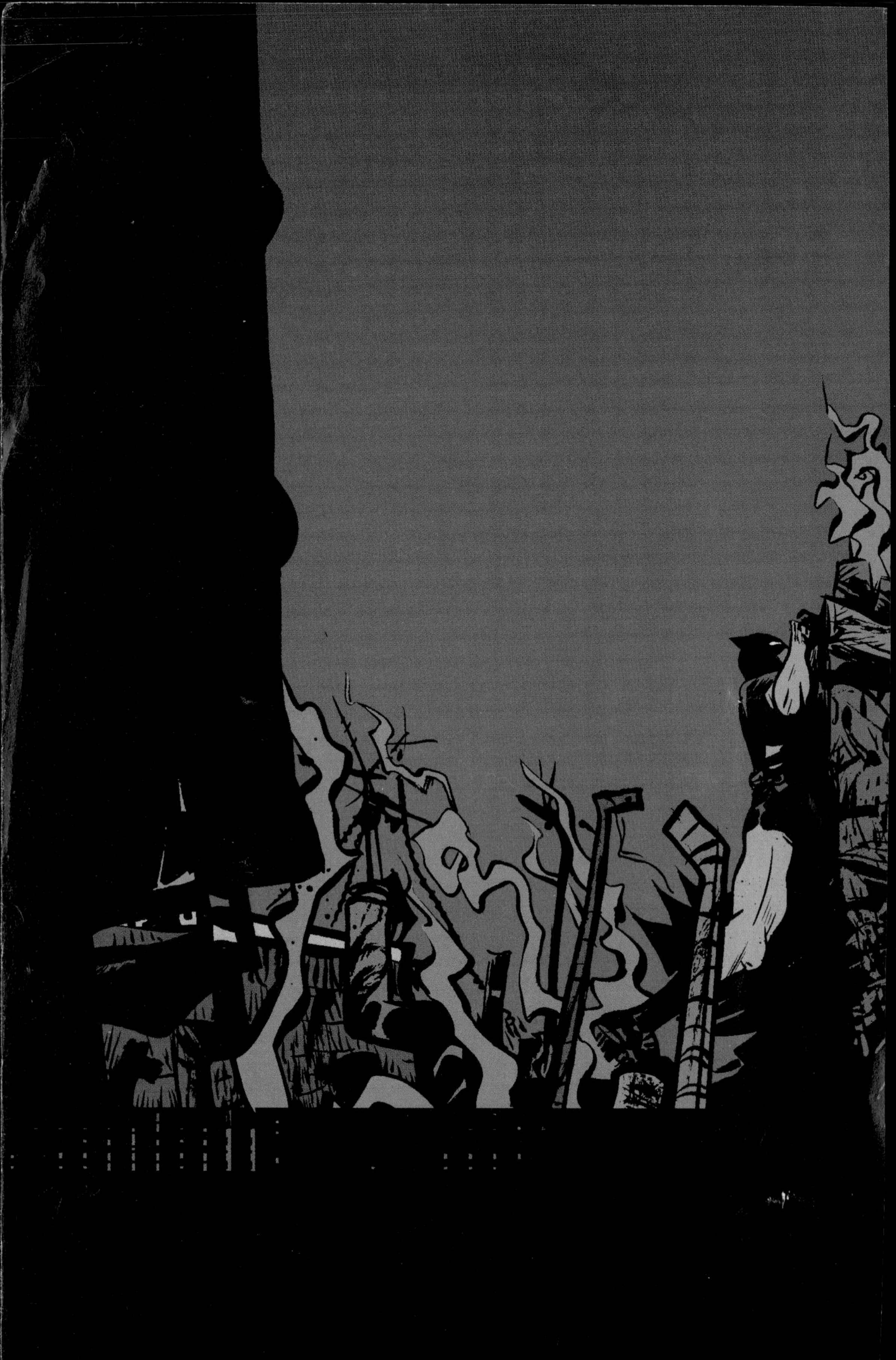

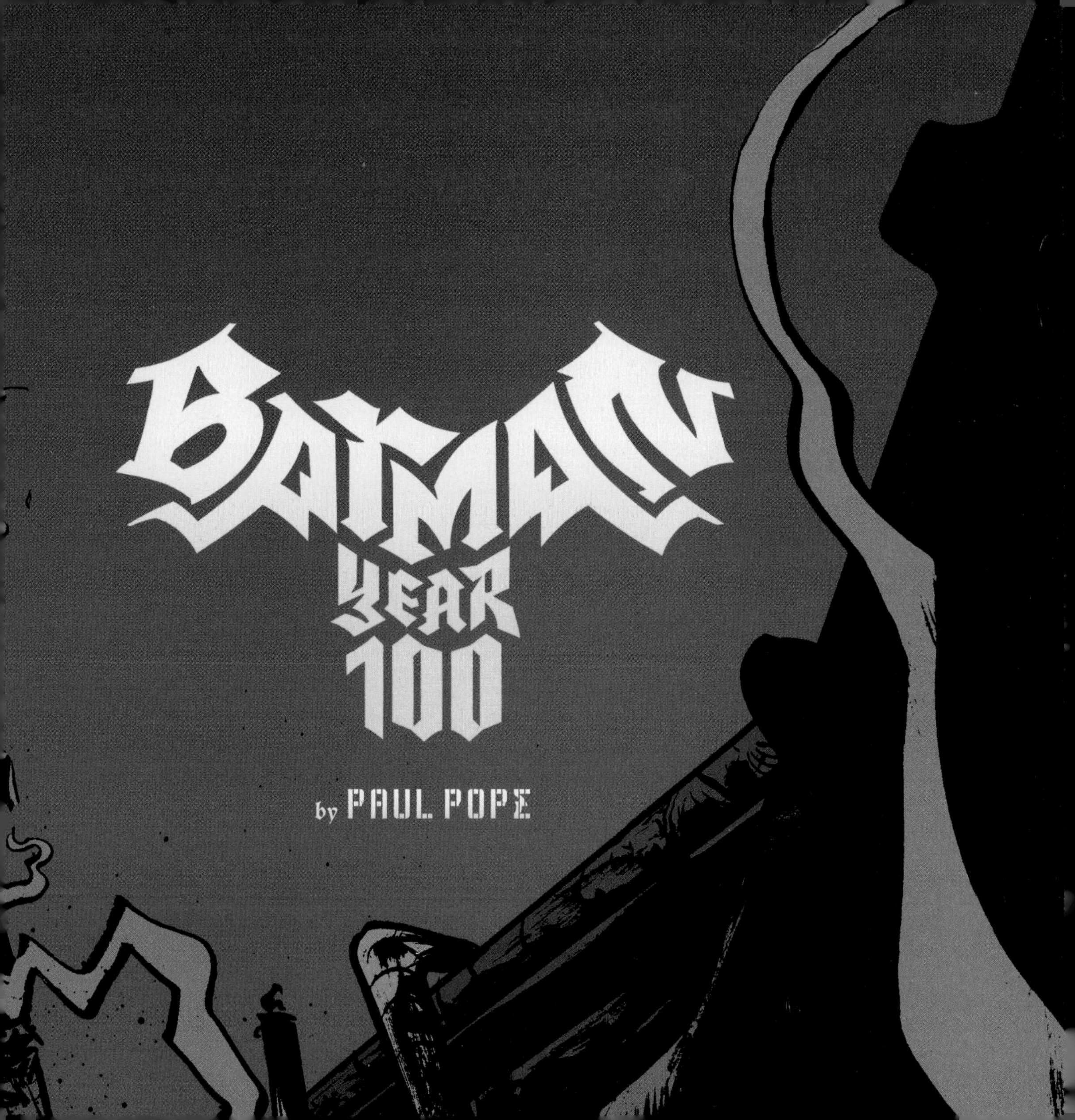
BATMAN
YEAR
100
by PAUL POPE

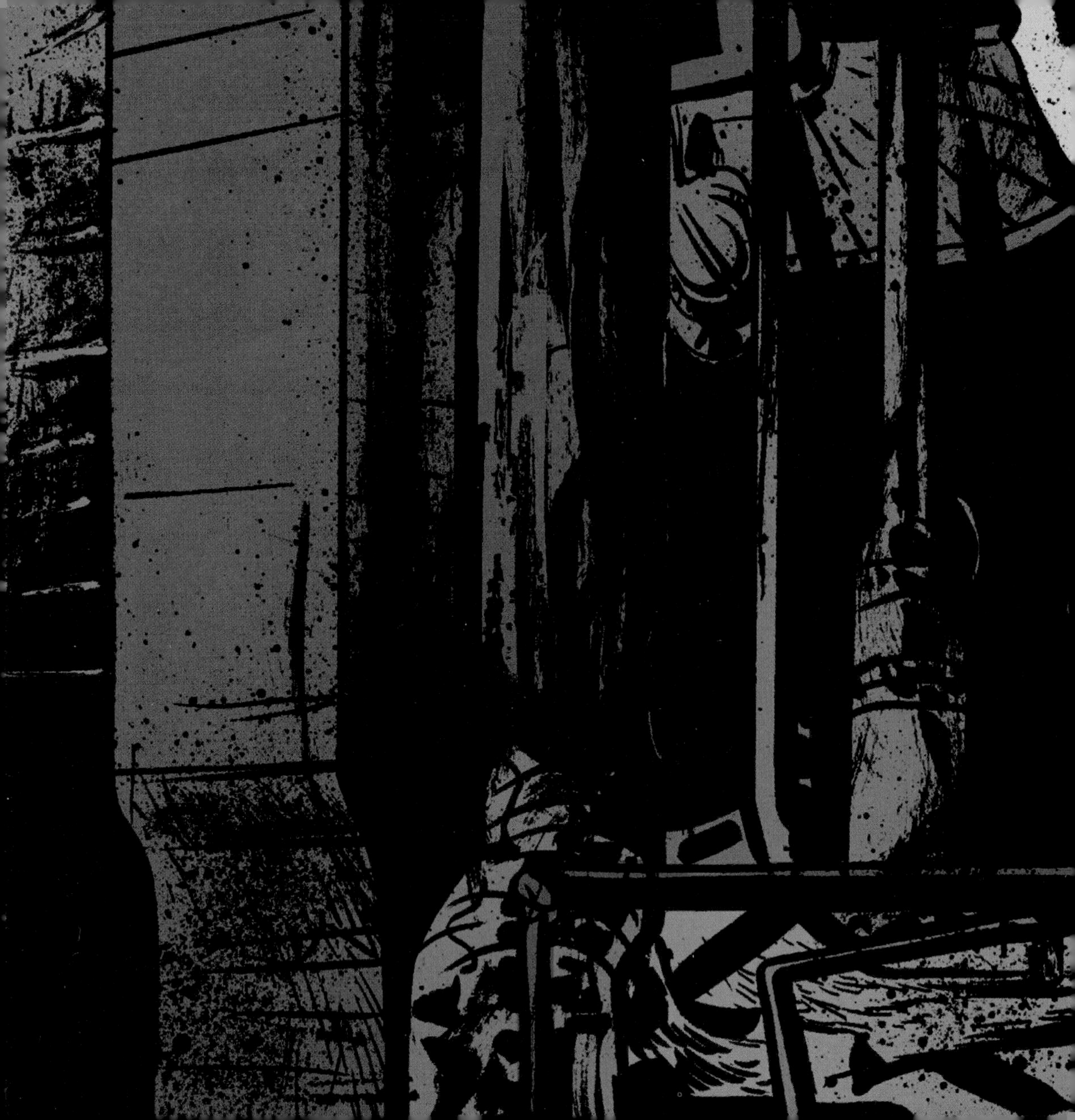

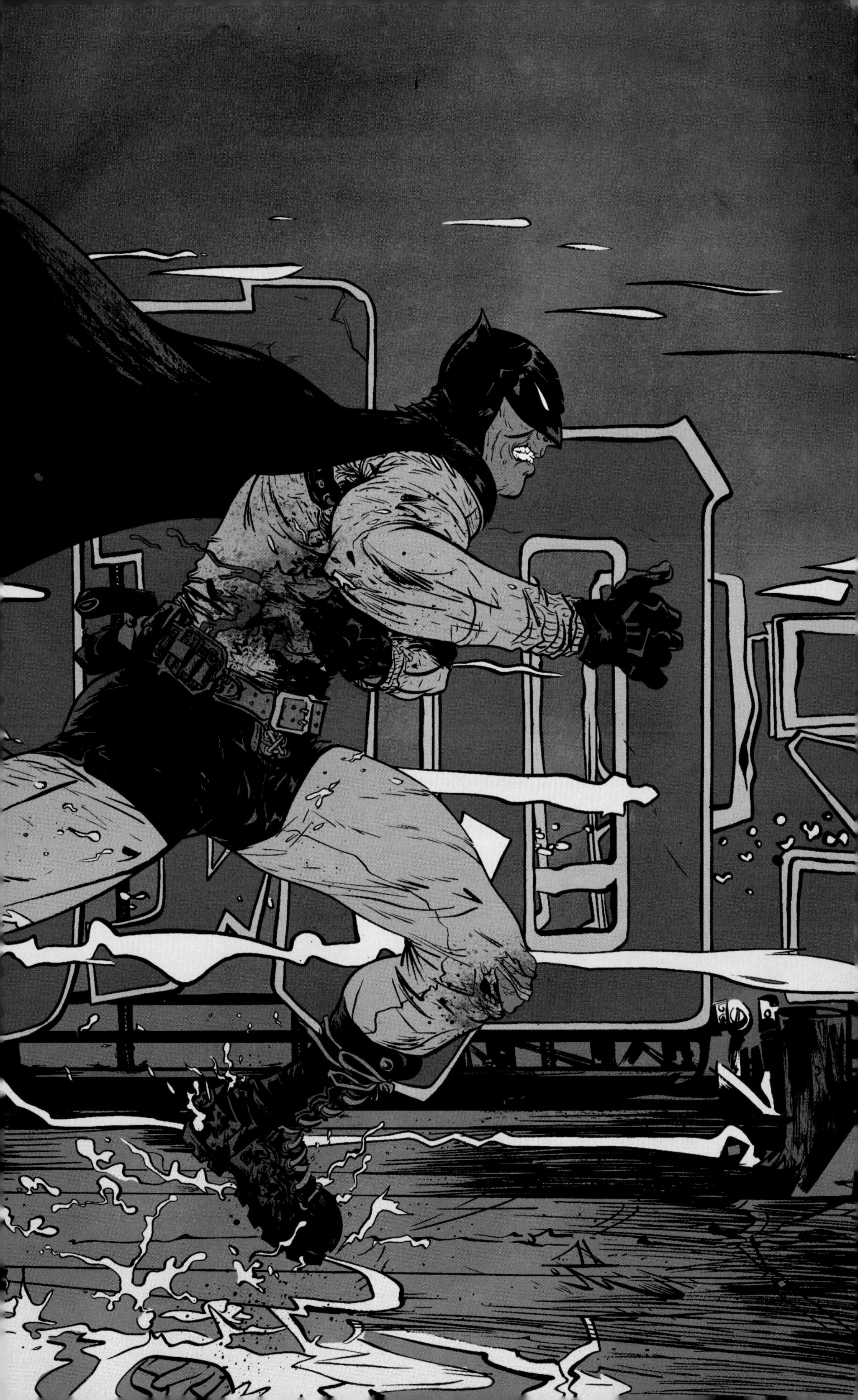

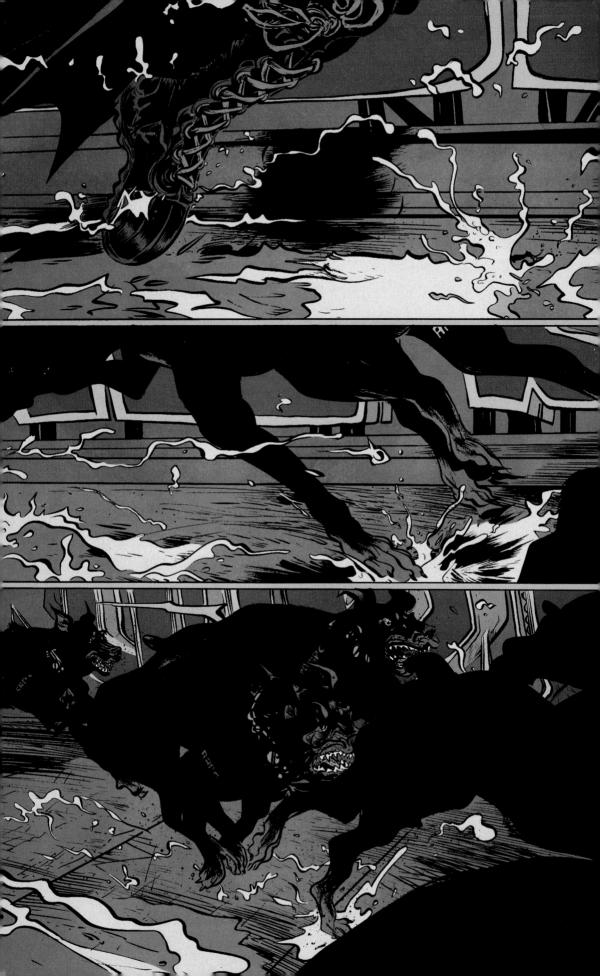

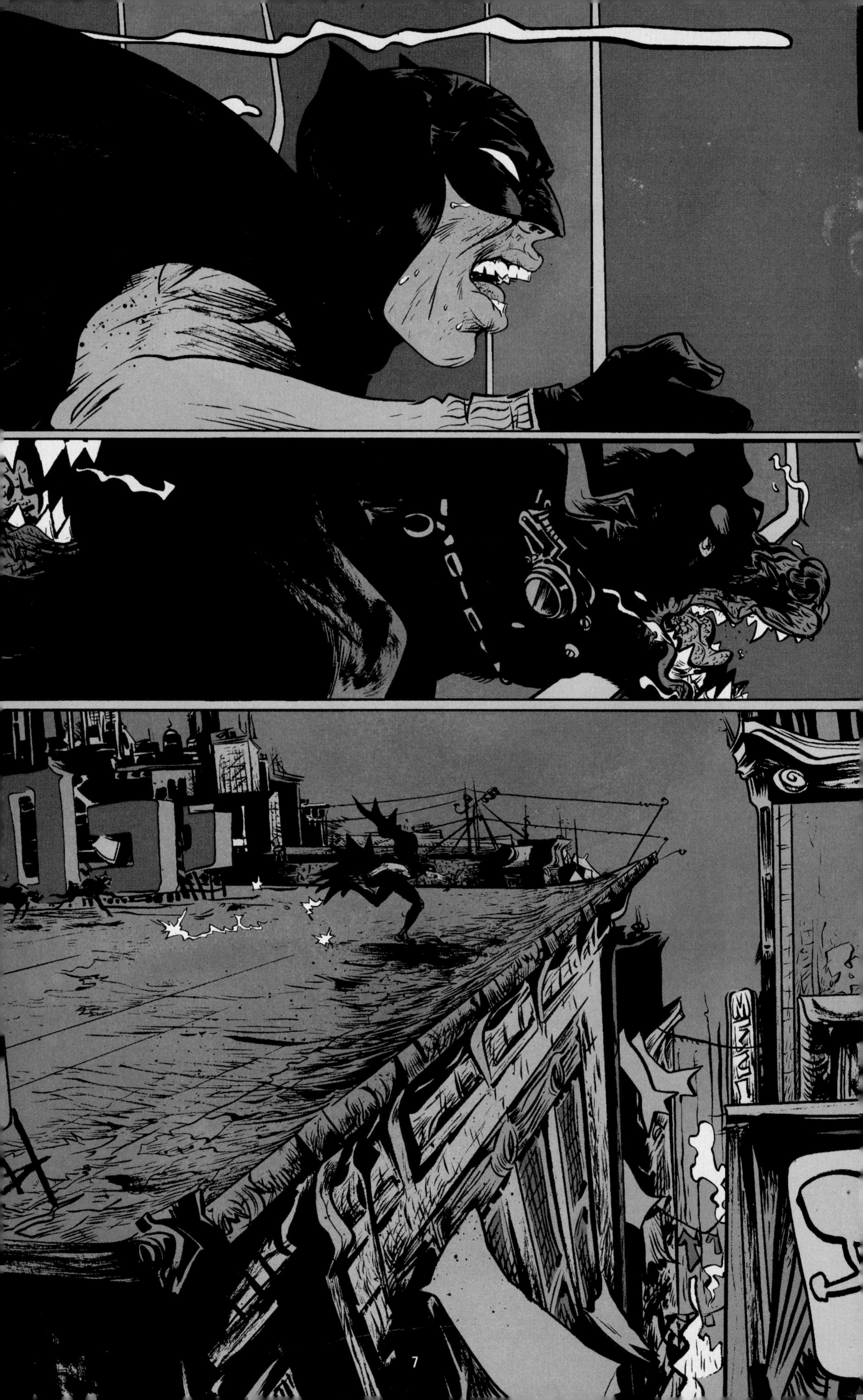

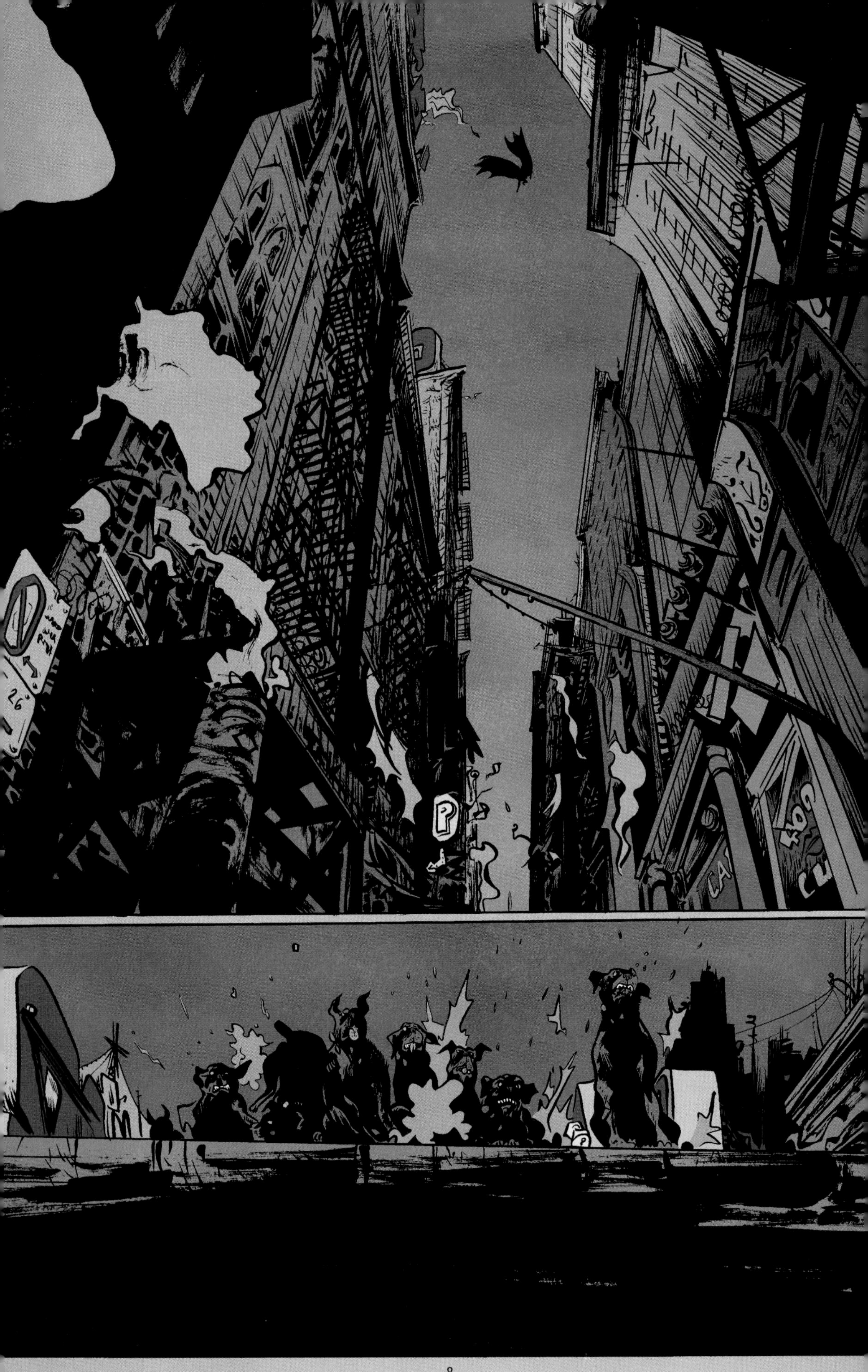

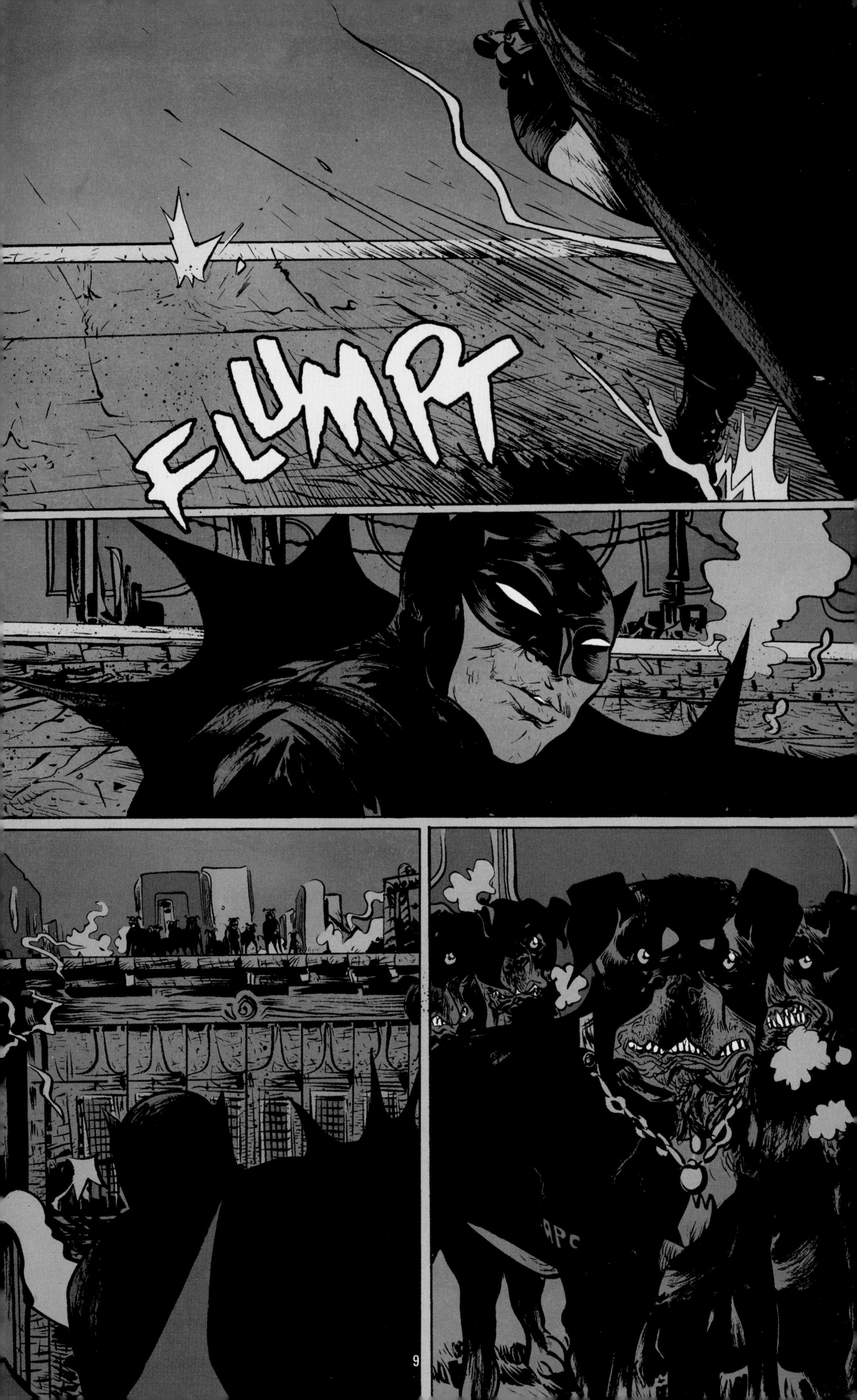
FLUMPT
APC

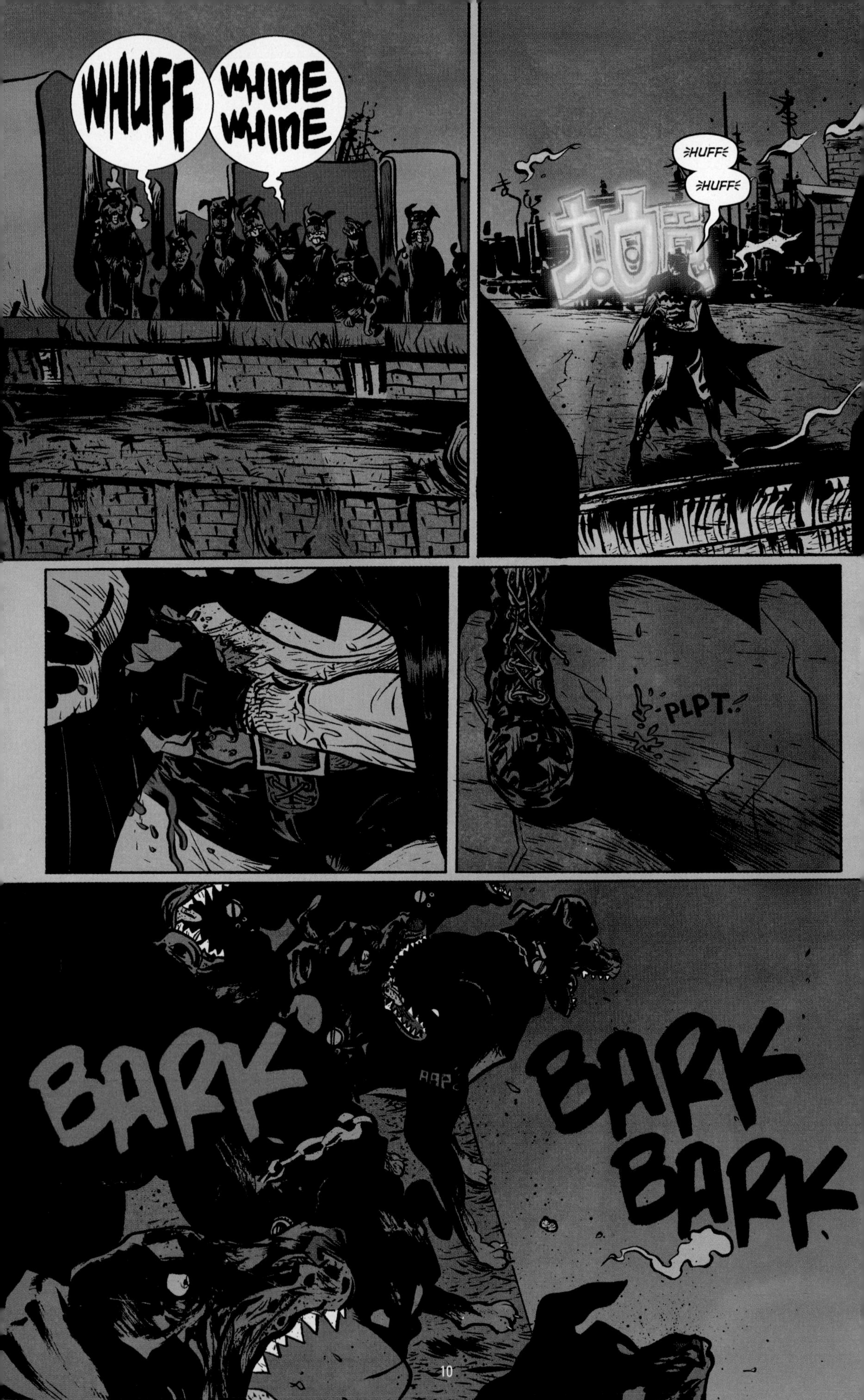

WHUFF
WHINE WHINE
HUFF
HUFF
PLPT.
BARK
BARK BARK

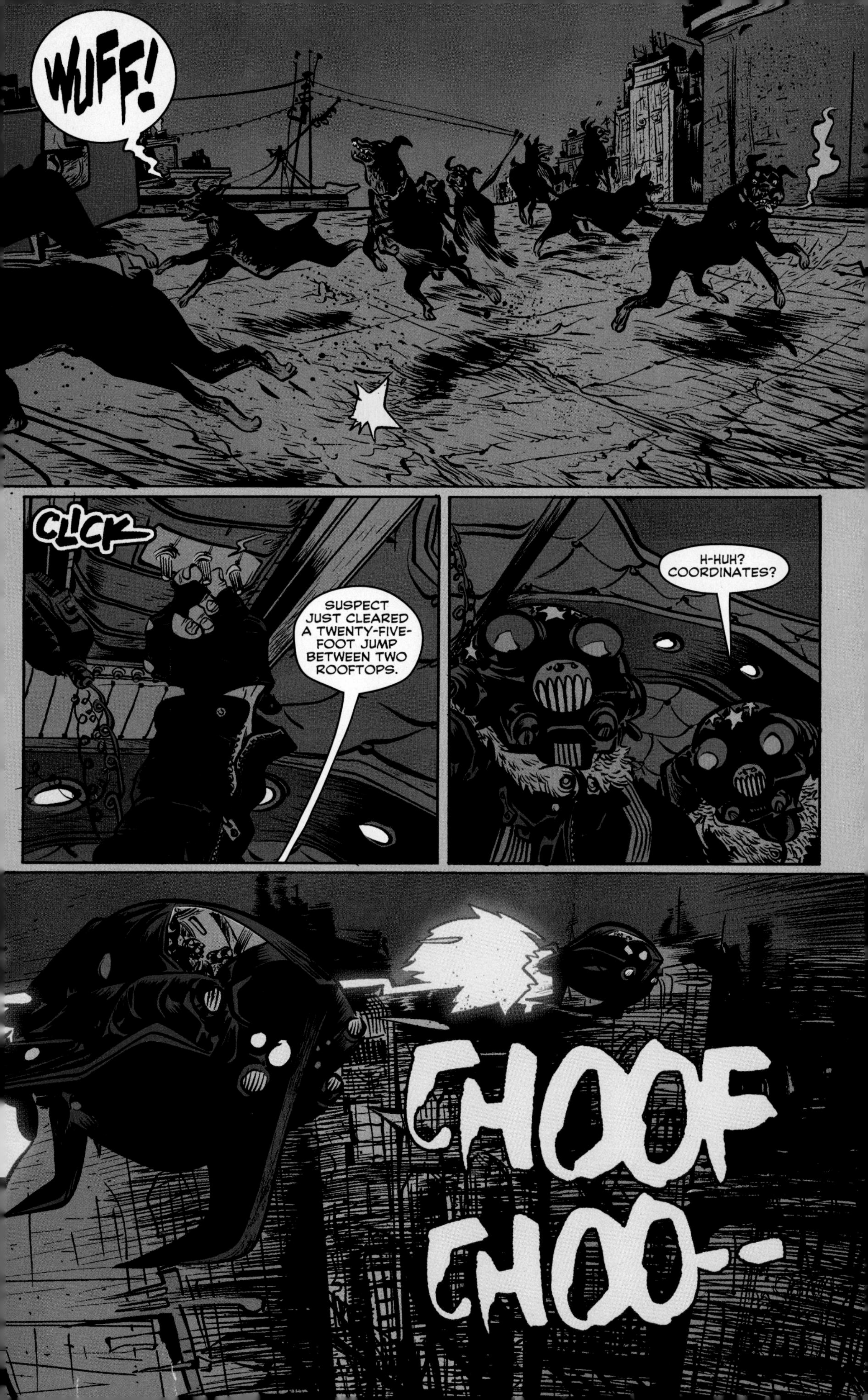
WUFF!
CLICK
SUSPECT JUST CLEARED A TWENTY-FIVE-FOOT JUMP BETWEEN TWO ROOFTOPS.
H-HUH? COORDINATES?
CHOOF CHOO-

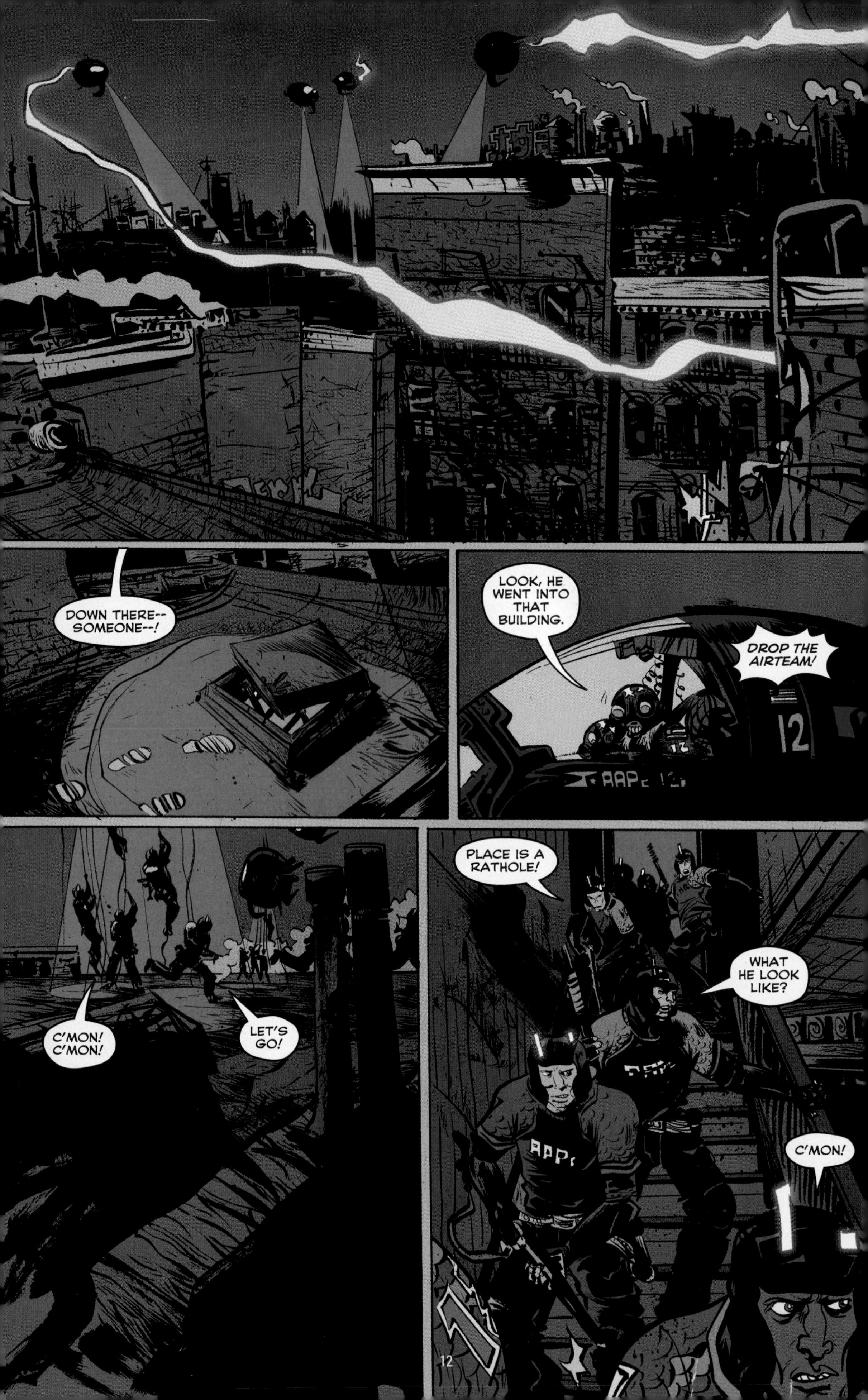

DOWN THERE--
SOMEONE--!
LOOK, HE WENT INTO THAT BUILDING.
DROP THE AIRTEAM!
C'MON! C'MON!
LET'S GO!
PLACE IS A RATHOLE!
WHAT HE LOOK LIKE?
C'MON!

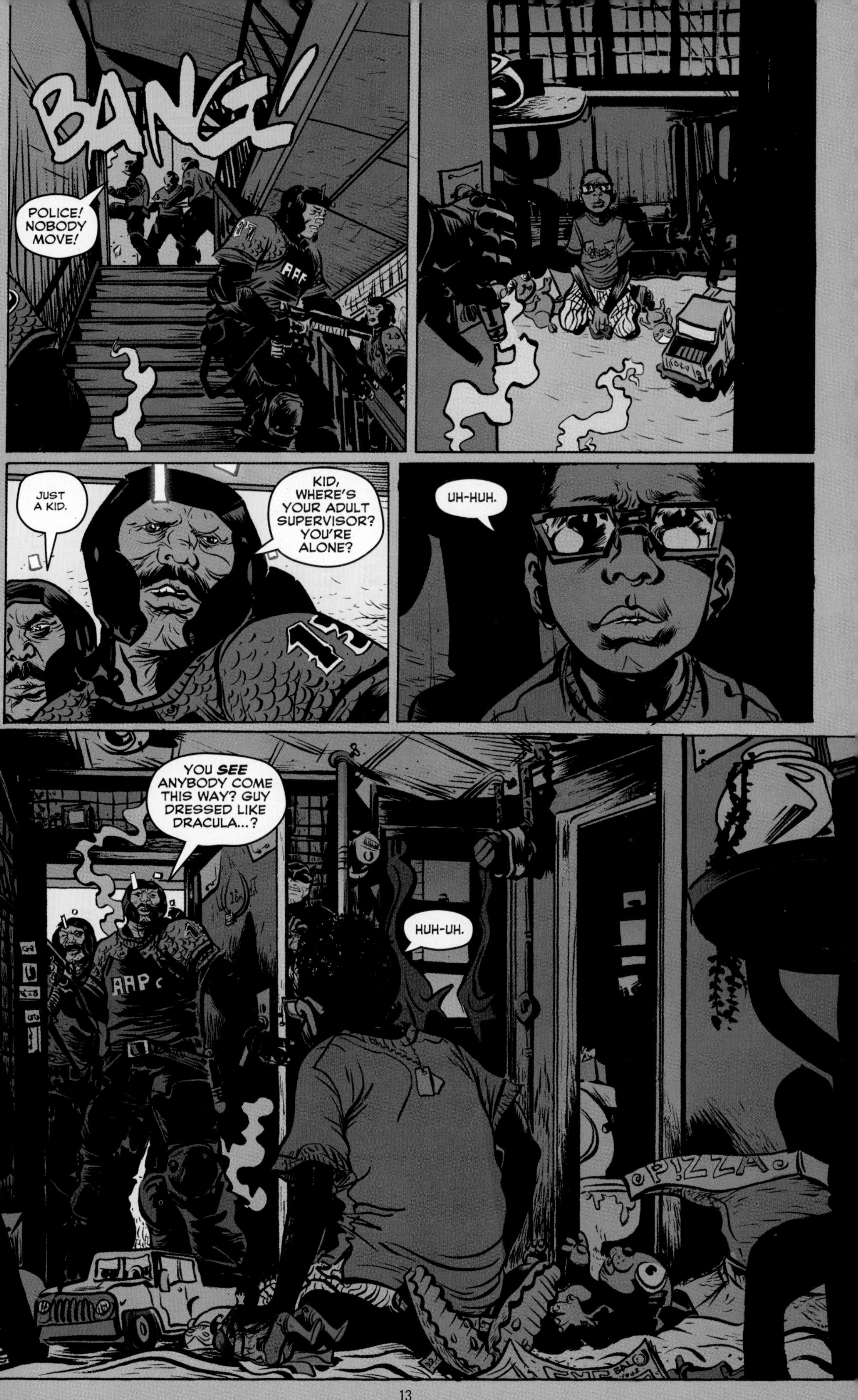
BANG!
POLICE! NOBODY MOVE!
JUST A KID.
KID, WHERE'S YOUR ADULT SUPERVISOR? YOU'RE ALONE?
UH-HUH.
YOU *SEE* ANYBODY COME THIS WAY? GUY DRESSED LIKE DRACULA...?
HUH-UH.
P!ZZA

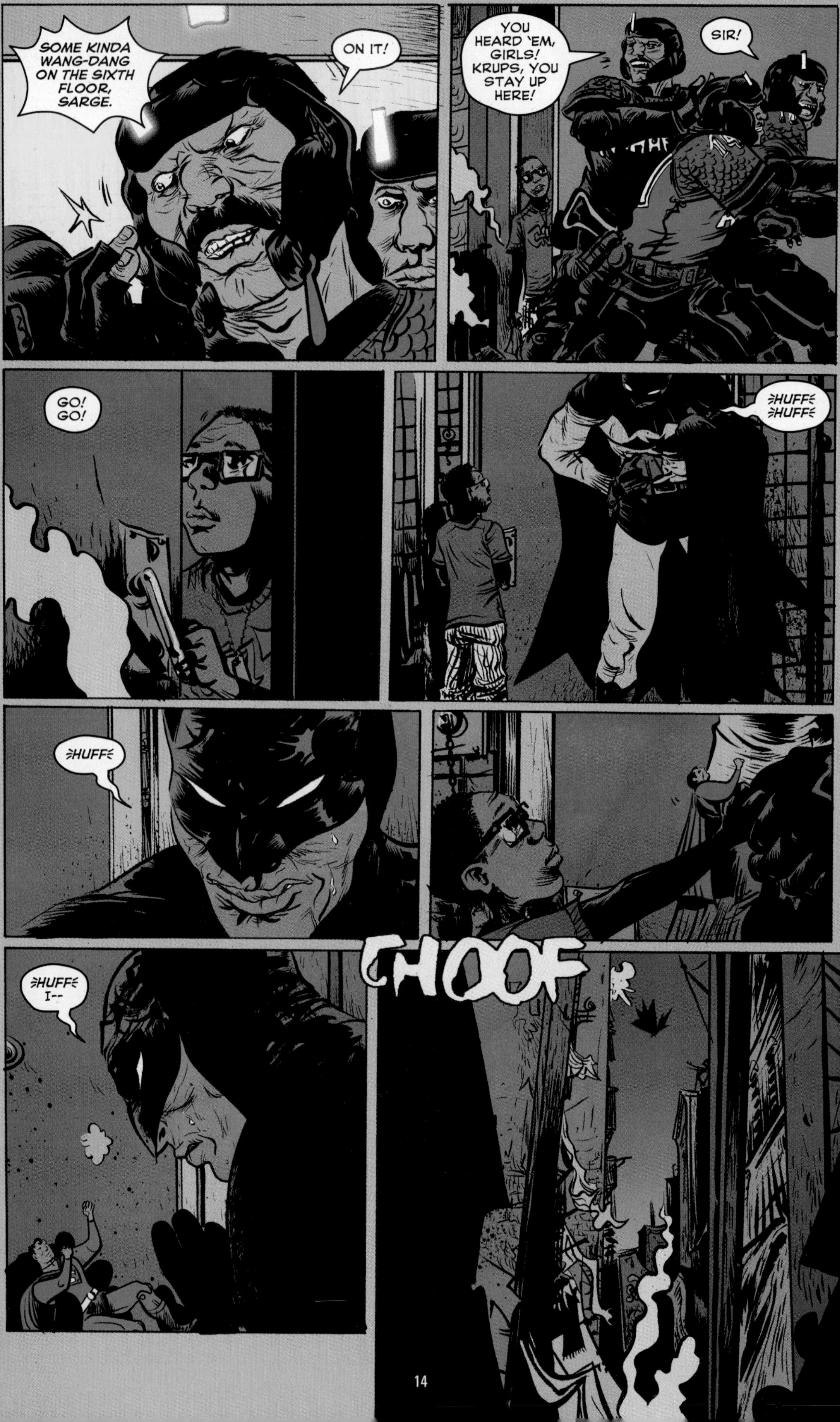
SOME KINDA WANG-DANG ON THE SIXTH FLOOR, SARGE.
ON IT!
YOU HEARD 'EM, GIRLS! KRUPS, YOU STAY UP HERE!
SIR!
GO! GO!
HUFF HUFF
HUFF
HUFF I--
CHOOF

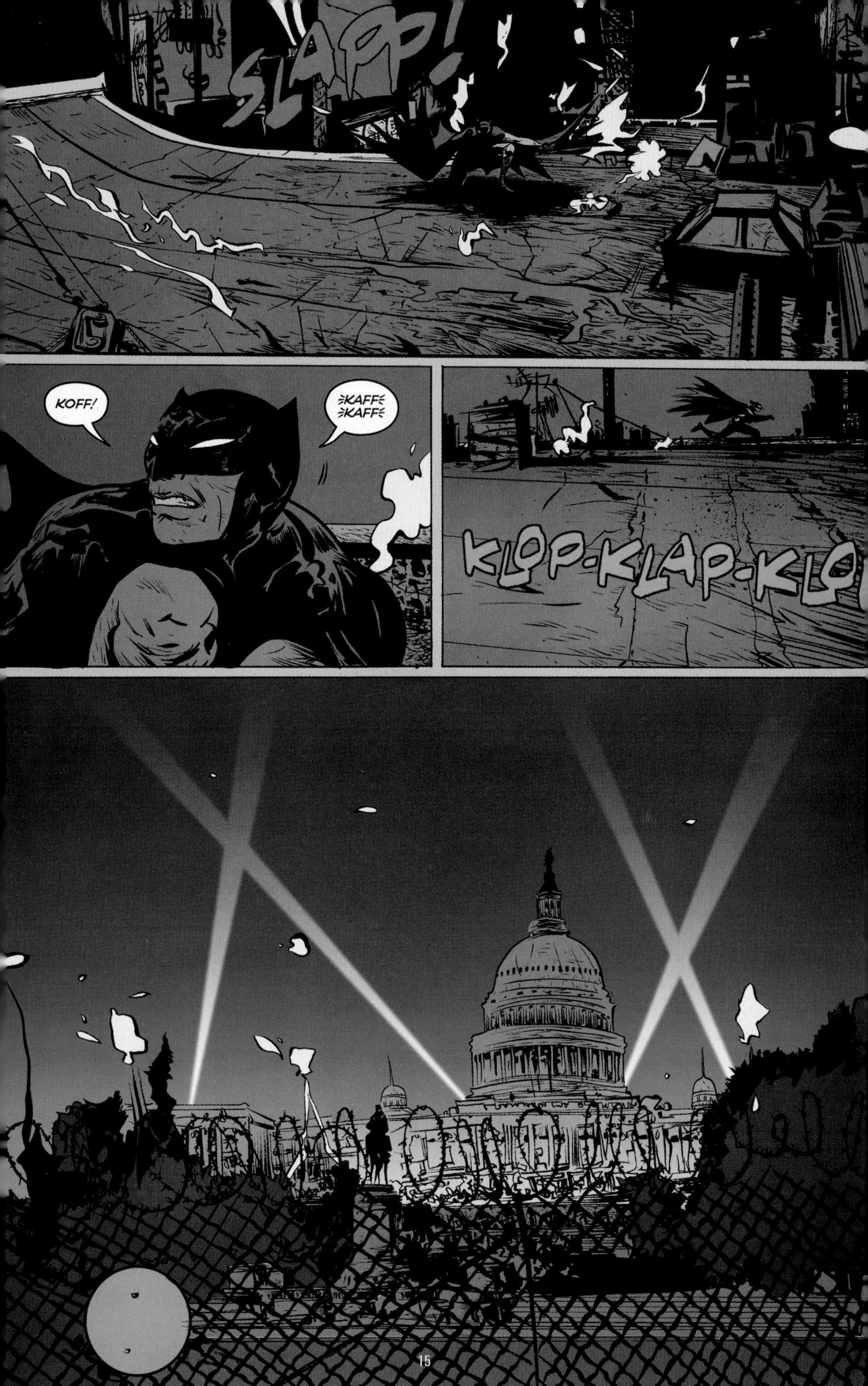
SLAPP!
KOFF!
KAFF KAFF
KLOP-KLAP-KLO

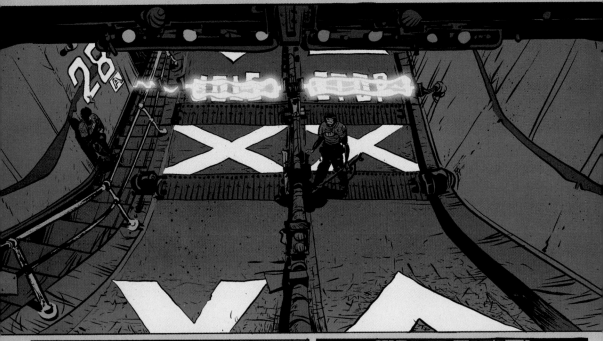

WHAT'S THIS-- GOTHAM CITY...

JUST COMING ACROSS NOW. RED HOT.

WE HAVE A DEAD MAN-- THREE, FOUR MINUTES AGO.

WE HAVE OUR LOCAL A.A.P.C. MEN THERE NOW-- GOTHAM PANTHERS.

DID ANYBODY SEE--?

NEGATIVE. THESE ARE FROM THE CAMERA REMOTES IN THE DOG RETINAS. HERE'S ANOTHER VIEW.

IMPOSSIBLE. THAT'S A TWENTY-FOOT JUMP. NOBODY CAN--

THIS PERSON'S A DOUBLE-U. UNCLASSIFIED, UNDOCUMENTED.

OBVIOUSLY SOME SORT OF EXO-SUIT. EVEN AN OLYMPIC--

I SEE NO EXO ON THIS DOUBLE-U. NO ENHANCEMENTS WHATSO--

BLACK COSTUME, MASK...

...TELLING ME WE CAN'T ESTABLISH HIS IDENTITY?

UNCLASSIFIED AND UNDOCUMENTED! THIS HASN'T HAPPENED FOR AT LEAST--

DRAW DOWN A CAPTURE OFF THE DOG LENSES, RUN IT THROUGH THE MAINFRAY-- LOOKS CAUCASIAN, SIX-TWO, OR THREE--

RUN IT BACK AT FOUR, FIVE, SIX YEARS. A MASK.

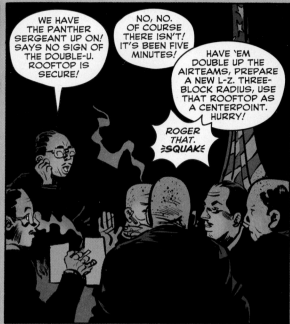

WE HAVE THE PANTHER SERGEANT UP ON! SAYS NO SIGN OF THE DOUBLE-U. ROOFTOP IS SECURE!

NO, NO. OF COURSE THERE ISN'T! IT'S BEEN FIVE MINUTES!

HAVE 'EM DOUBLE UP THE AIRTEAMS, PREPARE A NEW L-Z. THREE-BLOCK RADIUS, USE THAT ROOFTOP AS A CENTERPOINT. HURRY!

ROGER THAT. ⇒SQUAK⇐

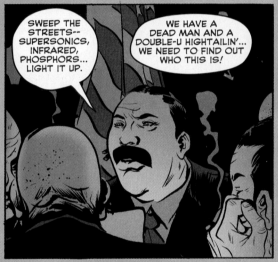

SWEEP THE STREETS-- SUPERSONICS, INFRARED, PHOSPHORS... LIGHT IT UP.

WE HAVE A DEAD MAN AND A DOUBLE-U HIGHTAILIN'... WE NEED TO FIND OUT WHO THIS IS!

SHFF

WHAT'S ALL THE HUBBUB?

A DOUBLE-U, SIR. GOTHAM.

ONE F.P.C. AGENT DOWN, HOT PURSUIT.

RUNNING-RUNNING.

IT'S OUR PANTHER-MAN, AGAIN. SAYS THE BUILDING'S SECURE. DOGS BACK, AIRTEAM TWELVE IS IN SWEEP.

IS THE DOUBLE-U THE SPOT-ON?

DON'T KNOW YET, SIR. HE FLED THE--

HOLD IT, WAIT. WAIT, THIS IS INTERESTING.

DONUT K

DON

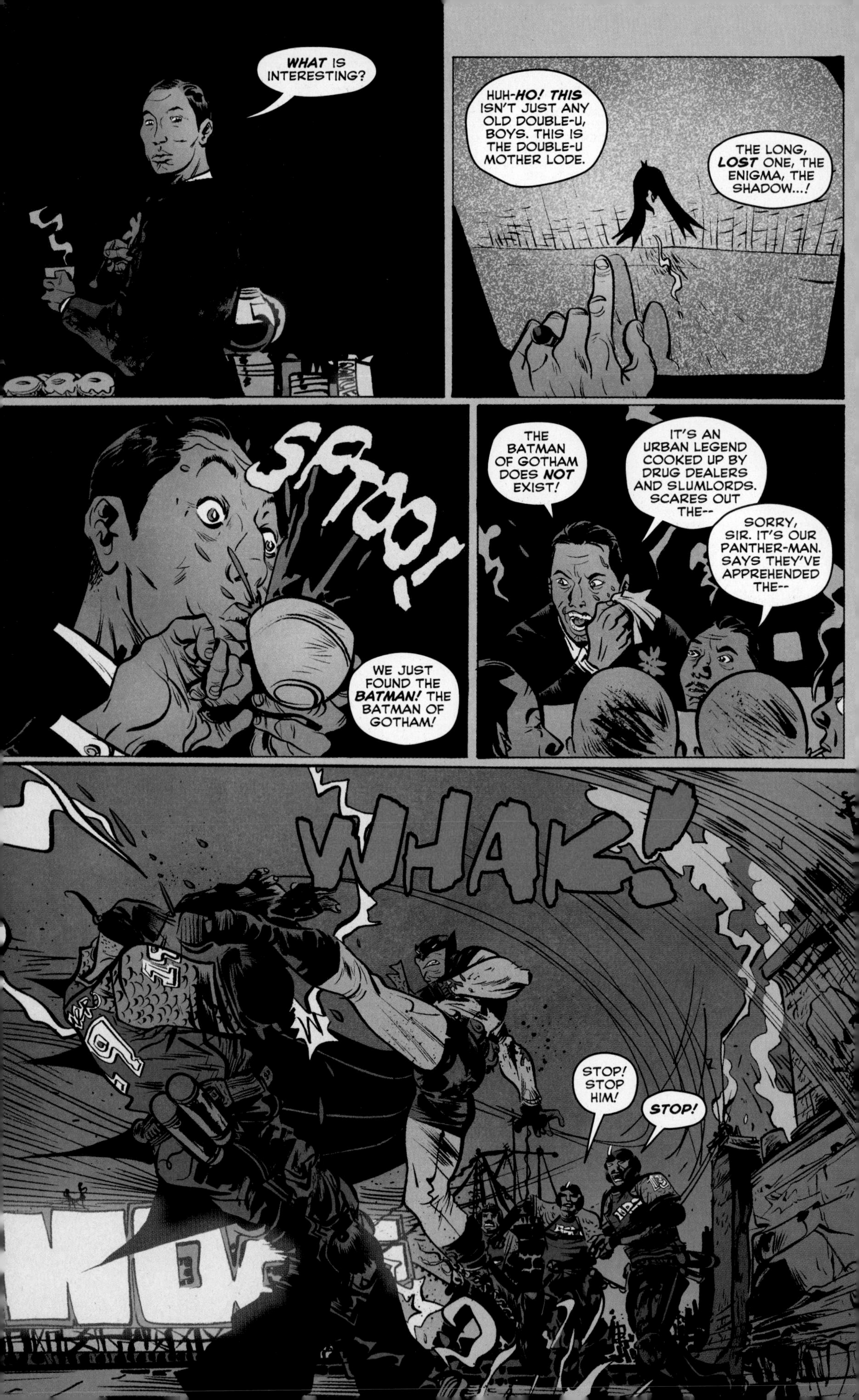
WHAT IS INTERESTING?
HUH-HO! THIS ISN'T JUST ANY OLD DOUBLE-U, BOYS. THIS IS THE DOUBLE-U MOTHER LODE.
THE LONG, LOST ONE, THE ENIGMA, THE SHADOW...!
SPTOO!
WE JUST FOUND THE BATMAN! THE BATMAN OF GOTHAM!
THE BATMAN OF GOTHAM DOES NOT EXIST!
IT'S AN URBAN LEGEND COOKED UP BY DRUG DEALERS AND SLUMLORDS. SCARES OUT THE--
SORRY, SIR. IT'S OUR PANTHER-MAN. SAYS THEY'VE APPREHENDED THE--
WHAK!
STOP! STOP HIM!
STOP!

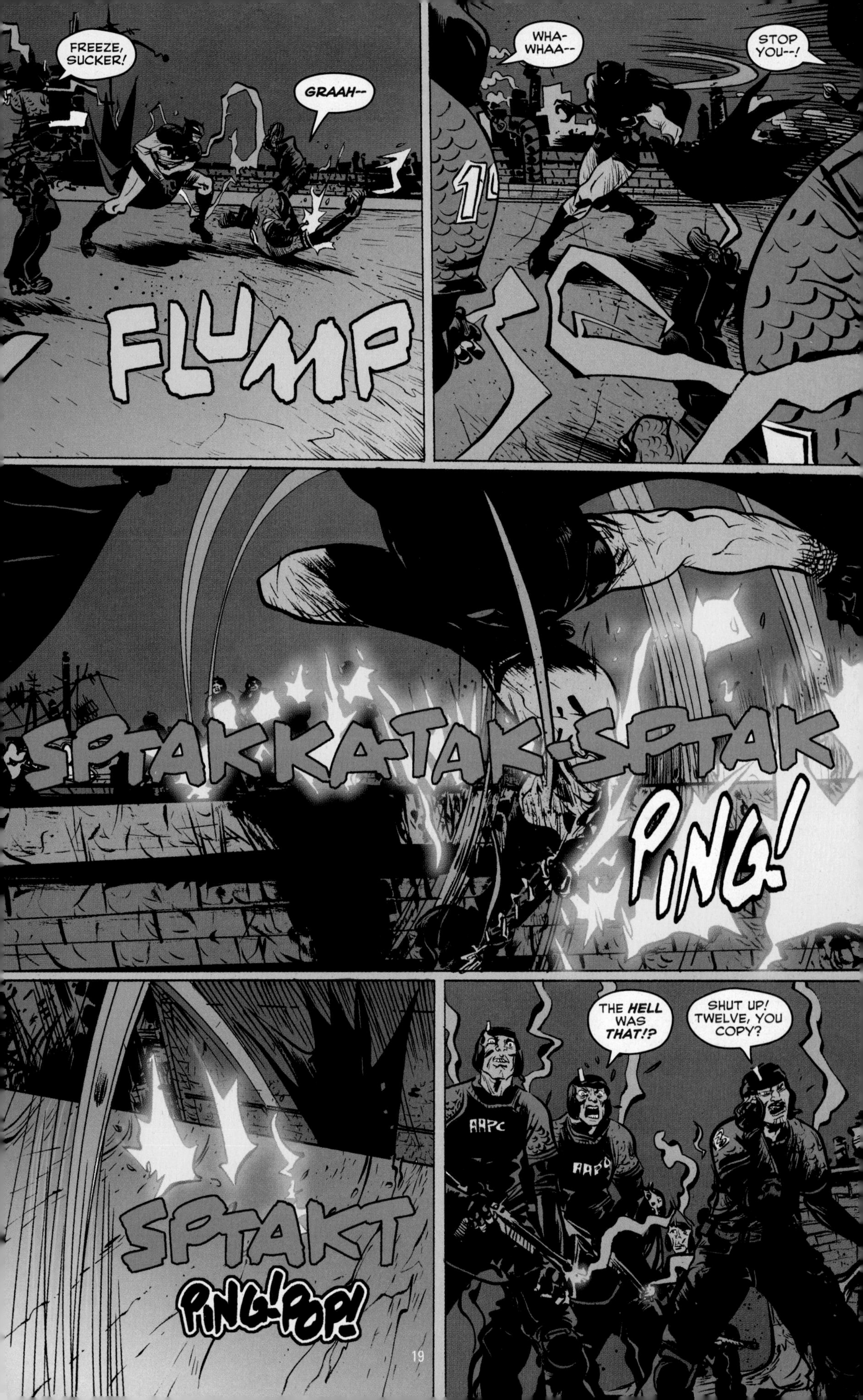
FREEZE, SUCKER!
GRAAH--
FLUMP
WHA- WHAA--
STOP YOU--!
SPTAKKA-TAK-SPTAK
PING!
SPTAKT
PING! POP!
THE HELL WAS THAT!?
SHUT UP! TWELVE, YOU COPY?

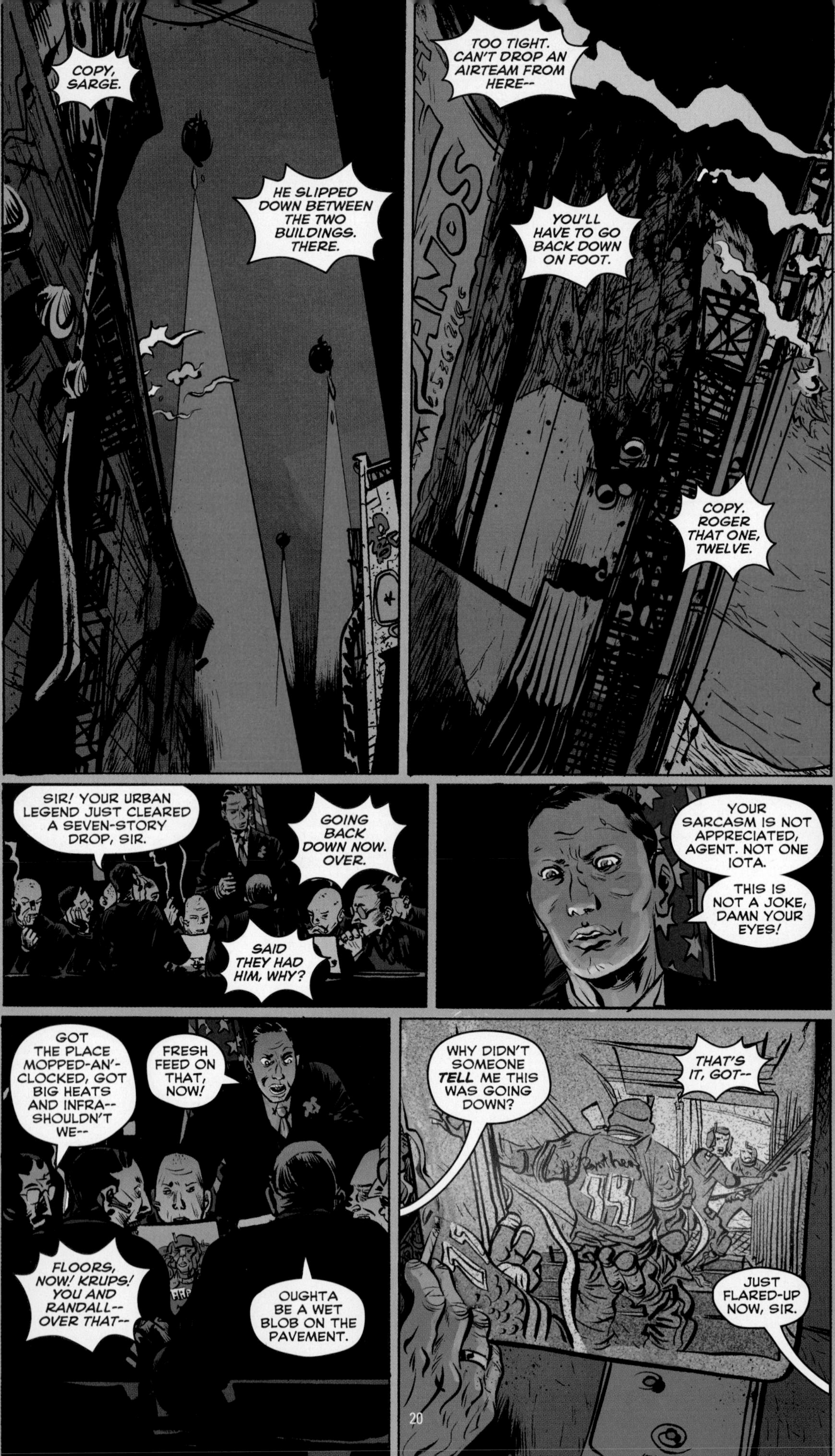
COPY, SARGE.
HE SLIPPED DOWN BETWEEN THE TWO BUILDINGS. THERE.
TOO TIGHT. CAN'T DROP AN AIRTEAM FROM HERE--
YOU'LL HAVE TO GO BACK DOWN ON FOOT.
COPY. ROGER THAT ONE, TWELVE.
SIR! YOUR URBAN LEGEND JUST CLEARED A SEVEN-STORY DROP, SIR.
GOING BACK DOWN NOW. OVER.
SAID THEY HAD HIM, WHY?
YOUR SARCASM IS NOT APPRECIATED, AGENT. NOT ONE IOTA.
THIS IS NOT A JOKE, DAMN YOUR EYES!
GOT THE PLACE MOPPED-AN'-CLOCKED, GOT BIG HEATS AND INFRA-- SHOULDN'T WE--
FRESH FEED ON THAT, NOW!
FLOORS, NOW! KRUPS! YOU AND RANDALL-- OVER THAT--
OUGHTA BE A WET BLOB ON THE PAVEMENT.
WHY DIDN'T SOMEONE TELL ME THIS WAS GOING DOWN?
THAT'S IT, GOT--
JUST FLARED-UP NOW, SIR.

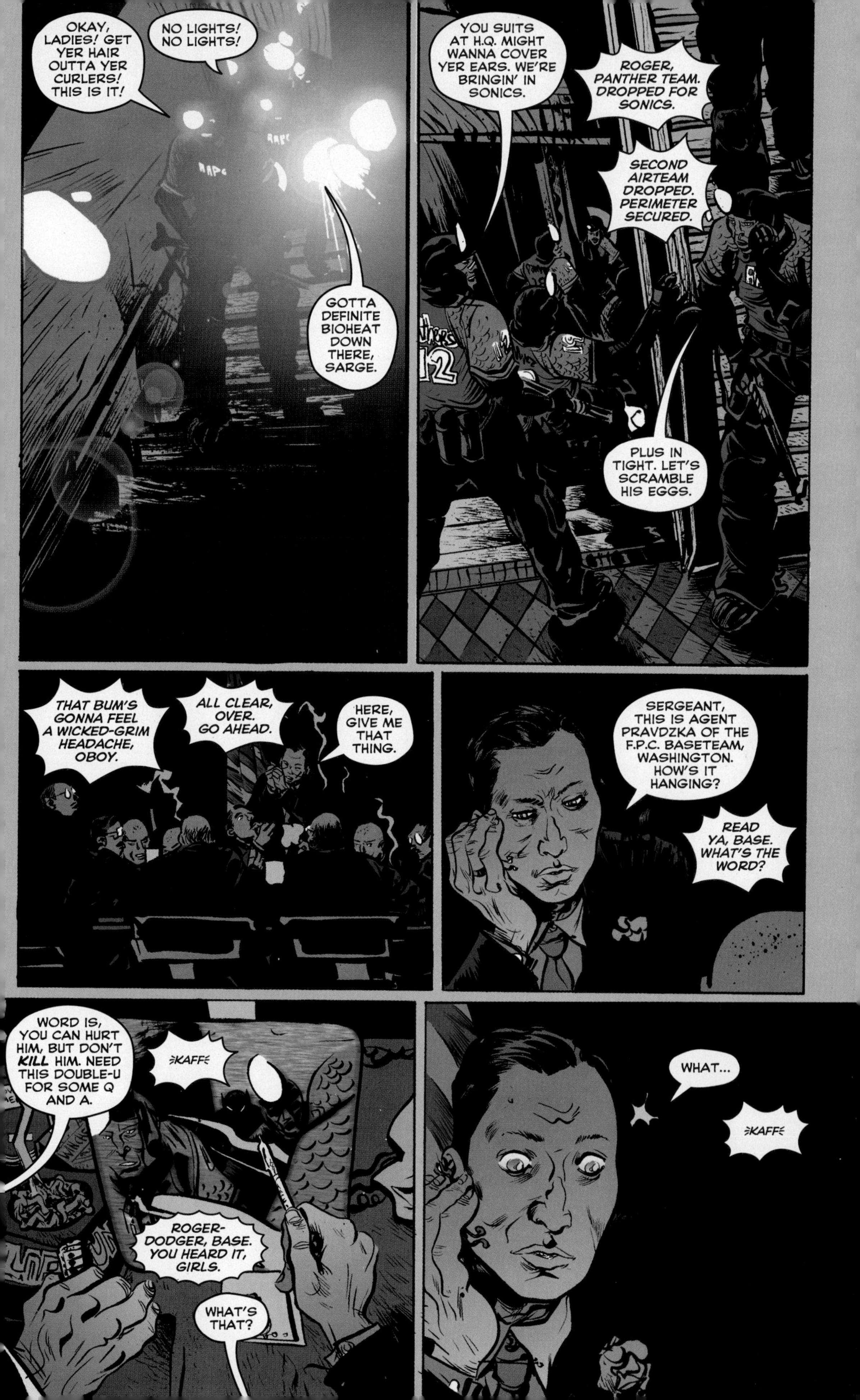
OKAY, LADIES! GET YER HAIR OUTTA YER CURLERS! THIS IS IT!
NO LIGHTS! NO LIGHTS!
GOTTA DEFINITE BIOHEAT DOWN THERE, SARGE.
YOU SUITS AT H.Q. MIGHT WANNA COVER YER EARS. WE'RE BRINGIN' IN SONICS.
ROGER, PANTHER TEAM. DROPPED FOR SONICS.
SECOND AIRTEAM DROPPED. PERIMETER SECURED.
PLUS IN TIGHT. LET'S SCRAMBLE HIS EGGS.
THAT BUM'S GONNA FEEL A WICKED-GRIM HEADACHE, OBOY.
ALL CLEAR, OVER. GO AHEAD.
HERE, GIVE ME THAT THING.
SERGEANT, THIS IS AGENT PRAVDZKA OF THE F.P.C. BASETEAM, WASHINGTON. HOW'S IT HANGING?
READ YA, BASE. WHAT'S THE WORD?
WORD IS, YOU CAN HURT HIM, BUT DON'T KILL HIM. NEED THIS DOUBLE-U FOR SOME Q AND A.
KAFF
ROGER-DODGER, BASE. YOU HEARD IT, GIRLS.
WHAT'S THAT?
WHAT...
KAFF

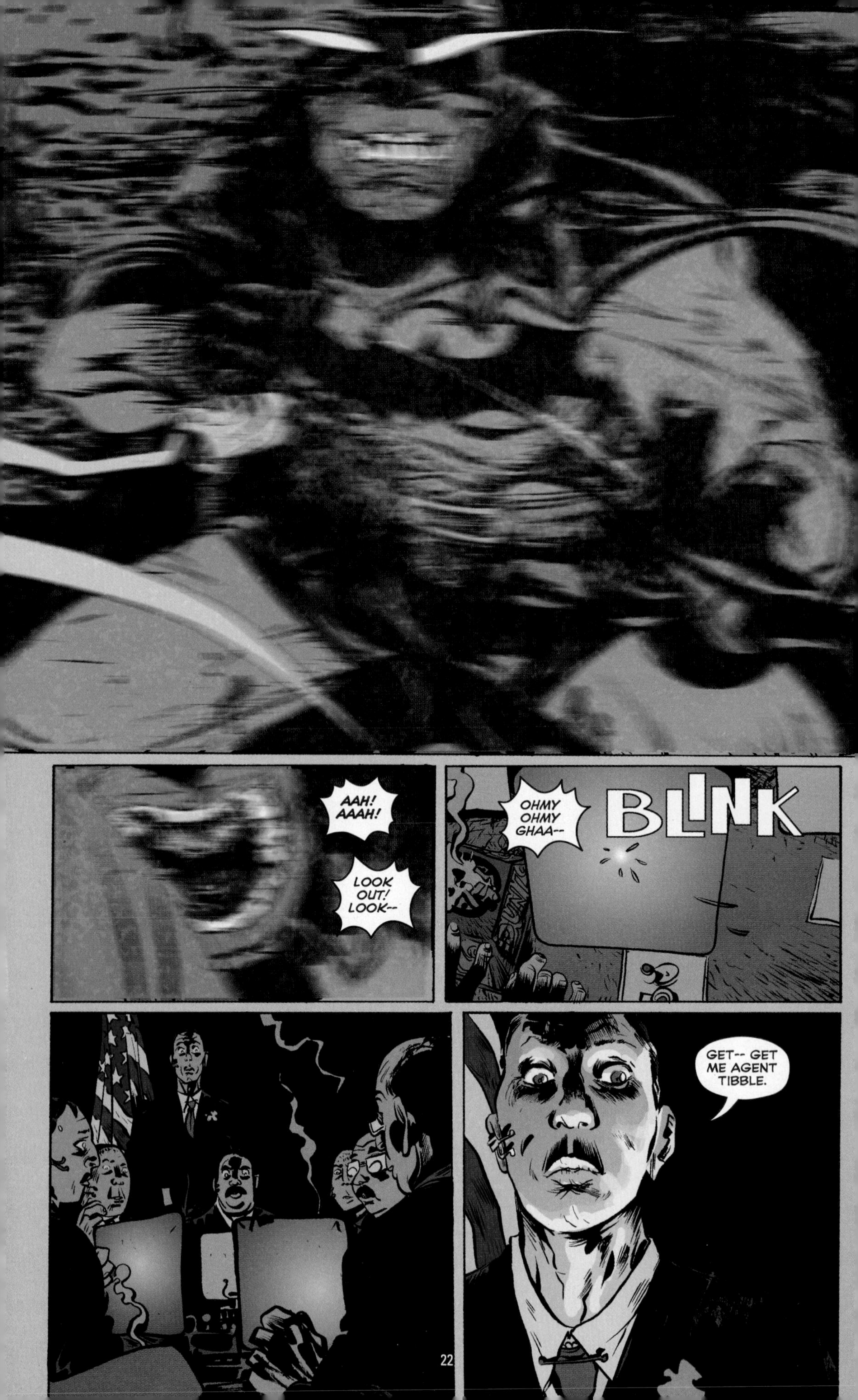
AAH! AAAH!
LOOK OUT! LOOK--
OHMY OHMY GHAA--
BLINK
GET-- GET ME AGENT TIBBLE.

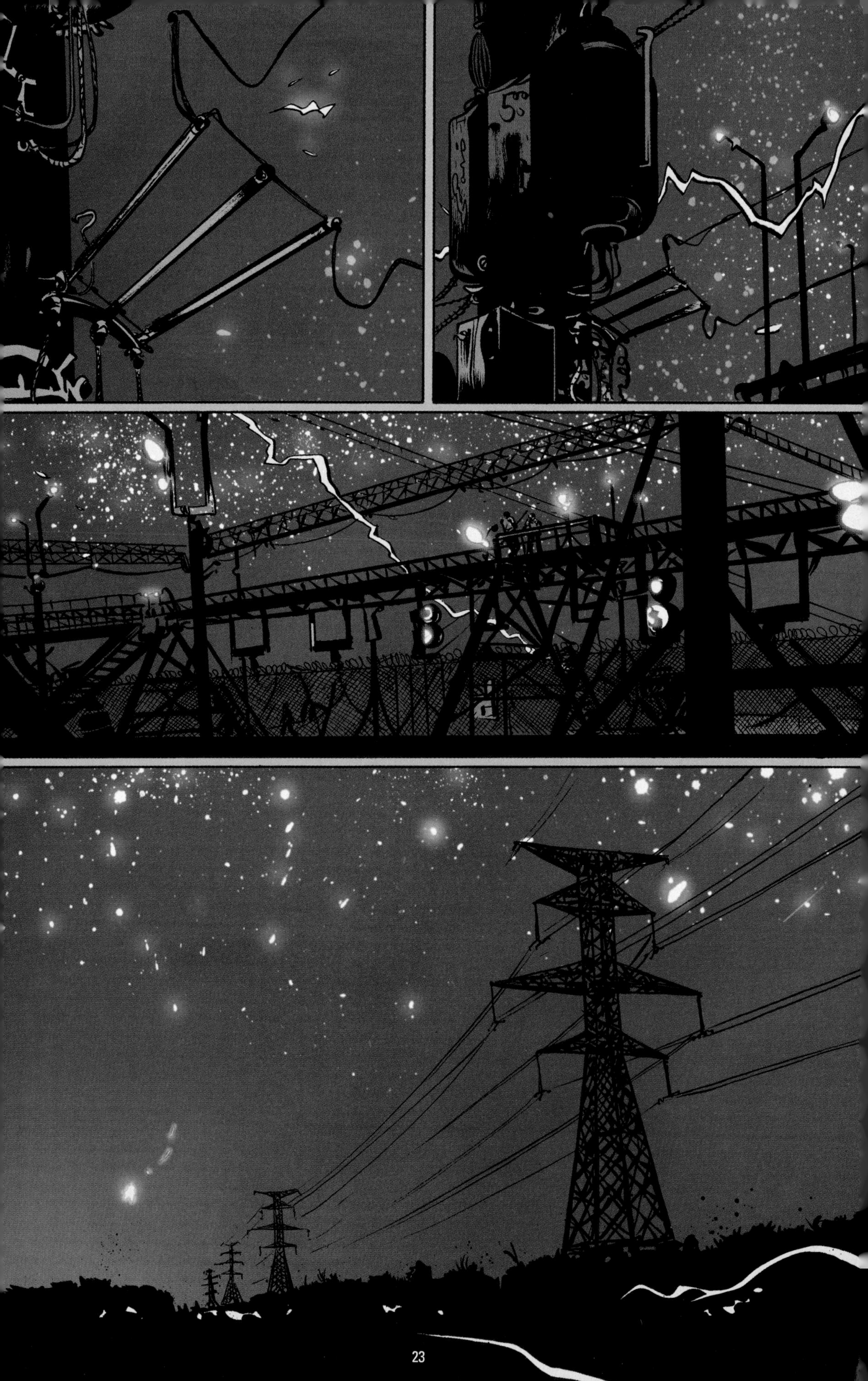

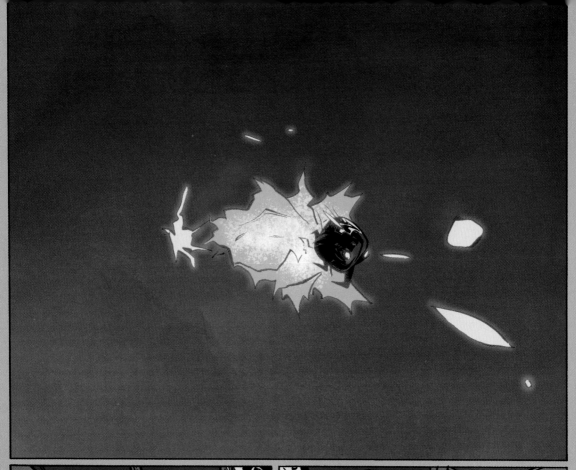

TIBBLE.

I SAW IT, SIR...

...WHOEVER HE IS, HE'S WEARING **ENHANCEMENTS.** THE PSYCHOLOGICAL ADVANTAGES ARE **OBVIOUS.**

THE BRAINS SAY NO ENHANCEMENTS.

YES, WELL, WITH ALL DUE RESPECT, THE BRAINS HAVE BEEN KNOWN TO MAKE MISTAKES...

...SIR.

WE GOT THE PANTHER BACK UP, SIR.

GOOD.

SERGEANT, IT'S BASE BACK'ACHA. WHAT THE **HELL.**

GONE, SIR. JUST GONE. DISAPPEARED.

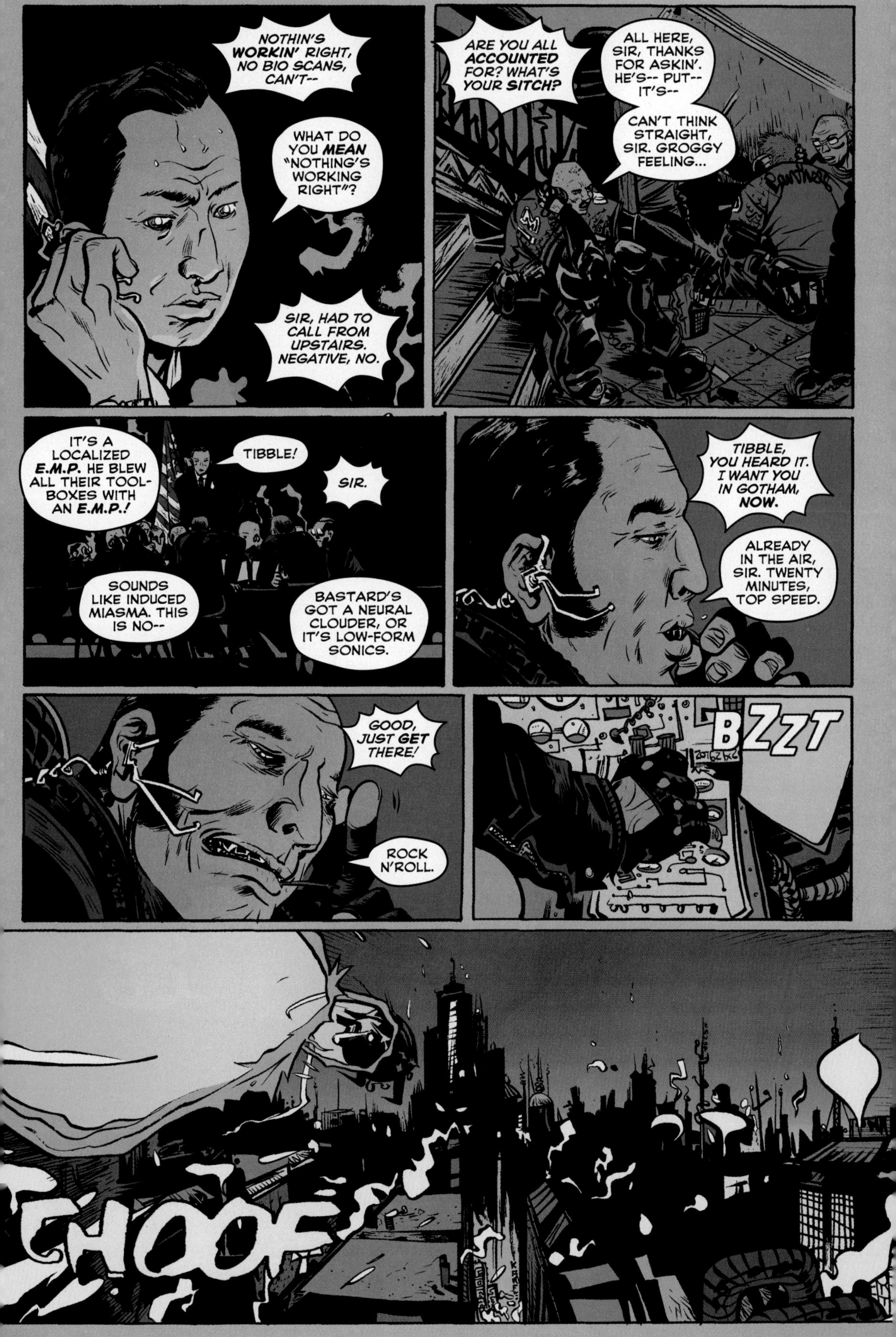
NOTHIN'S WORKIN' RIGHT, NO BIO SCANS, CAN'T--
WHAT DO YOU MEAN "NOTHING'S WORKING RIGHT"?
SIR, HAD TO CALL FROM UPSTAIRS. NEGATIVE, NO.
ARE YOU ALL ACCOUNTED FOR? WHAT'S YOUR SITCH?
ALL HERE, SIR, THANKS FOR ASKIN'. HE'S-- PUT-- IT'S--
CAN'T THINK STRAIGHT, SIR. GROGGY FEELING...
IT'S A LOCALIZED E.M.P. HE BLEW ALL THEIR TOOL-BOXES WITH AN E.M.P.!
TIBBLE!
SIR.
SOUNDS LIKE INDUCED MIASMA. THIS IS NO--
BASTARD'S GOT A NEURAL CLOUDER, OR IT'S LOW-FORM SONICS.
TIBBLE, YOU HEARD IT. I WANT YOU IN GOTHAM, NOW.
ALREADY IN THE AIR, SIR. TWENTY MINUTES, TOP SPEED.
GOOD, JUST GET THERE!
ROCK N'ROLL.
BZZT
CHOOF

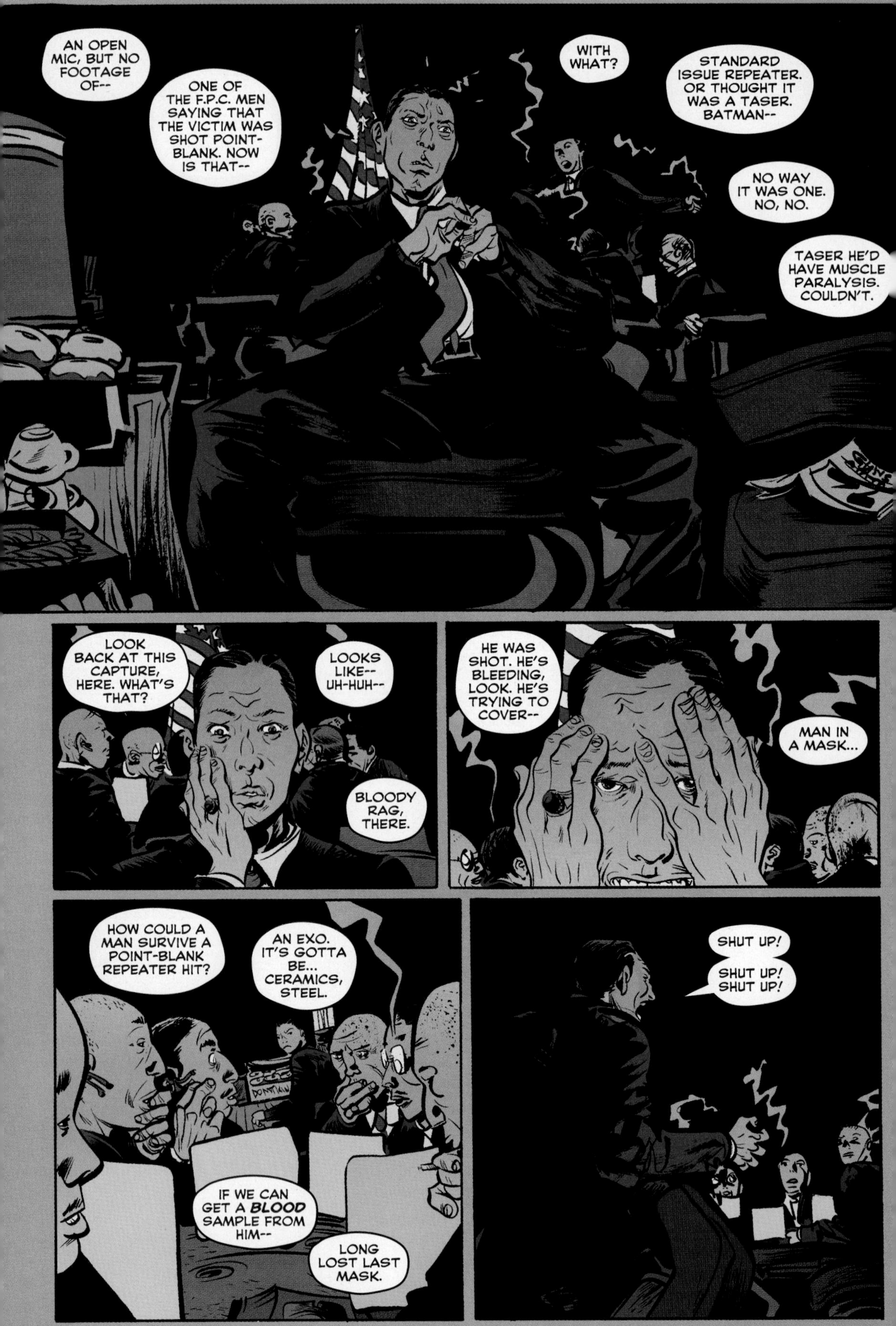

AN OPEN MIC, BUT NO FOOTAGE OF--
ONE OF THE F.P.C. MEN SAYING THAT THE VICTIM WAS SHOT POINT-BLANK. NOW IS THAT--
WITH WHAT?
STANDARD ISSUE REPEATER. OR THOUGHT IT WAS A TASER. BATMAN--
NO WAY IT WAS ONE. NO, NO.
TASER HE'D HAVE MUSCLE PARALYSIS. COULDN'T.
LOOK BACK AT THIS CAPTURE, HERE. WHAT'S THAT?
LOOKS LIKE-- UH-HUH--
BLOODY RAG, THERE.
HE WAS SHOT. HE'S BLEEDING, LOOK. HE'S TRYING TO COVER--
MAN IN A MASK...
HOW COULD A MAN SURVIVE A POINT-BLANK REPEATER HIT?
AN EXO. IT'S GOTTA BE... CERAMICS, STEEL.
IF WE CAN GET A ***BLOOD*** SAMPLE FROM HIM--
LONG LOST LAST MASK.
SHUT UP!
SHUT UP! SHUT UP!

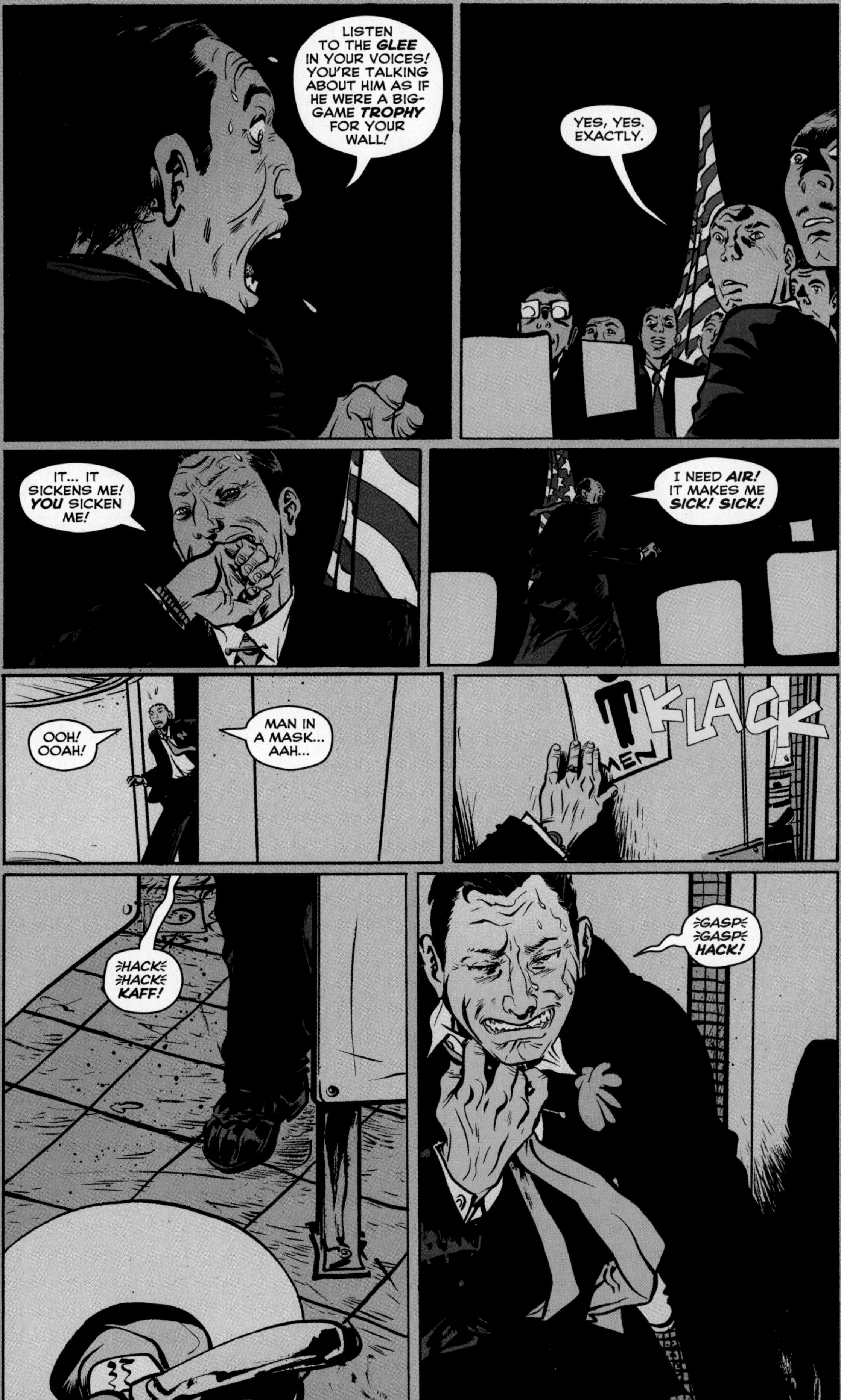
LISTEN TO THE ***GLEE*** IN YOUR VOICES! YOU'RE TALKING ABOUT HIM AS IF HE WERE A BIG-GAME ***TROPHY*** FOR YOUR WALL!
YES, YES. EXACTLY.
IT... IT SICKENS ME! ***YOU*** SICKEN ME!
I NEED ***AIR!*** IT MAKES ME ***SICK! SICK!***
OOH! OOAH!
MAN IN A MASK... AAH...
MEN
KLACK
HACK HACK ***KAFF!***
GASP GASP ***HACK!***

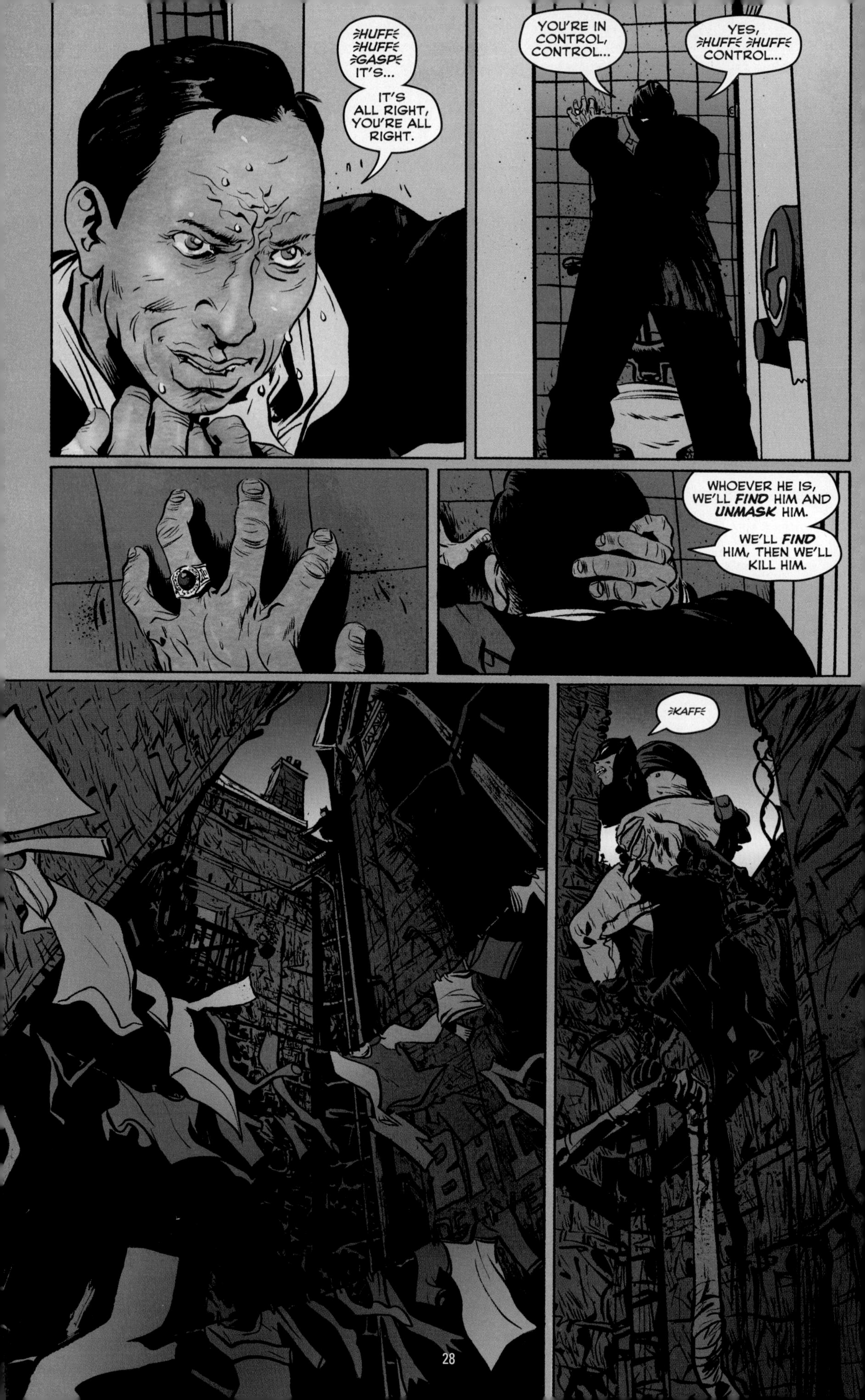

≥HUFF≤ ≥HUFF≤ ≥GASP≤ IT'S...
IT'S ALL RIGHT, YOU'RE ALL RIGHT.
YOU'RE IN CONTROL, CONTROL...
YES, ≥HUFF≤ ≥HUFF≤ CONTROL...
WHOEVER HE IS, WE'LL FIND HIM AND UNMASK HIM.
WE'LL FIND HIM, THEN WE'LL KILL HIM.
≥KAFF≤

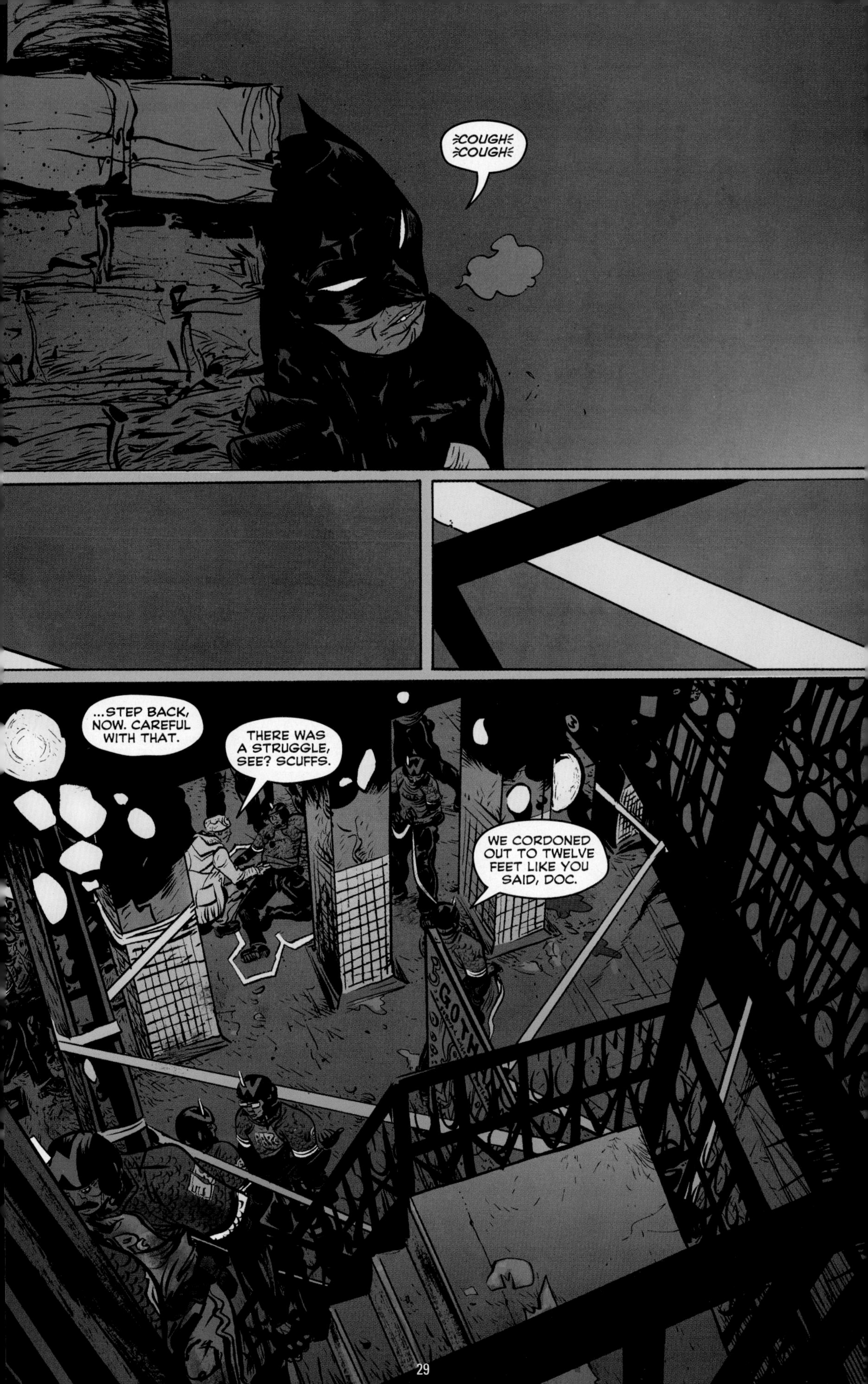

≥COUGH≤ ≥COUGH≤
...STEP BACK, NOW. CAREFUL WITH THAT.
THERE WAS A STRUGGLE, SEE? SCUFFS.
WE CORDONED OUT TO TWELVE FEET LIKE YOU SAID, DOC.

NOTING POSITION AND APPARENT LOCATION OF DEATH. VICTIM FULLY-SUITED, GLOVES AND HELMET INTACT, BOOTS LACED...

...AS FOR INITIAL EXTERNAL BODY EXAM, THERE ARE SOME ABRASIONS AROUND THE FACE. NO HEMATOMA, NO OTHER BRUISING.

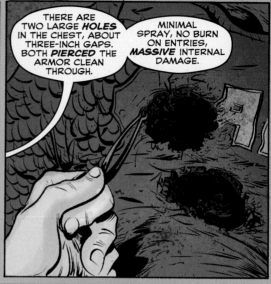

THERE ARE TWO LARGE **HOLES** IN THE CHEST, ABOUT THREE-INCH GAPS. BOTH **PIERCED** THE ARMOR CLEAN THROUGH.

MINIMAL SPRAY, NO BURN ON ENTRIES, **MASSIVE** INTERNAL DAMAGE.

TURNING HIM OVER, WE FIND THE **EXITS** COMPLETELY BLOWN **OUT**.

THE BLASTS MUST'VE BEEN FOUR FEET OFF OR LESS, GENTLE-MEN...

...ONE BLAST WOULD'A BEEN DEATH... HE HAS **TWO**. THAT'S GRIM.

AYE... **WICKED** GRIM.

NOTE, THE VIC'S CAMERA PAK IS **GONE**. LOOKS FORCIBLY SO...

...THUS, NO FIRST-PERSON FOOTAGE OF WHATEVER HAPPENED.

HE MUST'VE **NICKED** IT, THIS-THIS "BATMAN"!

WE'LL BREAK OFF HIS **HEAD**!

EASY, WOLF! TIME ENOUGH FOR THAT LATER!

THIS IS INTERESTING...

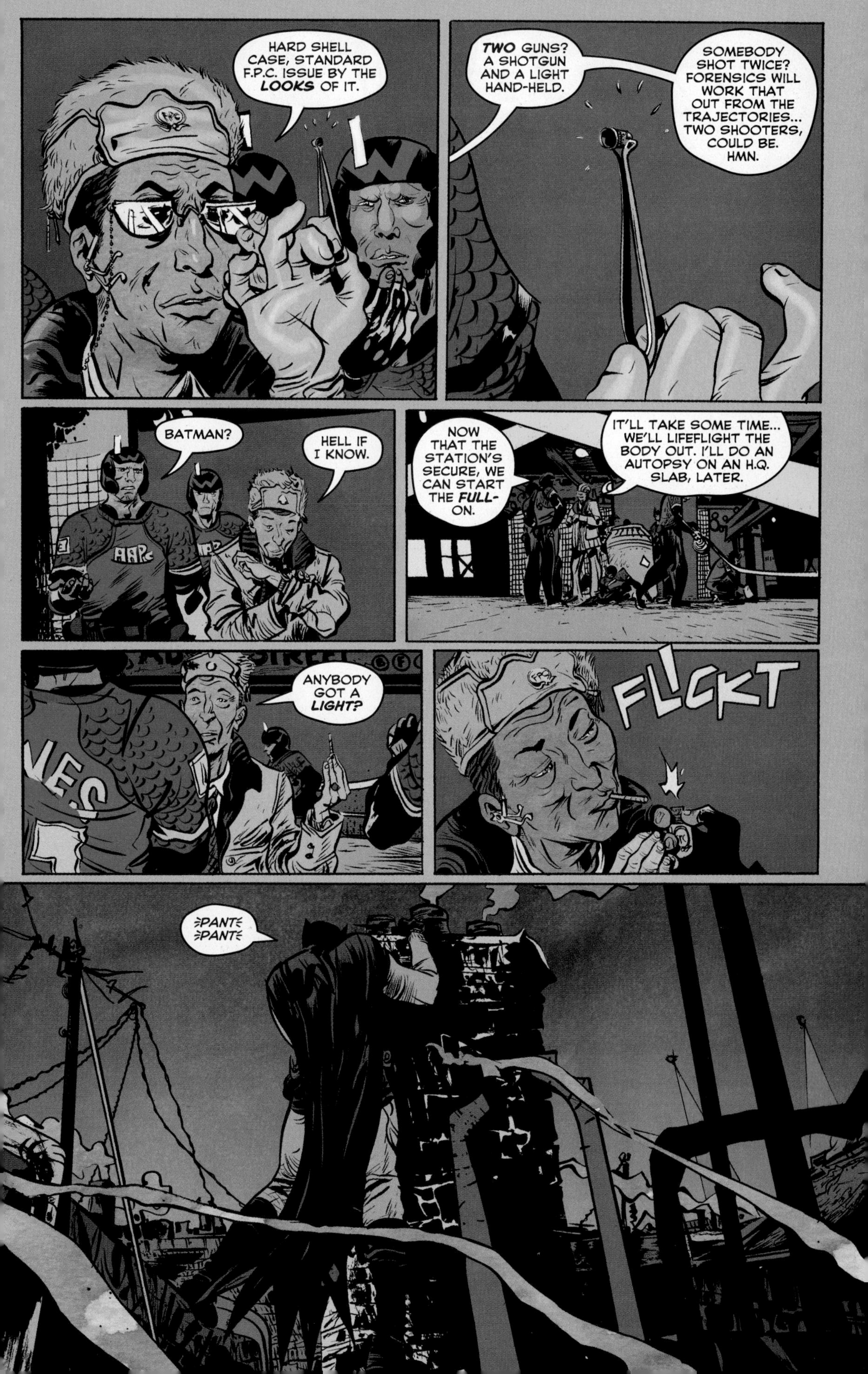
HARD SHELL CASE, STANDARD F.P.C. ISSUE BY THE LOOKS OF IT.
TWO GUNS? A SHOTGUN AND A LIGHT HAND-HELD.
SOMEBODY SHOT TWICE? FORENSICS WILL WORK THAT OUT FROM THE TRAJECTORIES... TWO SHOOTERS, COULD BE. HMN.
BATMAN?
HELL IF I KNOW.
NOW THAT THE STATION'S SECURE, WE CAN START THE FULL-ON.
IT'LL TAKE SOME TIME... WE'LL LIFEFLIGHT THE BODY OUT. I'LL DO AN AUTOPSY ON AN H.Q. SLAB, LATER.
ANYBODY GOT A LIGHT?
FLICKT
PANT PANT

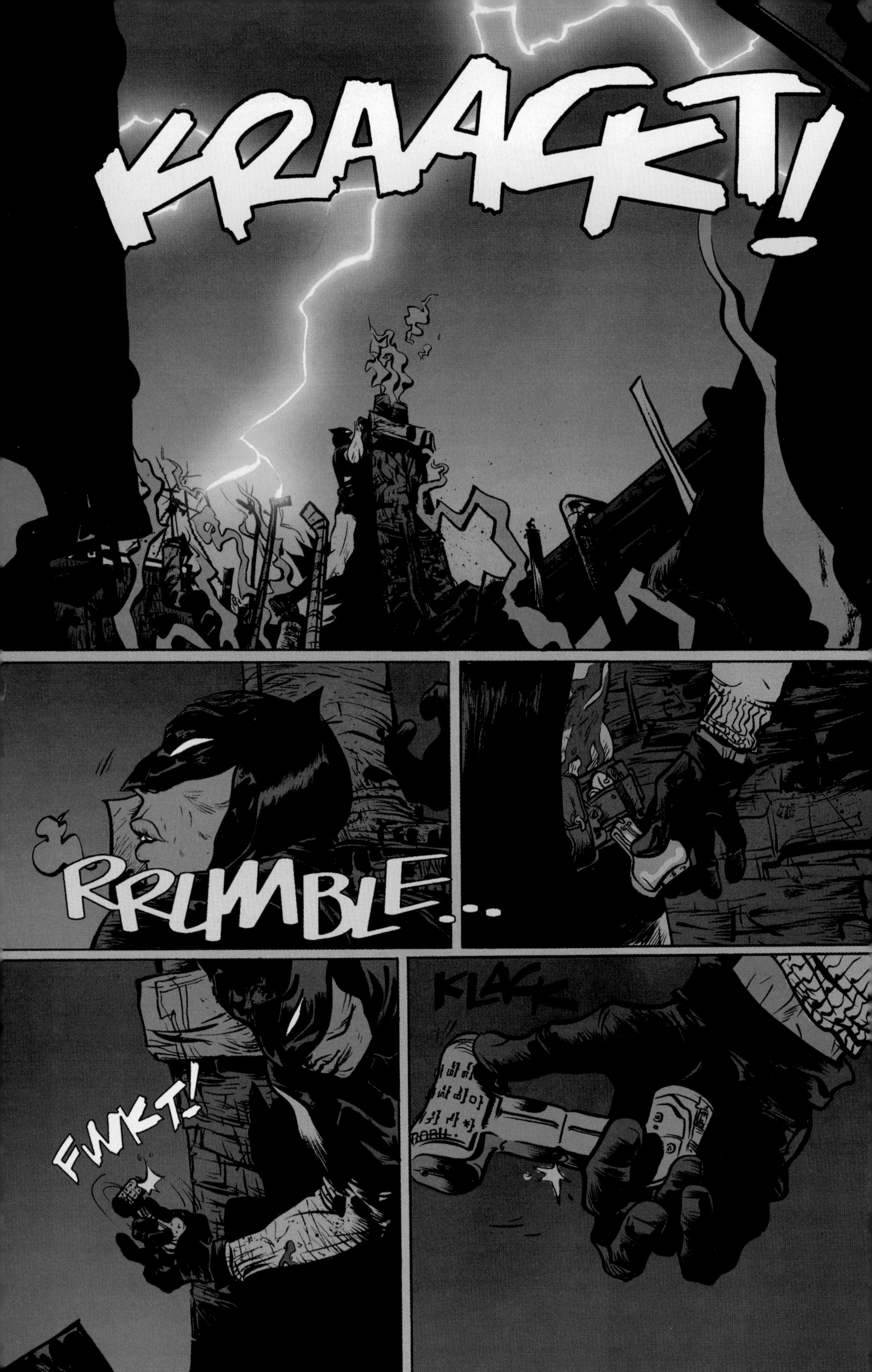
KRAAACKT!
RRUMBLE...
FWKT!
KLACK

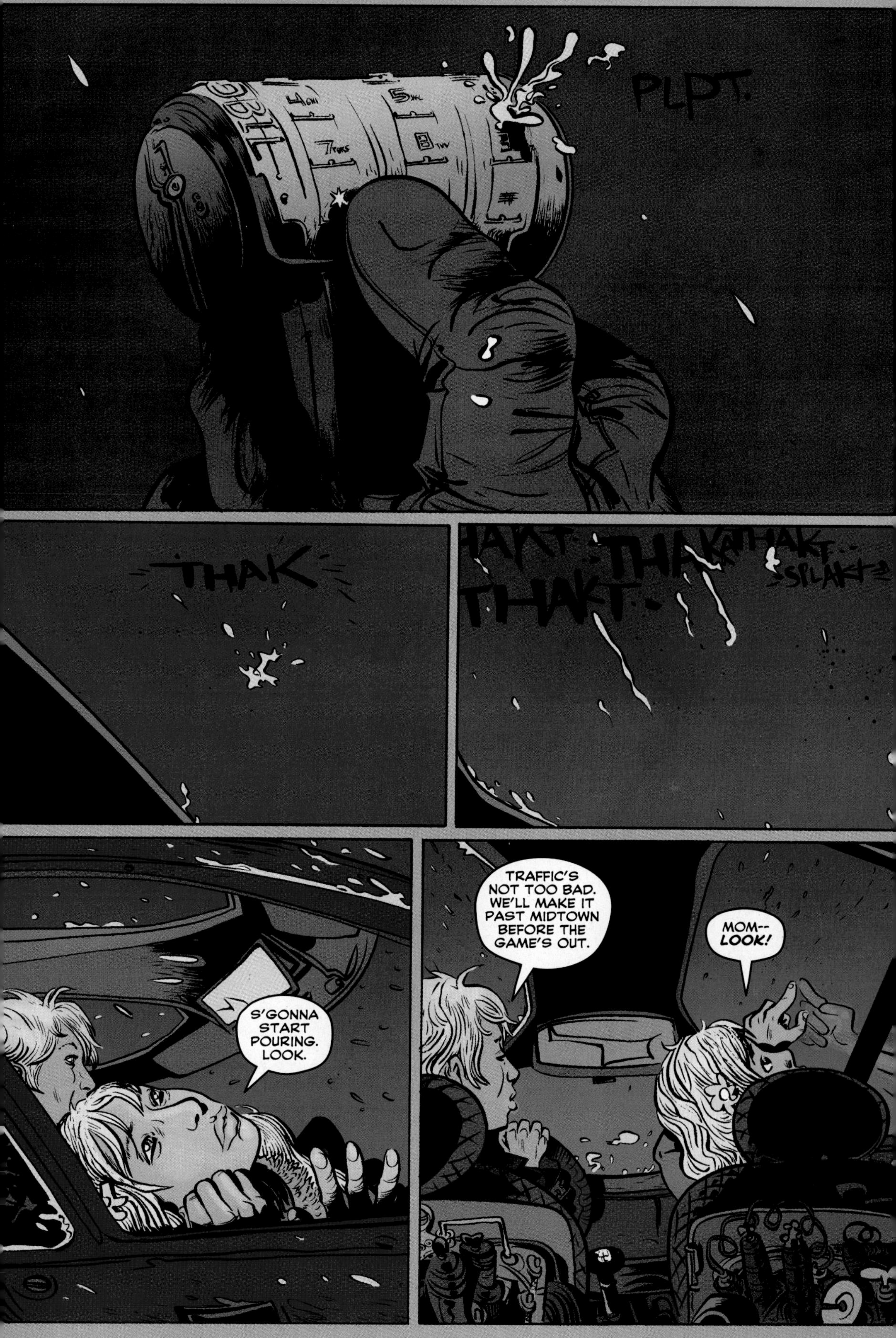
PLPT.
THAK
THAK
THAKTHAKT--
SPLAKT
THAKT
S'GONNA START POURING. LOOK.
TRAFFIC'S NOT TOO BAD. WE'LL MAKE IT PAST MIDTOWN BEFORE THE GAME'S OUT.
MOM-- **LOOK!**

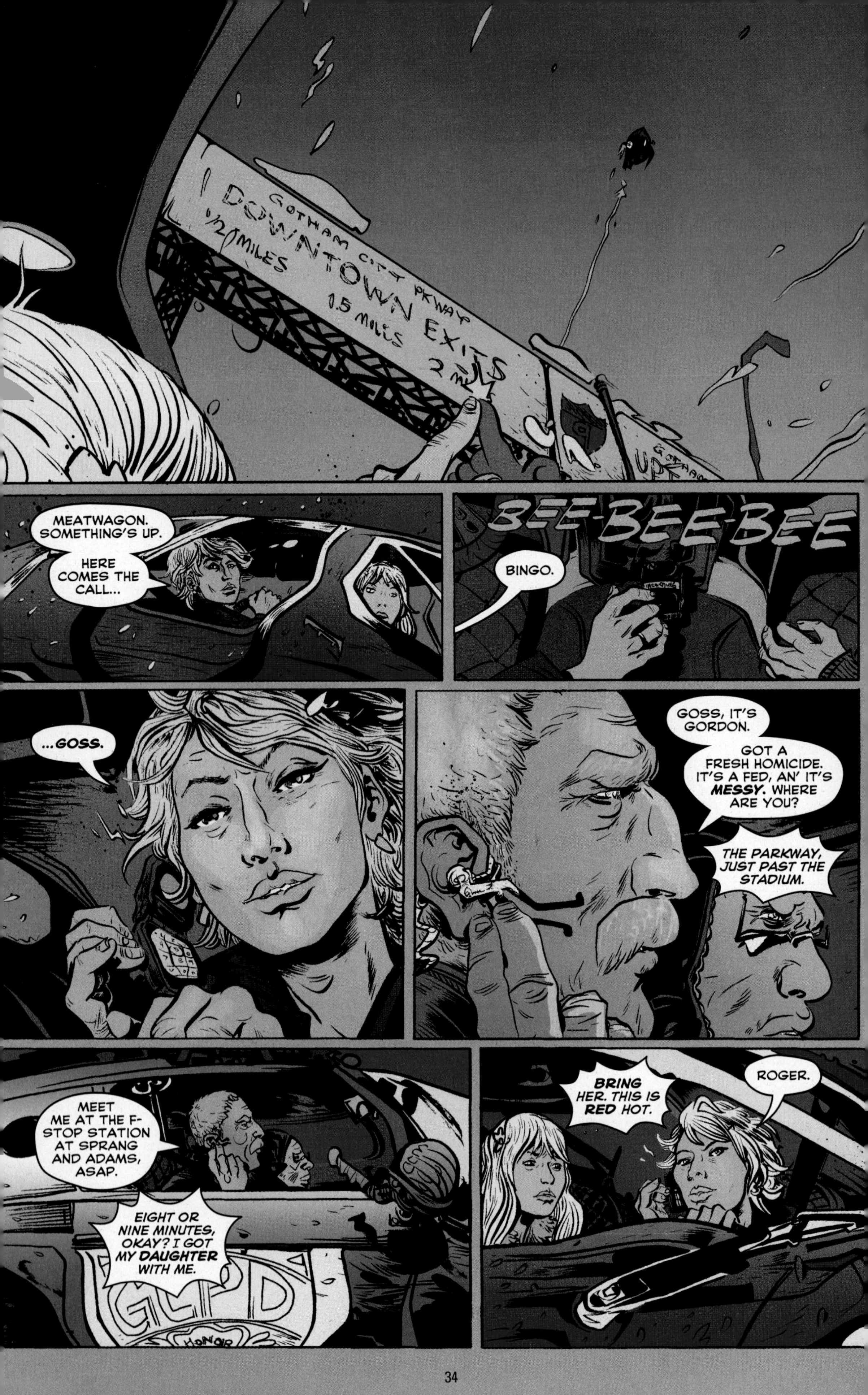
GOTHAM CITY PKWAY
DOWNTOWN EXITS
1/2 MILES
1.5 MILES
MEATWAGON. SOMETHING'S UP.
HERE COMES THE CALL...
BEE-BEE-BEE
BINGO.
...GOSS.
GOSS, IT'S GORDON.
GOT A FRESH HOMICIDE. IT'S A FED, AN' IT'S MESSY. WHERE ARE YOU?
THE PARKWAY, JUST PAST THE STADIUM.
MEET ME AT THE F-STOP STATION AT SPRANG AND ADAMS, ASAP.
EIGHT OR NINE MINUTES, OKAY? I GOT MY DAUGHTER WITH ME.
BRING HER. THIS IS RED HOT.
ROGER.
GCPD

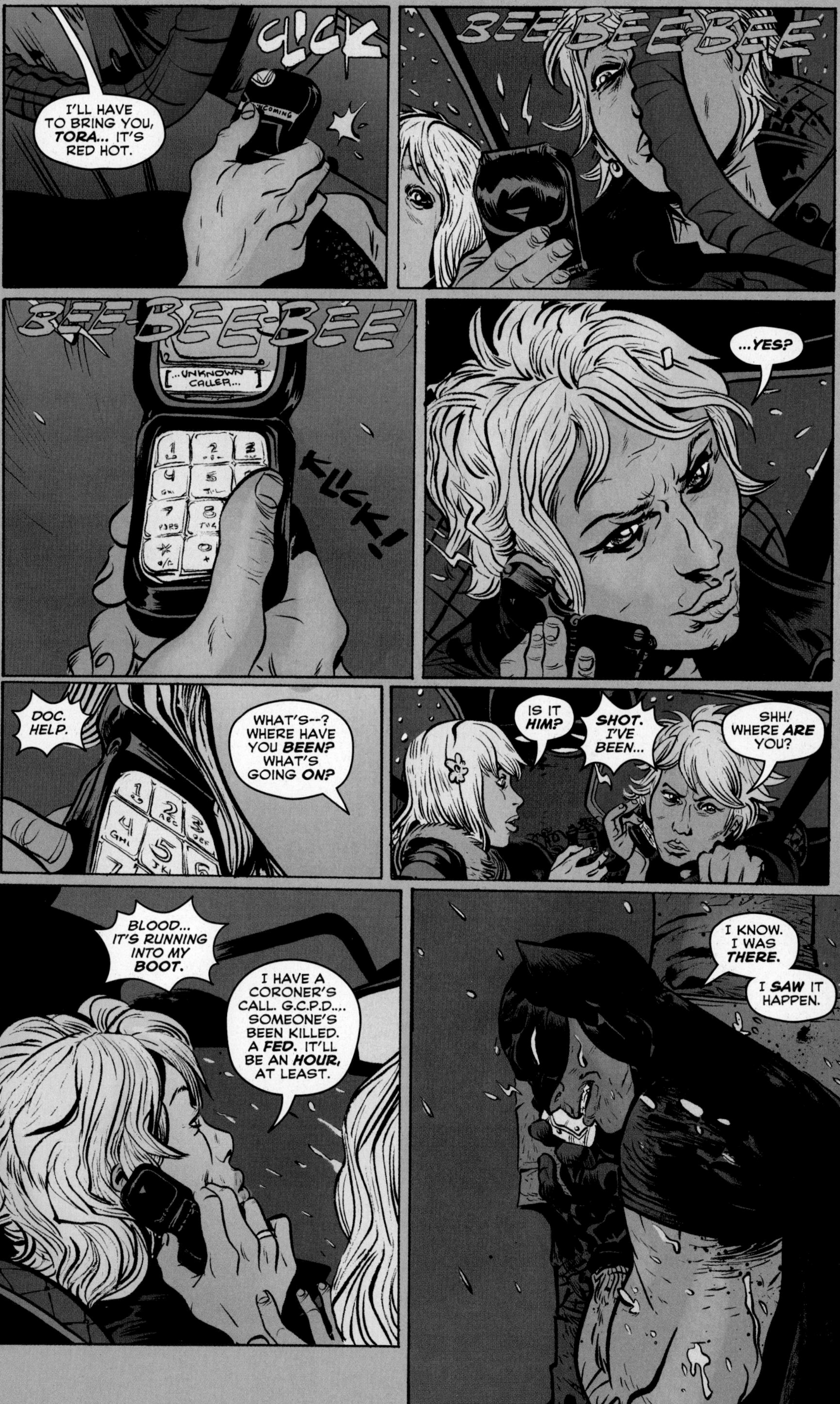
CLICK
I'LL HAVE TO BRING YOU, TORA... IT'S RED HOT.
BEE-BEE-BEE
BEE-BEE-BEE
[...UNKNOWN CALLER...]
KLICK!
...YES?
DOC. HELP.
WHAT'S--? WHERE HAVE YOU BEEN? WHAT'S GOING ON?
IS IT HIM?
SHOT. I'VE BEEN...
SHH! WHERE ARE YOU?
BLOOD... IT'S RUNNING INTO MY BOOT.
I HAVE A CORONER'S CALL. G.C.P.D.... SOMEONE'S BEEN KILLED. A FED. IT'LL BE AN HOUR, AT LEAST.
I KNOW. I WAS THERE.
I SAW IT HAPPEN.

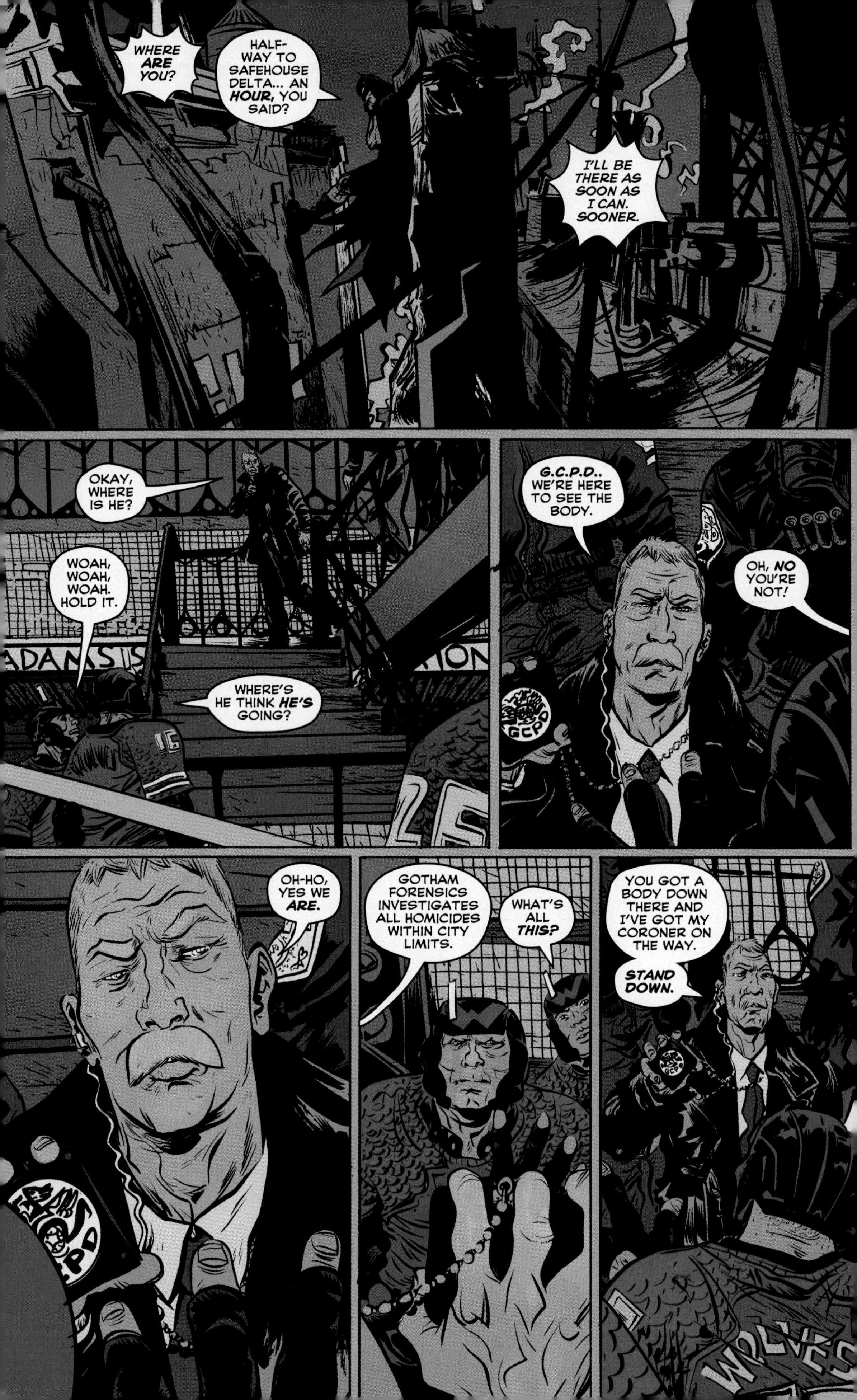
WHERE ARE YOU?
HALF-WAY TO SAFEHOUSE DELTA... AN HOUR, YOU SAID?
I'LL BE THERE AS SOON AS I CAN. SOONER.
OKAY, WHERE IS HE?
WOAH, WOAH, WOAH. HOLD IT.
WHERE'S HE THINK HE'S GOING?
G.C.P.D.. WE'RE HERE TO SEE THE BODY.
OH, NO YOU'RE NOT!
OH-HO, YES WE ARE.
GOTHAM FORENSICS INVESTIGATES ALL HOMICIDES WITHIN CITY LIMITS.
WHAT'S ALL THIS?
YOU GOT A BODY DOWN THERE AND I'VE GOT MY CORONER ON THE WAY.
STAND DOWN.

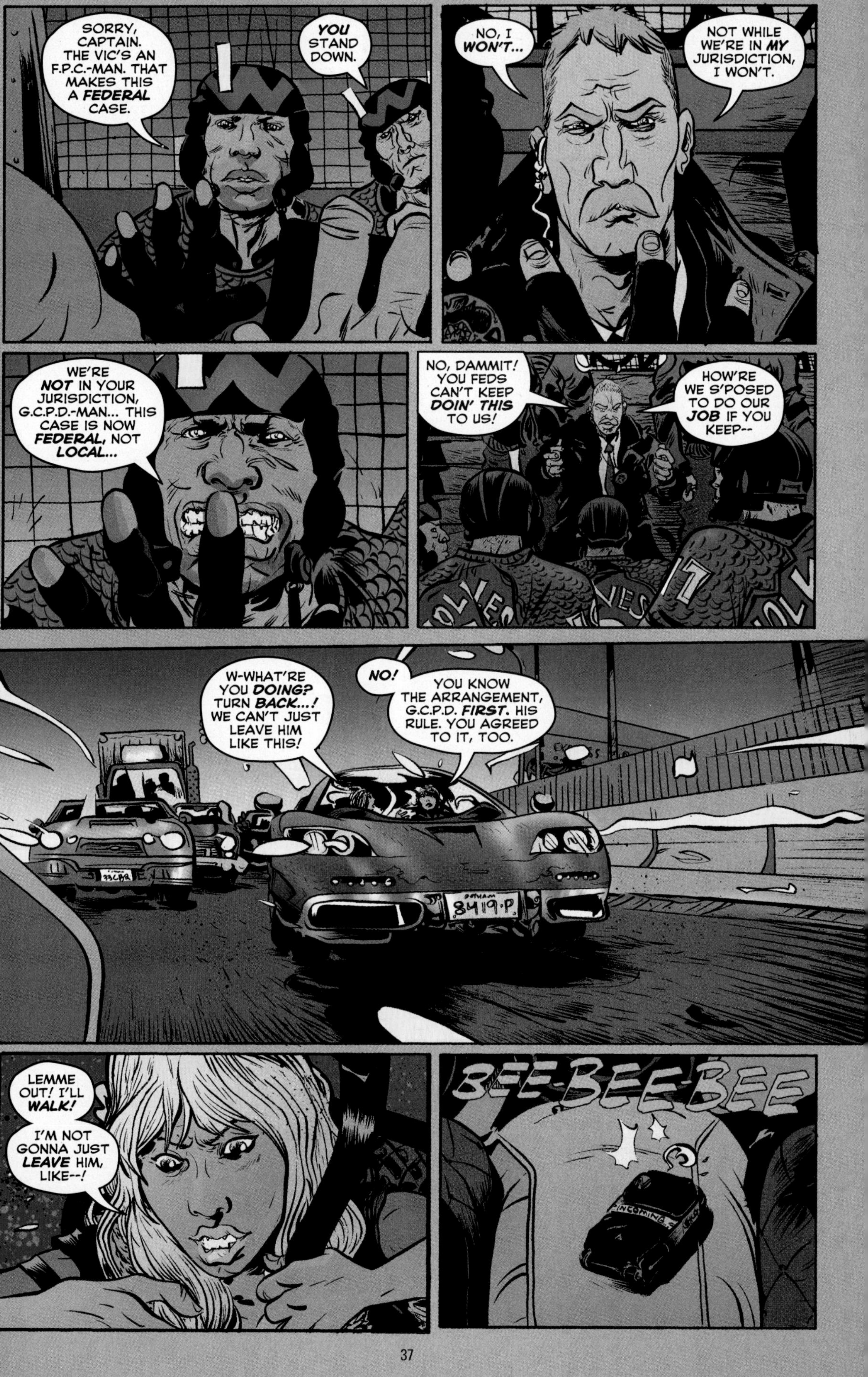
SORRY, CAPTAIN. THE VIC'S AN F.P.C.-MAN. THAT MAKES THIS A **FEDERAL** CASE.
YOU STAND DOWN.
NO, I ***WON'T...***
NOT WHILE WE'RE IN ***MY*** JURISDICTION, I WON'T.
WE'RE ***NOT*** IN YOUR JURISDICTION, G.C.P.D.-MAN... THIS CASE IS NOW ***FEDERAL,*** NOT ***LOCAL...***
NO, DAMMIT! YOU FEDS CAN'T KEEP ***DOIN' THIS*** TO US!
HOW'RE WE S'POSED TO DO OUR ***JOB*** IF YOU KEEP--
W-WHAT'RE YOU ***DOING?*** TURN ***BACK...!*** WE CAN'T JUST LEAVE HIM LIKE THIS!
NO!
YOU KNOW THE ARRANGEMENT, G.C.P.D. ***FIRST.*** HIS RULE. YOU AGREED TO IT, TOO.
LEMME OUT! I'LL ***WALK!***
I'M NOT GONNA JUST ***LEAVE*** HIM, LIKE--!
BEE-BEE-BEE

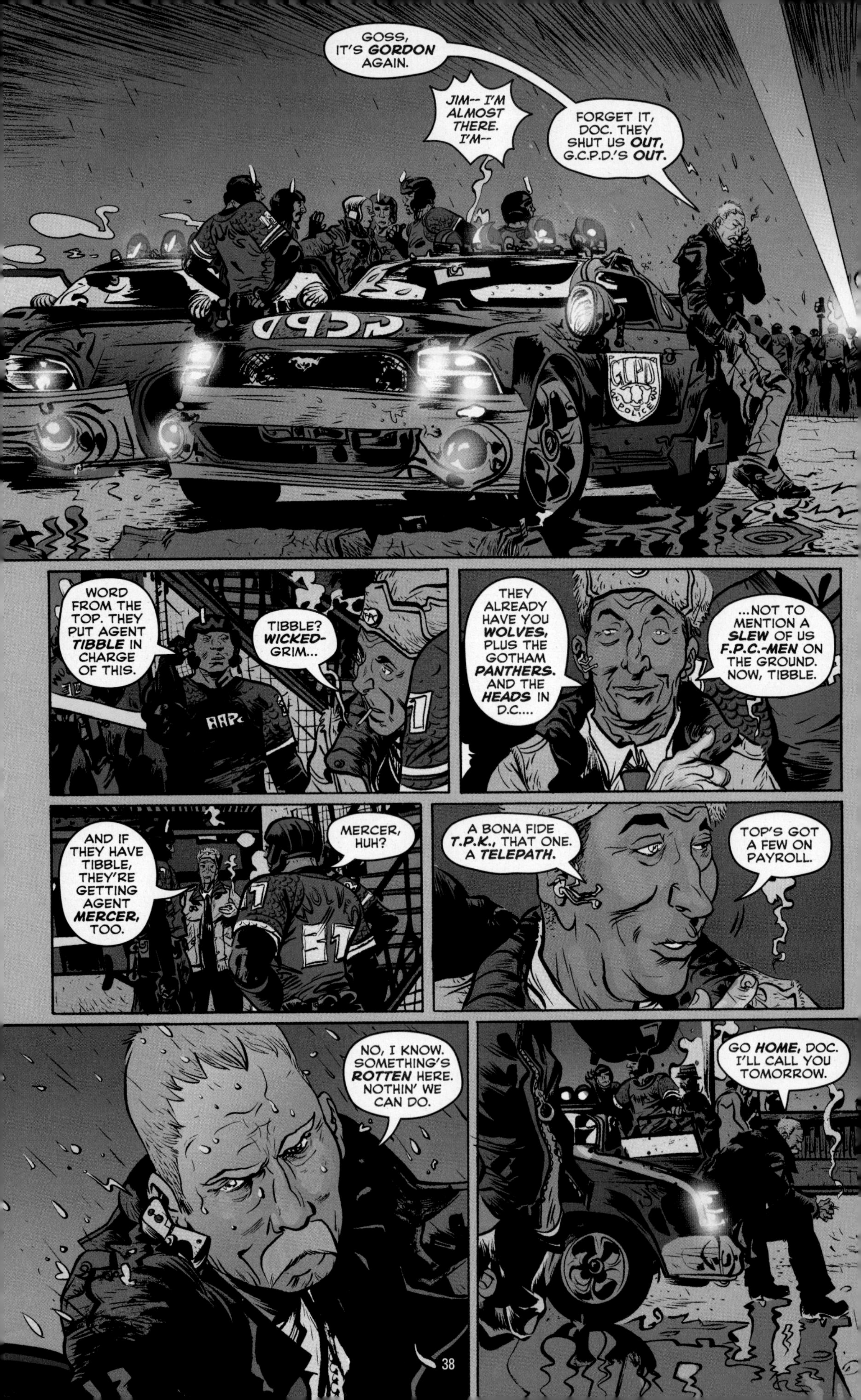
GOSS, IT'S GORDON AGAIN.
JIM-- I'M ALMOST THERE. I'M--
FORGET IT, DOC. THEY SHUT US OUT, G.C.P.D.'S OUT.
GCPD
WORD FROM THE TOP. THEY PUT AGENT TIBBLE IN CHARGE OF THIS.
TIBBLE? WICKED-GRIM...
THEY ALREADY HAVE YOU WOLVES, PLUS THE GOTHAM PANTHERS. AND THE HEADS IN D.C....
...NOT TO MENTION A SLEW OF US F.P.C.-MEN ON THE GROUND. NOW, TIBBLE.
AND IF THEY HAVE TIBBLE, THEY'RE GETTING AGENT MERCER, TOO.
MERCER, HUH?
A BONA FIDE T.P.K., THAT ONE. A TELEPATH.
TOP'S GOT A FEW ON PAYROLL.
NO, I KNOW. SOMETHING'S ROTTEN HERE. NOTHIN' WE CAN DO.
GO HOME, DOC. I'LL CALL YOU TOMORROW.

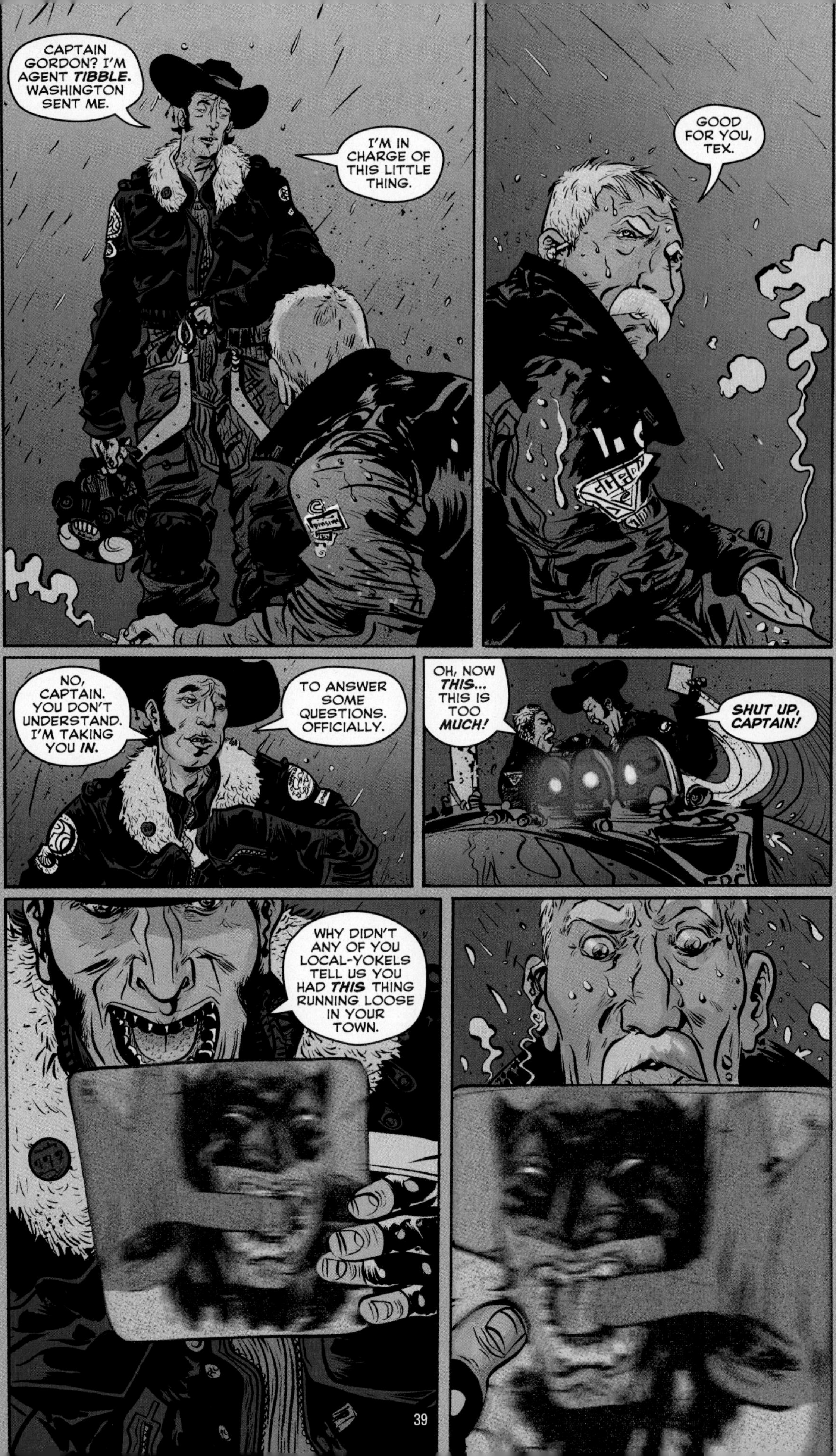
CAPTAIN GORDON? I'M AGENT TIBBLE. WASHINGTON SENT ME.
I'M IN CHARGE OF THIS LITTLE THING.
GOOD FOR YOU, TEX.
NO, CAPTAIN. YOU DON'T UNDERSTAND. I'M TAKING YOU IN.
TO ANSWER SOME QUESTIONS. OFFICIALLY.
OH, NOW THIS... THIS IS TOO MUCH!
SHUT UP, CAPTAIN!
WHY DIDN'T ANY OF YOU LOCAL-YOKELS TELL US YOU HAD THIS THING RUNNING LOOSE IN YOUR TOWN.

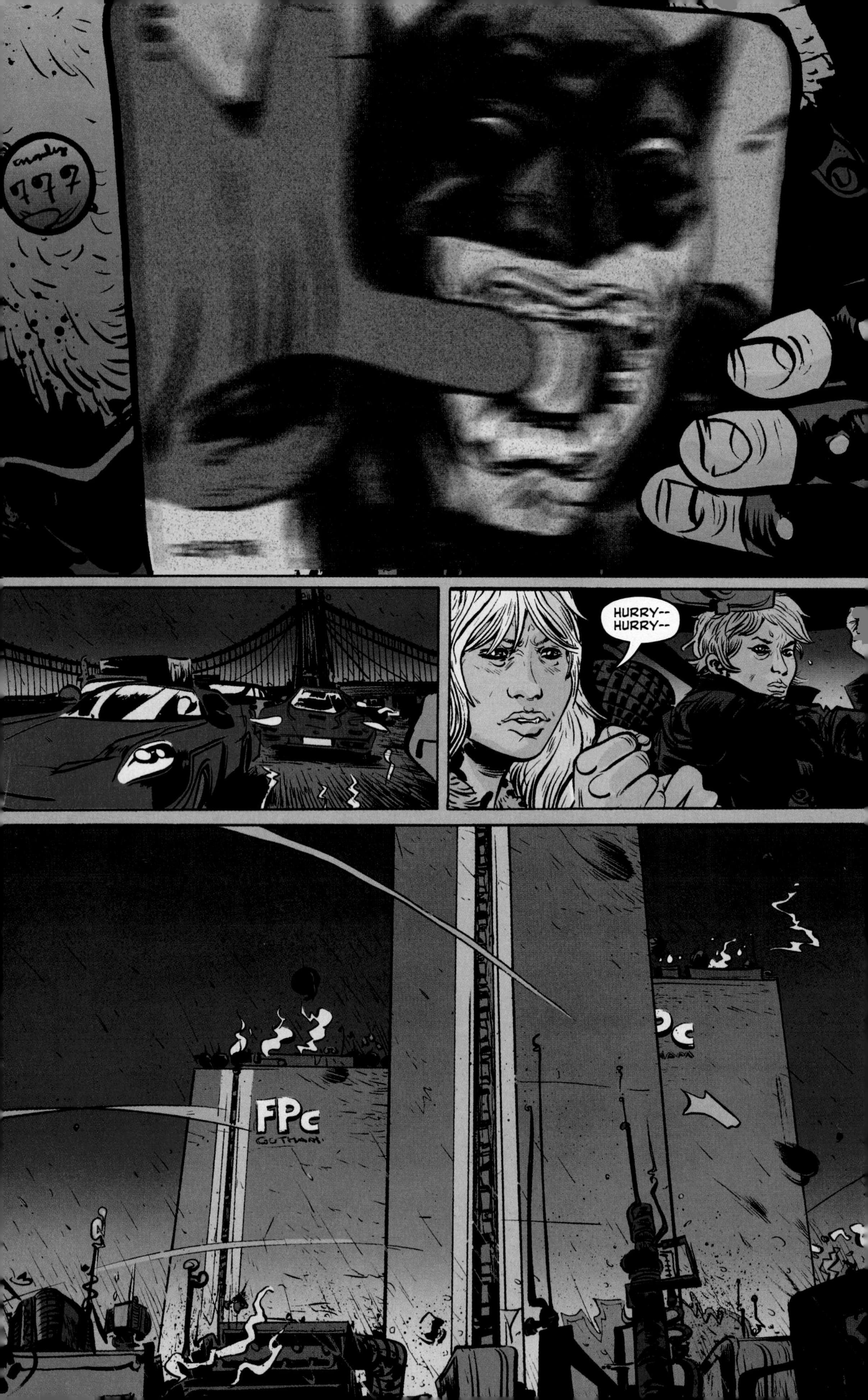
HURRY--
HURRY--
FPc
GOTHAM

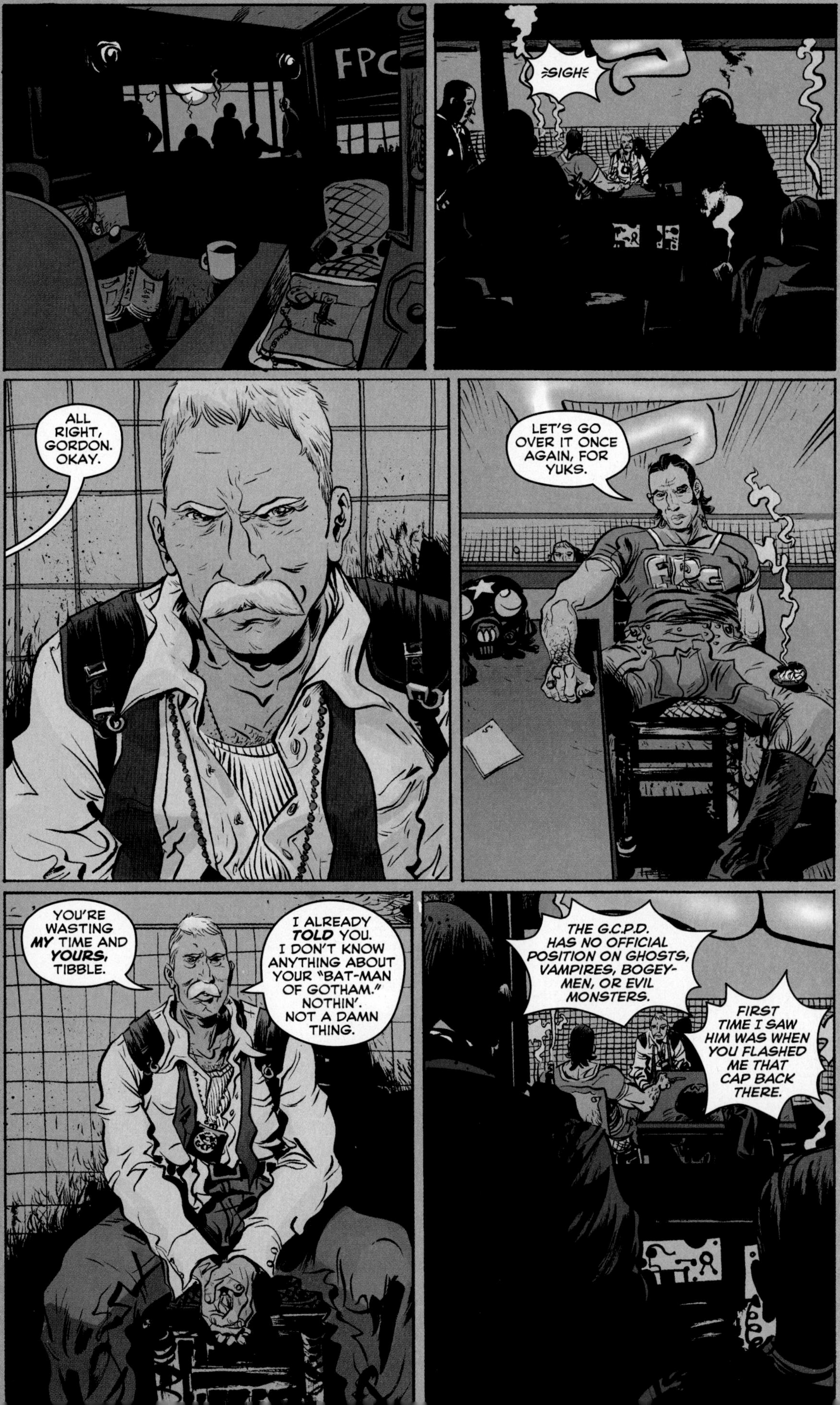

SIGH
ALL RIGHT, GORDON. OKAY.
LET'S GO OVER IT ONCE AGAIN, FOR YUKS.
YOU'RE WASTING MY TIME AND YOURS, TIBBLE.
I ALREADY TOLD YOU. I DON'T KNOW ANYTHING ABOUT YOUR "BAT-MAN OF GOTHAM." NOTHIN'. NOT A DAMN THING.
THE G.C.P.D. HAS NO OFFICIAL POSITION ON GHOSTS, VAMPIRES, BOGEY-MEN, OR EVIL MONSTERS.
FIRST TIME I SAW HIM WAS WHEN YOU FLASHED ME THAT CAP BACK THERE.

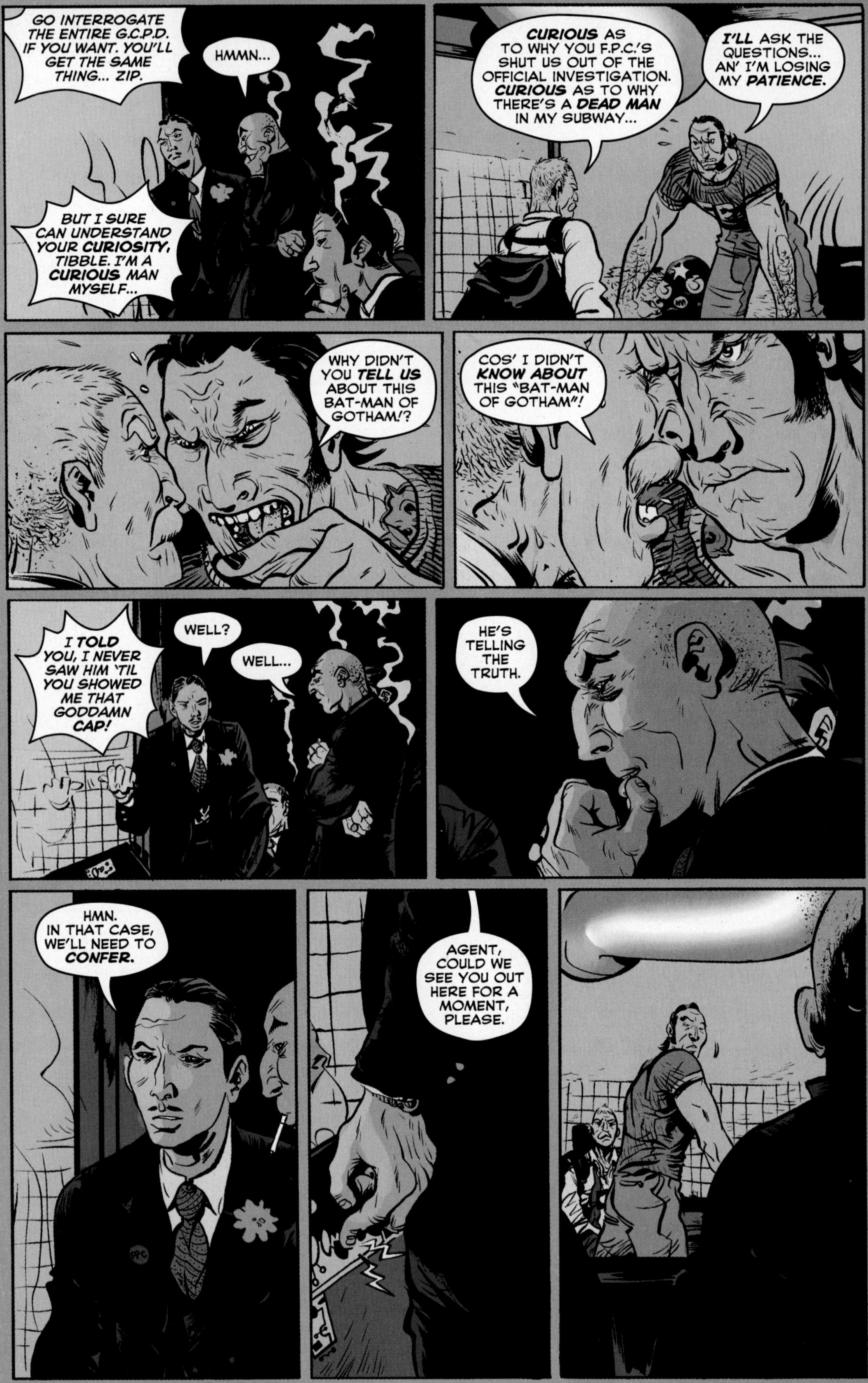
GO INTERROGATE THE ENTIRE G.C.P.D. IF YOU WANT. YOU'LL GET THE SAME THING... ZIP.
HMMN...
BUT I SURE CAN UNDERSTAND YOUR CURIOSITY, TIBBLE. I'M A CURIOUS MAN MYSELF...
CURIOUS AS TO WHY YOU F.P.C.'S SHUT US OUT OF THE OFFICIAL INVESTIGATION. CURIOUS AS TO WHY THERE'S A DEAD MAN IN MY SUBWAY...
I'LL ASK THE QUESTIONS... AN' I'M LOSING MY PATIENCE.
WHY DIDN'T YOU TELL US ABOUT THIS BAT-MAN OF GOTHAM!?
COS' I DIDN'T KNOW ABOUT THIS "BAT-MAN OF GOTHAM"!
I TOLD YOU, I NEVER SAW HIM 'TIL YOU SHOWED ME THAT GODDAMN CAP!
WELL?
WELL...
HE'S TELLING THE TRUTH.
HMN. IN THAT CASE, WE'LL NEED TO CONFER.
AGENT, COULD WE SEE YOU OUT HERE FOR A MOMENT, PLEASE.

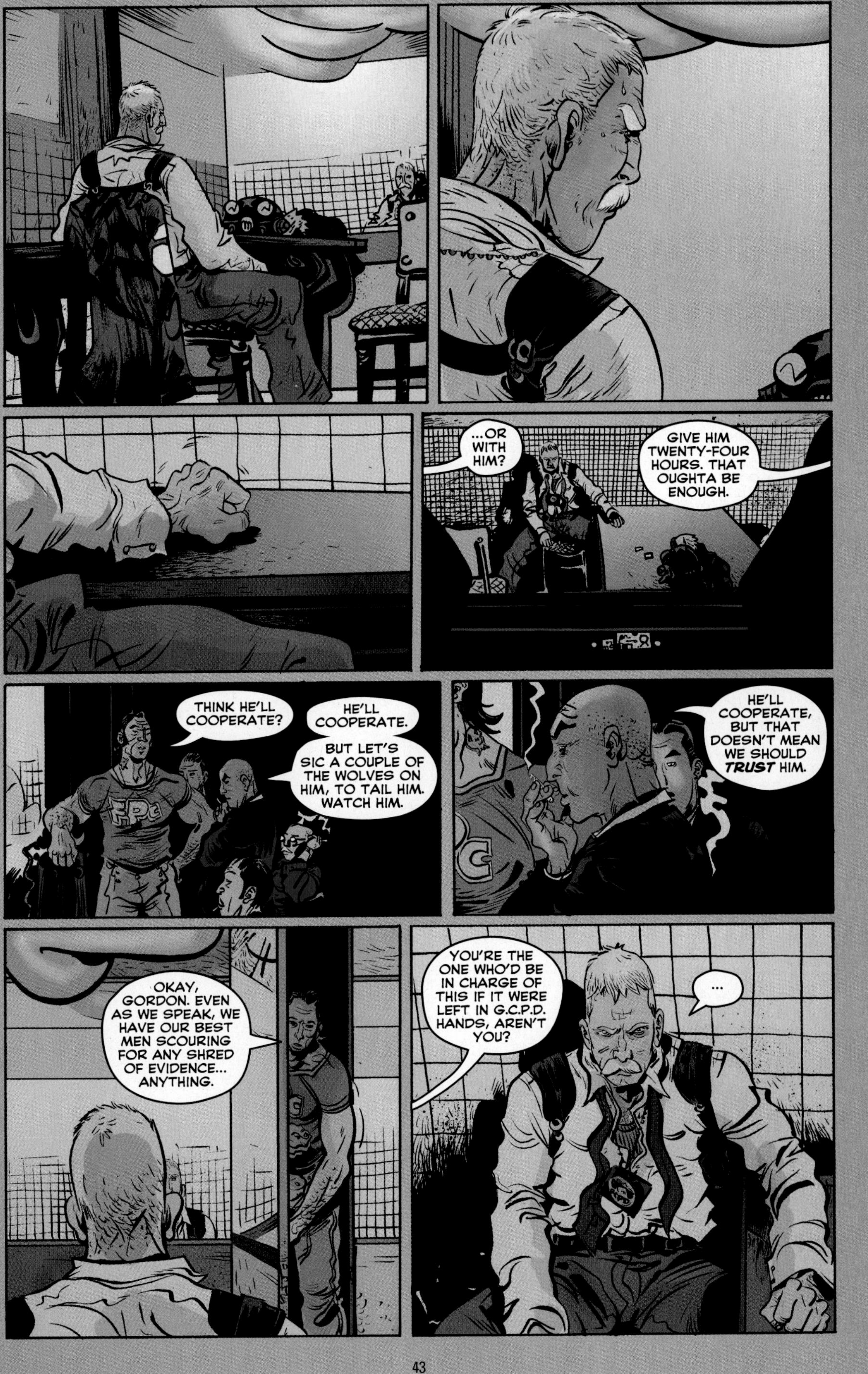
...OR WITH HIM?
GIVE HIM TWENTY-FOUR HOURS. THAT OUGHTA BE ENOUGH.
THINK HE'LL COOPERATE?
HE'LL COOPERATE.
BUT LET'S SIC A COUPLE OF THE WOLVES ON HIM, TO TAIL HIM. WATCH HIM.
HE'LL COOPERATE, BUT THAT DOESN'T MEAN WE SHOULD *TRUST* HIM.
OKAY, GORDON. EVEN AS WE SPEAK, WE HAVE OUR BEST MEN SCOURING FOR ANY SHRED OF EVIDENCE... ANYTHING.
YOU'RE THE ONE WHO'D BE IN CHARGE OF THIS IF IT WERE LEFT IN G.C.P.D. HANDS, AREN'T YOU?
...

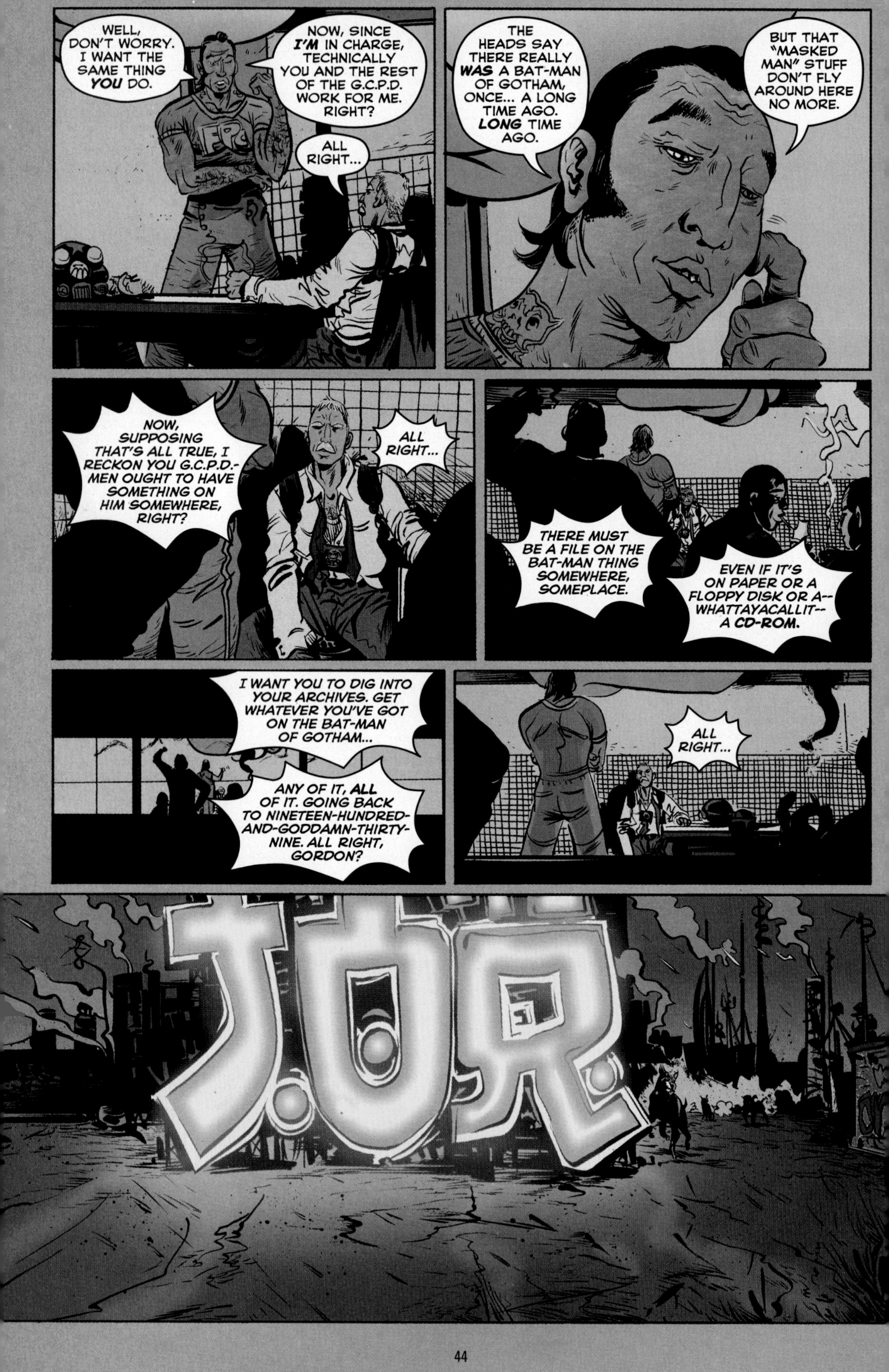

WELL, DON'T WORRY. I WANT THE SAME THING YOU DO.
NOW, SINCE I'M IN CHARGE, TECHNICALLY YOU AND THE REST OF THE G.C.P.D. WORK FOR ME. RIGHT?
ALL RIGHT...
THE HEADS SAY THERE REALLY WAS A BAT-MAN OF GOTHAM, ONCE... A LONG TIME AGO. LONG TIME AGO.
BUT THAT "MASKED MAN" STUFF DON'T FLY AROUND HERE NO MORE.
NOW, SUPPOSING THAT'S ALL TRUE, I RECKON YOU G.C.P.D.-MEN OUGHT TO HAVE SOMETHING ON HIM SOMEWHERE, RIGHT?
ALL RIGHT...
THERE MUST BE A FILE ON THE BAT-MAN THING SOMEWHERE, SOMEPLACE.
EVEN IF IT'S ON PAPER OR A FLOPPY DISK OR A--WHATTAYACALLIT--A CD-ROM.
I WANT YOU TO DIG INTO YOUR ARCHIVES. GET WHATEVER YOU'VE GOT ON THE BAT-MAN OF GOTHAM...
ANY OF IT, ALL OF IT. GOING BACK TO NINETEEN-HUNDRED-AND-GODDAMN-THIRTY-NINE. ALL RIGHT, GORDON?
ALL RIGHT...
J.O.R.

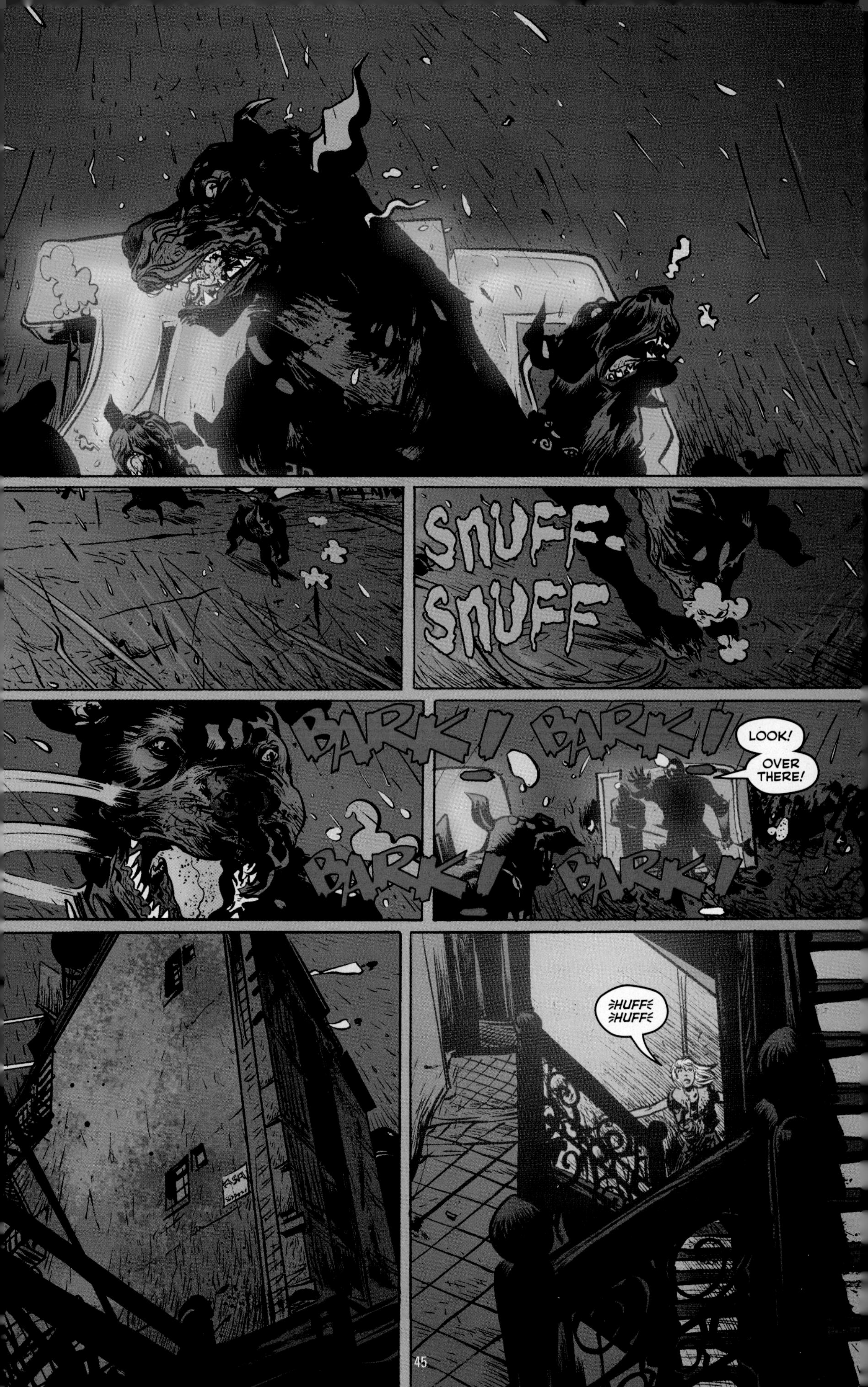
SNUFF SNUFF
BARK! BARK!
LOOK!
OVER THERE!
BARK! BARK!
HUFF HUFF

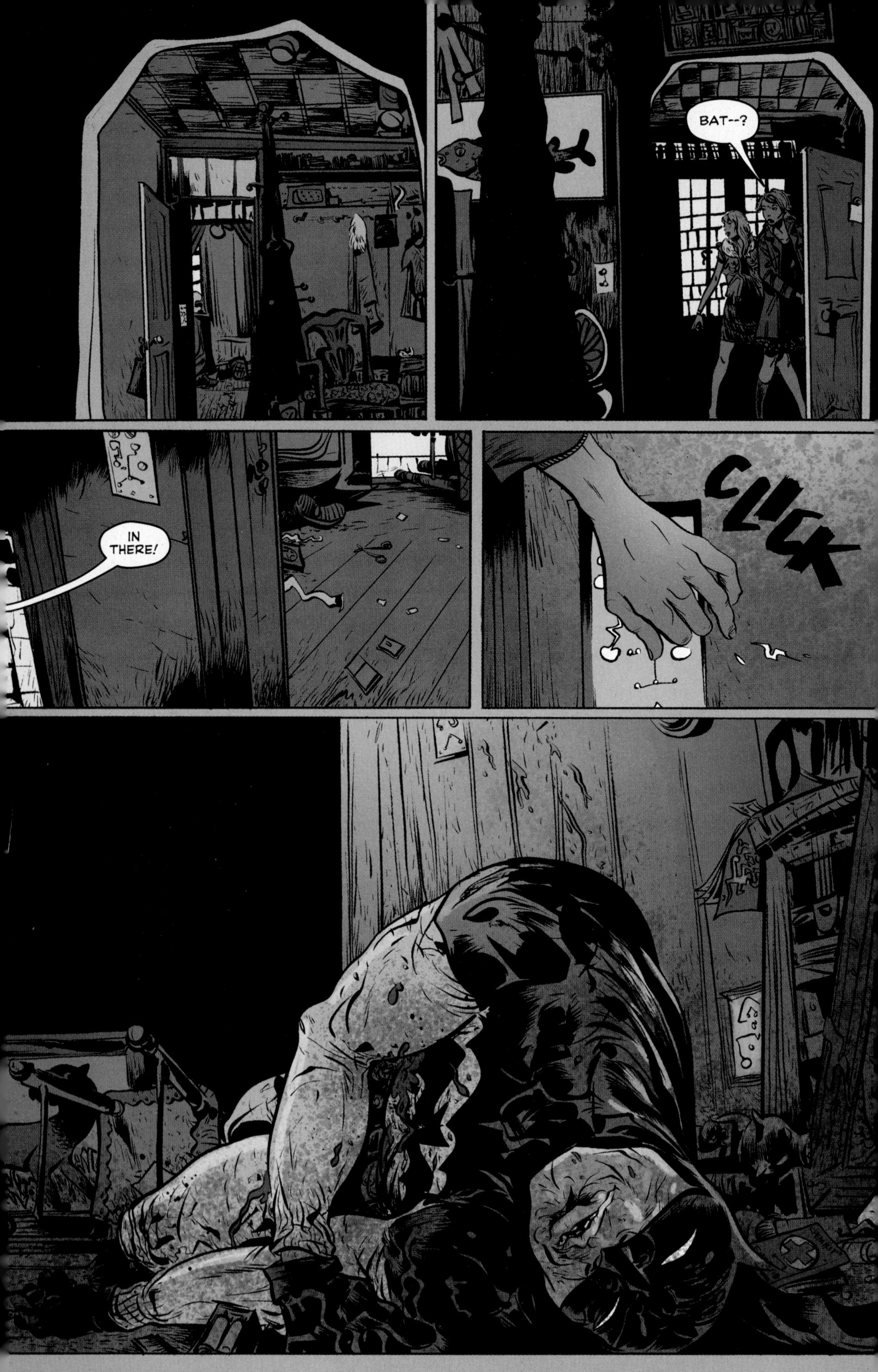
BAT--?
IN THERE!
CLICK

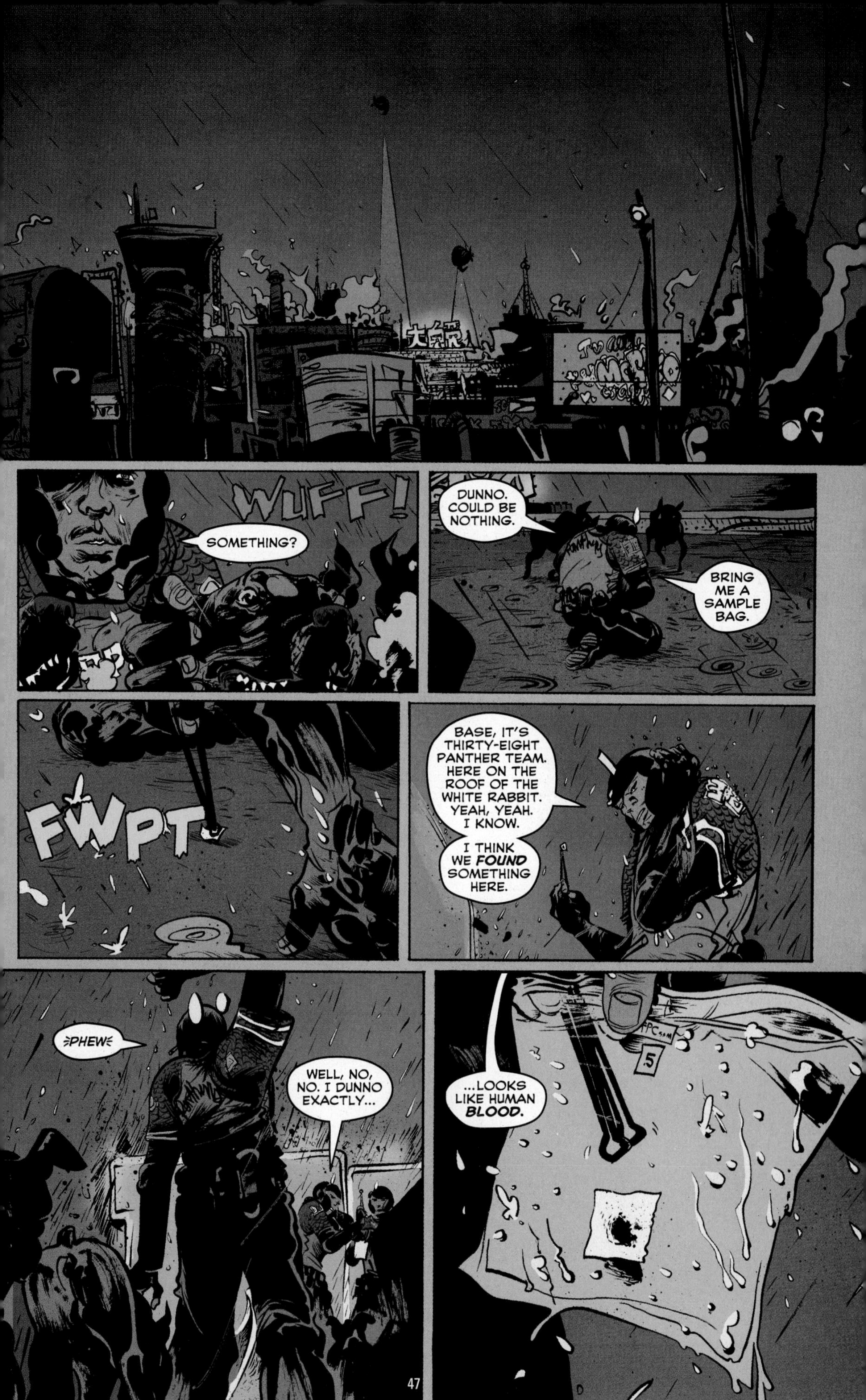
WUFF!
SOMETHING?
DUNNO. COULD BE NOTHING.
BRING ME A SAMPLE BAG.
FWPT
BASE, IT'S THIRTY-EIGHT PANTHER TEAM. HERE ON THE ROOF OF THE WHITE RABBIT. YEAH, YEAH. I KNOW.
I THINK WE *FOUND* SOMETHING HERE.
PHEW
WELL, NO, NO. I DUNNO EXACTLY...
...LOOKS LIKE HUMAN *BLOOD.*

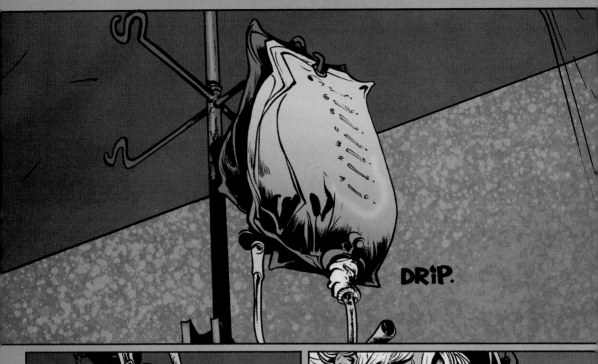

DRIP.

DRIP.
DRIP.

HE'S LOST A LOT, MAYBE TWO UNITS. I'M STARTING HIM ON A LITER OF SALINE, THEN PLASMA. C'MON.

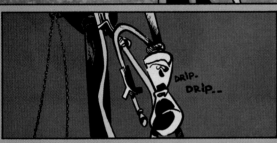

WHAT D'YA THINK *HAPPENED* TO HIM?

IT'S A SELF-LIMITED GUNSHOT WOUND.

LOOKS LIKE IT WAS A SMALL GAUGE HARD-SHELL.

AND IT FEELS LIKE HE HAS A COUPLE FRACTURES HERE, RIGHT MIDSIDE.

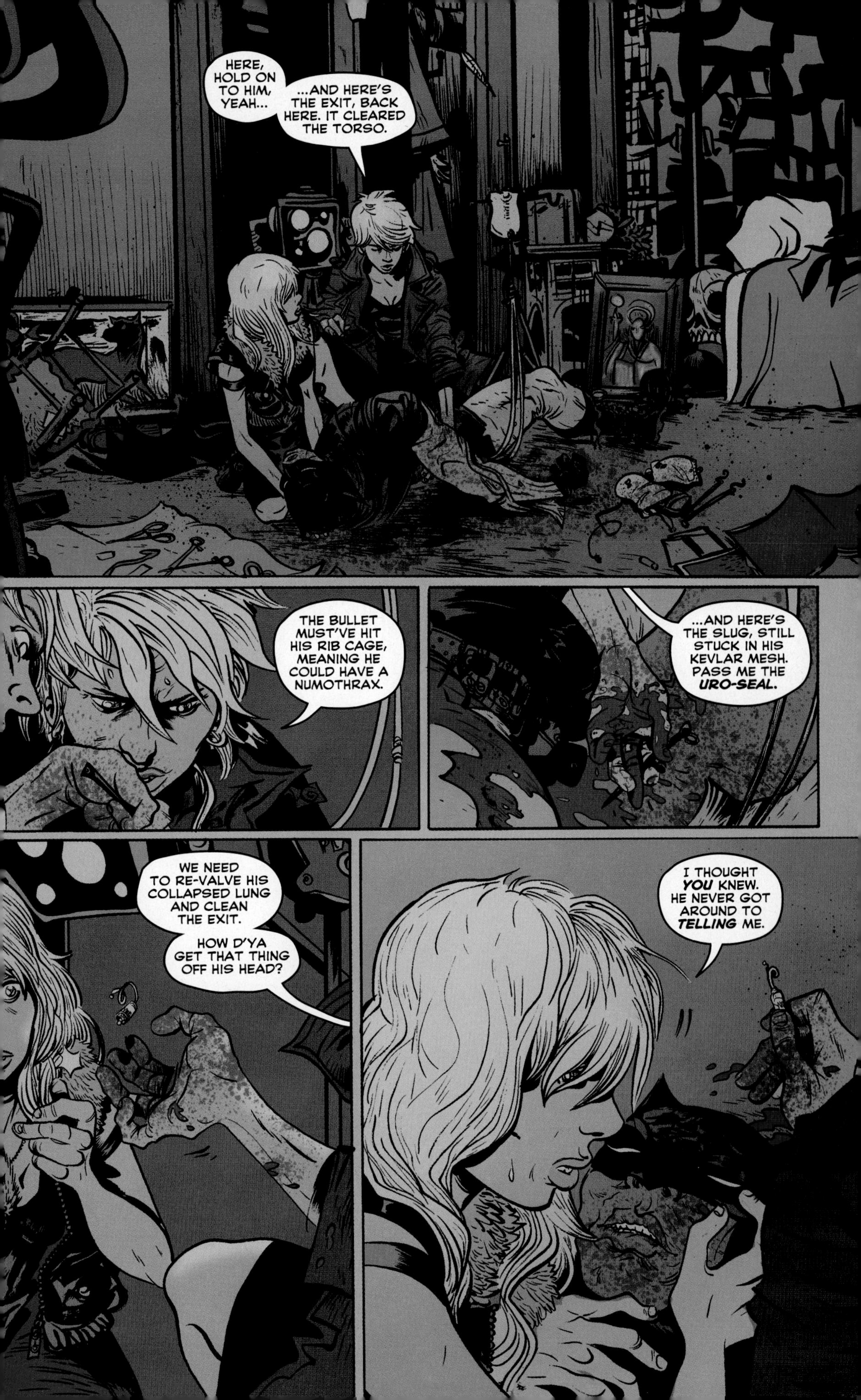
HERE, HOLD ON TO HIM, YEAH...
...AND HERE'S THE EXIT, BACK HERE. IT CLEARED THE TORSO.
THE BULLET MUST'VE HIT HIS RIB CAGE, MEANING HE COULD HAVE A NUMOTHRAX.
...AND HERE'S THE SLUG, STILL STUCK IN HIS KEVLAR MESH. PASS ME THE *URO-SEAL.*
WE NEED TO RE-VALVE HIS COLLAPSED LUNG AND CLEAN THE EXIT.
HOW D'YA GET THAT THING OFF HIS HEAD?
I THOUGHT *YOU* KNEW. HE NEVER GOT AROUND TO *TELLING* ME.

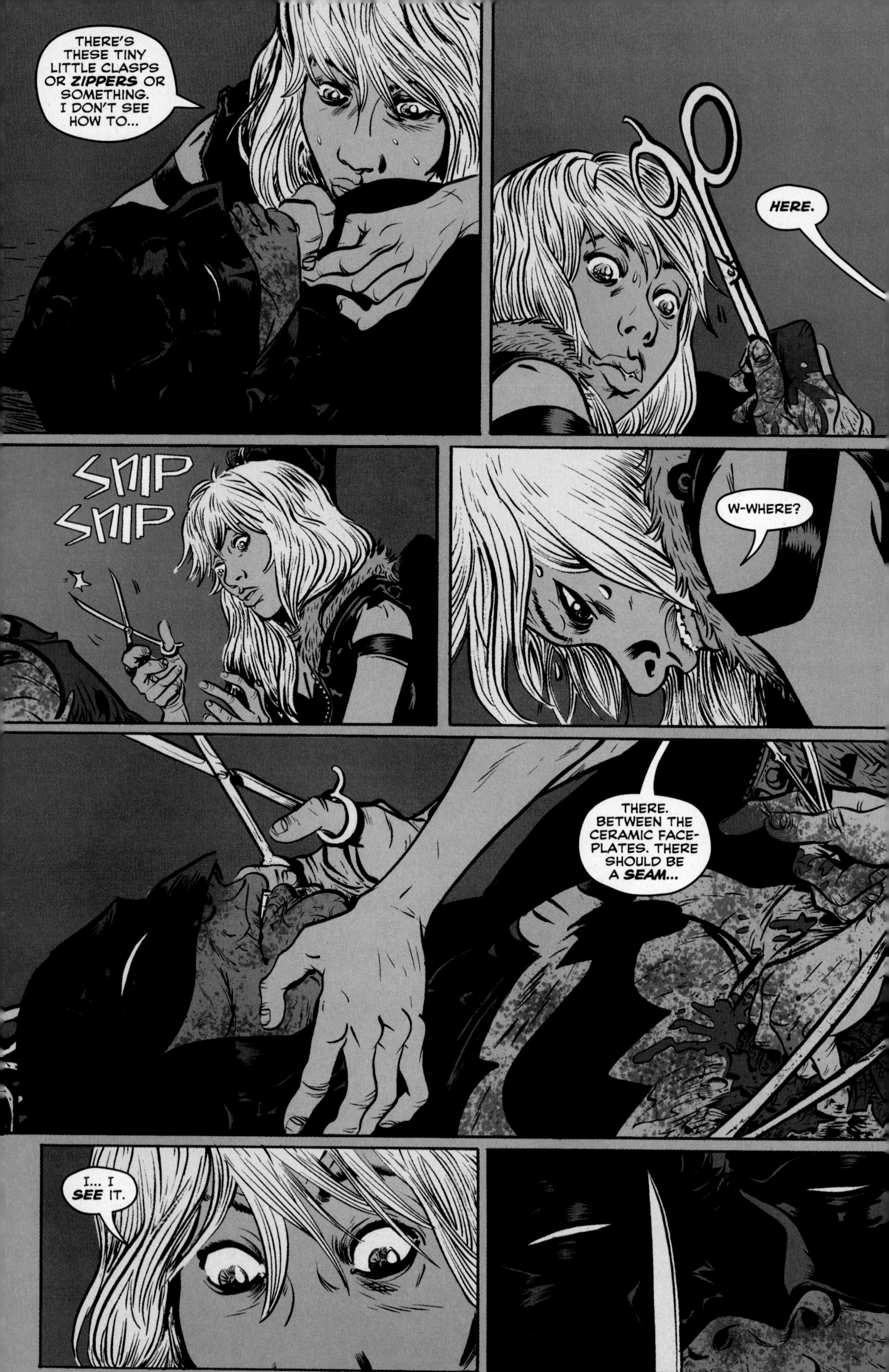
THERE'S THESE TINY LITTLE CLASPS OR *ZIPPERS* OR SOMETHING. I DON'T SEE HOW TO...
HERE.
SNIP SNIP
W-WHERE?
THERE. BETWEEN THE CERAMIC FACE-PLATES. THERE SHOULD BE A *SEAM*...
I... I *SEE* IT.

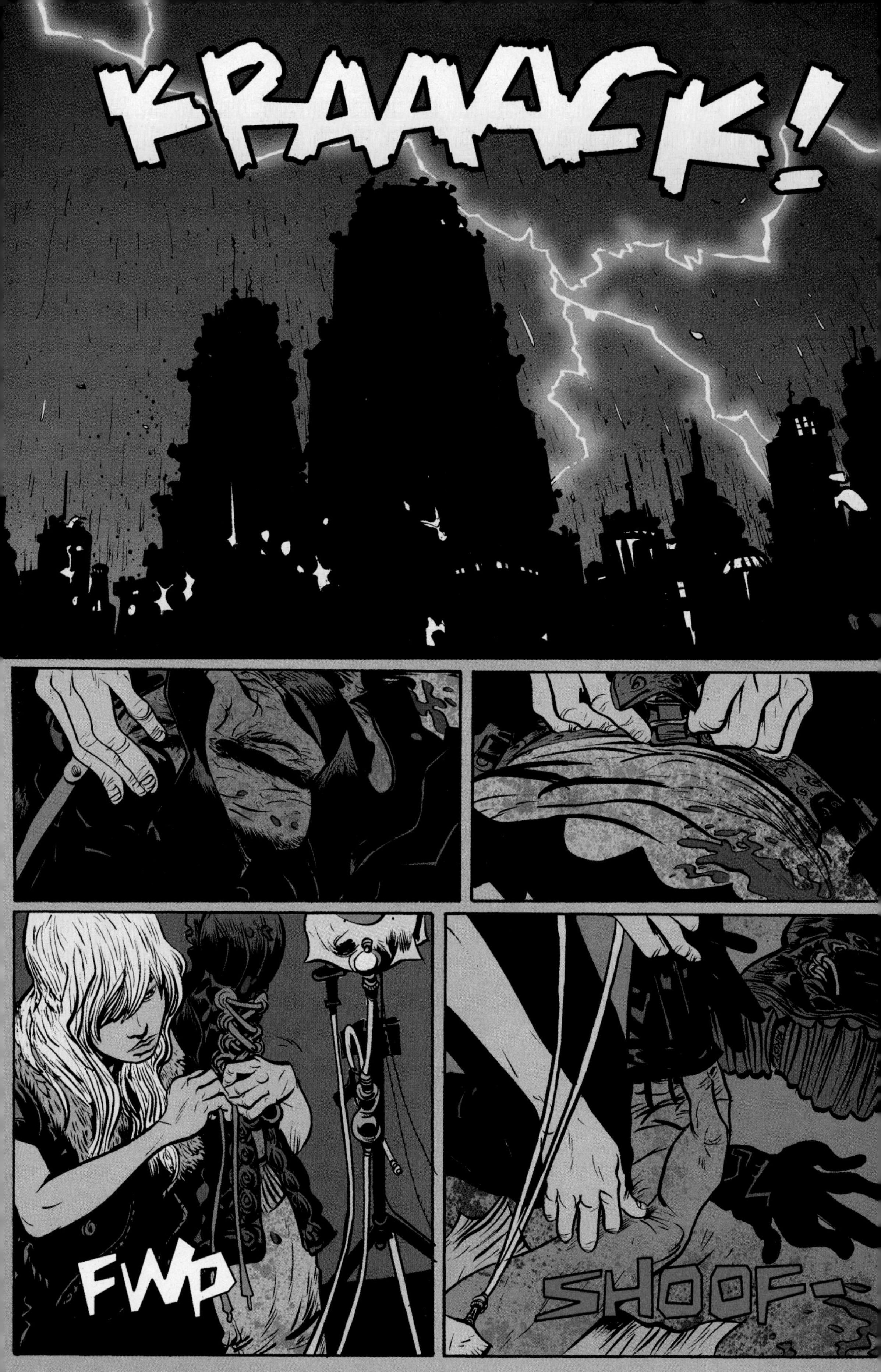
KRAAACK!
FWP
SHOOF--

THE LUCKY FOOL. THE LUCKY, LUCKY FOOL...

...DRIP.

DRIP. DRIP.

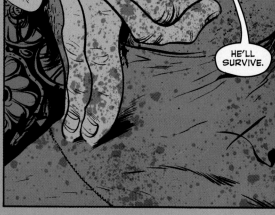

HE'LL SURVIVE.

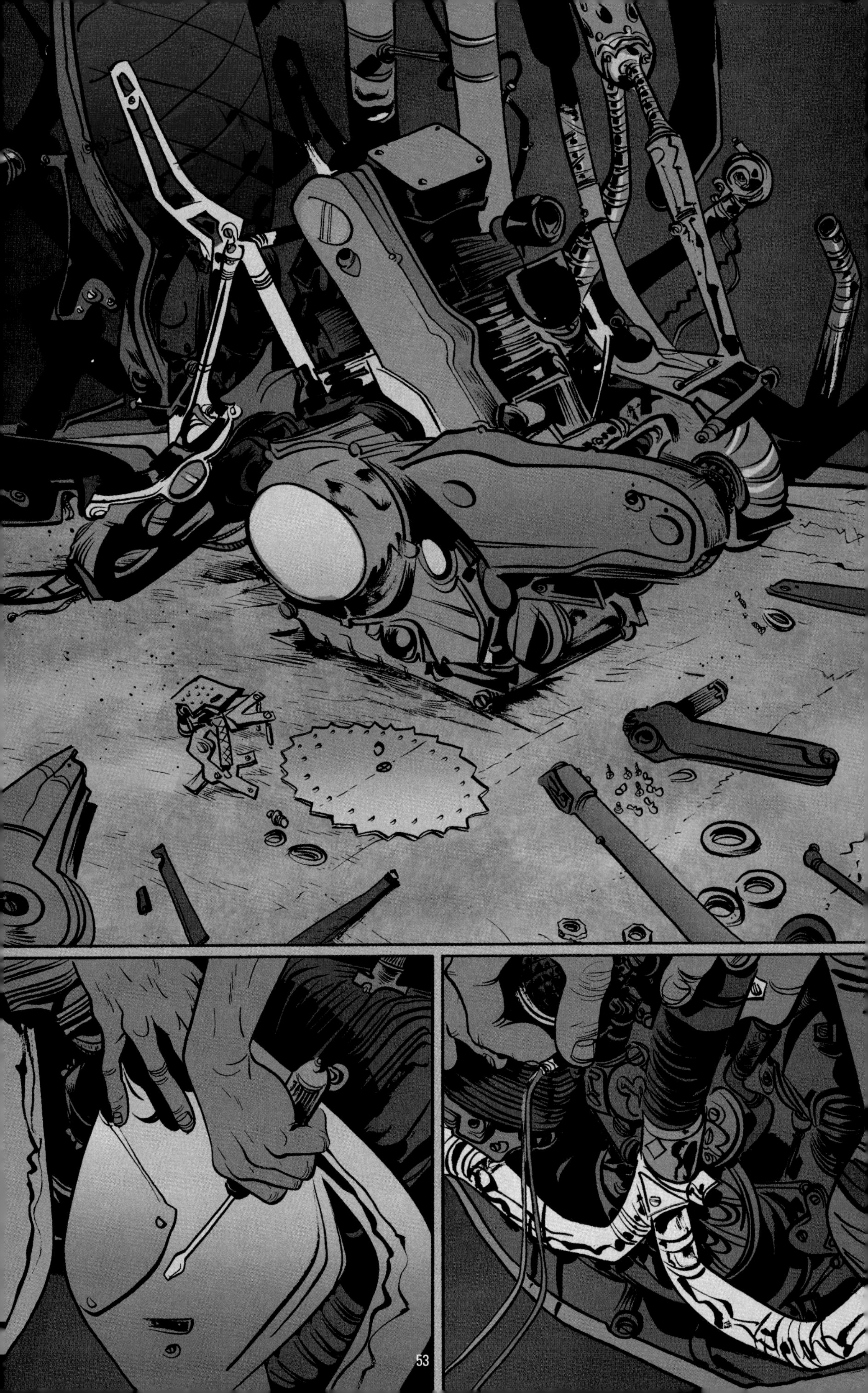

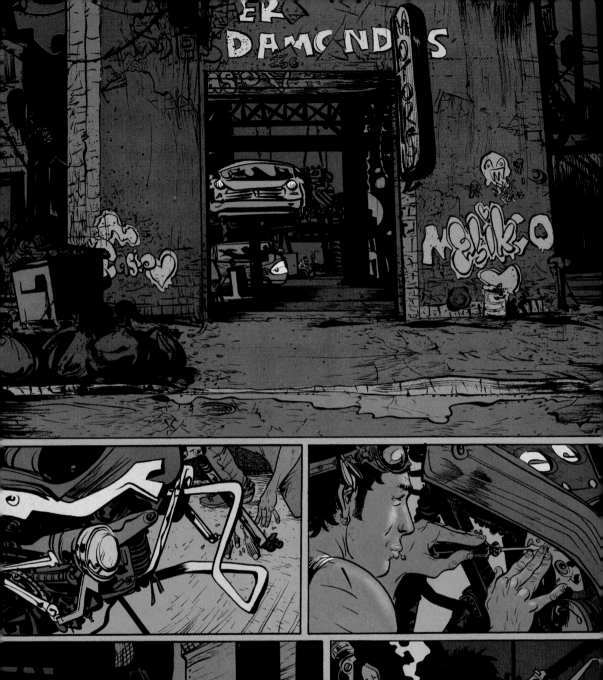

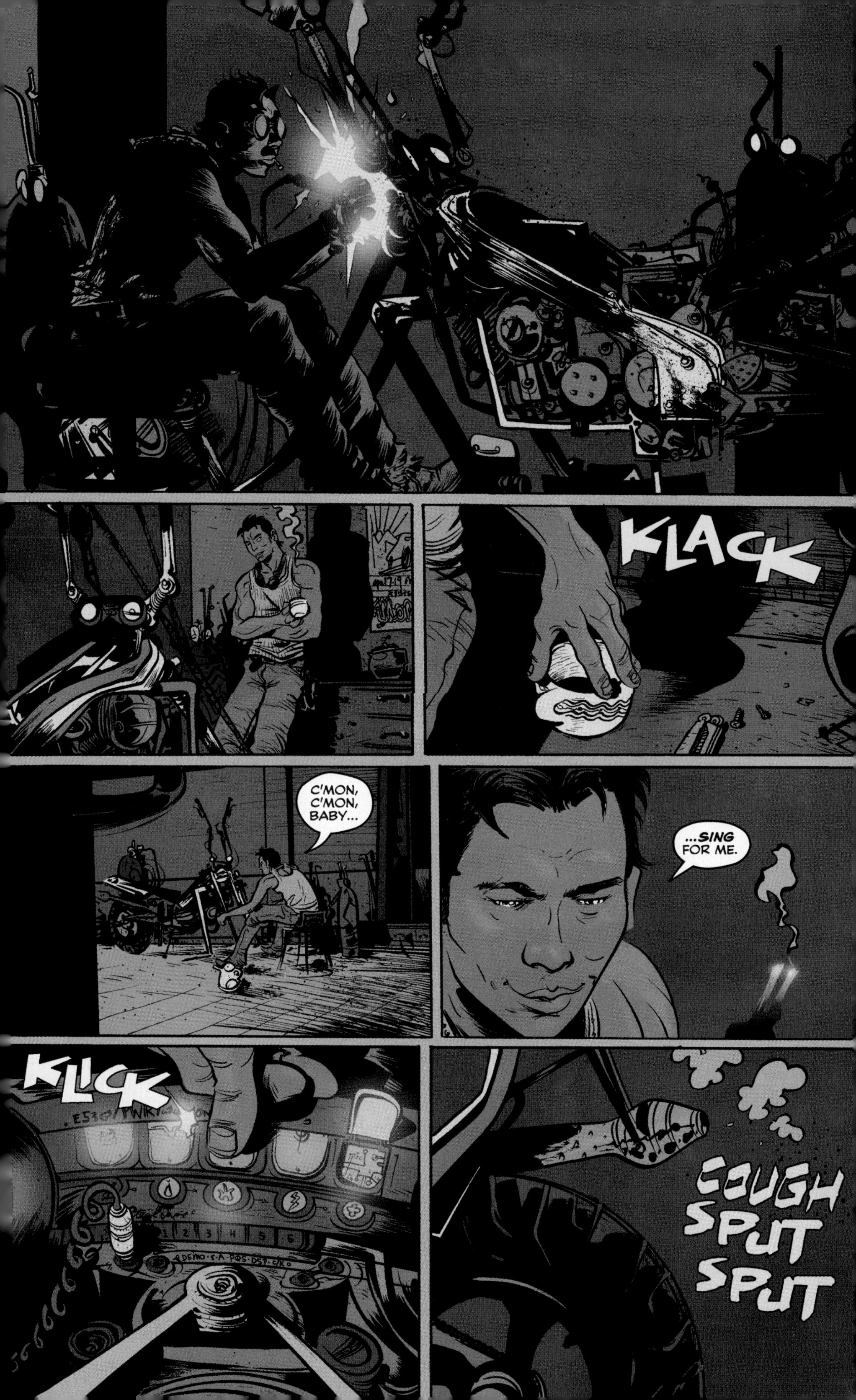
KLACK
C'MON, C'MON, BABY...
...SING FOR ME.
KLICK
COUGH SPUT SPUT

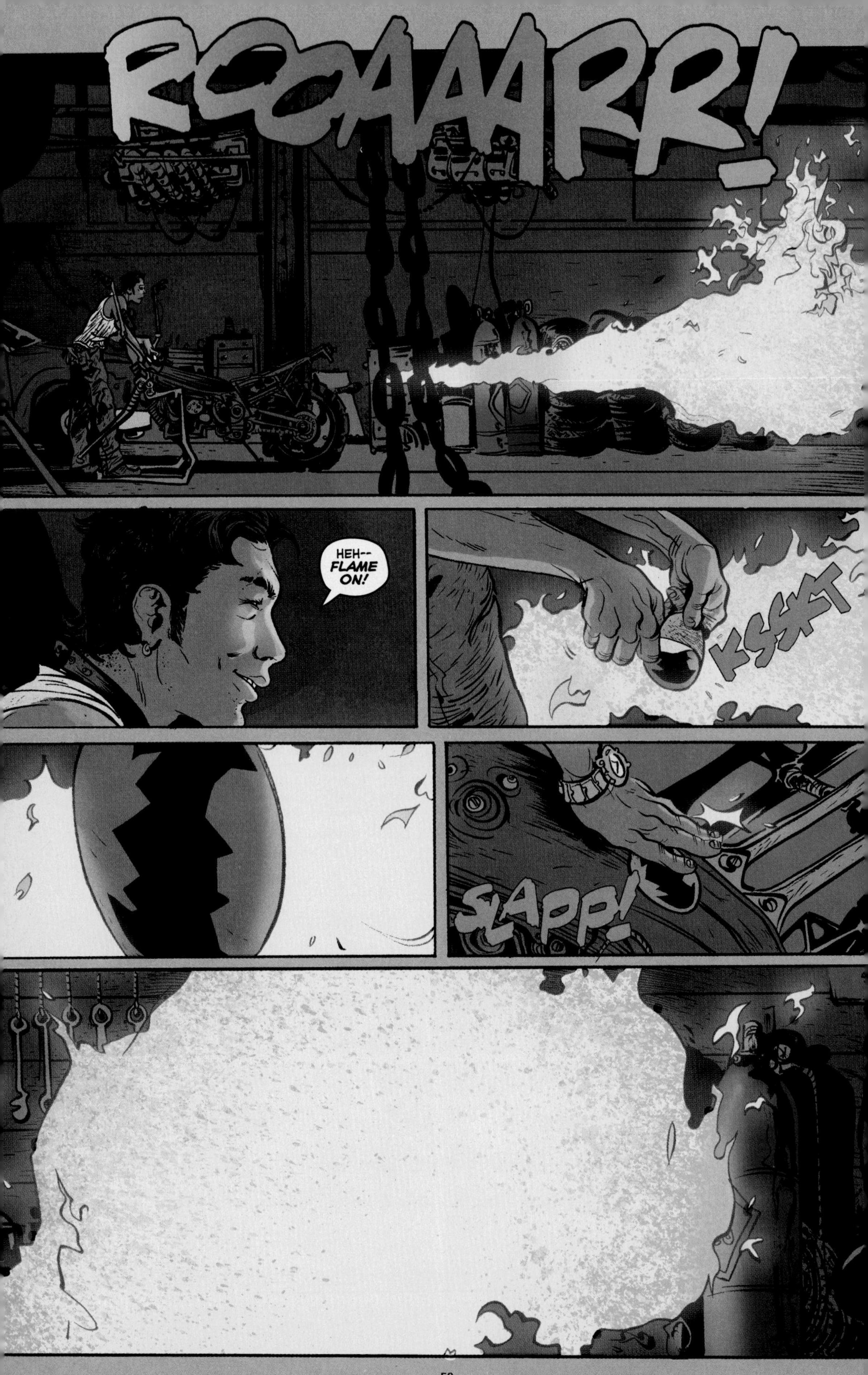
RCOAAARR!
HEH-- FLAME ON!
KSSKT
SLAPP!

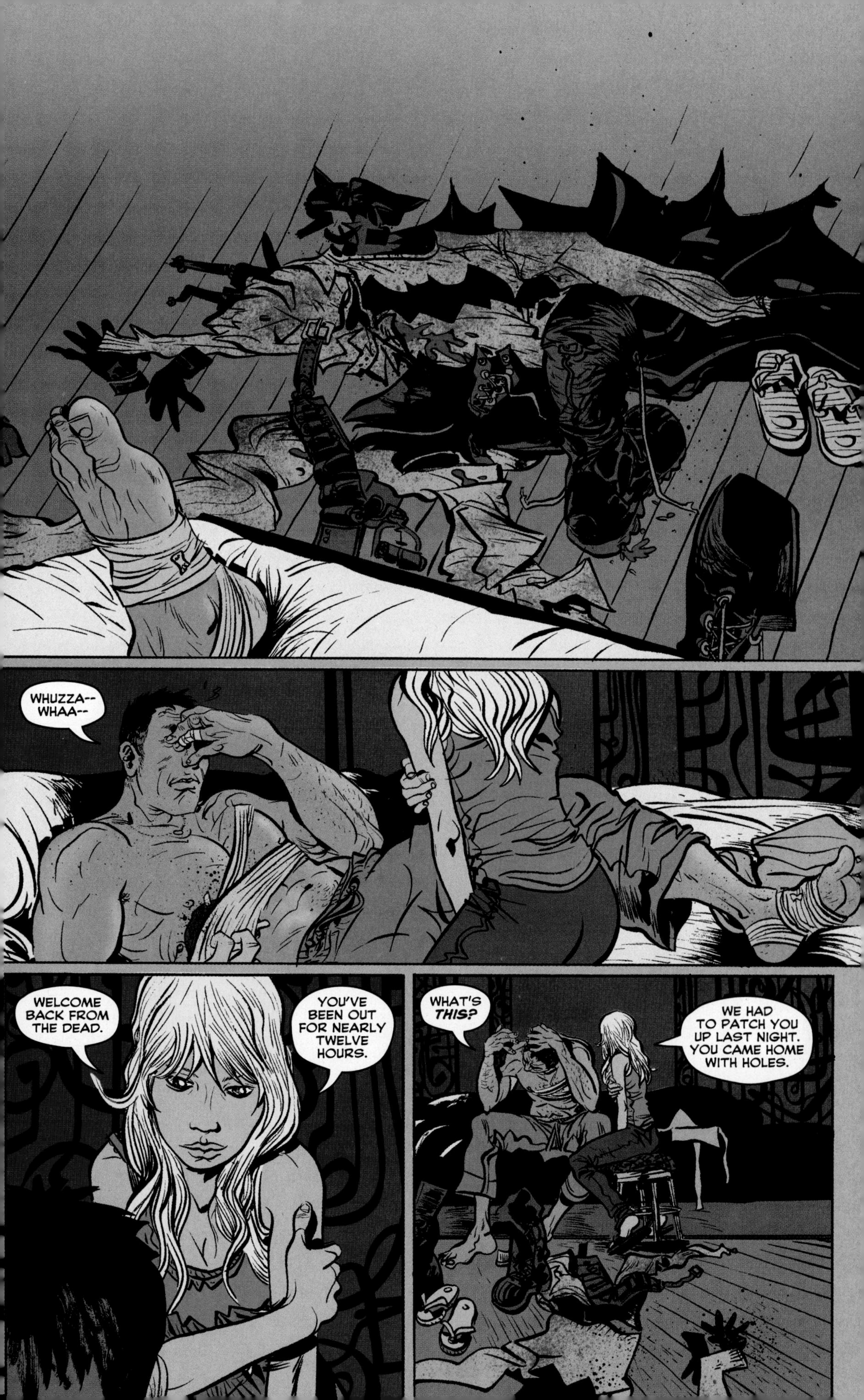
WHUZZA--
WHAA--
WELCOME BACK FROM THE DEAD.
YOU'VE BEEN OUT FOR NEARLY TWELVE HOURS.
WHAT'S *THIS?*
WE HAD TO PATCH YOU UP LAST NIGHT. YOU CAME HOME WITH HOLES.

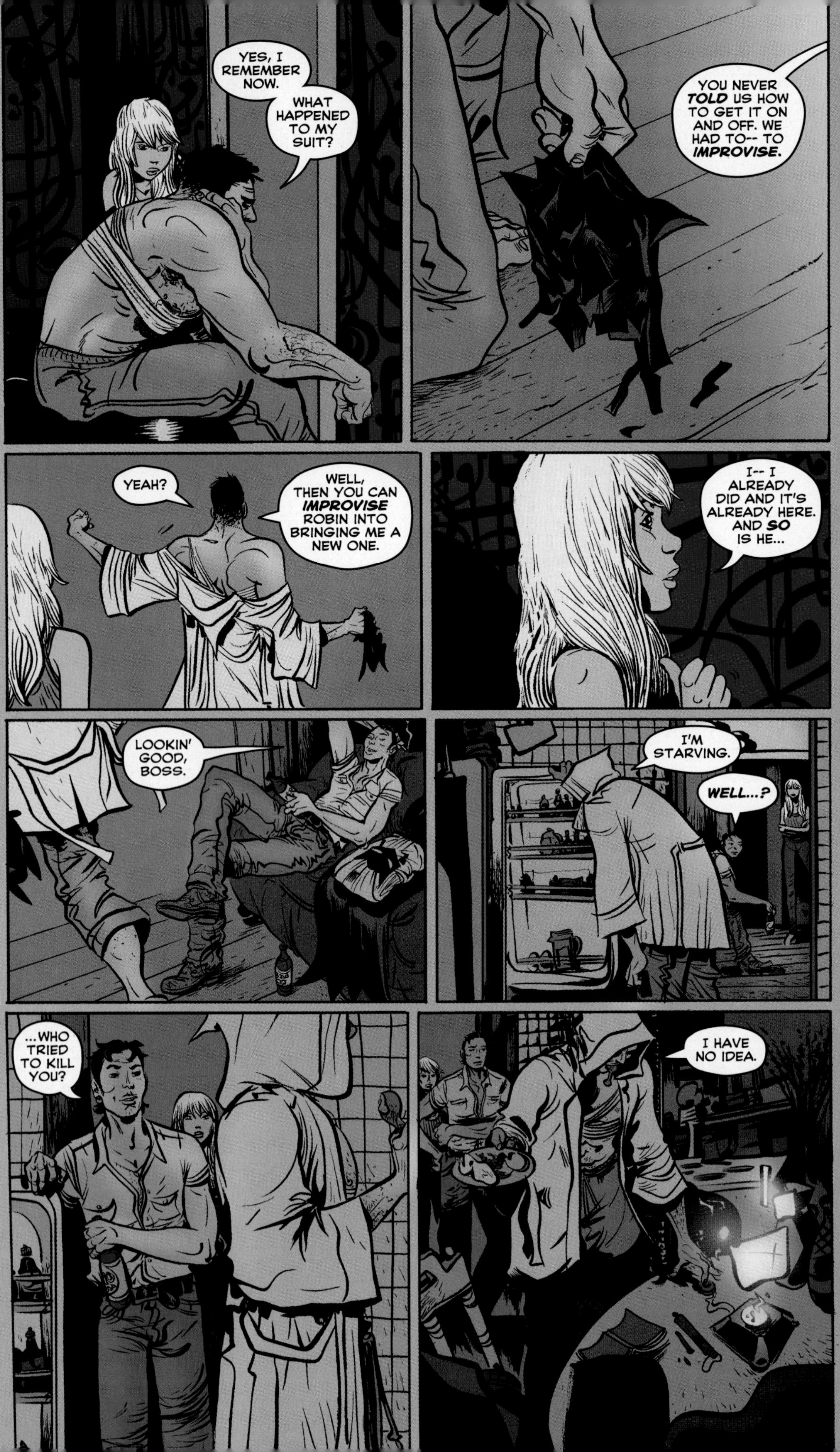
YES, I REMEMBER NOW.
WHAT HAPPENED TO MY SUIT?
YOU NEVER TOLD US HOW TO GET IT ON AND OFF. WE HAD TO-- TO IMPROVISE.
YEAH?
WELL, THEN YOU CAN IMPROVISE ROBIN INTO BRINGING ME A NEW ONE.
I-- I ALREADY DID AND IT'S ALREADY HERE. AND SO IS HE...
LOOKIN' GOOD, BOSS.
I'M STARVING.
WELL...?
...WHO TRIED TO KILL YOU?
I HAVE NO IDEA.

THAT'S STRANGE. LAST NIGHT I SAW A MAN GUNNED DOWN IN THE ADAMS STREET SUBWAY STATION. A FEDERAL MAN. IT *SHOULD'VE* MADE THE NEWS BY NOW.

THERE'S NOT A *WORD* OF IT ON ANY OF THE INSTANETS OR THE BLOTTERS.

...SO, THIS FIRST ONE'S FROM THEIR DOGS' RETINA REMOTES, LAST NIGHT.

WHAT *IS* THAT? IS THAT A *MAN* JUMPING BETWEEN TWO ROOFTOPS? THAT'S A GOOD *TWENTY-FOOT* LEAP.

UH-HUH. AND THIS ONE'S FROM A FEW MINUTES LATER, FROM INSIDE. FROM THEIR PANTHER TEAM CAMERAS. *THAT'S* HIM.

IT'S THE *ONLY* CLEAN IMAGE WE HAVE. AFTER THIS THE CAMERAS GO DEAD. THREE SECONDS OF GOOD FOOTAGE. *THREE SECONDS.*

WE'VE ALREADY SEEN THESE. WHAT ELSE IS THERE? WHAT'S THE *OLDEST?*

THIS ONE, MAY SIX, NINETEEN-THIRTY-NINE. LOOKS LIKE HE'S ON A WIRE, THERE.

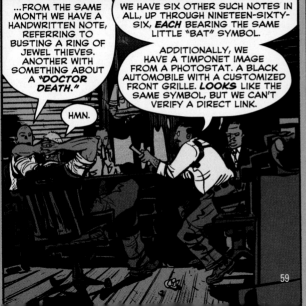

...FROM THE SAME MONTH WE HAVE A HANDWRITTEN NOTE, REFERRING TO BUSTING A RING OF JEWEL THIEVES. ANOTHER WITH SOMETHING ABOUT A *"DOCTOR DEATH."*

HMN.

WE HAVE SIX OTHER SUCH NOTES IN ALL, UP THROUGH NINETEEN-SIXTY-SIX, *EACH* BEARING THE SAME LITTLE "BAT" SYMBOL.

ADDITIONALLY, WE HAVE A TIMPONET IMAGE FROM A PHOTOSTAT. A BLACK AUTOMOBILE WITH A CUSTOMIZED FRONT GRILLE. *LOOKS* LIKE THE SAME SYMBOL, BUT WE CAN'T VERIFY A DIRECT LINK.

THIS CLEAR IMAGE IS FROM 'SIXTY-EIGHT. NO EXPLANATION OR ACCOMPANYING REPORT ATTACHED.

WHAT ARE *THOSE* THINGS? BUBBLES?

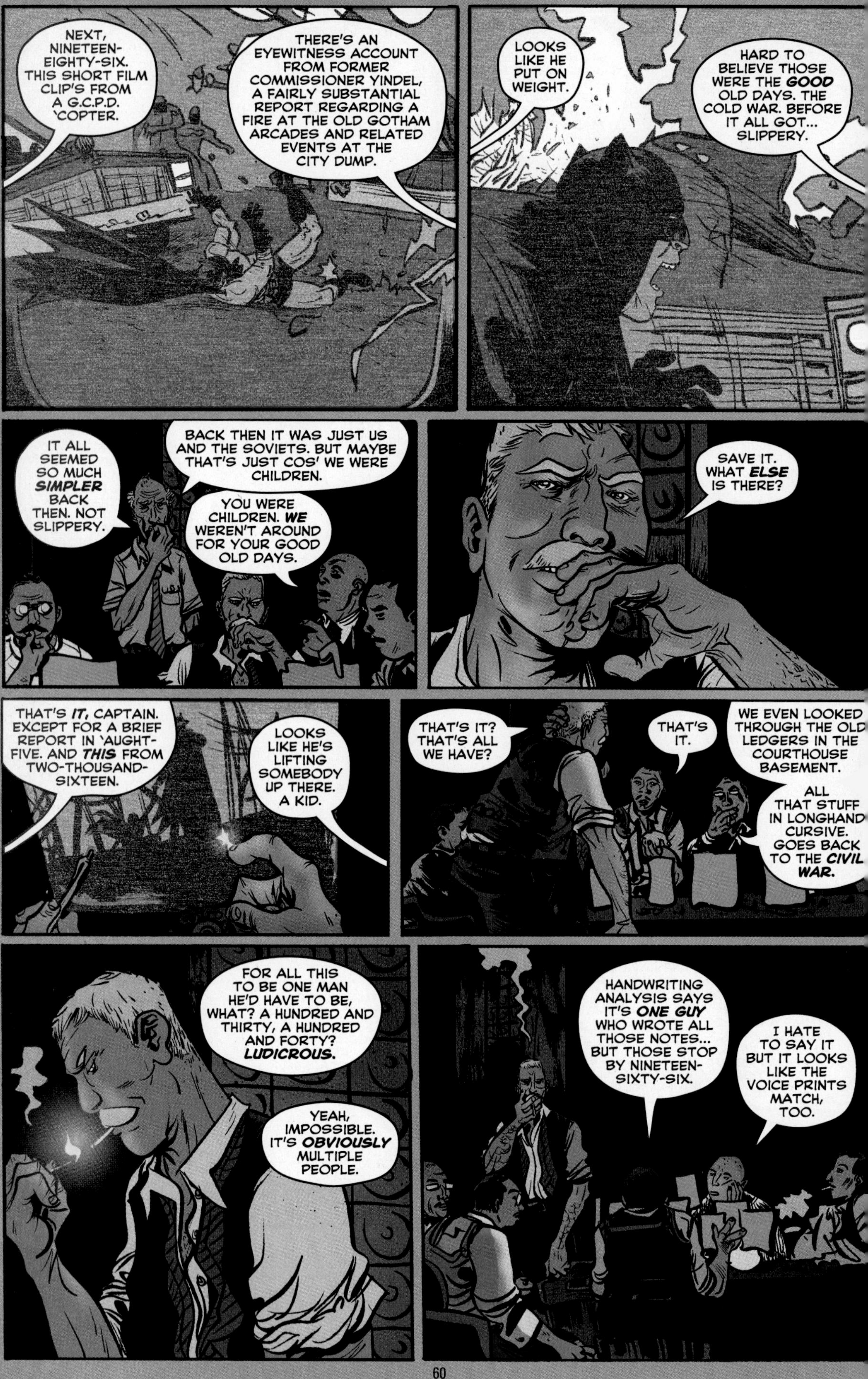
NEXT, NINETEEN-EIGHTY-SIX. THIS SHORT FILM CLIP'S FROM A G.C.P.D. 'COPTER.
THERE'S AN EYEWITNESS ACCOUNT FROM FORMER COMMISSIONER YINDEL, A FAIRLY SUBSTANTIAL REPORT REGARDING A FIRE AT THE OLD GOTHAM ARCADES AND RELATED EVENTS AT THE CITY DUMP.
LOOKS LIKE HE PUT ON WEIGHT.
HARD TO BELIEVE THOSE WERE THE GOOD OLD DAYS. THE COLD WAR. BEFORE IT ALL GOT... SLIPPERY.
IT ALL SEEMED SO MUCH SIMPLER BACK THEN. NOT SLIPPERY.
BACK THEN IT WAS JUST US AND THE SOVIETS. BUT MAYBE THAT'S JUST COS' WE WERE CHILDREN.
YOU WERE CHILDREN. WE WEREN'T AROUND FOR YOUR GOOD OLD DAYS.
SAVE IT. WHAT ELSE IS THERE?
THAT'S IT, CAPTAIN. EXCEPT FOR A BRIEF REPORT IN 'AUGHT-FIVE. AND THIS FROM TWO-THOUSAND-SIXTEEN.
LOOKS LIKE HE'S LIFTING SOMEBODY UP THERE. A KID.
THAT'S IT? THAT'S ALL WE HAVE?
THAT'S IT.
WE EVEN LOOKED THROUGH THE OLD LEDGERS IN THE COURTHOUSE BASEMENT.
ALL THAT STUFF IN LONGHAND CURSIVE. GOES BACK TO THE CIVIL WAR.
FOR ALL THIS TO BE ONE MAN HE'D HAVE TO BE, WHAT? A HUNDRED AND THIRTY, A HUNDRED AND FORTY? LUDICROUS.
YEAH, IMPOSSIBLE. IT'S OBVIOUSLY MULTIPLE PEOPLE.
HANDWRITING ANALYSIS SAYS IT'S ONE GUY WHO WROTE ALL THOSE NOTES... BUT THOSE STOP BY NINETEEN-SIXTY-SIX.
I HATE TO SAY IT BUT IT LOOKS LIKE THE VOICE PRINTS MATCH, TOO.

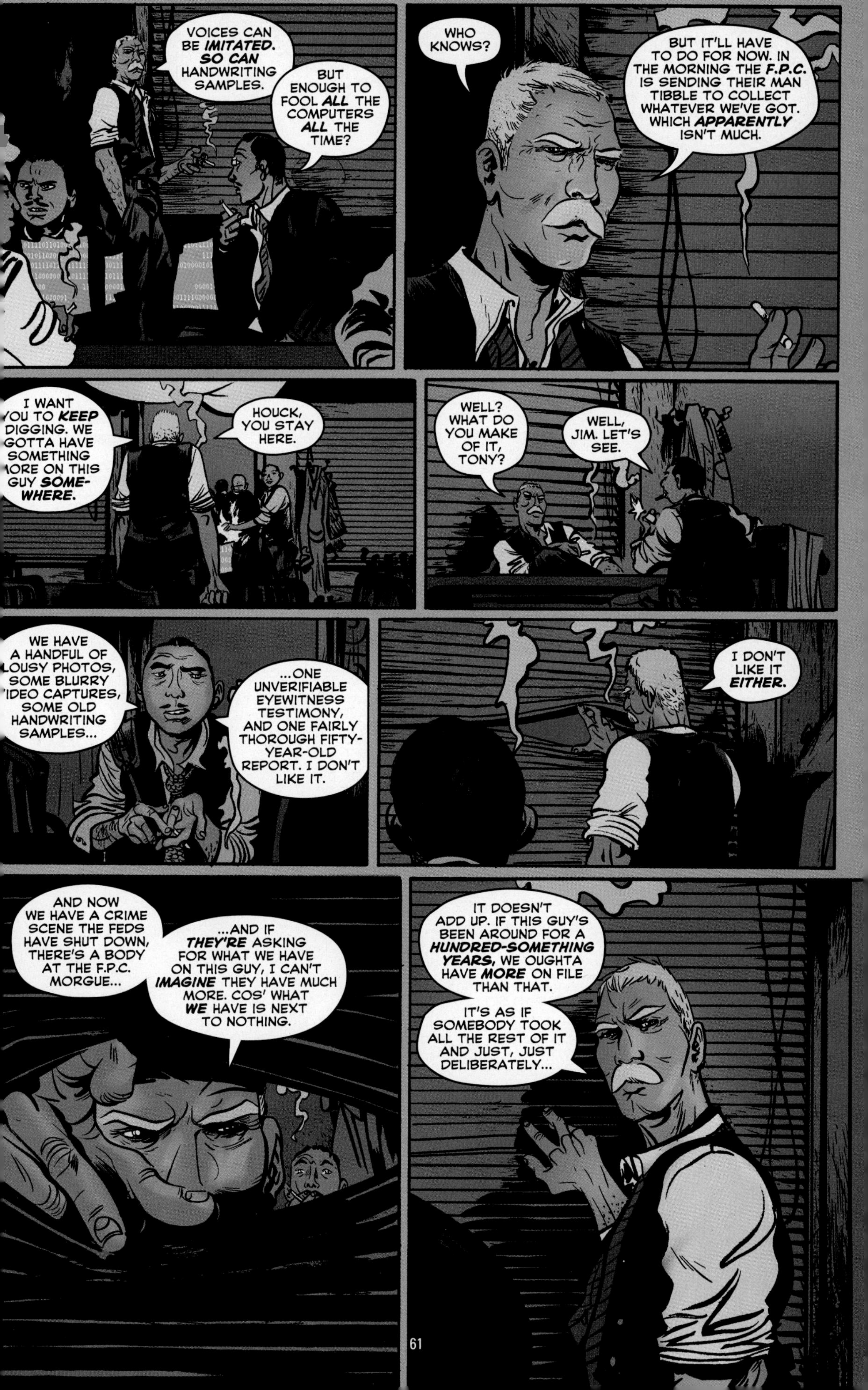

VOICES CAN BE *IMITATED.* ***SO CAN*** HANDWRITING SAMPLES.
BUT ENOUGH TO FOOL ***ALL*** THE COMPUTERS ***ALL*** THE TIME?
WHO KNOWS?
BUT IT'LL HAVE TO DO FOR NOW. IN THE MORNING THE ***F.P.C.*** IS SENDING THEIR MAN TIBBLE TO COLLECT WHATEVER WE'VE GOT. WHICH ***APPARENTLY*** ISN'T MUCH.
I WANT YOU TO ***KEEP*** DIGGING. WE GOTTA HAVE SOMETHING MORE ON THIS GUY ***SOME-WHERE.***
HOUCK, YOU STAY HERE.
WELL? WHAT DO YOU MAKE OF IT, TONY?
WELL, JIM. LET'S SEE.
WE HAVE A HANDFUL OF LOUSY PHOTOS, SOME BLURRY VIDEO CAPTURES, SOME OLD HANDWRITING SAMPLES...
...ONE UNVERIFIABLE EYEWITNESS TESTIMONY, AND ONE FAIRLY THOROUGH FIFTY-YEAR-OLD REPORT. I DON'T LIKE IT.
I DON'T LIKE IT ***EITHER.***
AND NOW WE HAVE A CRIME SCENE THE FEDS HAVE SHUT DOWN, THERE'S A BODY AT THE F.P.C. MORGUE...
...AND IF ***THEY'RE*** ASKING FOR WHAT WE HAVE ON THIS GUY, I CAN'T ***IMAGINE*** THEY HAVE MUCH MORE. COS' WHAT ***WE*** HAVE IS NEXT TO NOTHING.
IT DOESN'T ADD UP. IF THIS GUY'S BEEN AROUND FOR A ***HUNDRED-SOMETHING YEARS,*** WE OUGHTA HAVE ***MORE*** ON FILE THAN THAT.
IT'S AS IF SOMEBODY TOOK ALL THE REST OF IT AND JUST, JUST DELIBERATELY...

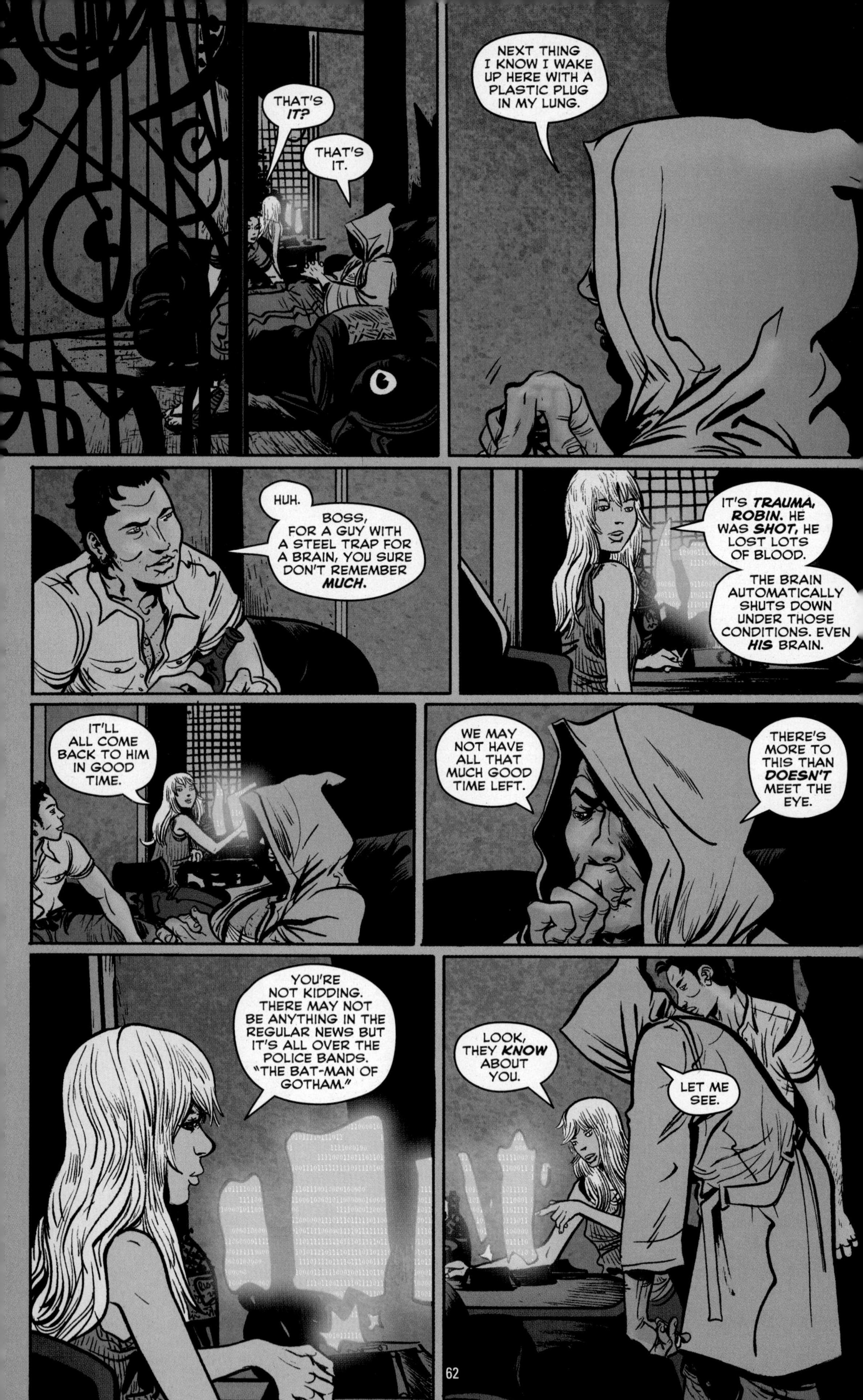
THAT'S *IT?*
THAT'S IT.
NEXT THING I KNOW I WAKE UP HERE WITH A PLASTIC PLUG IN MY LUNG.
HUH.
BOSS, FOR A GUY WITH A STEEL TRAP FOR A BRAIN, YOU SURE DON'T REMEMBER ***MUCH.***
IT'S ***TRAUMA, ROBIN.*** HE WAS ***SHOT,*** HE LOST LOTS OF BLOOD.
THE BRAIN AUTOMATICALLY SHUTS DOWN UNDER THOSE CONDITIONS. EVEN ***HIS*** BRAIN.
IT'LL ALL COME BACK TO HIM IN GOOD TIME.
WE MAY NOT HAVE ALL THAT MUCH GOOD TIME LEFT.
THERE'S MORE TO THIS THAN ***DOESN'T*** MEET THE EYE.
YOU'RE NOT KIDDING. THERE MAY NOT BE ANYTHING IN THE REGULAR NEWS BUT IT'S ALL OVER THE POLICE BANDS. "THE BAT-MAN OF GOTHAM."
LOOK, THEY ***KNOW*** ABOUT YOU.
LET ME SEE.

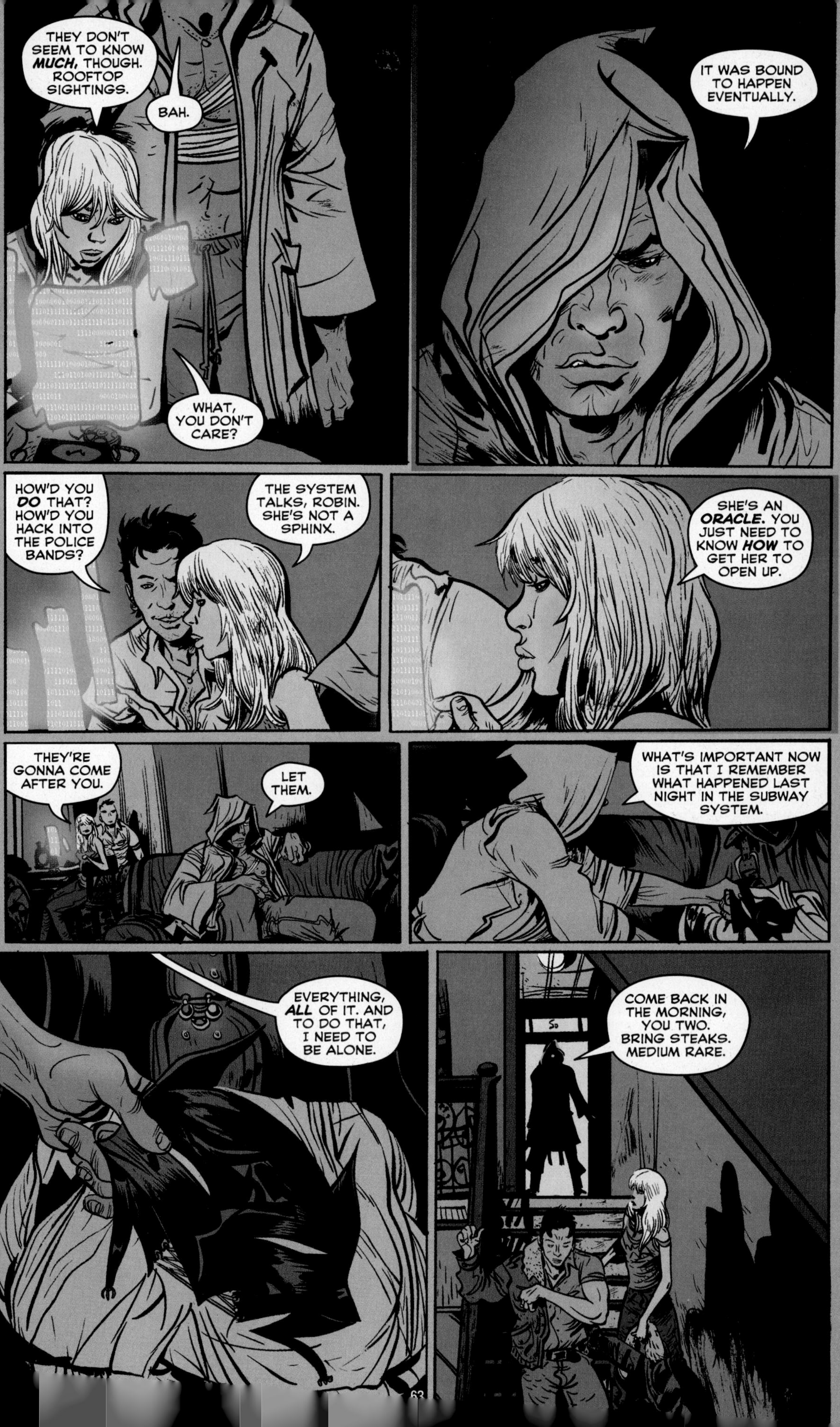
THEY DON'T SEEM TO KNOW MUCH, THOUGH. ROOFTOP SIGHTINGS.
BAH.
WHAT, YOU DON'T CARE?
IT WAS BOUND TO HAPPEN EVENTUALLY.
HOW'D YOU DO THAT? HOW'D YOU HACK INTO THE POLICE BANDS?
THE SYSTEM TALKS, ROBIN. SHE'S NOT A SPHINX.
SHE'S AN ORACLE. YOU JUST NEED TO KNOW HOW TO GET HER TO OPEN UP.
THEY'RE GONNA COME AFTER YOU.
LET THEM.
WHAT'S IMPORTANT NOW IS THAT I REMEMBER WHAT HAPPENED LAST NIGHT IN THE SUBWAY SYSTEM.
EVERYTHING, ALL OF IT. AND TO DO THAT, I NEED TO BE ALONE.
COME BACK IN THE MORNING, YOU TWO. BRING STEAKS. MEDIUM RARE.

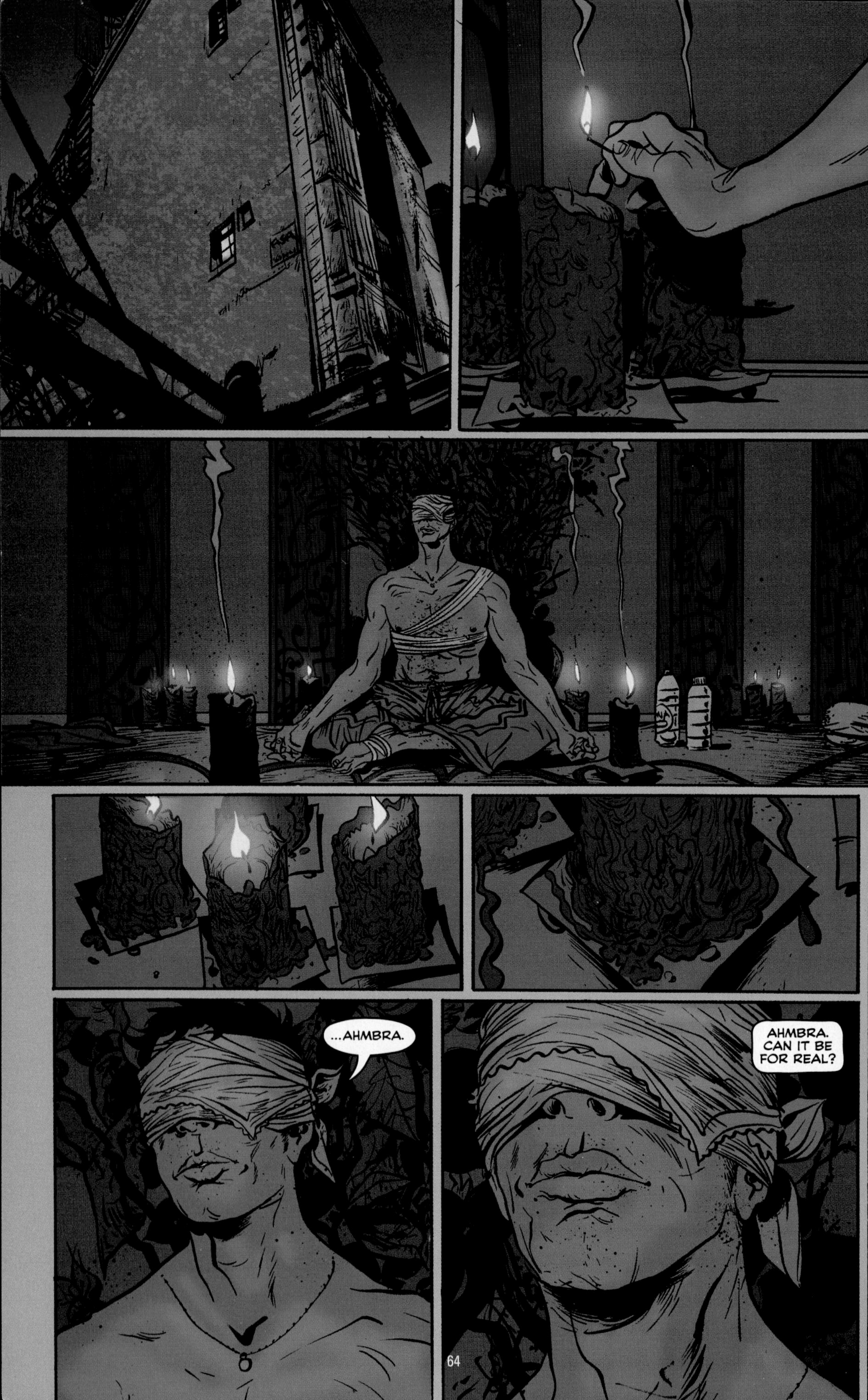
...AHMBRA.
AHMBRA. CAN IT BE FOR REAL?

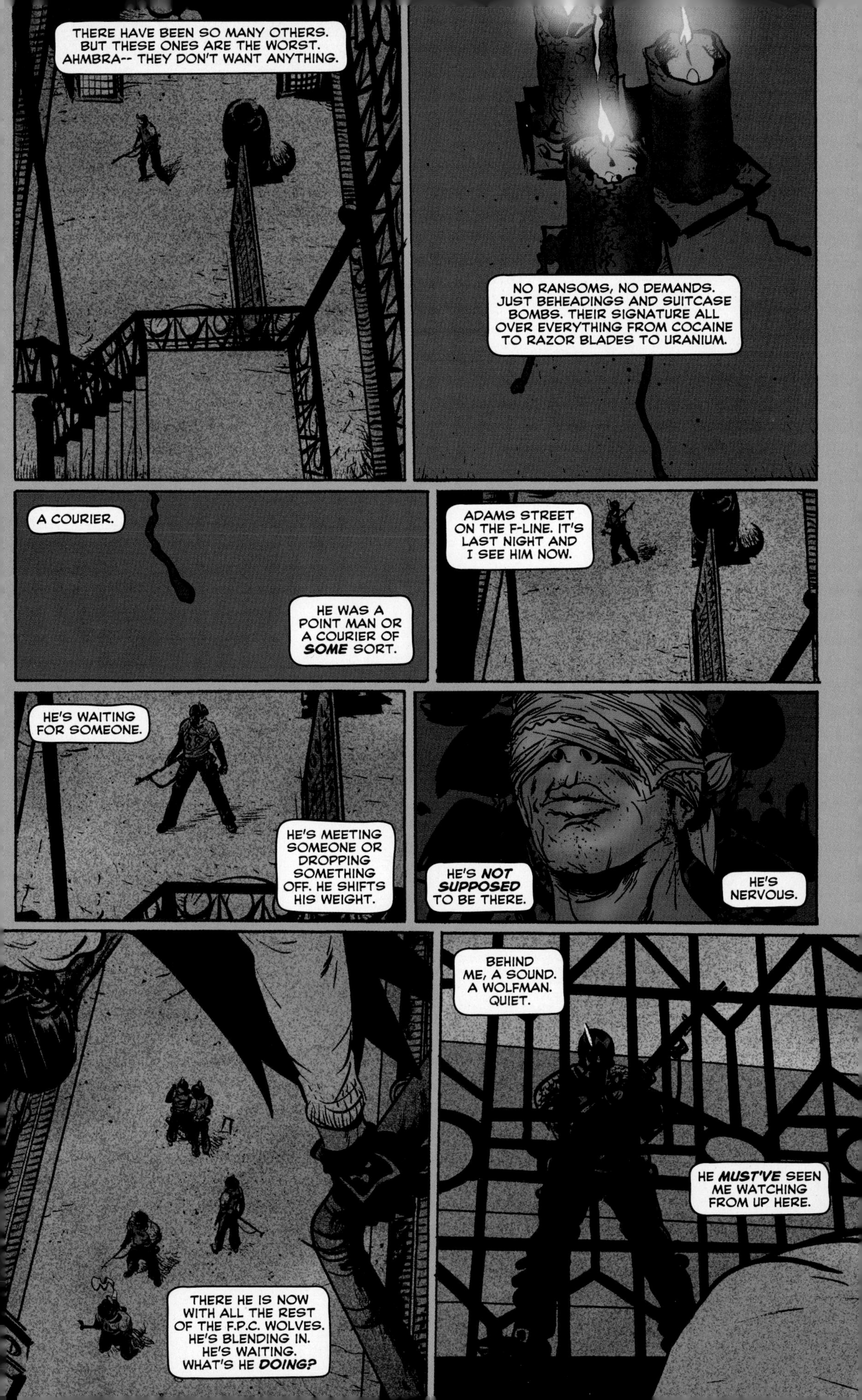
THERE HAVE BEEN SO MANY OTHERS. BUT THESE ONES ARE THE WORST. AHMBRA-- THEY DON'T WANT ANYTHING.
NO RANSOMS, NO DEMANDS. JUST BEHEADINGS AND SUITCASE BOMBS. THEIR SIGNATURE ALL OVER EVERYTHING FROM COCAINE TO RAZOR BLADES TO URANIUM.
A COURIER.
HE WAS A POINT MAN OR A COURIER OF *SOME* SORT.
ADAMS STREET ON THE F-LINE. IT'S LAST NIGHT AND I SEE HIM NOW.
HE'S WAITING FOR SOMEONE.
HE'S MEETING SOMEONE OR DROPPING SOMETHING OFF. HE SHIFTS HIS WEIGHT.
HE'S *NOT SUPPOSED* TO BE THERE.
HE'S NERVOUS.
THERE HE IS NOW WITH ALL THE REST OF THE F.P.C. WOLVES. HE'S BLENDING IN. HE'S WAITING. WHAT'S HE *DOING?*
BEHIND ME, A SOUND. A WOLFMAN. QUIET.
HE *MUST'VE* SEEN ME WATCHING FROM UP HERE.

WHY DOESN'T HE ALERT THE OTHERS? WHY DOESN'T HE...?

I CAN'T SEE HIS FACE.

THEN THE NOISE. BROKEN CONCENTRATION.

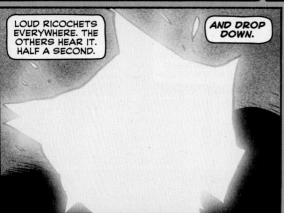

LOUD RICOCHETS EVERYWHERE. THE OTHERS HEAR IT. HALF A SECOND.

AND DROP DOWN.

THE THICK OF IT. *SO MUCH, TOO FAST.* SLOW IT DOWN.

SLOW IT DOWN, *SLOWER.*

SLOWER.

THERE, THAT'S THE ONE. THAT *MUST* BE HIM.

HE'S HOLDING A TWENTY-TWO.

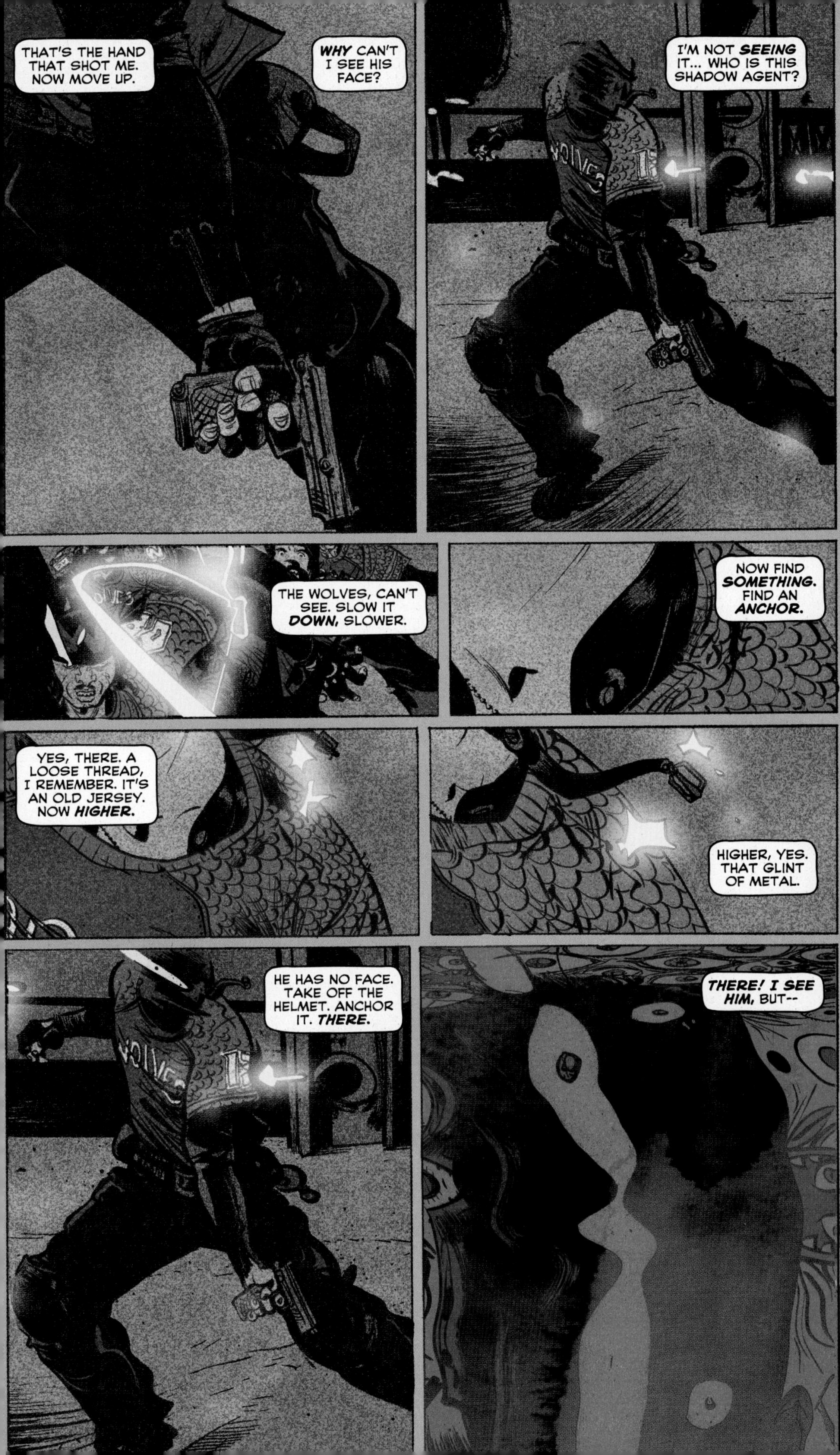
THAT'S THE HAND THAT SHOT ME. NOW MOVE UP.
WHY CAN'T I SEE HIS FACE?
I'M NOT SEEING IT... WHO IS THIS SHADOW AGENT?
THE WOLVES, CAN'T SEE. SLOW IT DOWN, SLOWER.
NOW FIND SOMETHING. FIND AN ANCHOR.
YES, THERE. A LOOSE THREAD, I REMEMBER. IT'S AN OLD JERSEY. NOW HIGHER.
HIGHER, YES. THAT GLINT OF METAL.
HE HAS NO FACE. TAKE OFF THE HELMET. ANCHOR IT. THERE.
THERE! I SEE HIM, BUT--

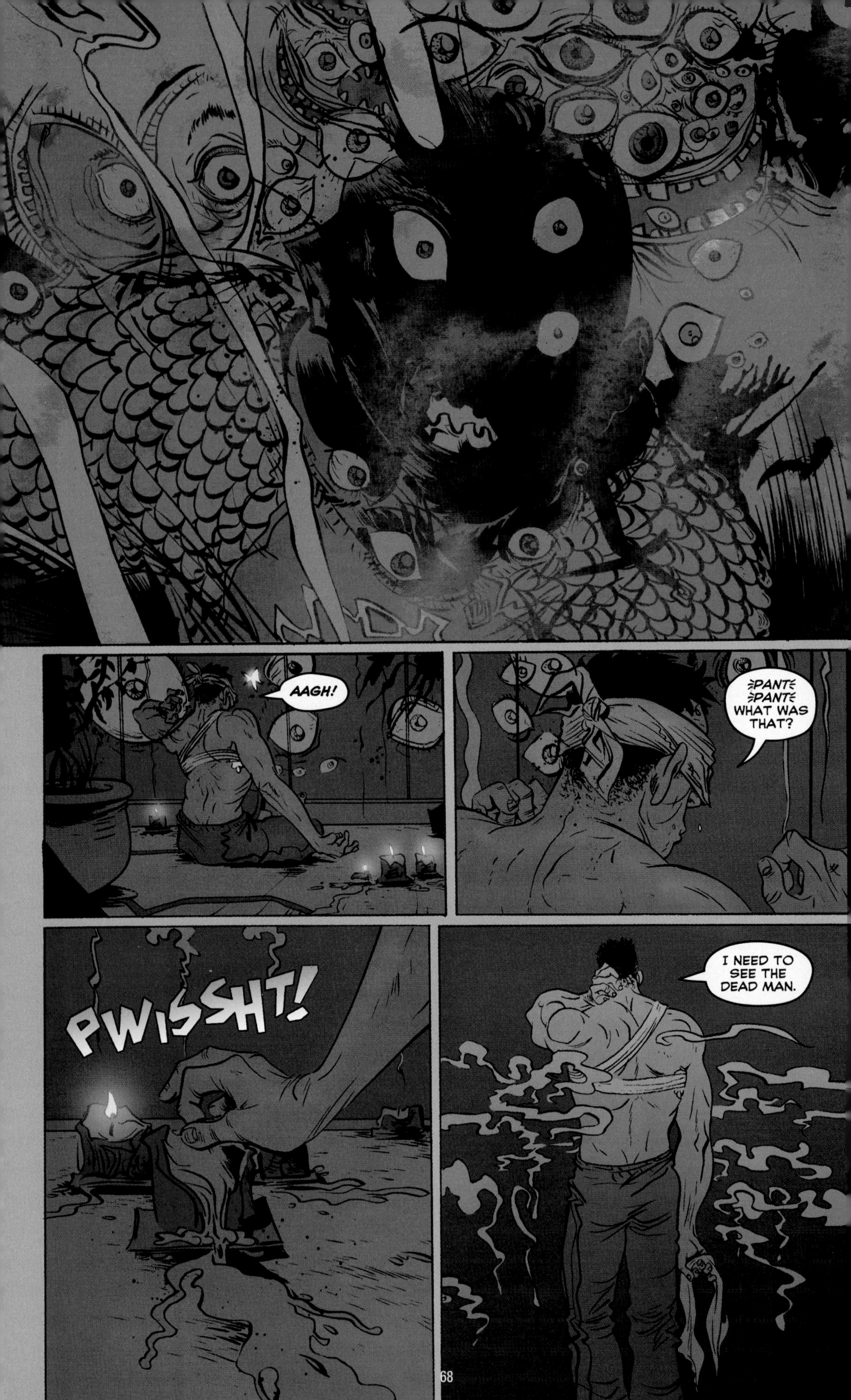
AAGH!
PANT
PANT
WHAT WAS THAT?
PWISSHT!
I NEED TO SEE THE DEAD MAN.

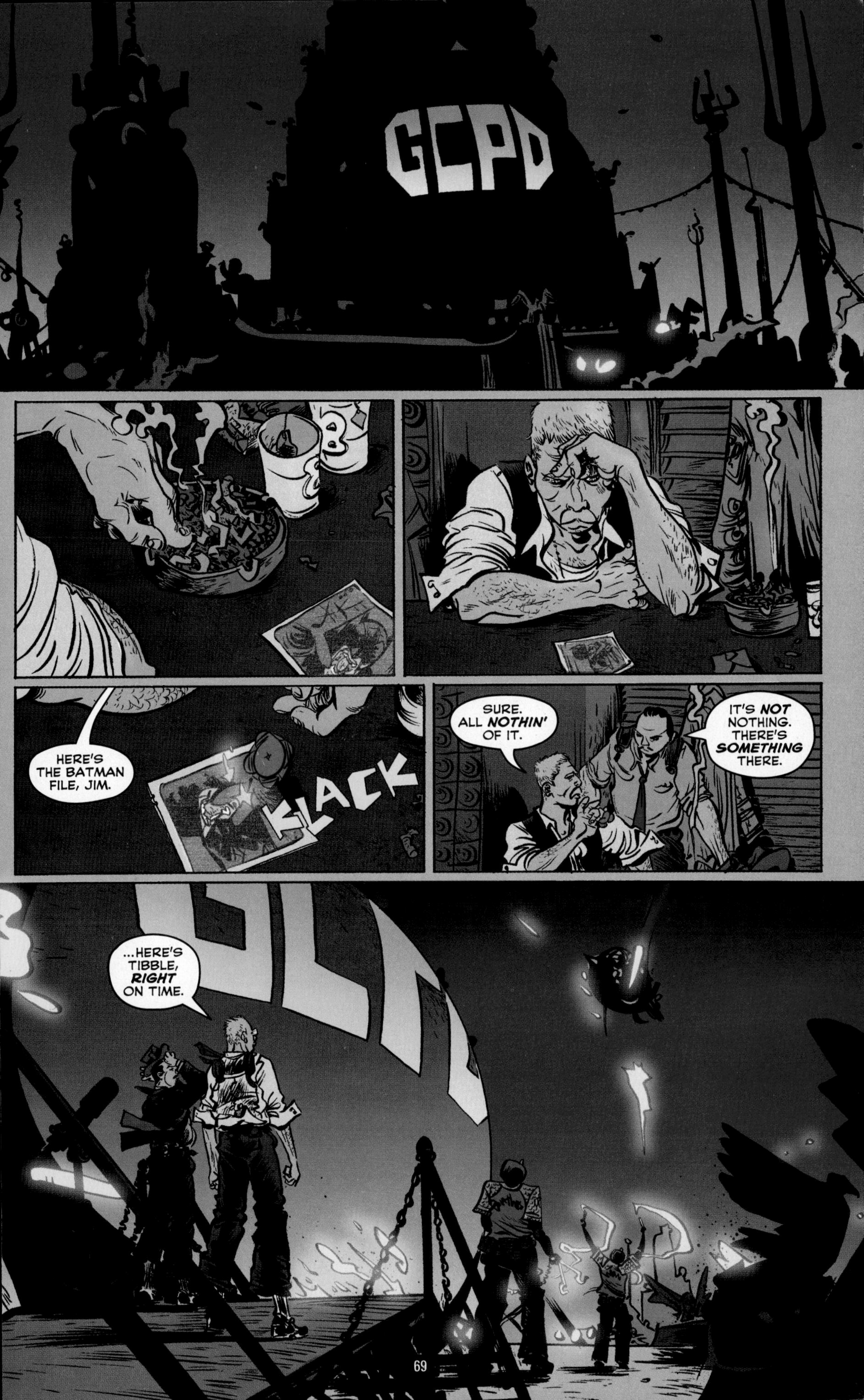
GCPD
HERE'S THE BATMAN FILE, JIM.
KLACK
SURE. ALL **NOTHIN'** OF IT.
IT'S **NOT** NOTHING. THERE'S **SOMETHING** THERE.
...HERE'S TIBBLE, **RIGHT** ON TIME.

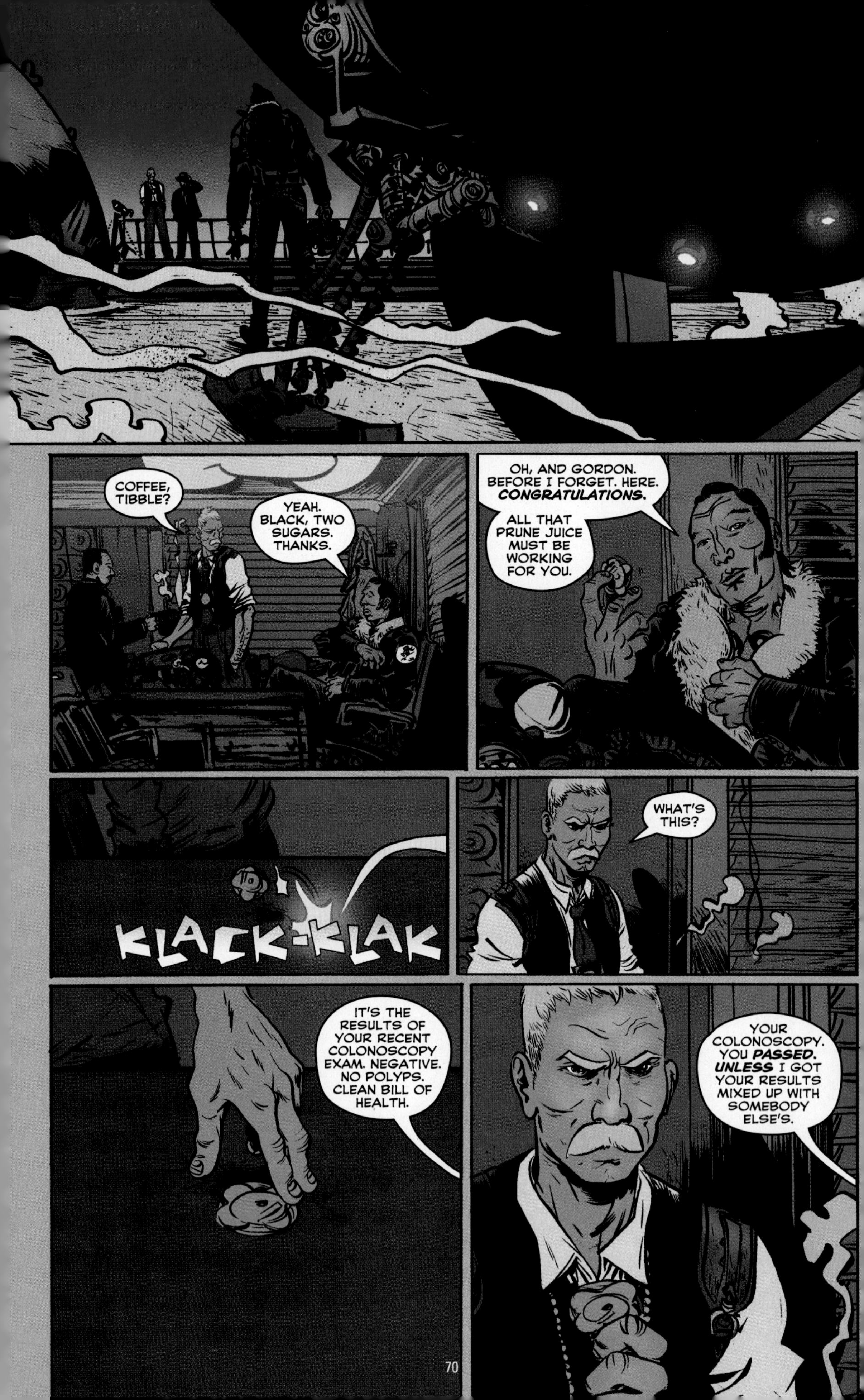
COFFEE, TIBBLE?
YEAH. BLACK, TWO SUGARS. THANKS.
OH, AND GORDON. BEFORE I FORGET. HERE. CONGRATULATIONS.
ALL THAT PRUNE JUICE MUST BE WORKING FOR YOU.
KLACK-KLAK
WHAT'S THIS?
IT'S THE RESULTS OF YOUR RECENT COLONOSCOPY EXAM. NEGATIVE. NO POLYPS. CLEAN BILL OF HEALTH.
YOUR COLONOSCOPY. YOU PASSED. UNLESS I GOT YOUR RESULTS MIXED UP WITH SOMEBODY ELSE'S.

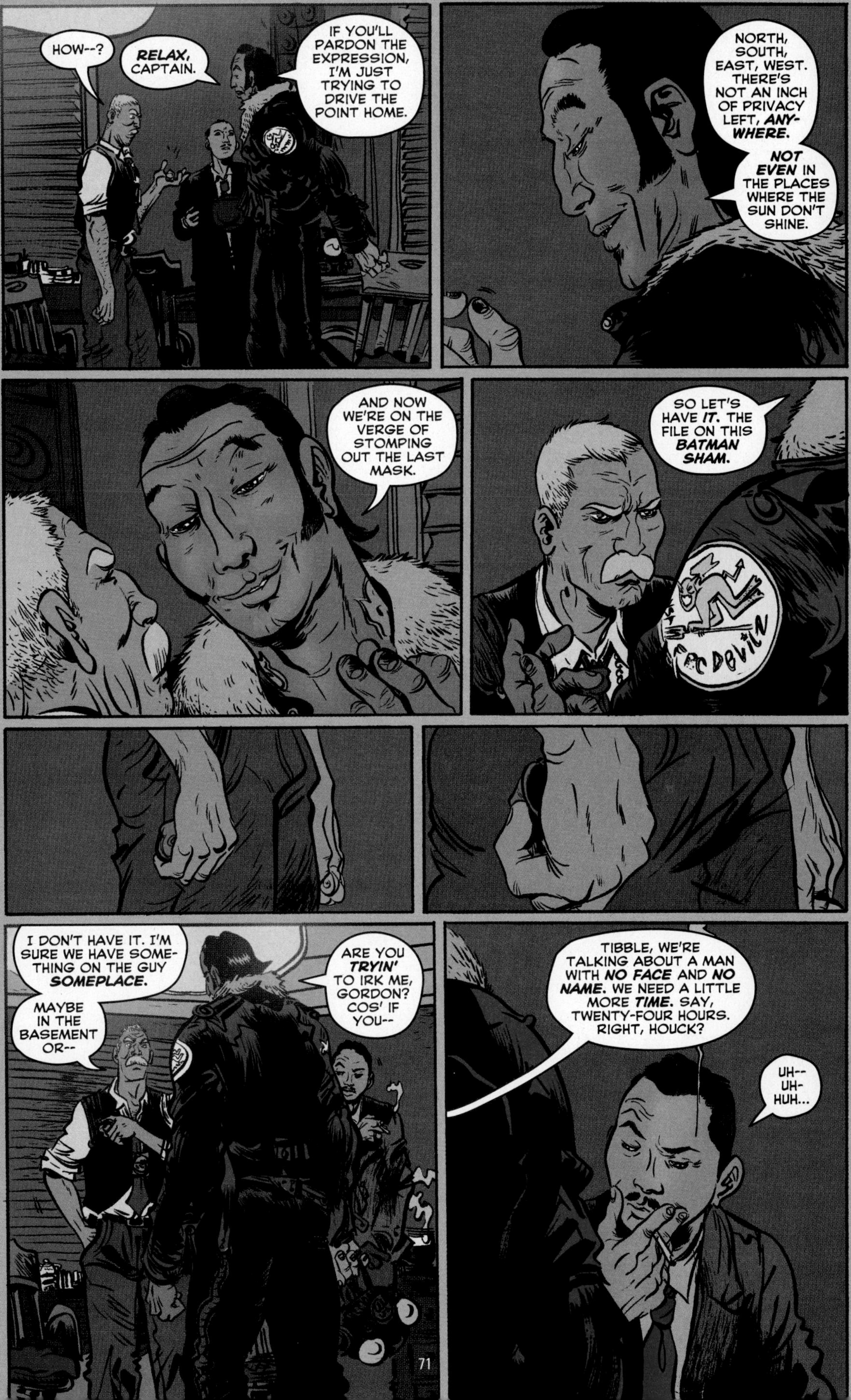
HOW--?
RELAX, CAPTAIN.
IF YOU'LL PARDON THE EXPRESSION, I'M JUST TRYING TO DRIVE THE POINT HOME.
NORTH, SOUTH, EAST, WEST. THERE'S NOT AN INCH OF PRIVACY LEFT, ANY-WHERE.
NOT EVEN IN THE PLACES WHERE THE SUN DON'T SHINE.
AND NOW WE'RE ON THE VERGE OF STOMPING OUT THE LAST MASK.
SO LET'S HAVE IT. THE FILE ON THIS BATMAN SHAM.
I DON'T HAVE IT. I'M SURE WE HAVE SOME-THING ON THE GUY SOMEPLACE.
MAYBE IN THE BASEMENT OR--
ARE YOU TRYIN' TO IRK ME, GORDON? COS' IF YOU--
TIBBLE, WE'RE TALKING ABOUT A MAN WITH NO FACE AND NO NAME. WE NEED A LITTLE MORE TIME. SAY, TWENTY-FOUR HOURS. RIGHT, HOUCK?
UH-- UH-HUH...

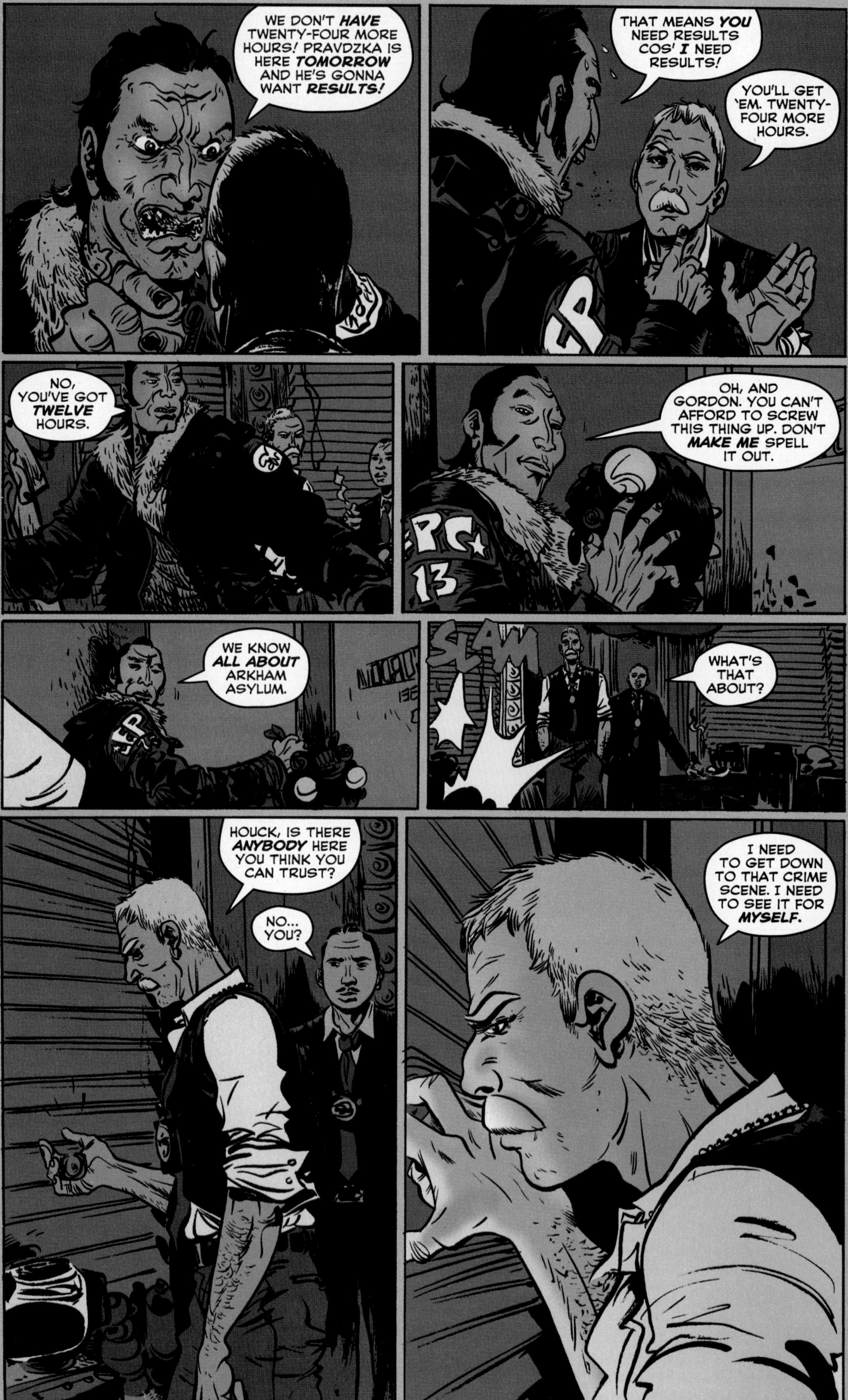
WE DON'T *HAVE* TWENTY-FOUR MORE HOURS! PRAVDZKA IS HERE *TOMORROW* AND HE'S GONNA WANT *RESULTS!*
THAT MEANS *YOU* NEED RESULTS COS' *I* NEED RESULTS!
YOU'LL GET 'EM. TWENTY-FOUR MORE HOURS.
NO, YOU'VE GOT *TWELVE* HOURS.
OH, AND GORDON. YOU CAN'T AFFORD TO SCREW THIS THING UP. DON'T *MAKE ME* SPELL IT OUT.
WE KNOW *ALL ABOUT* ARKHAM ASYLUM.
SLAM
WHAT'S THAT ABOUT?
HOUCK, IS THERE *ANYBODY* HERE YOU THINK YOU CAN TRUST?
NO... YOU?
I NEED TO GET DOWN TO THAT CRIME SCENE. I NEED TO SEE IT FOR *MYSELF.*

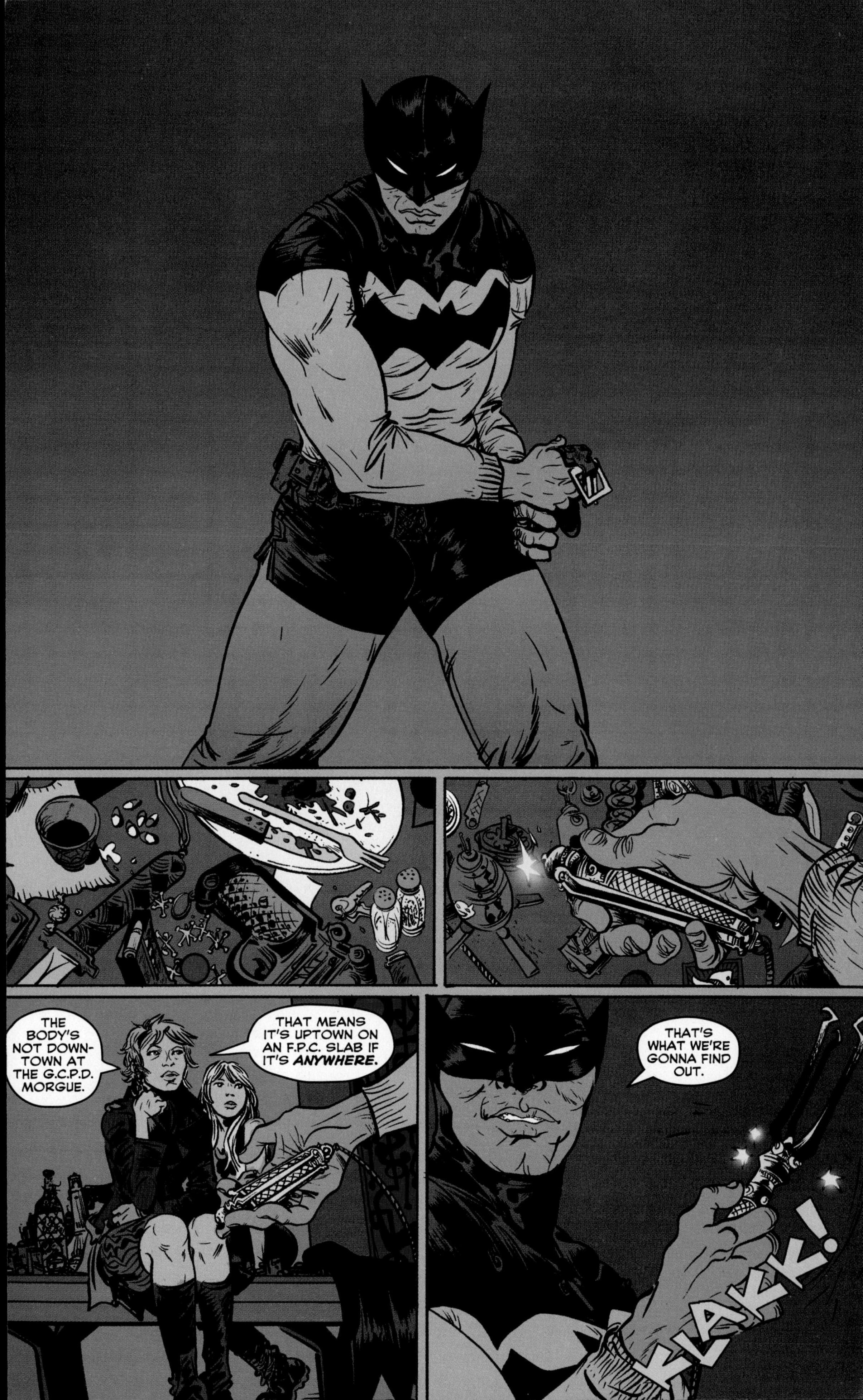

THE BODY'S NOT DOWN-TOWN AT THE G.C.P.D. MORGUE.
THAT MEANS IT'S UPTOWN ON AN F.P.C. SLAB IF IT'S ***ANYWHERE.***
THAT'S WHAT WE'RE GONNA FIND OUT.
KLAKK!

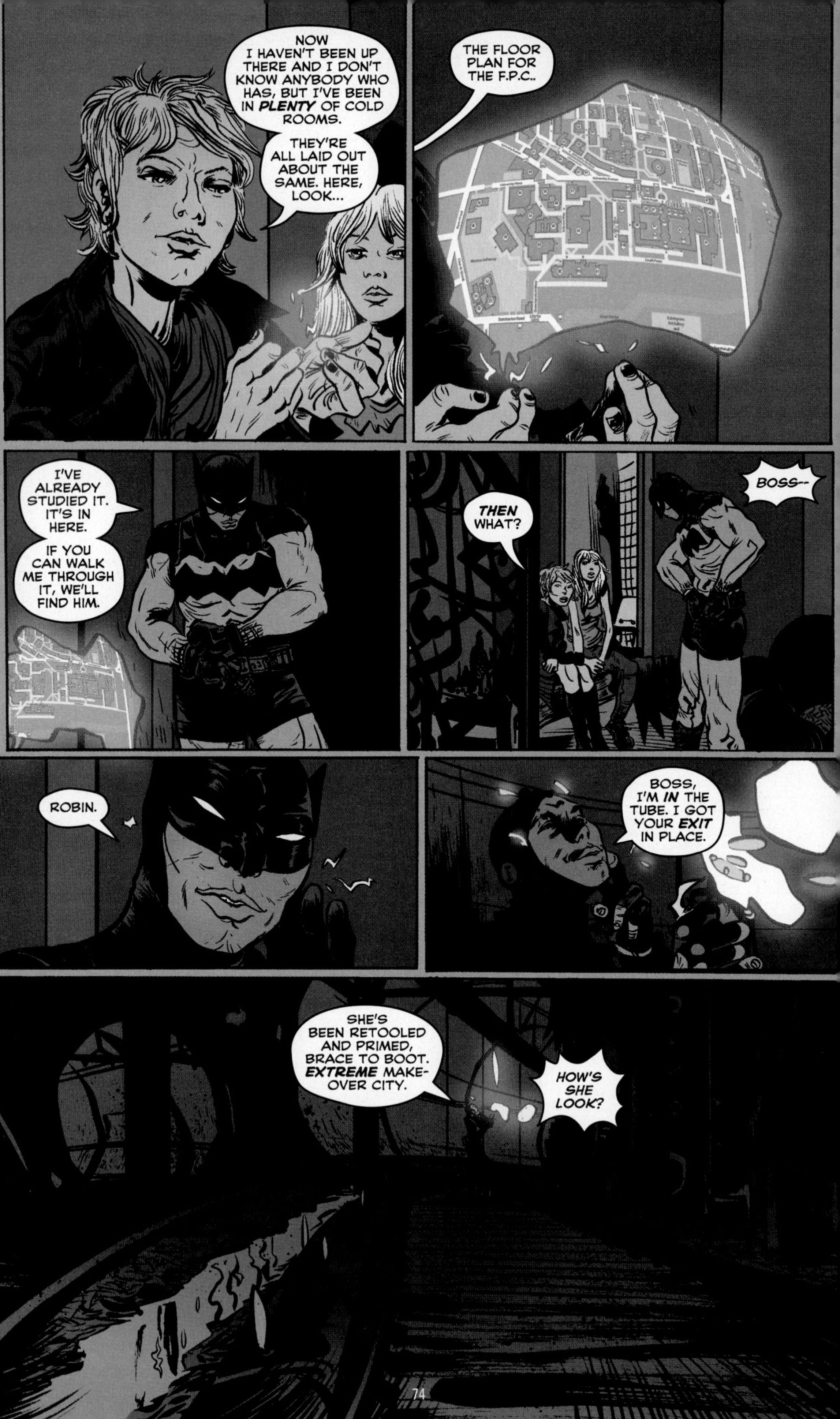
NOW I HAVEN'T BEEN UP THERE AND I DON'T KNOW ANYBODY WHO HAS, BUT I'VE BEEN IN *PLENTY* OF COLD ROOMS.
THEY'RE ALL LAID OUT ABOUT THE SAME. HERE, LOOK...
THE FLOOR PLAN FOR THE F.P.C..
I'VE ALREADY STUDIED IT. IT'S IN HERE.
IF YOU CAN WALK ME THROUGH IT, WE'LL FIND HIM.
THEN WHAT?
BOSS--
ROBIN.
BOSS, I'M *IN* THE TUBE. I GOT YOUR *EXIT* IN PLACE.
HOW'S SHE LOOK?
SHE'S BEEN RETOOLED AND PRIMED, BRACE TO BOOT. *EXTREME* MAKE-OVER CITY.

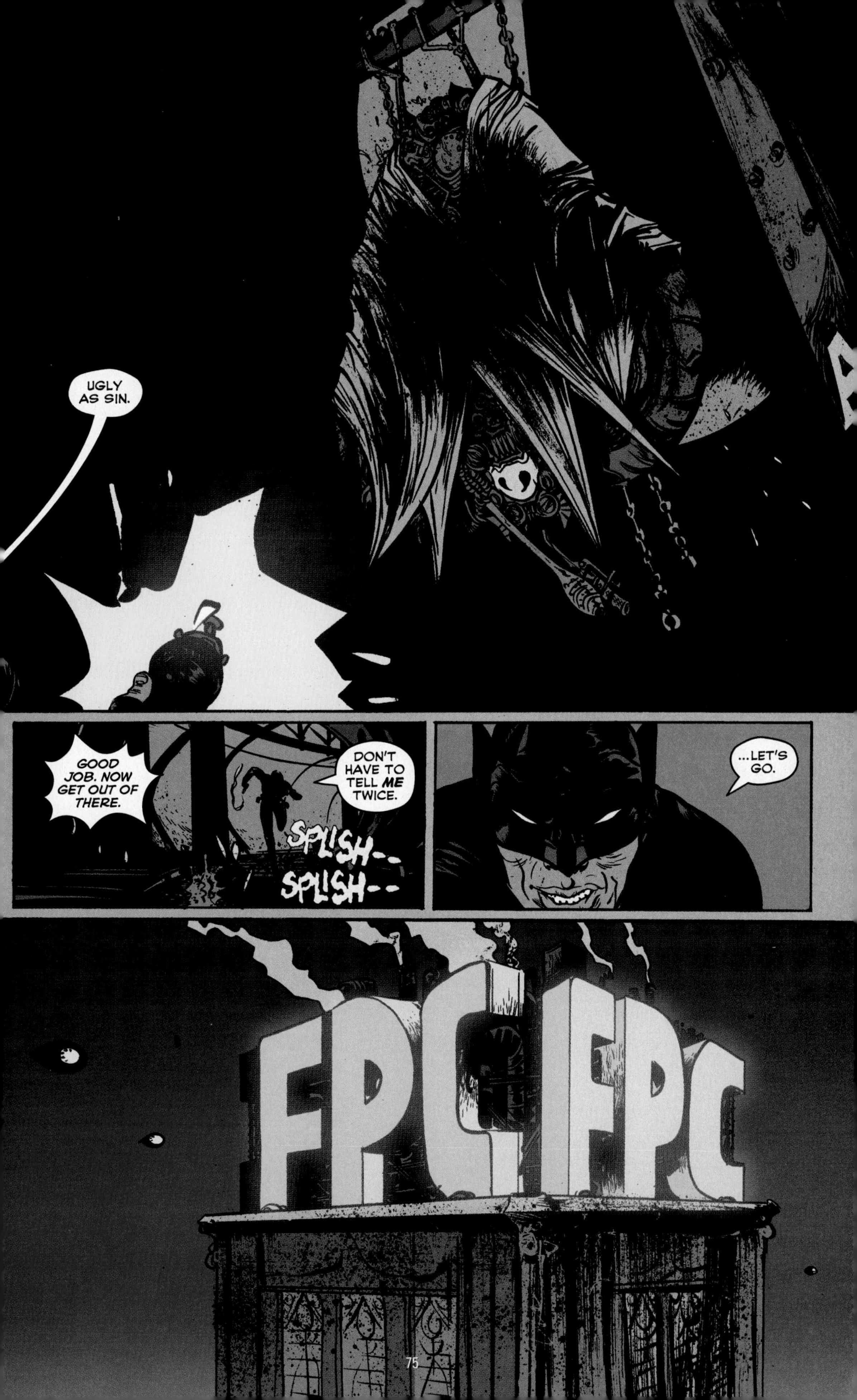
UGLY AS SIN.
GOOD JOB. NOW GET OUT OF THERE.
DON'T HAVE TO TELL *ME* TWICE.
SPLISH--
SPLISH--
...LET'S GO.
FPC FPC

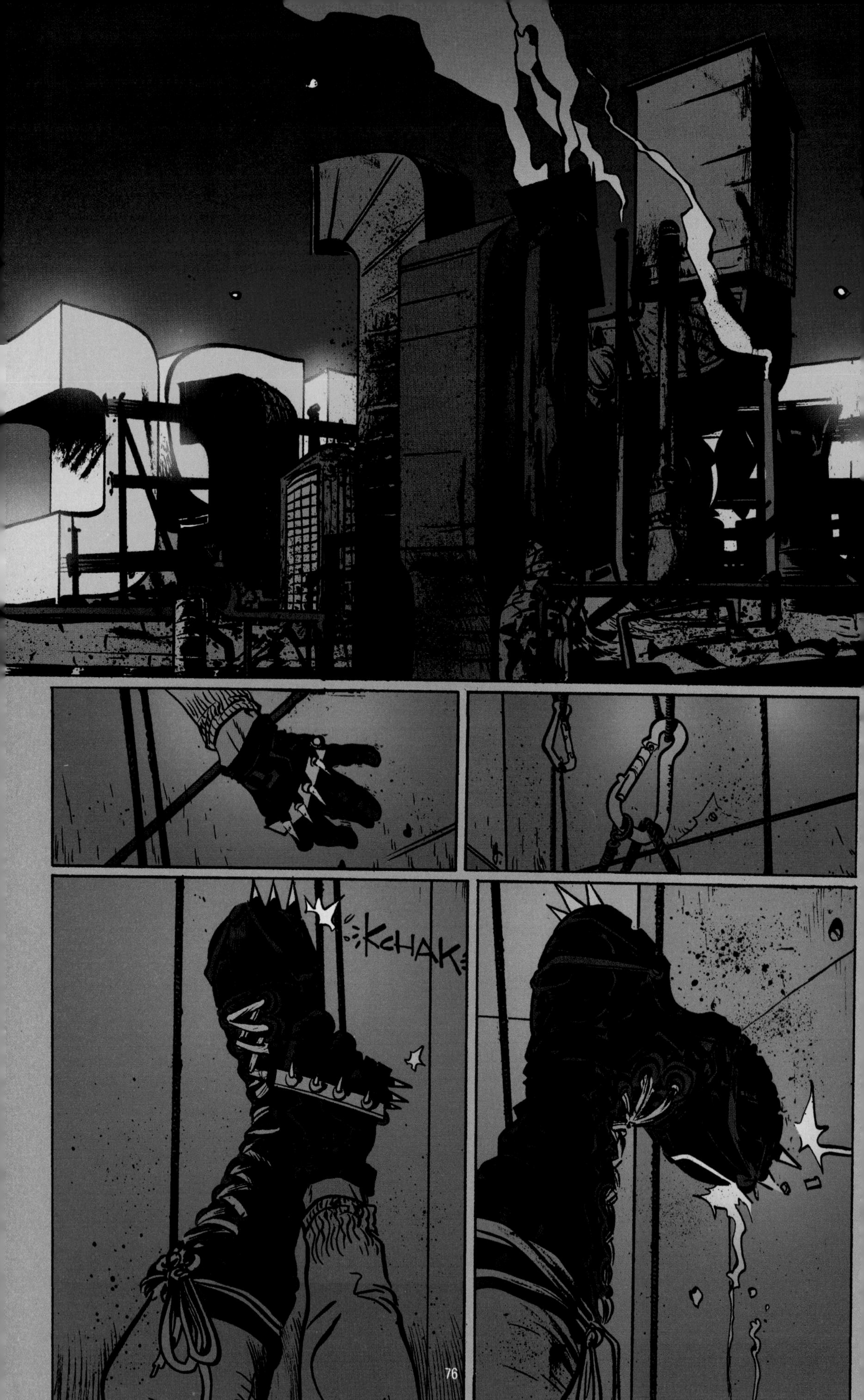
KCHAK

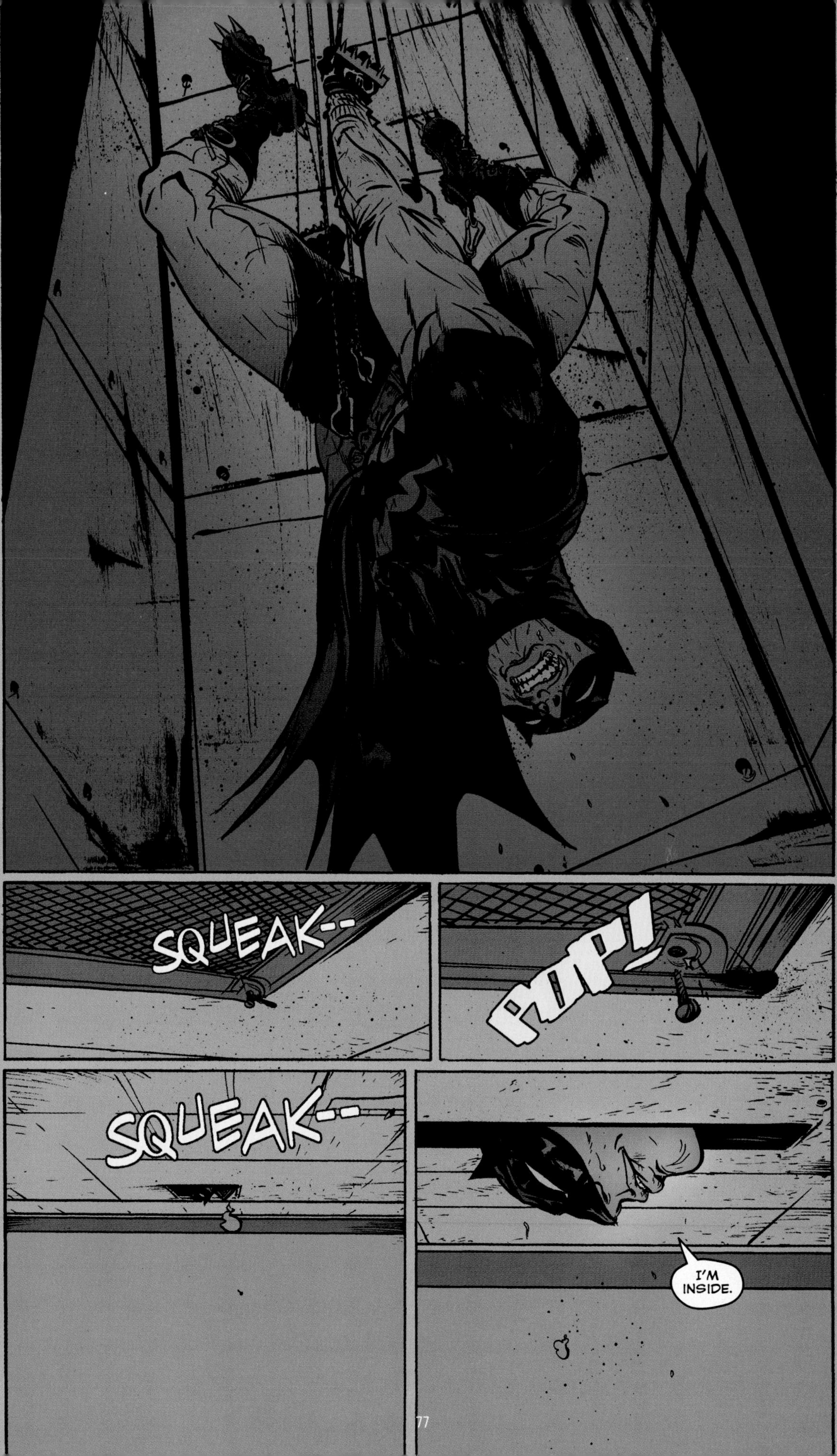

SQUEAK--
POP!
SQUEAK--
I'M INSIDE.

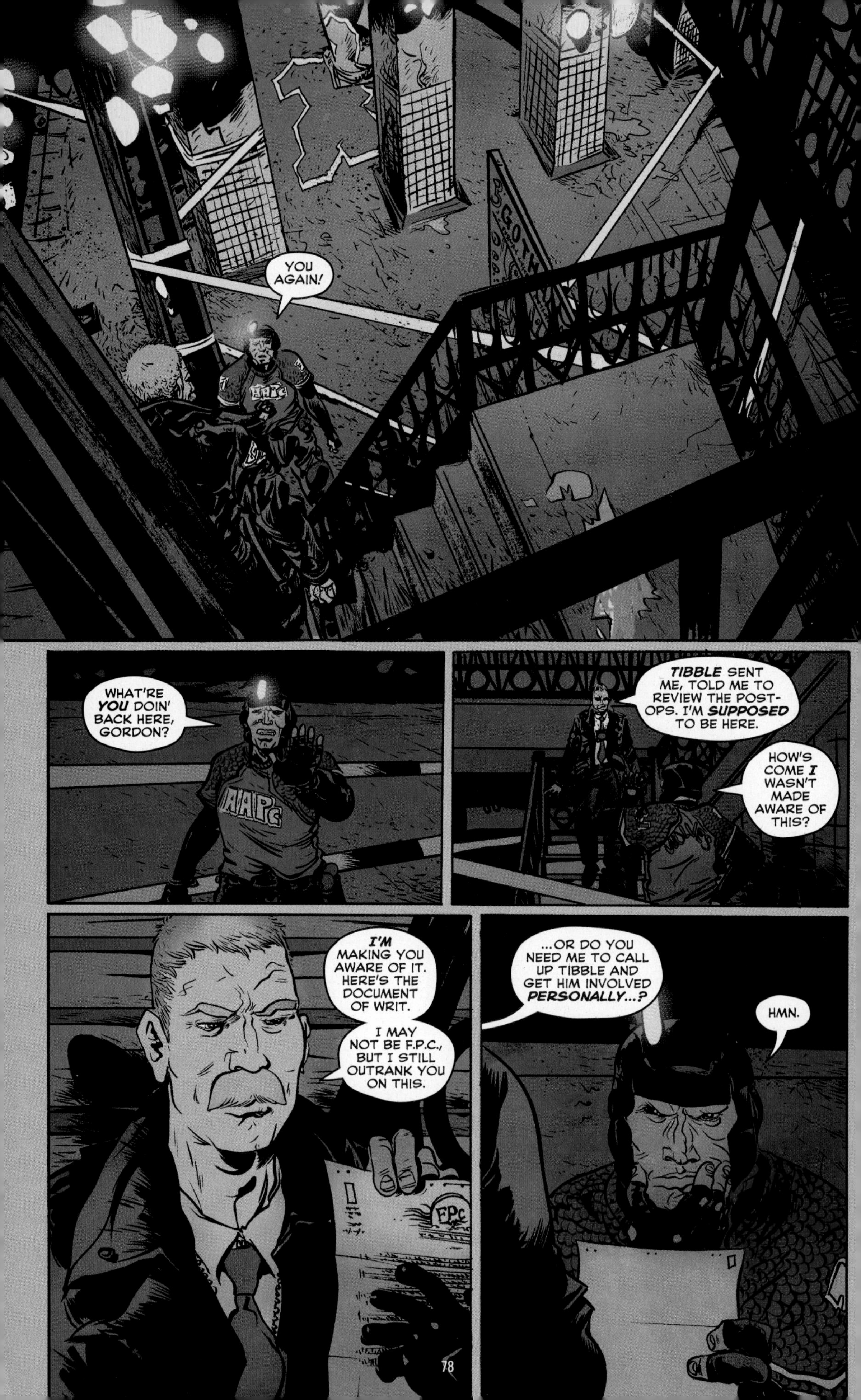
YOU AGAIN!
WHAT'RE YOU DOIN' BACK HERE, GORDON?
TIBBLE SENT ME, TOLD ME TO REVIEW THE POST-OPS. I'M SUPPOSED TO BE HERE.
HOW'S COME I WASN'T MADE AWARE OF THIS?
I'M MAKING YOU AWARE OF IT. HERE'S THE DOCUMENT OF WRIT.
I MAY NOT BE F.P.C., BUT I STILL OUTRANK YOU ON THIS.
...OR DO YOU NEED ME TO CALL UP TIBBLE AND GET HIM INVOLVED PERSONALLY...?
HMN.

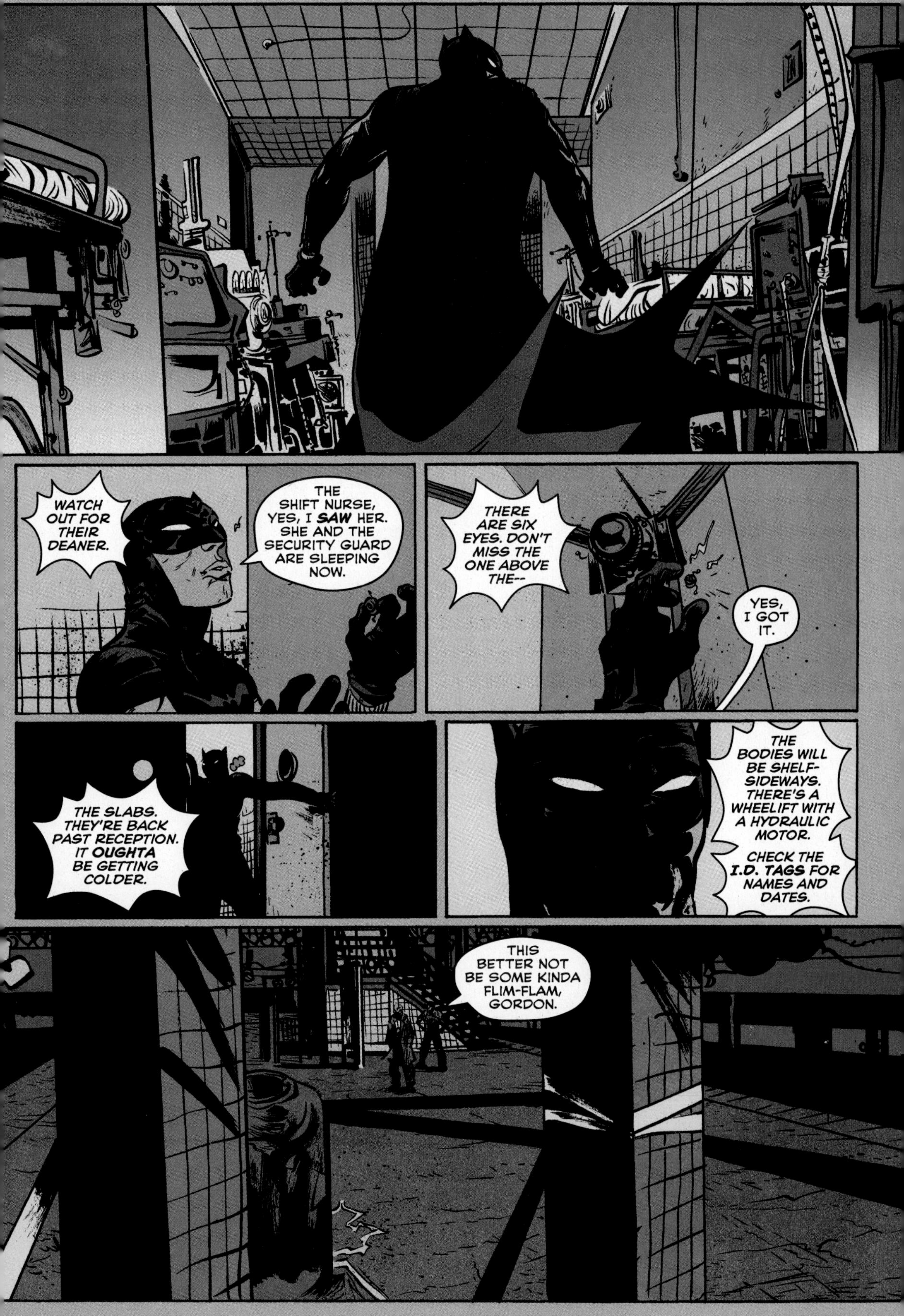
WATCH OUT FOR THEIR DEANER.
THE SHIFT NURSE, YES, I SAW HER. SHE AND THE SECURITY GUARD ARE SLEEPING NOW.
THERE ARE SIX EYES. DON'T MISS THE ONE ABOVE THE--
YES, I GOT IT.
THE SLABS. THEY'RE BACK PAST RECEPTION. IT OUGHTA BE GETTING COLDER.
THE BODIES WILL BE SHELF-SIDEWAYS. THERE'S A WHEELIFT WITH A HYDRAULIC MOTOR.
CHECK THE I.D. TAGS FOR NAMES AND DATES.
THIS BETTER NOT BE SOME KINDA FLIM-FLAM, GORDON.

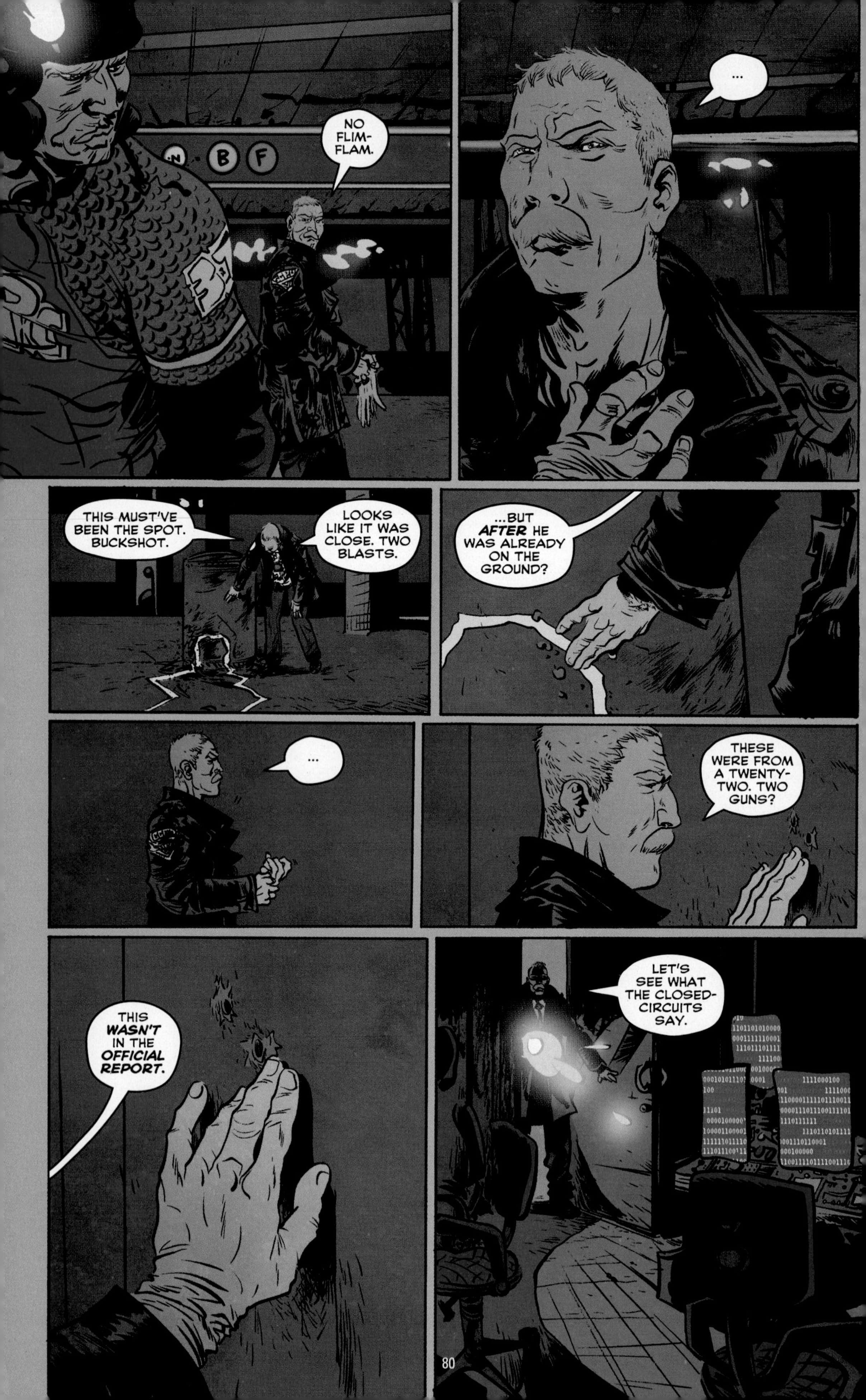
NO FLIM-FLAM.
...
THIS MUST'VE BEEN THE SPOT. BUCKSHOT.
LOOKS LIKE IT WAS CLOSE. TWO BLASTS.
...BUT *AFTER* HE WAS ALREADY ON THE GROUND?
...
THESE WERE FROM A TWENTY-TWO. TWO GUNS?
THIS *WASN'T* IN THE *OFFICIAL REPORT*.
LET'S SEE WHAT THE CLOSED-CIRCUITS SAY.

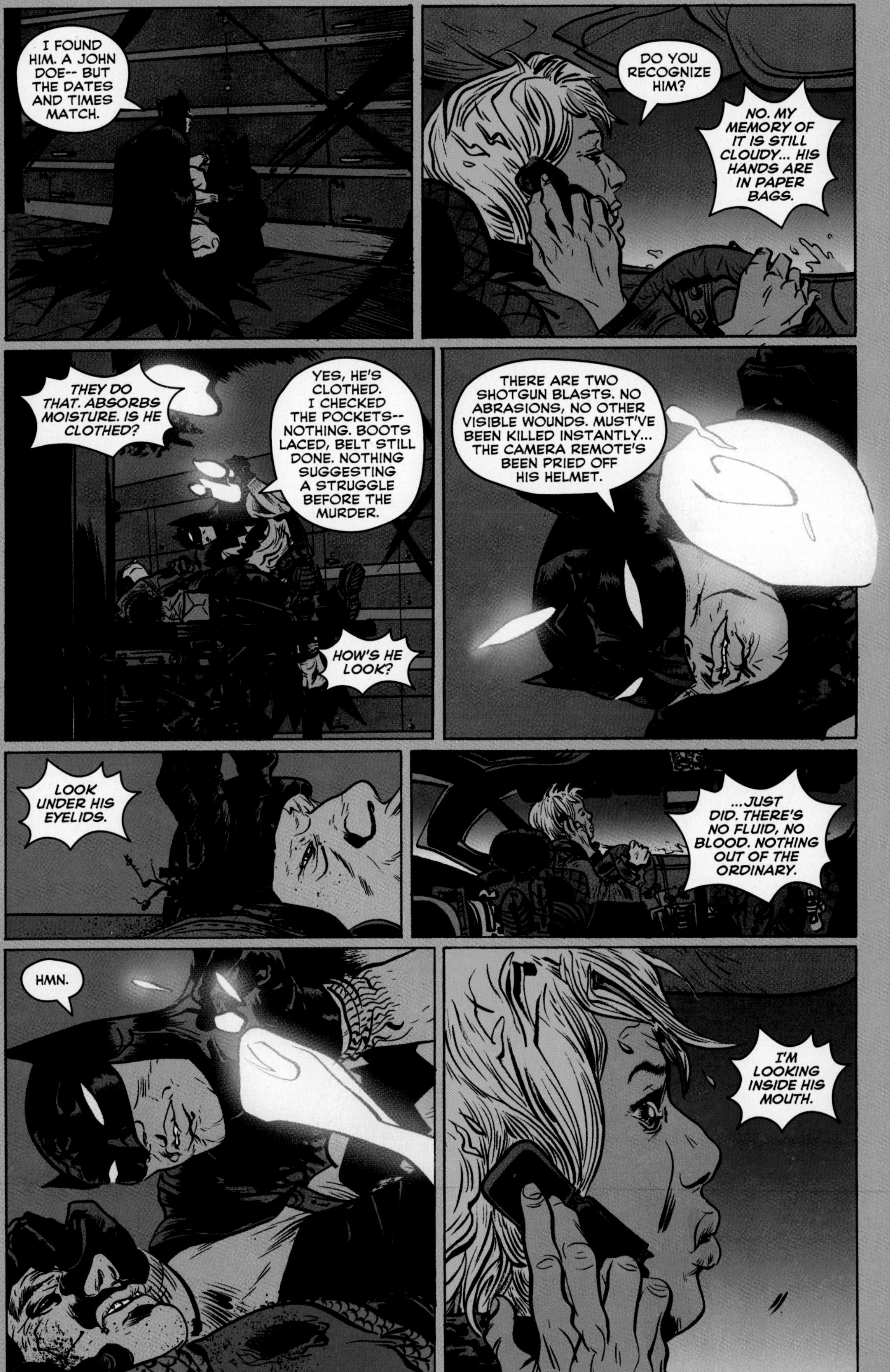
I FOUND HIM. A JOHN DOE-- BUT THE DATES AND TIMES MATCH.
DO YOU RECOGNIZE HIM?
NO. MY MEMORY OF IT IS STILL CLOUDY... HIS HANDS ARE IN PAPER BAGS.
THEY DO THAT. ABSORBS MOISTURE. IS HE CLOTHED?
YES, HE'S CLOTHED. I CHECKED THE POCKETS-- NOTHING. BOOTS LACED, BELT STILL DONE. NOTHING SUGGESTING A STRUGGLE BEFORE THE MURDER.
HOW'S HE LOOK?
THERE ARE TWO SHOTGUN BLASTS. NO ABRASIONS, NO OTHER VISIBLE WOUNDS. MUST'VE BEEN KILLED INSTANTLY... THE CAMERA REMOTE'S BEEN PRIED OFF HIS HELMET.
LOOK UNDER HIS EYELIDS.
...JUST DID. THERE'S NO FLUID, NO BLOOD. NOTHING OUT OF THE ORDINARY.
HMN.
I'M LOOKING INSIDE HIS MOUTH.

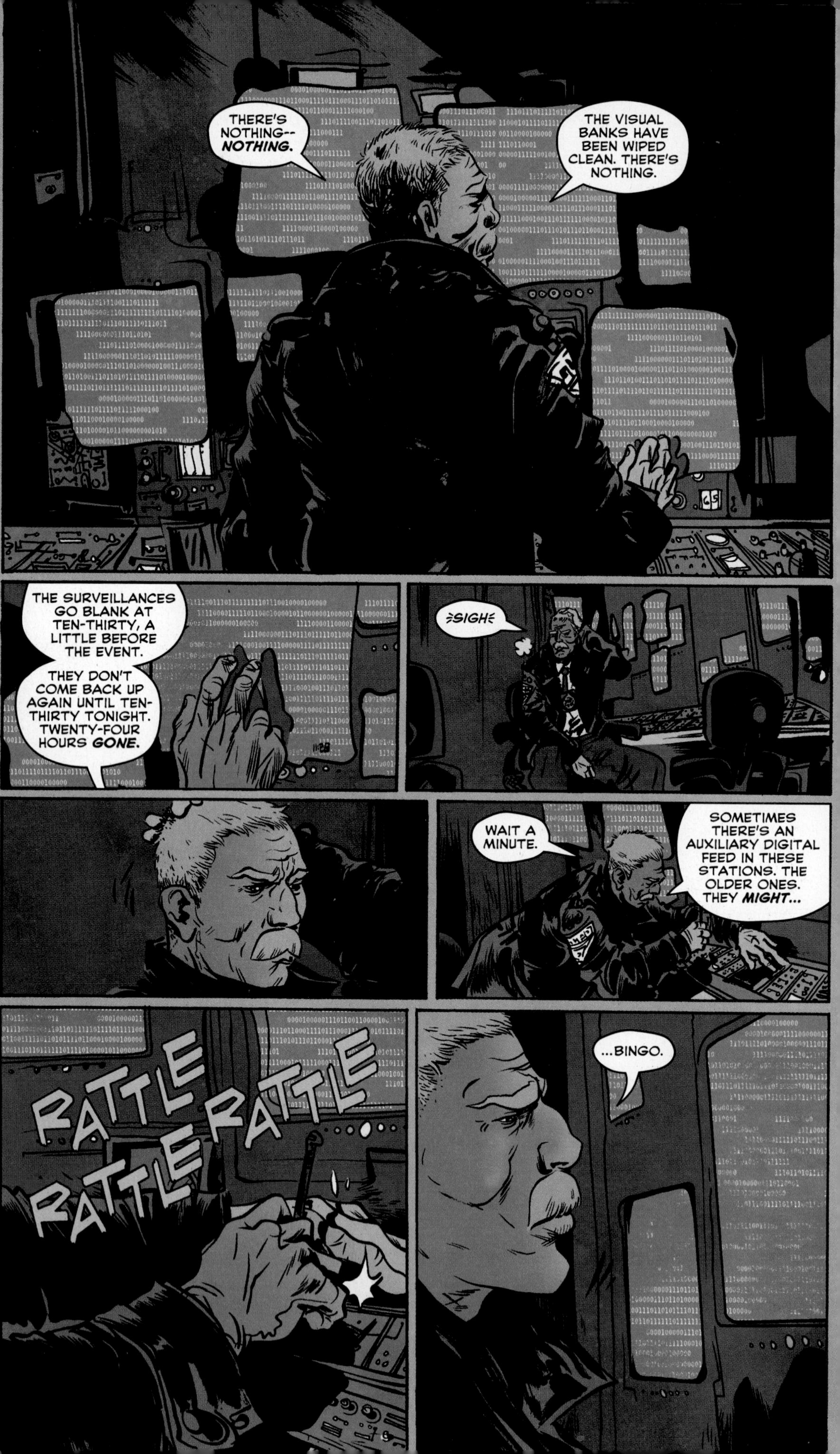
THERE'S NOTHING-- *NOTHING.*
THE VISUAL BANKS HAVE BEEN WIPED CLEAN. THERE'S NOTHING.
THE SURVEILLANCES GO BLANK AT TEN-THIRTY, A LITTLE BEFORE THE EVENT.
THEY DON'T COME BACK UP AGAIN UNTIL TEN-THIRTY TONIGHT. TWENTY-FOUR HOURS *GONE.*
SIGH
WAIT A MINUTE.
SOMETIMES THERE'S AN AUXILIARY DIGITAL FEED IN THESE STATIONS. THE OLDER ONES. THEY *MIGHT...*
RATTLE RATTLE RATTLE
...BINGO.

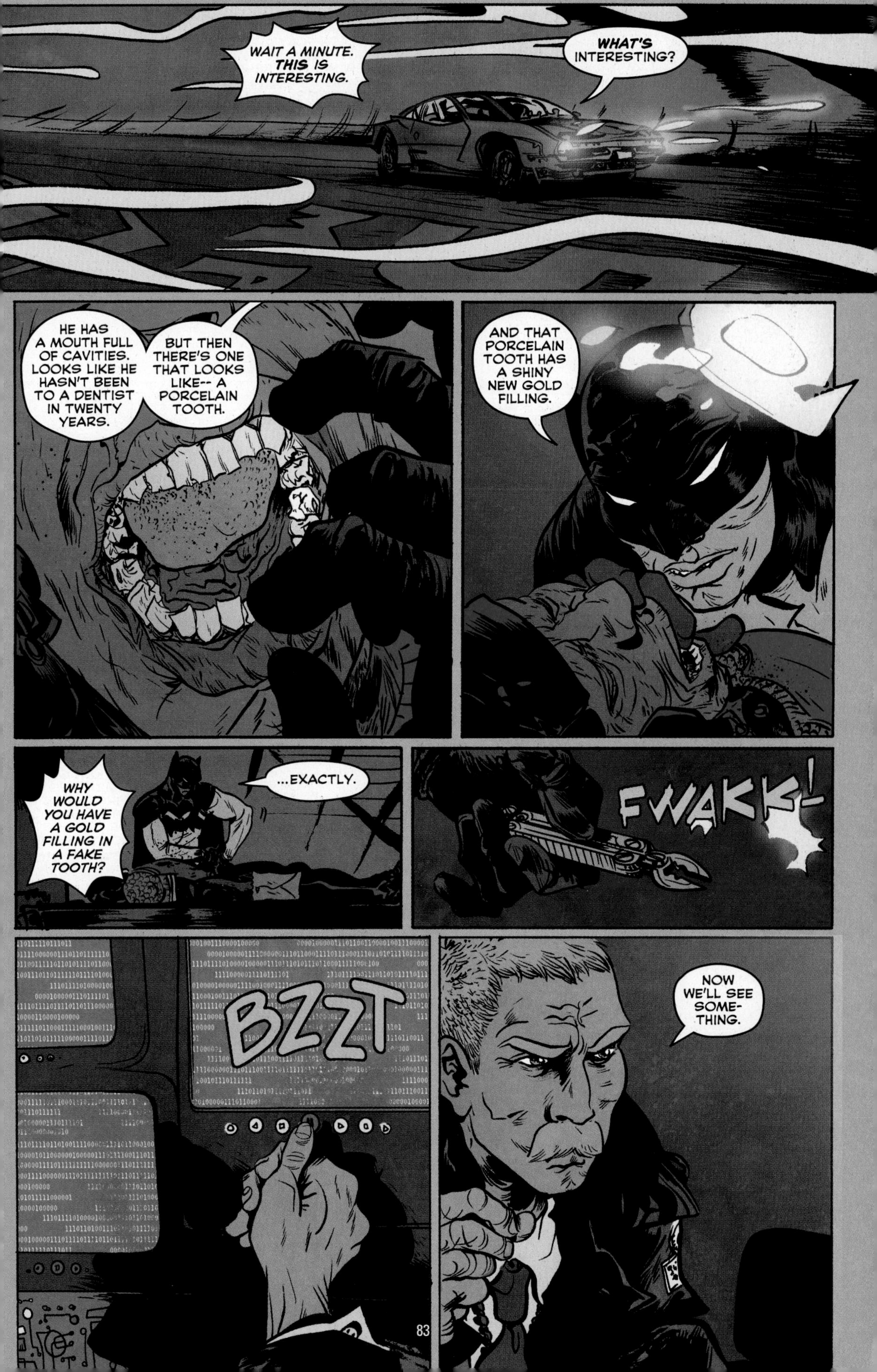

WAIT A MINUTE. THIS IS INTERESTING.
WHAT'S INTERESTING?
HE HAS A MOUTH FULL OF CAVITIES. LOOKS LIKE HE HASN'T BEEN TO A DENTIST IN TWENTY YEARS.
BUT THEN THERE'S ONE THAT LOOKS LIKE-- A PORCELAIN TOOTH.
AND THAT PORCELAIN TOOTH HAS A SHINY NEW GOLD FILLING.
WHY WOULD YOU HAVE A GOLD FILLING IN A FAKE TOOTH?
...EXACTLY.
FWAKK!
BZZT
NOW WE'LL SEE SOME-THING.

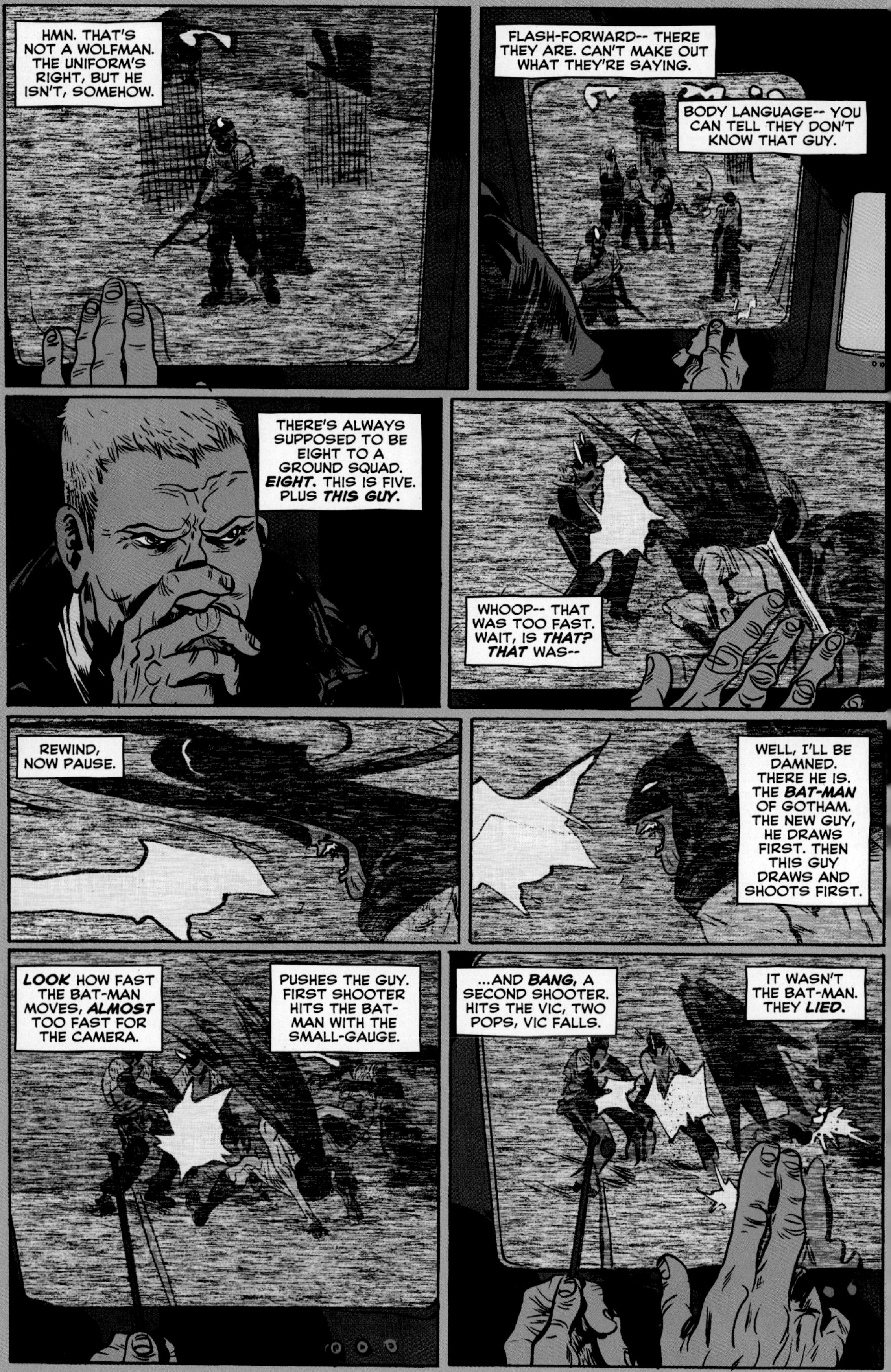
HMN. THAT'S NOT A WOLFMAN. THE UNIFORM'S RIGHT, BUT HE ISN'T, SOMEHOW.
FLASH-FORWARD-- THERE THEY ARE. CAN'T MAKE OUT WHAT THEY'RE SAYING.
BODY LANGUAGE-- YOU CAN TELL THEY DON'T KNOW THAT GUY.
THERE'S ALWAYS SUPPOSED TO BE EIGHT TO A GROUND SQUAD. EIGHT. THIS IS FIVE. PLUS THIS GUY.
WHOOP-- THAT WAS TOO FAST. WAIT, IS THAT? THAT WAS--
REWIND, NOW PAUSE.
WELL, I'LL BE DAMNED. THERE HE IS. THE BAT-MAN OF GOTHAM. THE NEW GUY, HE DRAWS FIRST. THEN THIS GUY DRAWS AND SHOOTS FIRST.
LOOK HOW FAST THE BAT-MAN MOVES, ALMOST TOO FAST FOR THE CAMERA.
PUSHES THE GUY. FIRST SHOOTER HITS THE BAT-MAN WITH THE SMALL-GAUGE.
...AND BANG, A SECOND SHOOTER. HITS THE VIC, TWO POPS, VIC FALLS.
IT WASN'T THE BAT-MAN. THEY LIED.

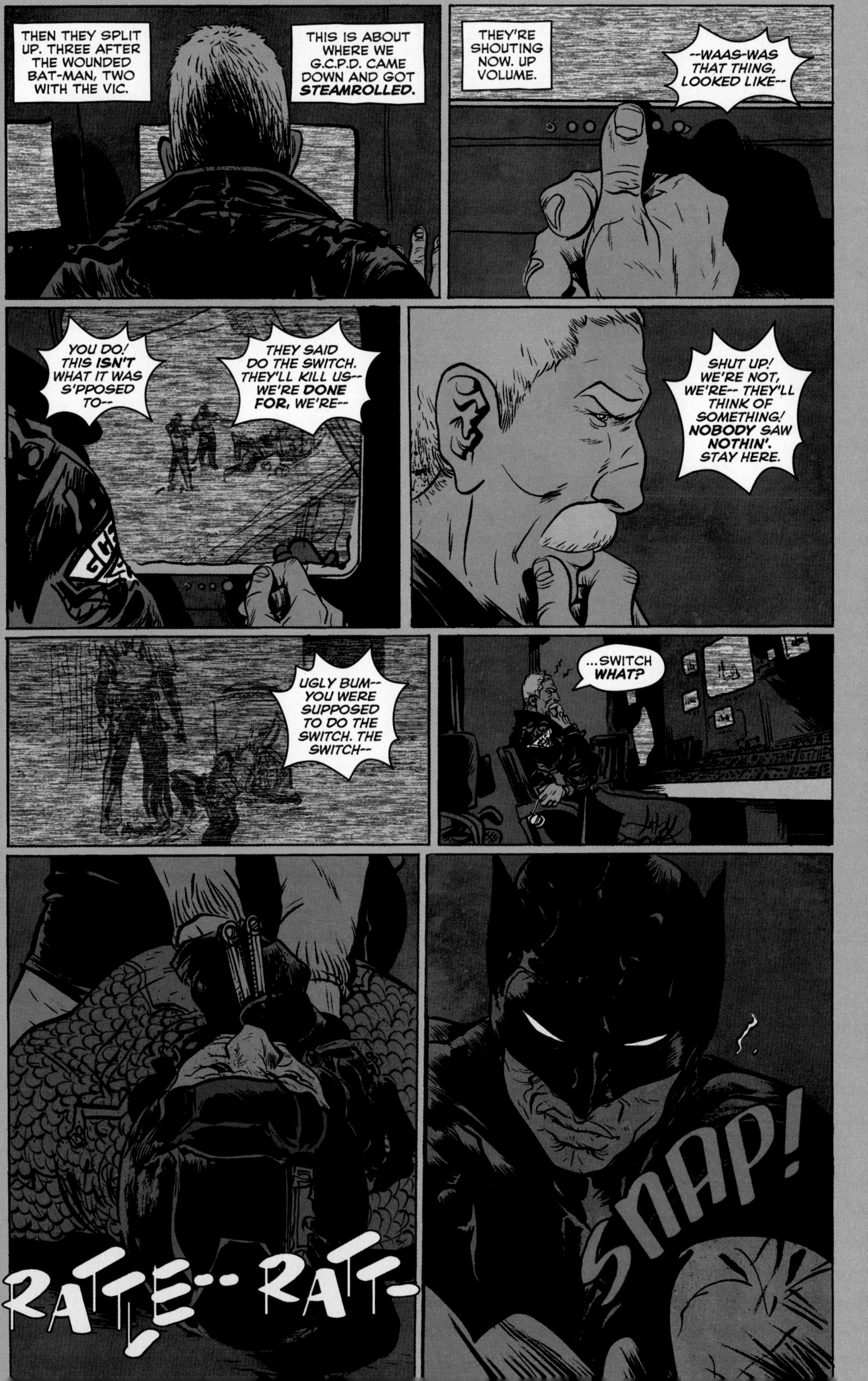

THEN THEY SPLIT UP. THREE AFTER THE WOUNDED BAT-MAN, TWO WITH THE VIC.
THIS IS ABOUT WHERE WE G.C.P.D. CAME DOWN AND GOT STEAMROLLED.
THEY'RE SHOUTING NOW. UP VOLUME.
--WAAS-WAS THAT THING, LOOKED LIKE--
YOU DO! THIS ISN'T WHAT IT WAS S'PPOSED TO--
THEY SAID DO THE SWITCH. THEY'LL KILL US-- WE'RE DONE FOR, WE'RE--
SHUT UP! WE'RE NOT, WE'RE-- THEY'LL THINK OF SOMETHING! NOBODY SAW NOTHIN'. STAY HERE.
UGLY BUM-- YOU WERE SUPPOSED TO DO THE SWITCH. THE SWITCH--
...SWITCH WHAT?
RATTLE-- RATT-
SNAP!

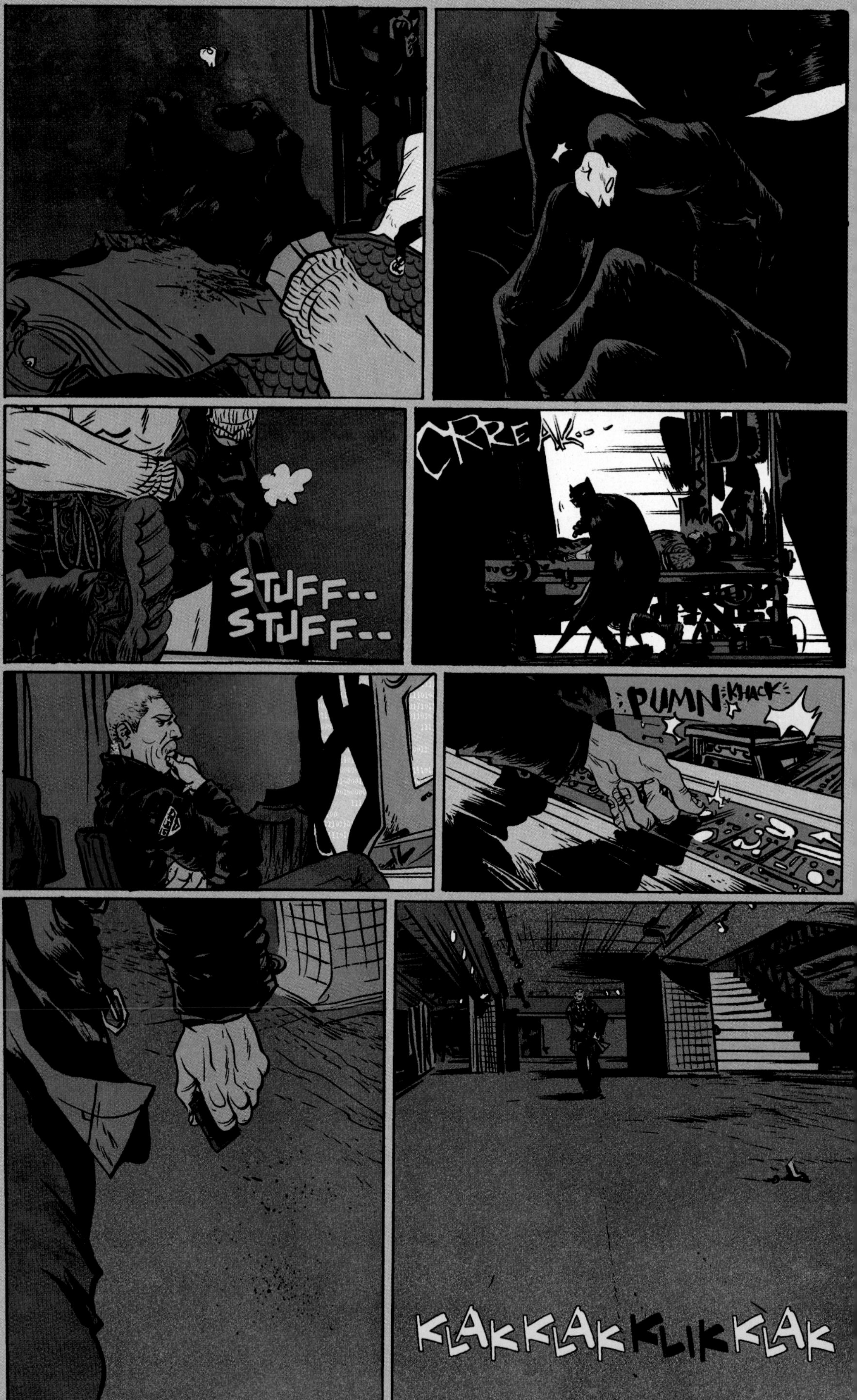
STUFF..
STUFF..
CRREAK...
PUMN
KHACK
KLAKKLAKKLIKKLAK

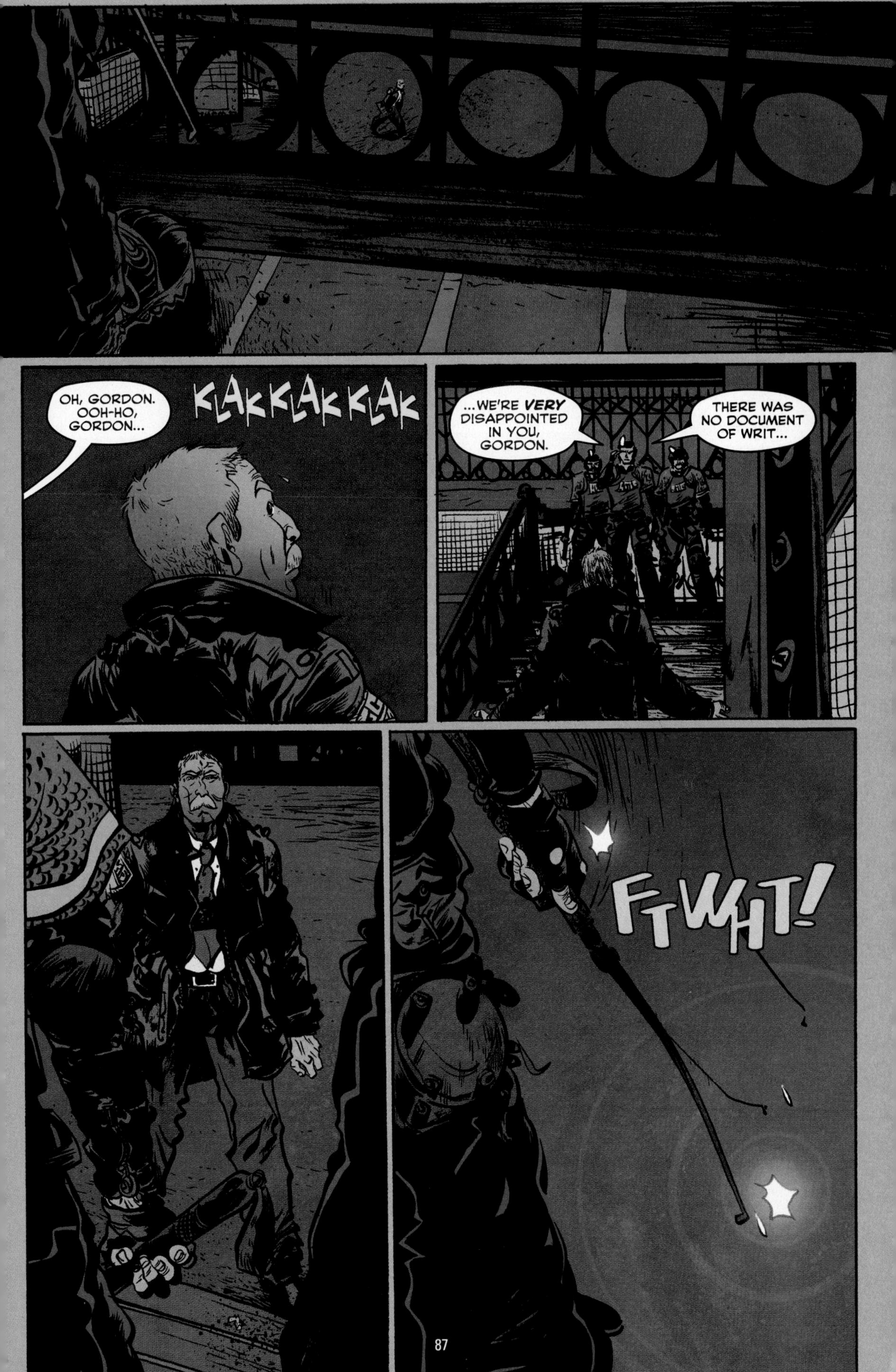
OH, GORDON. OOH-HO, GORDON...
KLAK KLAK KLAK
...WE'RE VERY DISAPPOINTED IN YOU, GORDON.
THERE WAS NO DOCUMENT OF WRIT...
FTWHT!

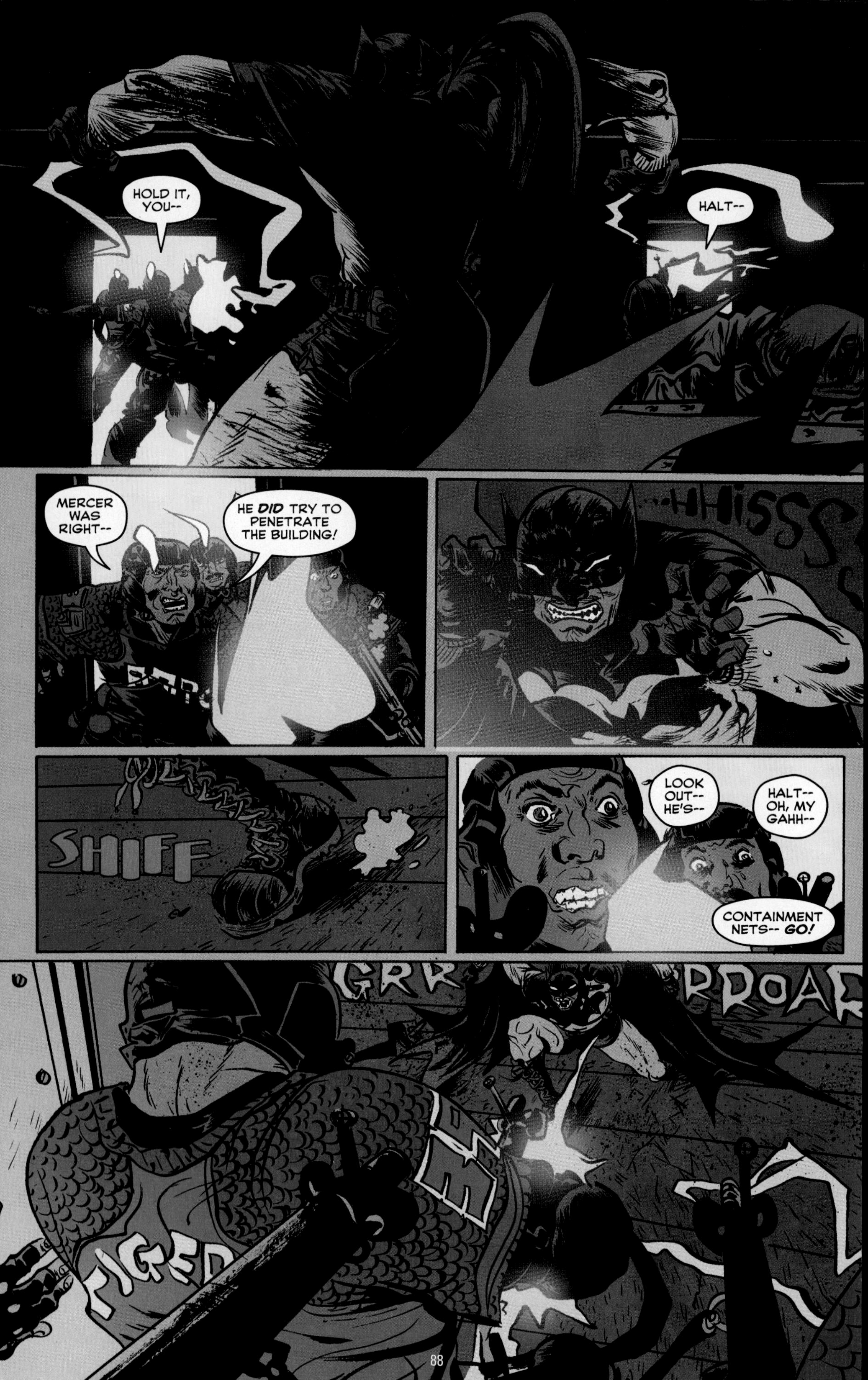
HOLD IT, YOU--
HALT--
MERCER WAS RIGHT--
HE DID TRY TO PENETRATE THE BUILDING!
HHISSS
SHIFF
LOOK OUT-- HE'S--
HALT-- OH, MY GAHH--
CONTAINMENT NETS-- GO!
GRR
RROAR
TIGER

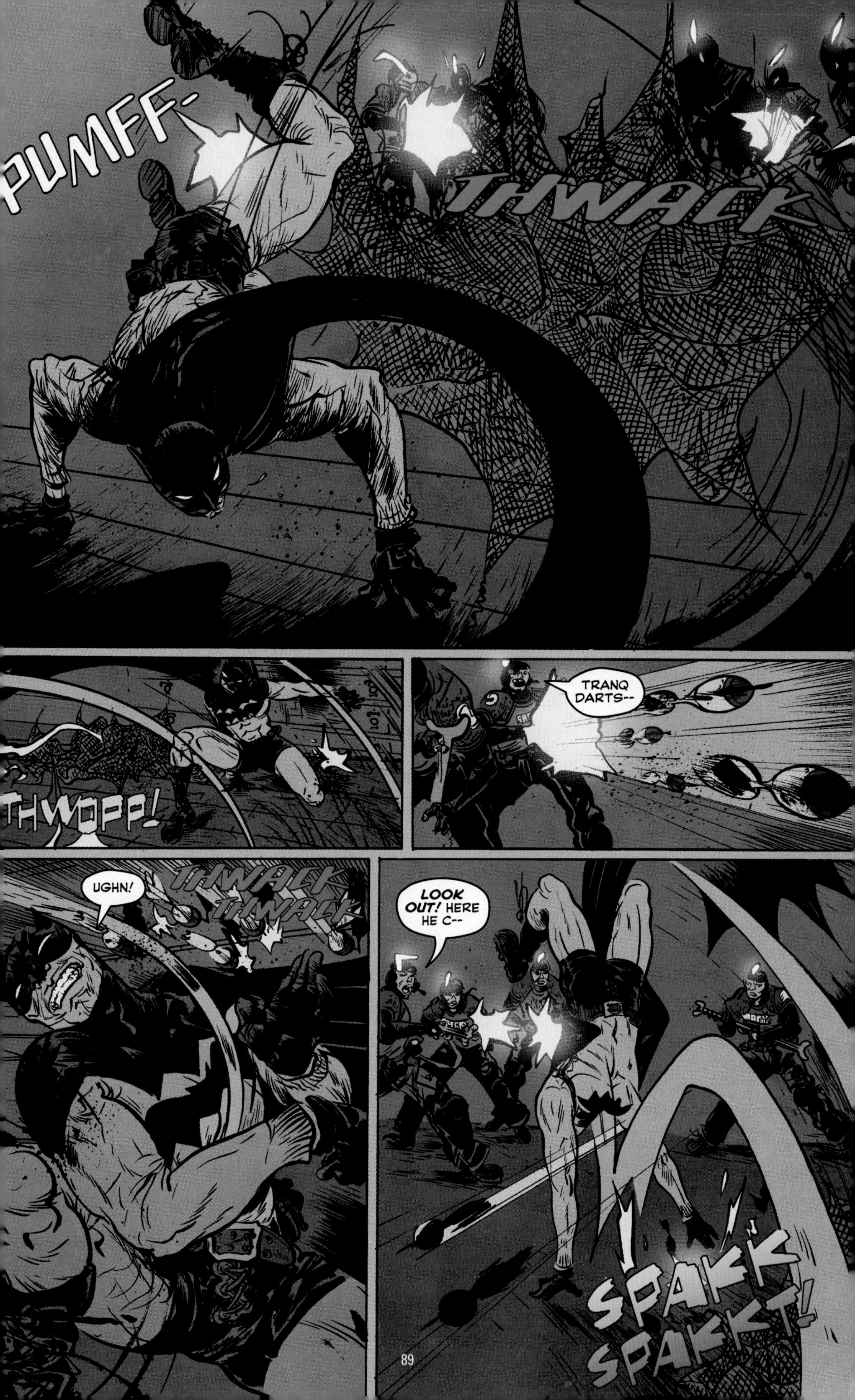
PUMFF-
THWACK
THWOPP!
TRANQ DARTS--
UGHN!
THWACK
THWACK
LOOK OUT! HERE HE C--
SPAKK
SPAKKT!

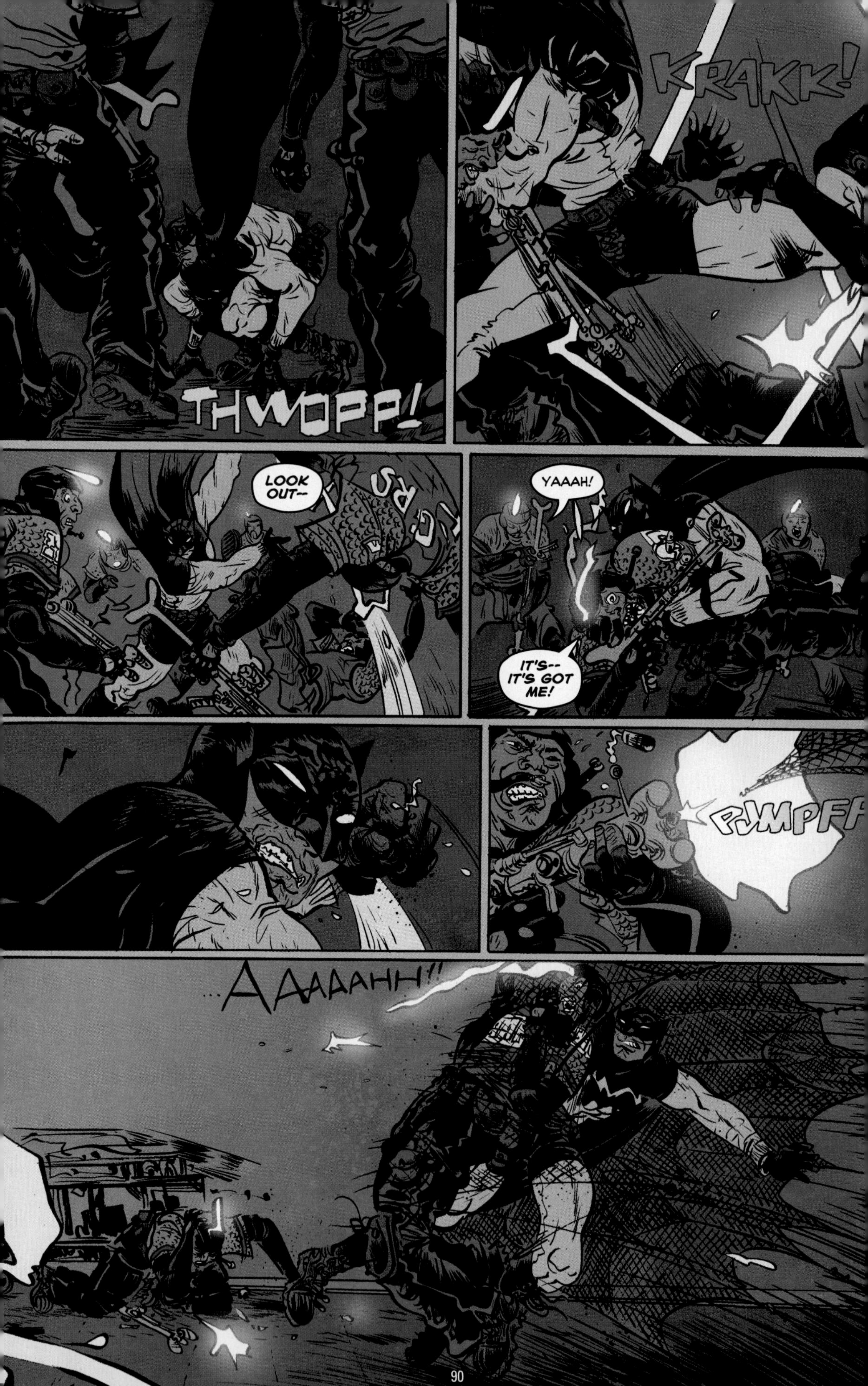
THWOPP!
KRAKK!
LOOK OUT--
YAAAH!
IT'S-- IT'S GOT ME!
PJMPFF
...AAAAAHH!!

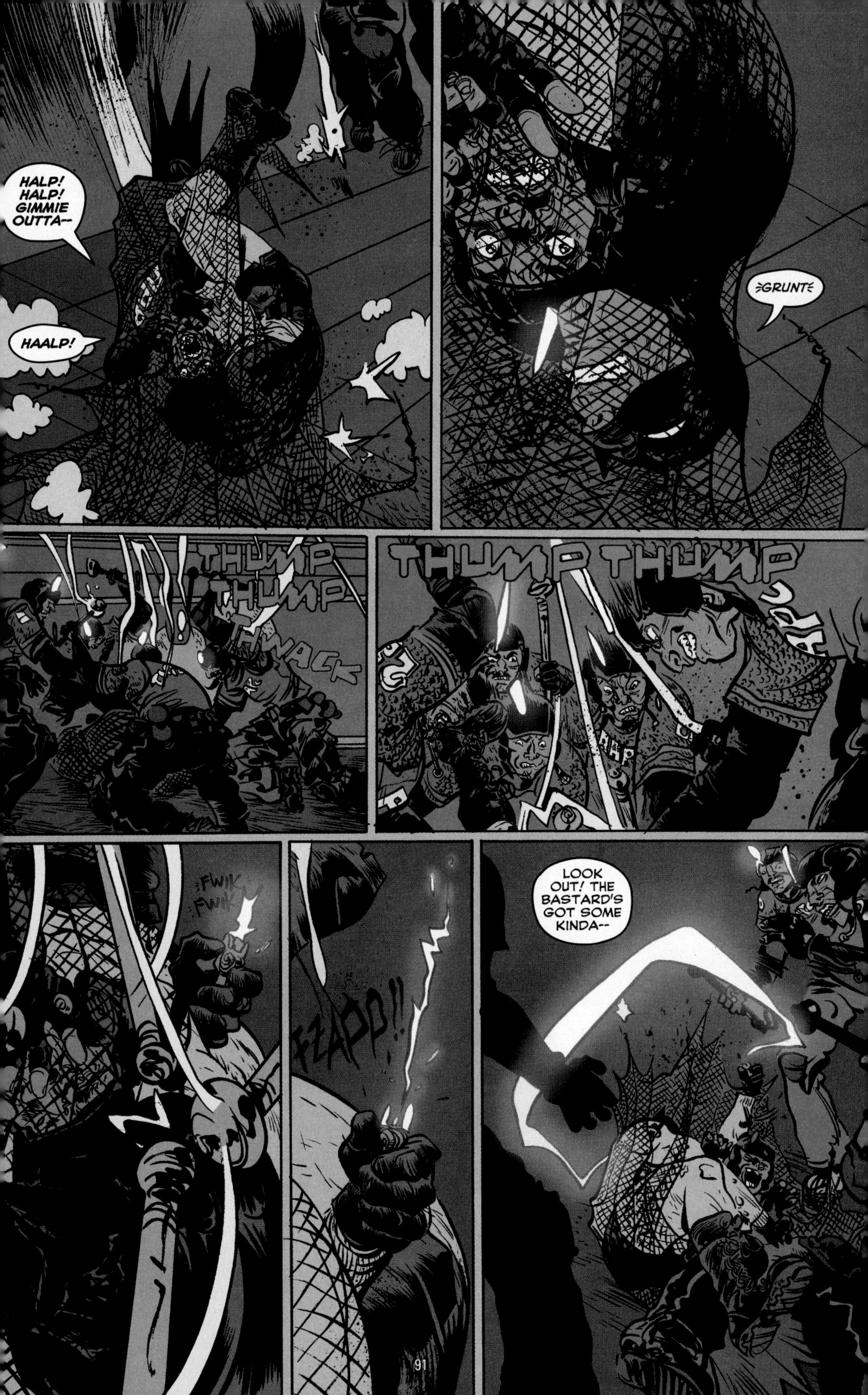
HALP! HALP! GIMMIE OUTTA--
HAALP!
GRUNT
THUMP THUMP
WHACK
THUMP THUMP
FWIK FWIK
FZAPP!!
LOOK OUT! THE BASTARD'S GOT SOME KINDA--

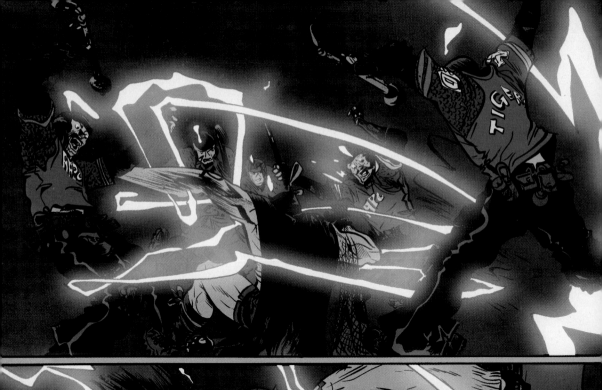

POKT!

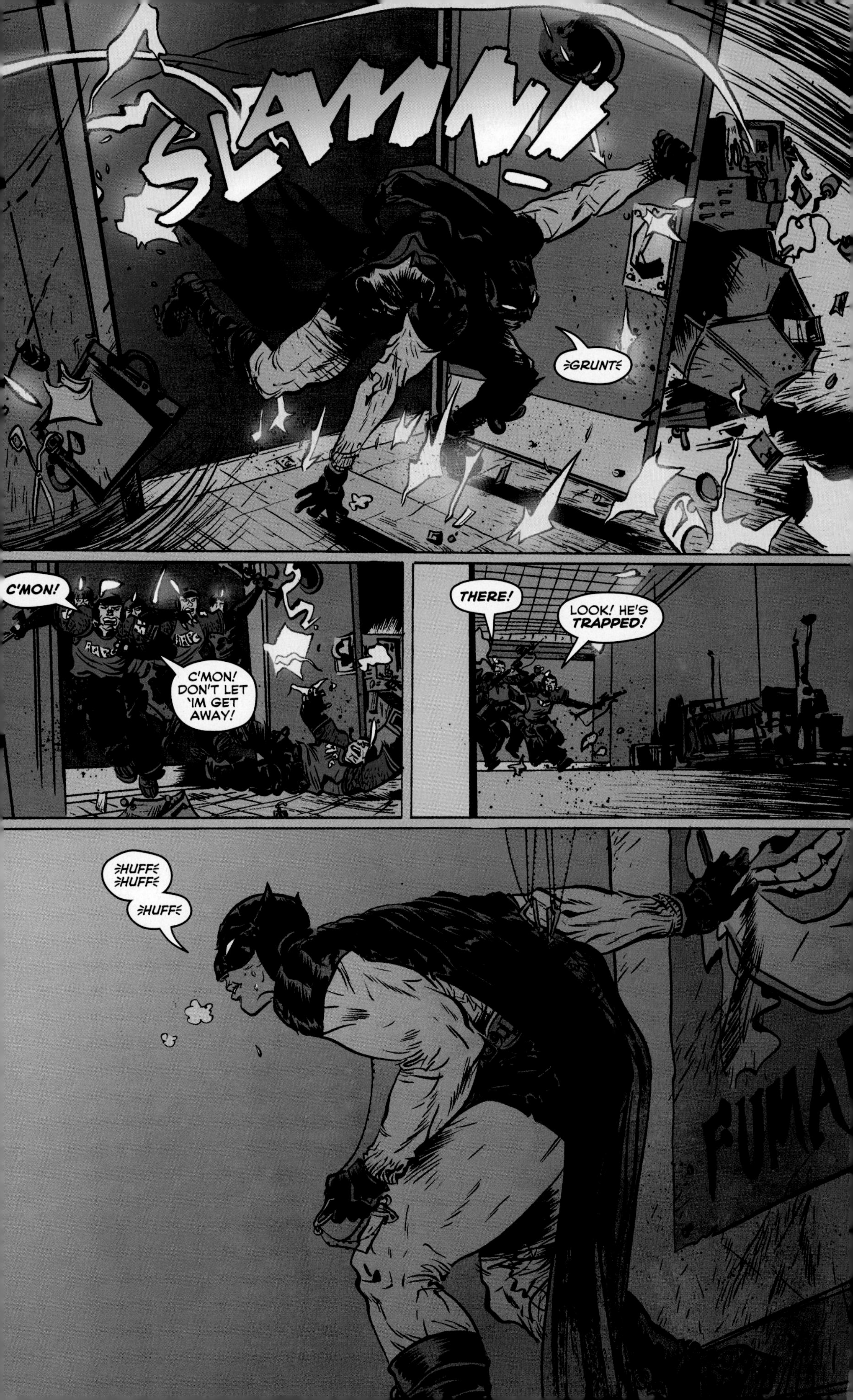
SLAM!
GRUNT
C'MON!
C'MON! DON'T LET 'IM GET AWAY!
THERE!
LOOK! HE'S TRAPPED!
HUFF HUFF
HUFF

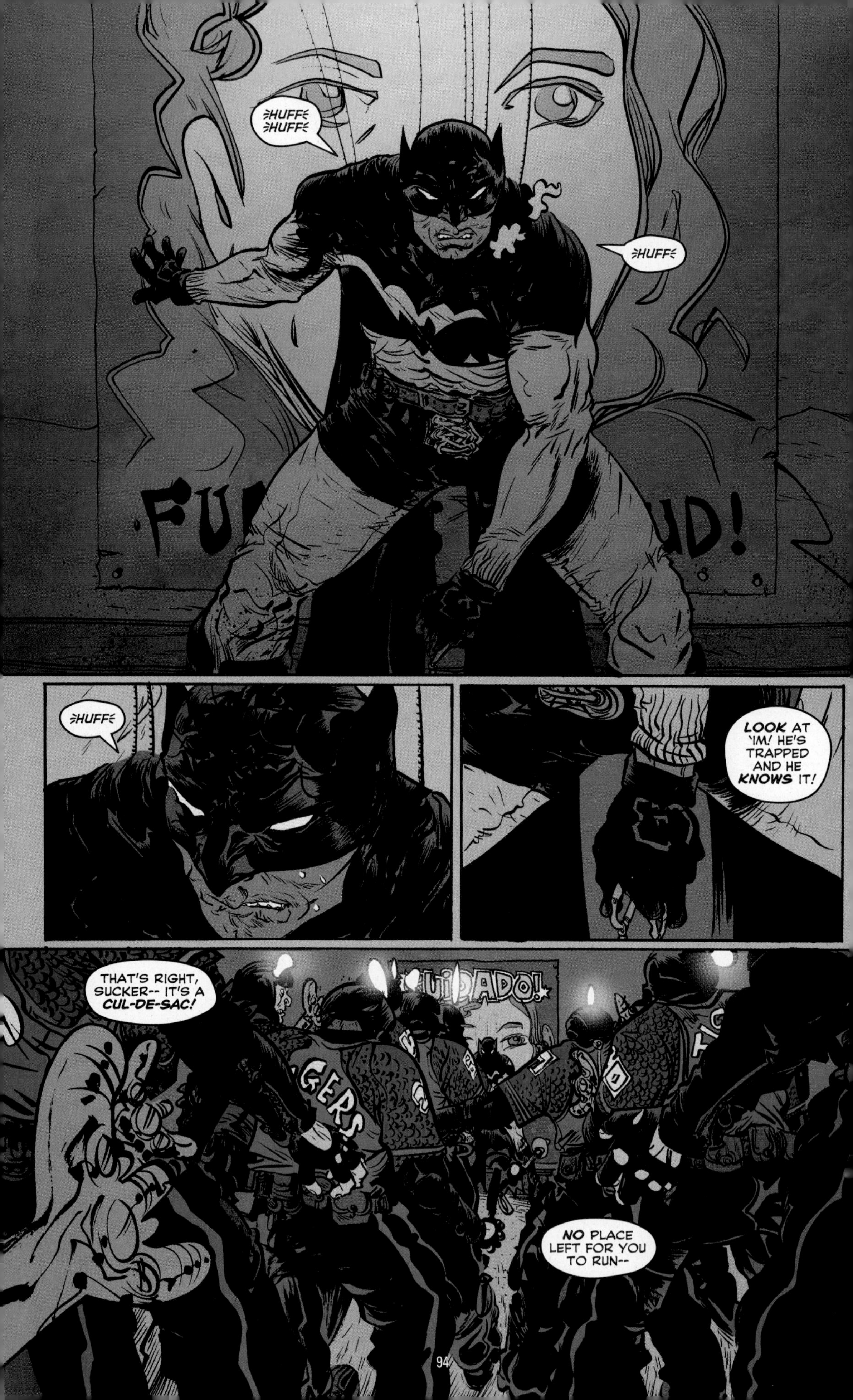

HUFF
HUFF
HUFF
HUFF
LOOK AT 'IM! HE'S TRAPPED AND HE KNOWS IT!
THAT'S RIGHT, SUCKER-- IT'S A CUL-DE-SAC!
NO PLACE LEFT FOR YOU TO RUN--

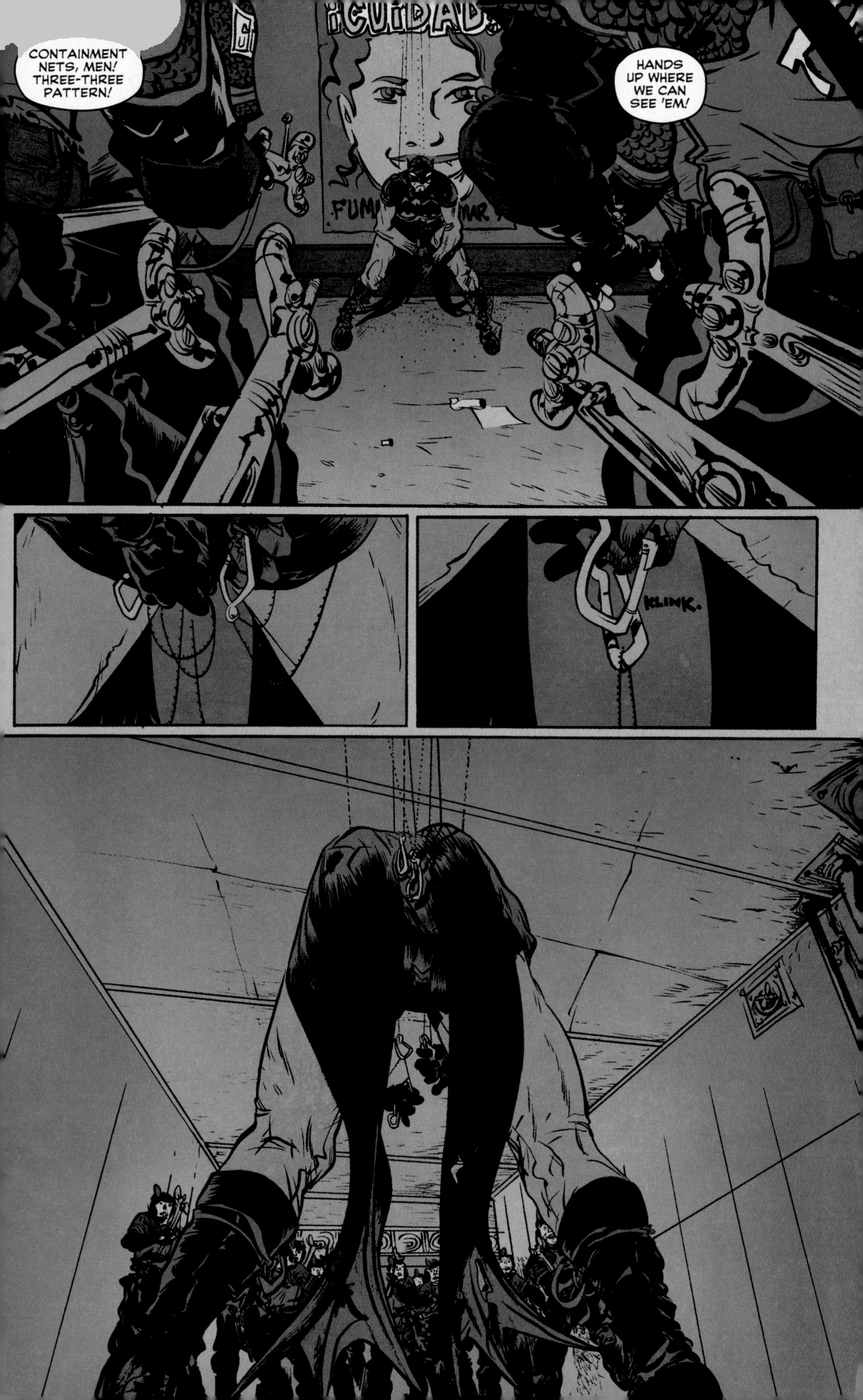
¡CUIDAD
FUM MAR
CONTAINMENT NETS, MEN! THREE-THREE PATTERN!
HANDS UP WHERE WE CAN SEE 'EM!
KLINK.

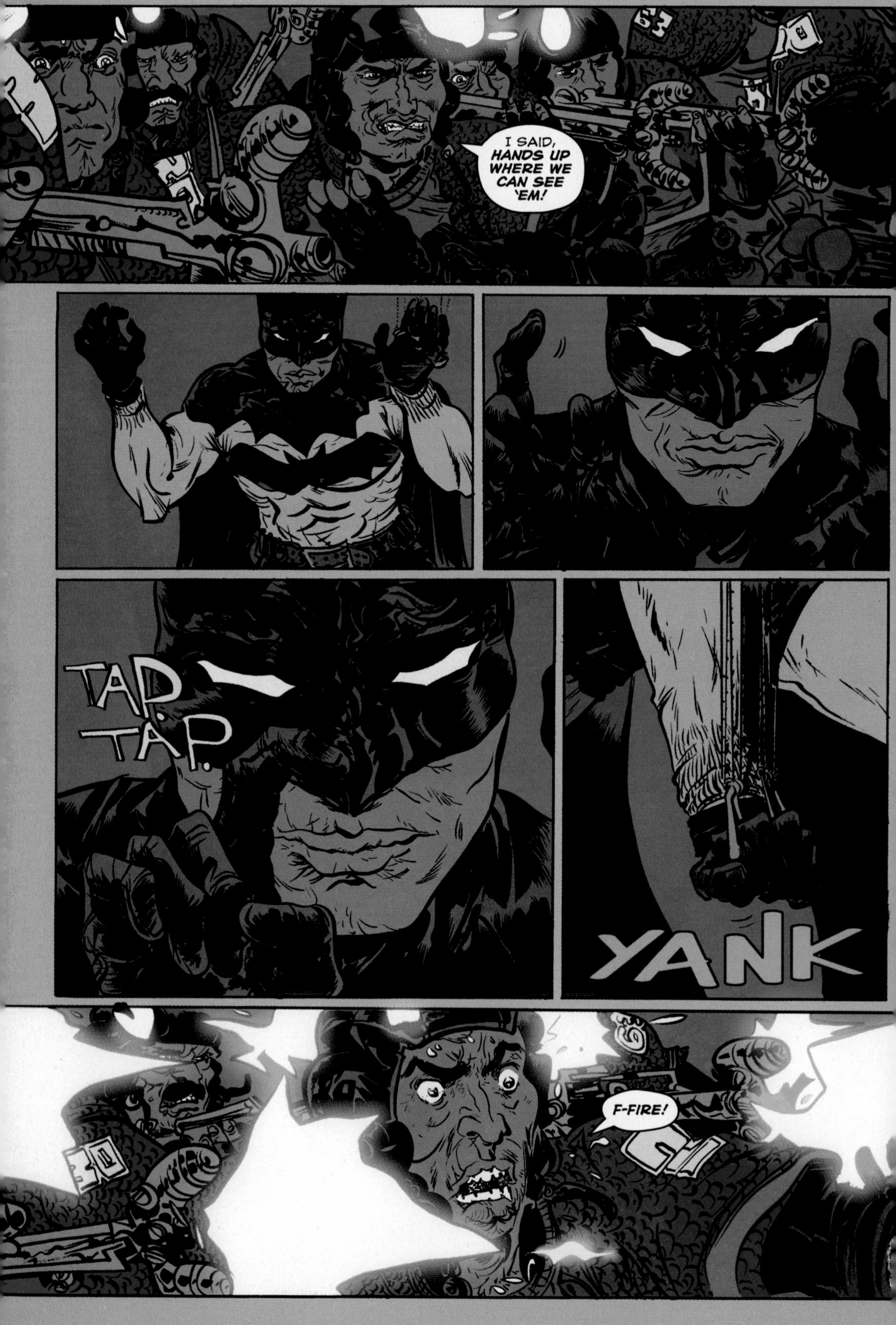
I SAID, HANDS UP WHERE WE CAN SEE 'EM!
TAP. TAP.
YANK
F-FIRE!

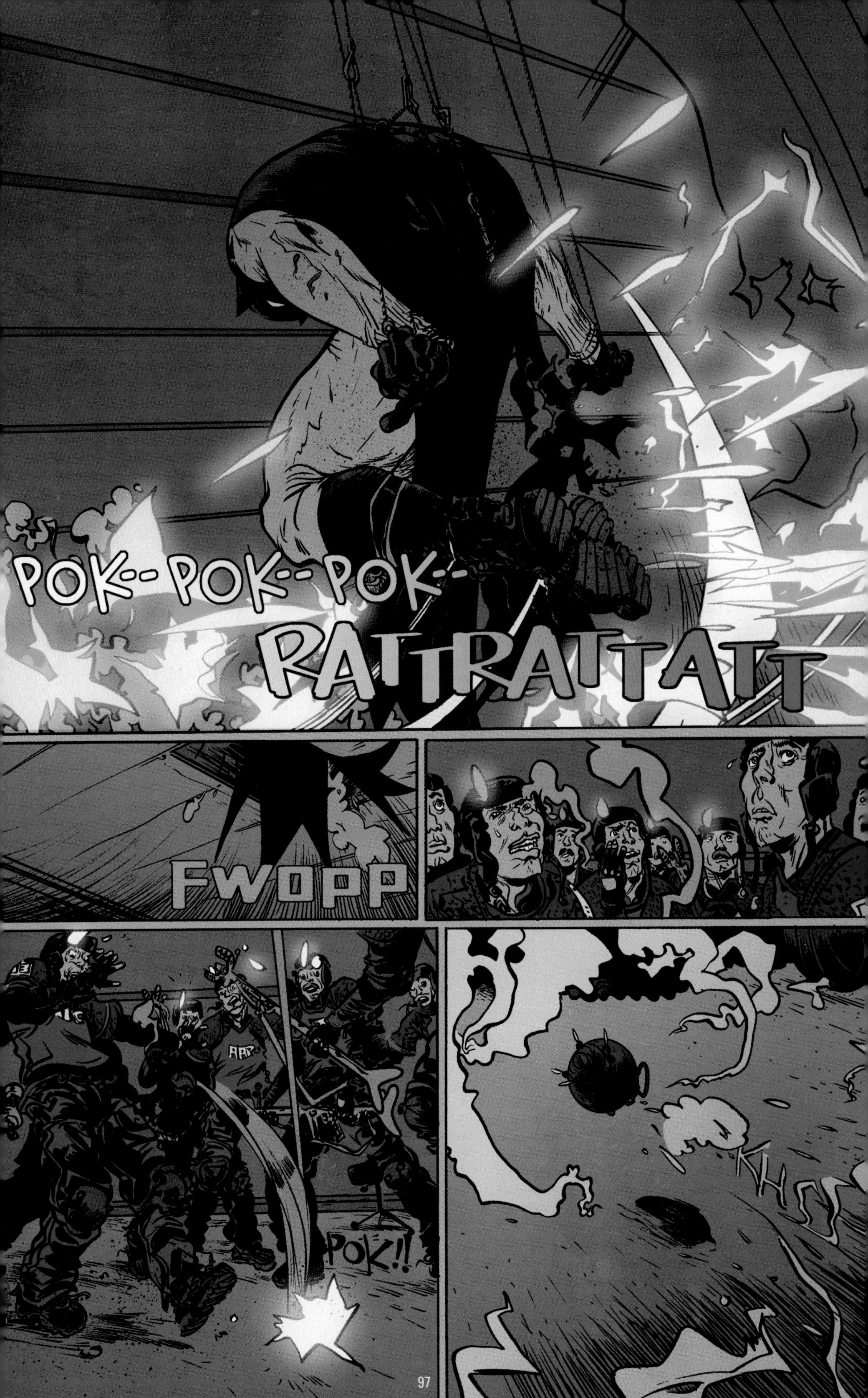
POK--POK--POK--
RATTRATTATT
FWOPP
POK!!
KHOOM

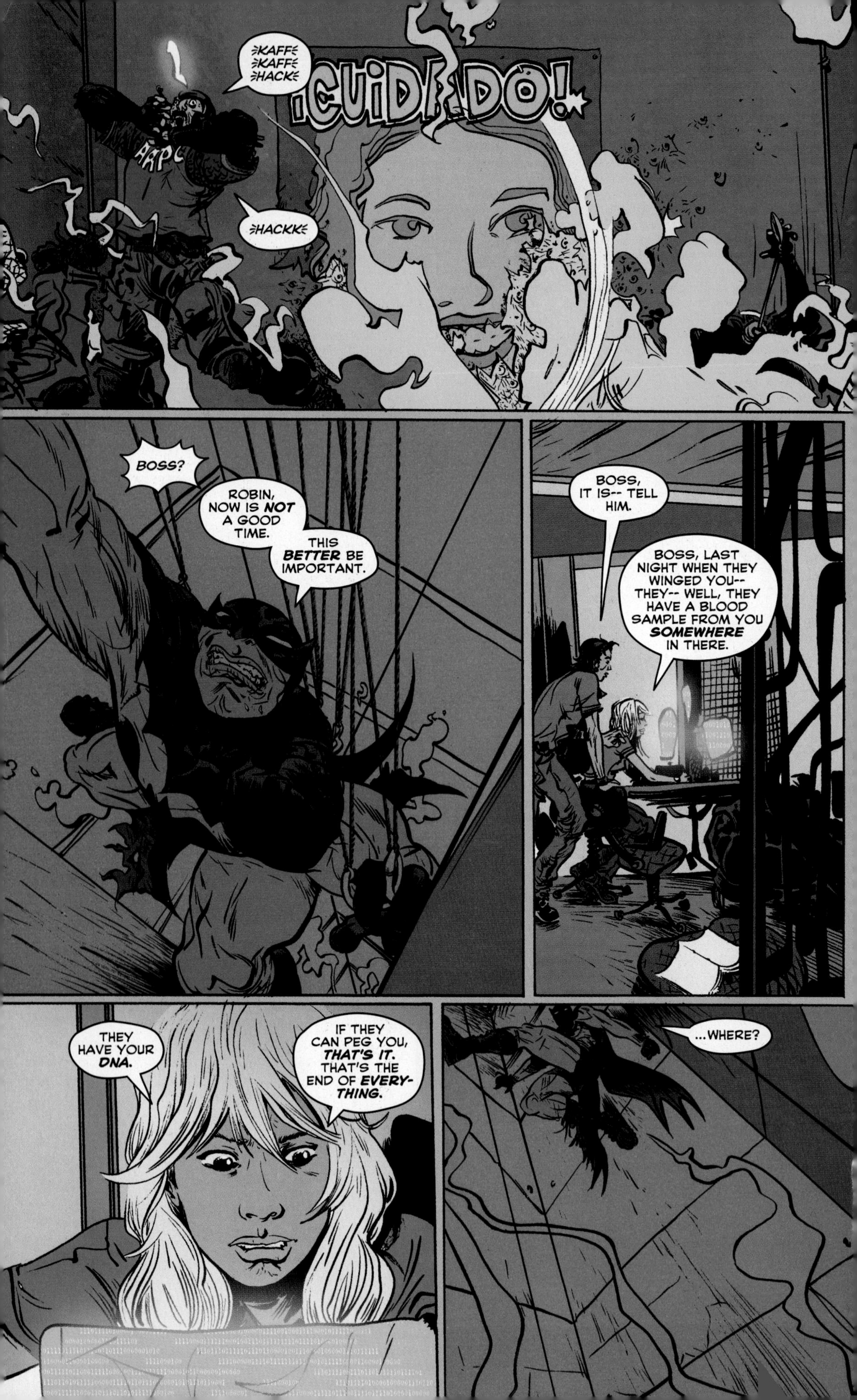
KAFF KAFF HACK
¡CUIDADO!
HACKK
BOSS?
ROBIN, NOW IS NOT A GOOD TIME.
THIS BETTER BE IMPORTANT.
BOSS, IT IS-- TELL HIM.
BOSS, LAST NIGHT WHEN THEY WINGED YOU-- THEY-- WELL, THEY HAVE A BLOOD SAMPLE FROM YOU SOMEWHERE IN THERE.
THEY HAVE YOUR DNA.
IF THEY CAN PEG YOU, THAT'S IT. THAT'S THE END OF EVERYTHING.
...WHERE?

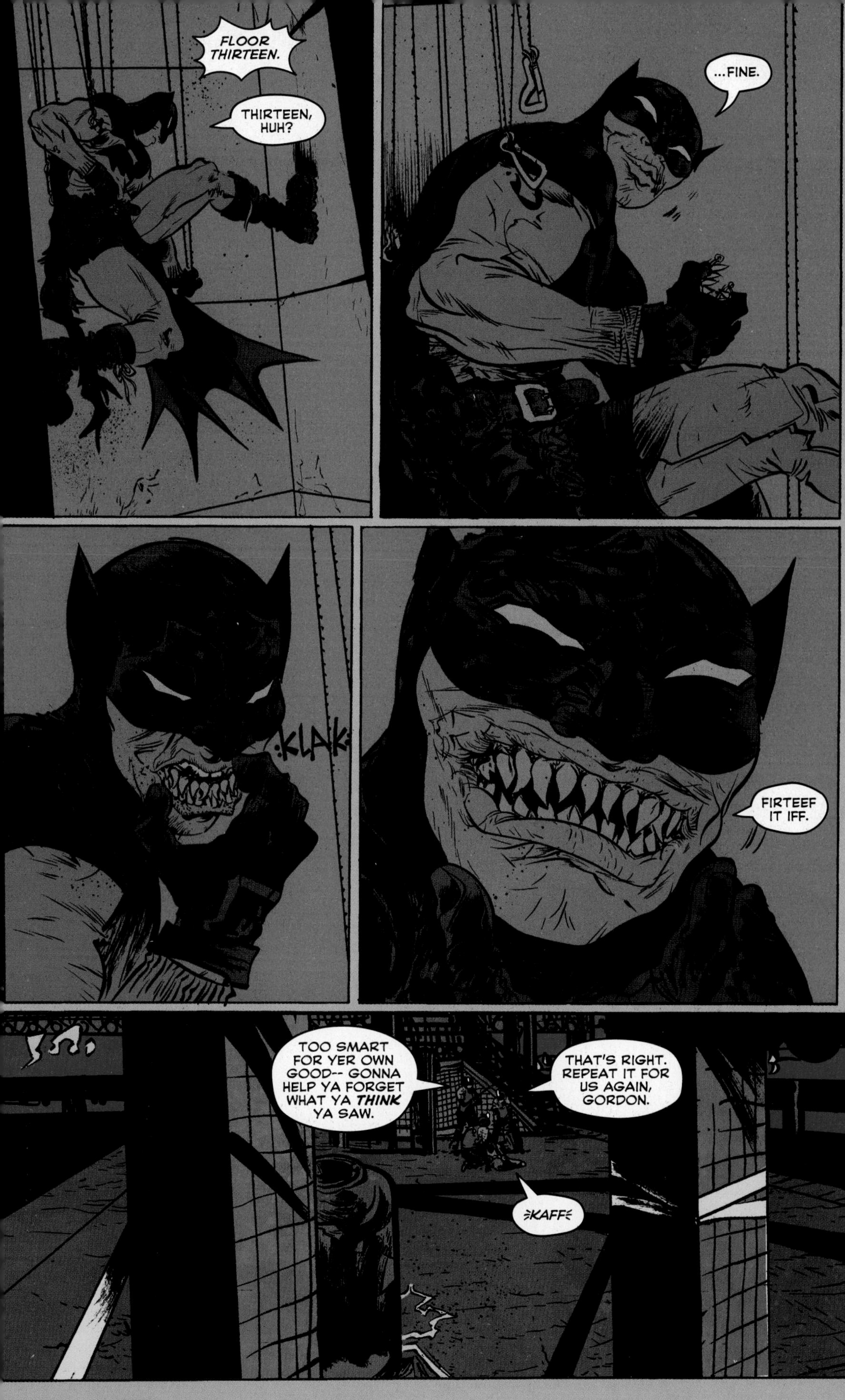
FLOOR THIRTEEN.
THIRTEEN, HUH?
...FINE.
KLAK
FIRTEEF IT IFF.
TOO SMART FOR YER OWN GOOD-- GONNA HELP YA FORGET WHAT YA *THINK* YA SAW.
THAT'S RIGHT. REPEAT IT FOR US AGAIN, GORDON.
KAFF

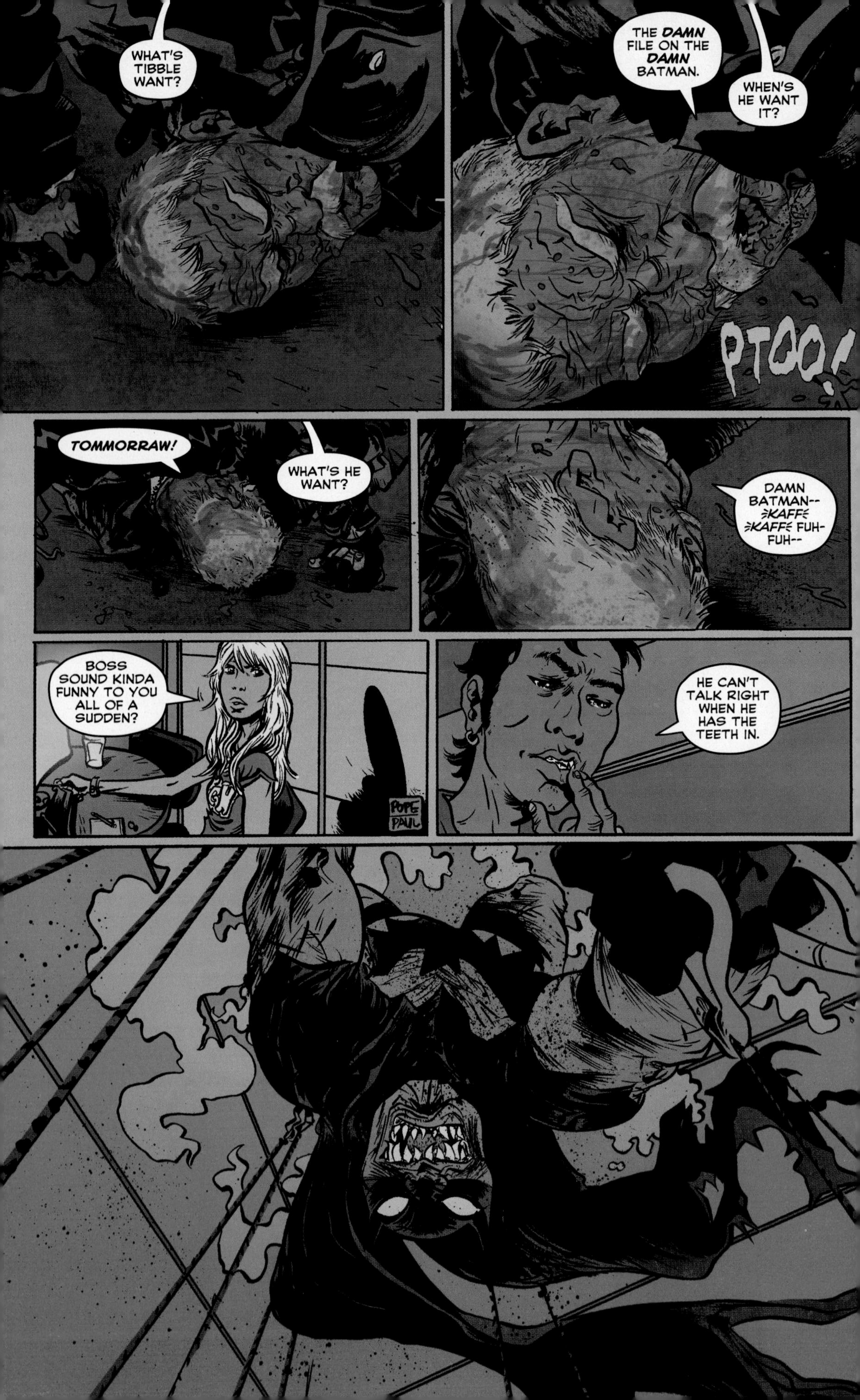
WHAT'S TIBBLE WANT?
THE DAMN FILE ON THE DAMN BATMAN.
WHEN'S HE WANT IT?
PTOO!
TOMMORRAW!
WHAT'S HE WANT?
DAMN BATMAN-- KAFF KAFF FUH-FUH--
BOSS SOUND KINDA FUNNY TO YOU ALL OF A SUDDEN?
POPE PAUL
HE CAN'T TALK RIGHT WHEN HE HAS THE TEETH IN.

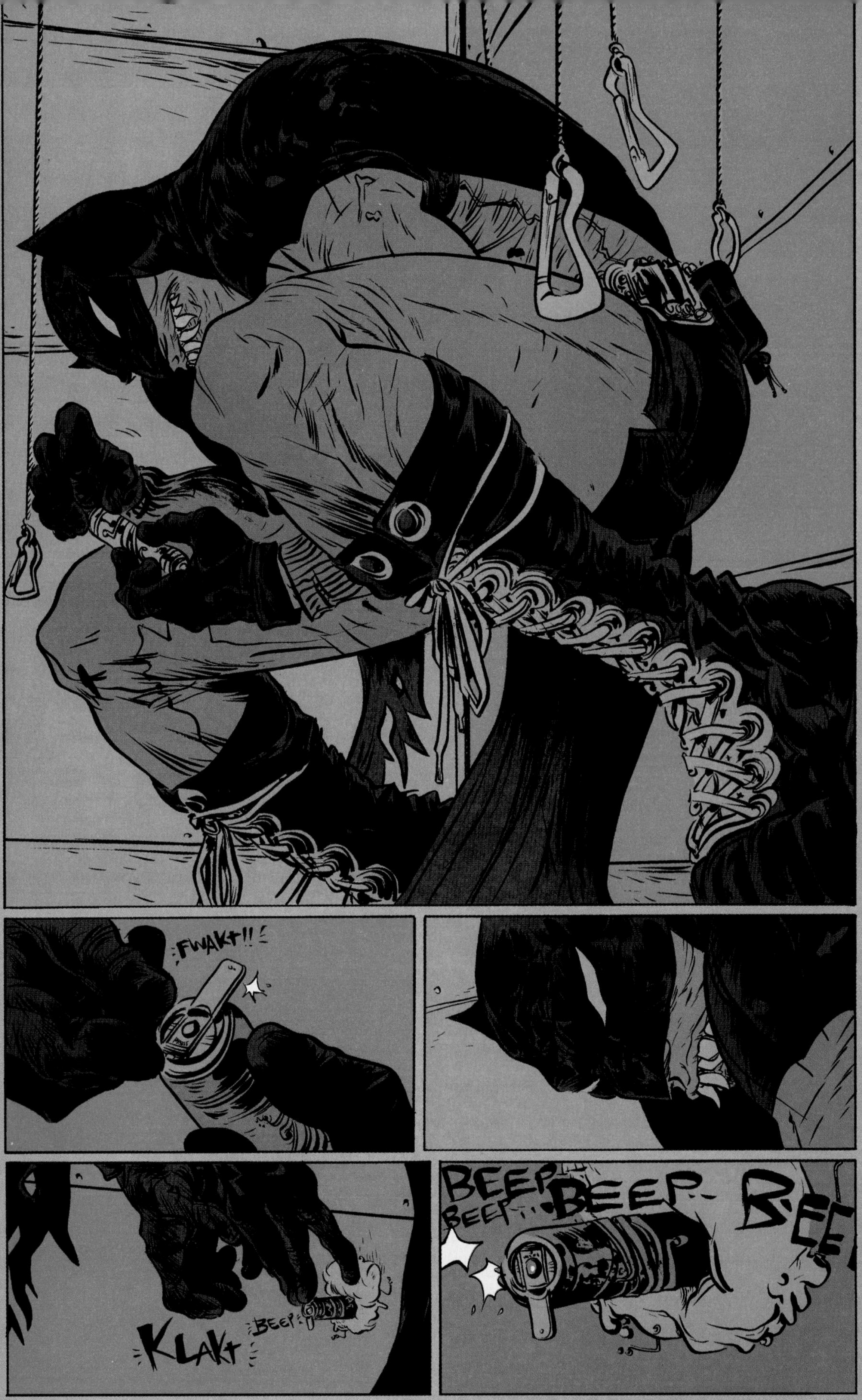
FWAKT!!
KLAKT
BEEP
BEEP
BEEP
BEEP

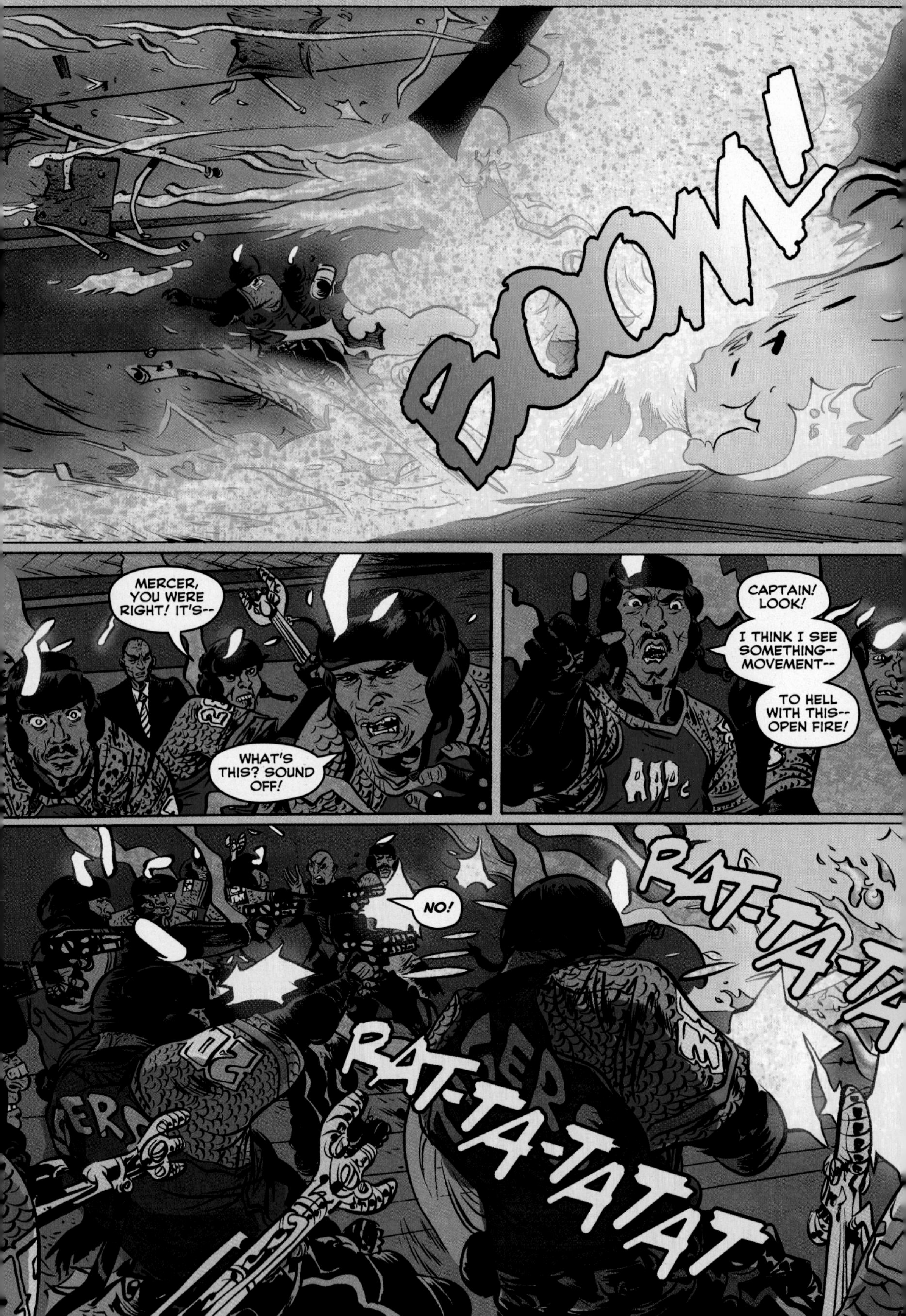
BOOM!
MERCER, YOU WERE RIGHT! IT'S--
WHAT'S THIS? SOUND OFF!
CAPTAIN! LOOK!
I THINK I SEE SOMETHING-- MOVEMENT--
TO HELL WITH THIS-- OPEN FIRE!
NO!
RAT-TA-TA
RAT-TA-TATAT

AIM LOW!

STOP, YOU FOOLS! STOP! WE'RE NOT AUTHORIZED TO-- *STOP!*

STOP SHOOTING!

≥PANT≥ ≥PANT≥

PLINK-TINK-TINK

HEADS ARE GONNA ROLL--

"GOTHAM TIGERS"-- YOU SHOULD BE ASHAMED. IF HE'S BEEN KILLED--

GOT CARRIED AWAY, SIR!

ORDERS ARE TO LET ME *TALK* TO HIM--

NOTHIN' COULD'A SURVIVED THAT-- MUST'A BEEN A--

C'MON, LET'S--

JUST WAIT 'TIL I FILL OUT THE REPORT... YOU'RE GONNA HAVE A HELL OF A TIME EXPLAINING THIS IF--

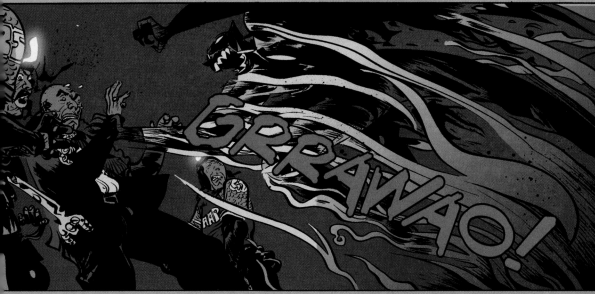

GRRAWAO!

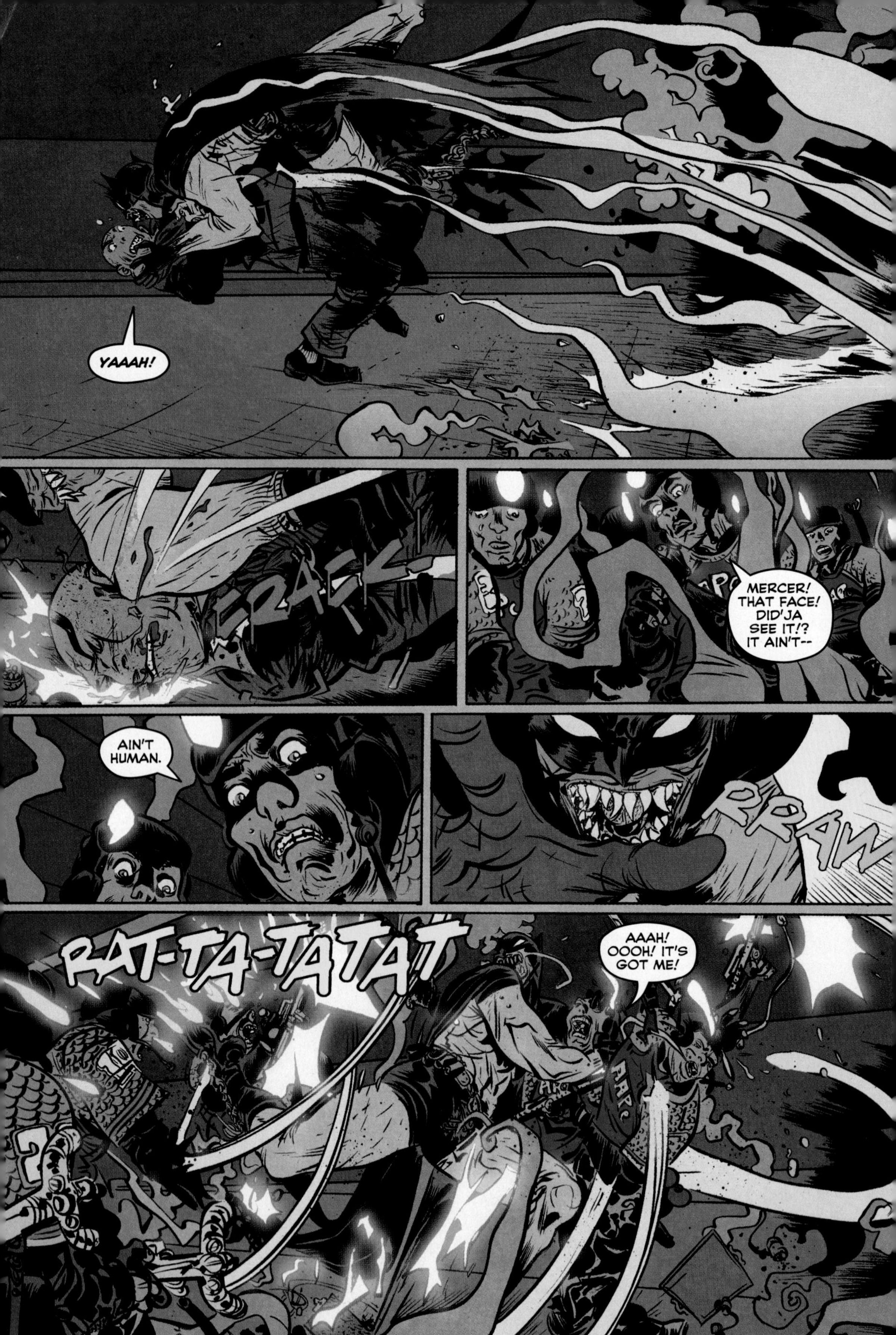

YAAAH!
CRACK!
MERCER! THAT FACE! DID'JA SEE IT!? IT AIN'T--
AIN'T HUMAN.
RRAW
RAT-TA-TATAT
AAAH! OOOH! IT'S GOT ME!

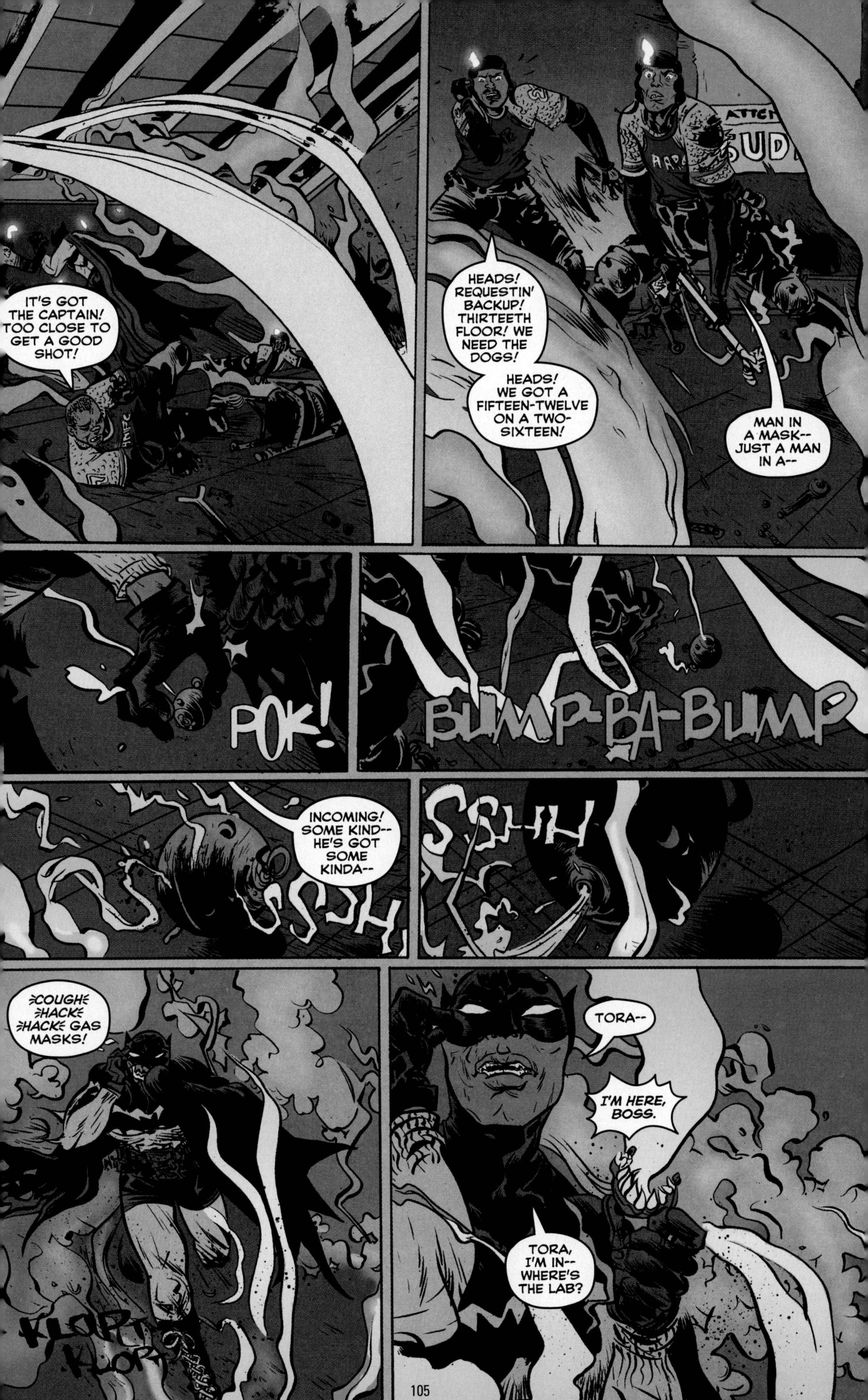
IT'S GOT THE CAPTAIN! TOO CLOSE TO GET A GOOD SHOT!
HEADS! REQUESTIN' BACKUP! THIRTEETH FLOOR! WE NEED THE DOGS!
HEADS! WE GOT A FIFTEEN-TWELVE ON A TWO-SIXTEEN!
MAN IN A MASK-- JUST A MAN IN A--
POK!
BUMP-BA-BUMP
INCOMING! SOME KIND-- HE'S GOT SOME KINDA--
SSSH
SSSH
COUGH HACK HACK GAS MASKS!
KLOP KLOP
TORA--
I'M HERE, BOSS.
TORA, I'M IN-- WHERE'S THE LAB?

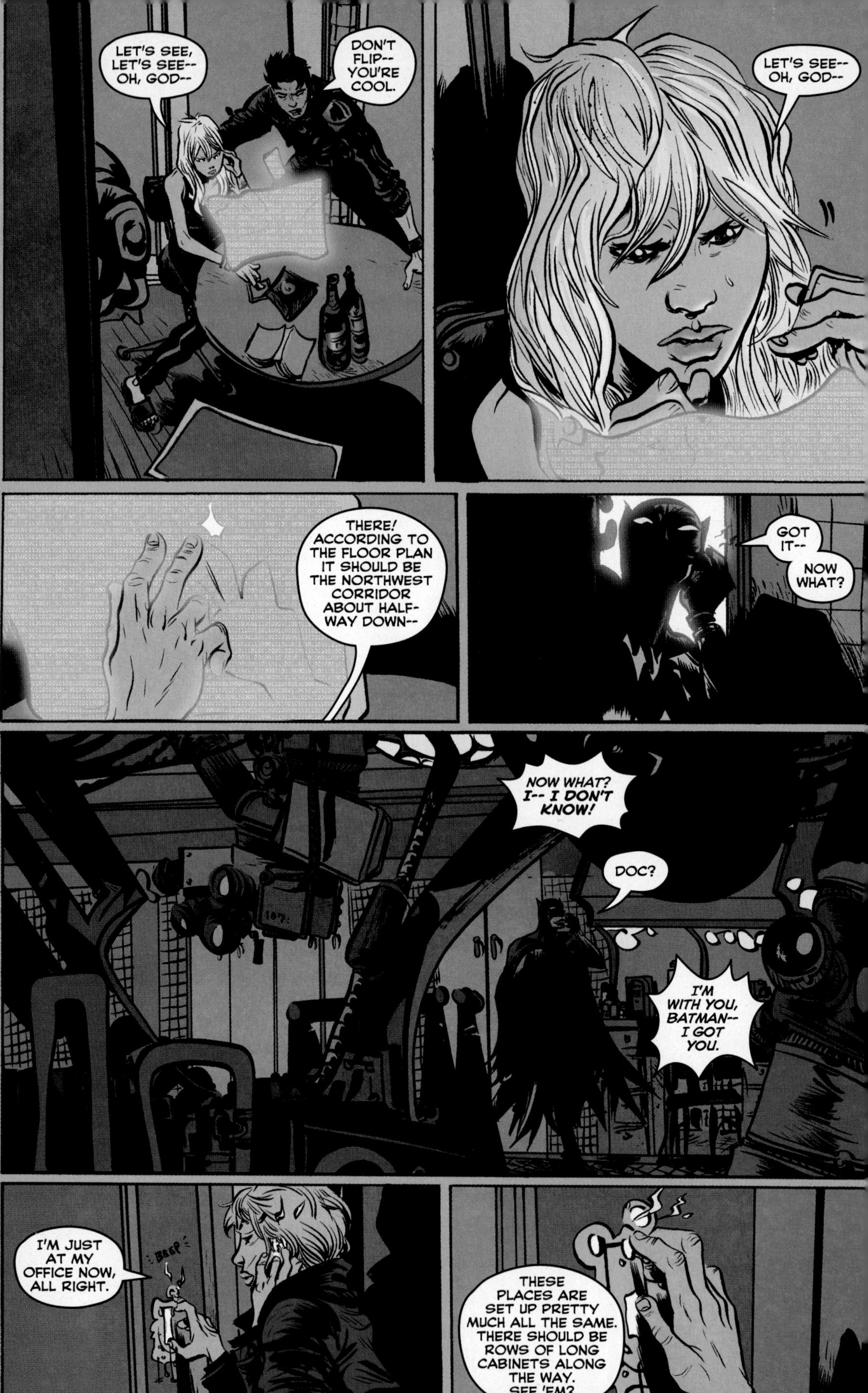
LET'S SEE, LET'S SEE-- OH, GOD--
DON'T FLIP-- YOU'RE COOL.
LET'S SEE-- OH, GOD--
THERE! ACCORDING TO THE FLOOR PLAN IT SHOULD BE THE NORTHWEST CORRIDOR ABOUT HALF-WAY DOWN--
GOT IT--
NOW WHAT?
NOW WHAT? I-- I DON'T KNOW!
DOC?
I'M WITH YOU, BATMAN-- I GOT YOU.
I'M JUST AT MY OFFICE NOW, ALL RIGHT.
BEEP
THESE PLACES ARE SET UP PRETTY MUCH ALL THE SAME. THERE SHOULD BE ROWS OF LONG CABINETS ALONG THE WAY. SEE 'EM?
I DO.

NOTHING BUT MEDICAL JUNK.

HANG ON.

THERE'S A LOT OF CABINETS.

TRY THE OTHER SIDE. TRY ALL OF 'EM.

WHAT'S THAT SOUND? BAT--

RATTLE-RATTLE-

PWSSHT

PWSSHT

HE'S SEALING THE DOOR, DOC. BUYING TIME.

SO THEY CAN'T BUST IN.

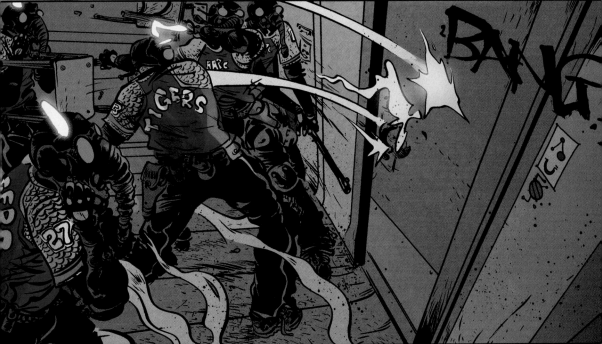

BANG

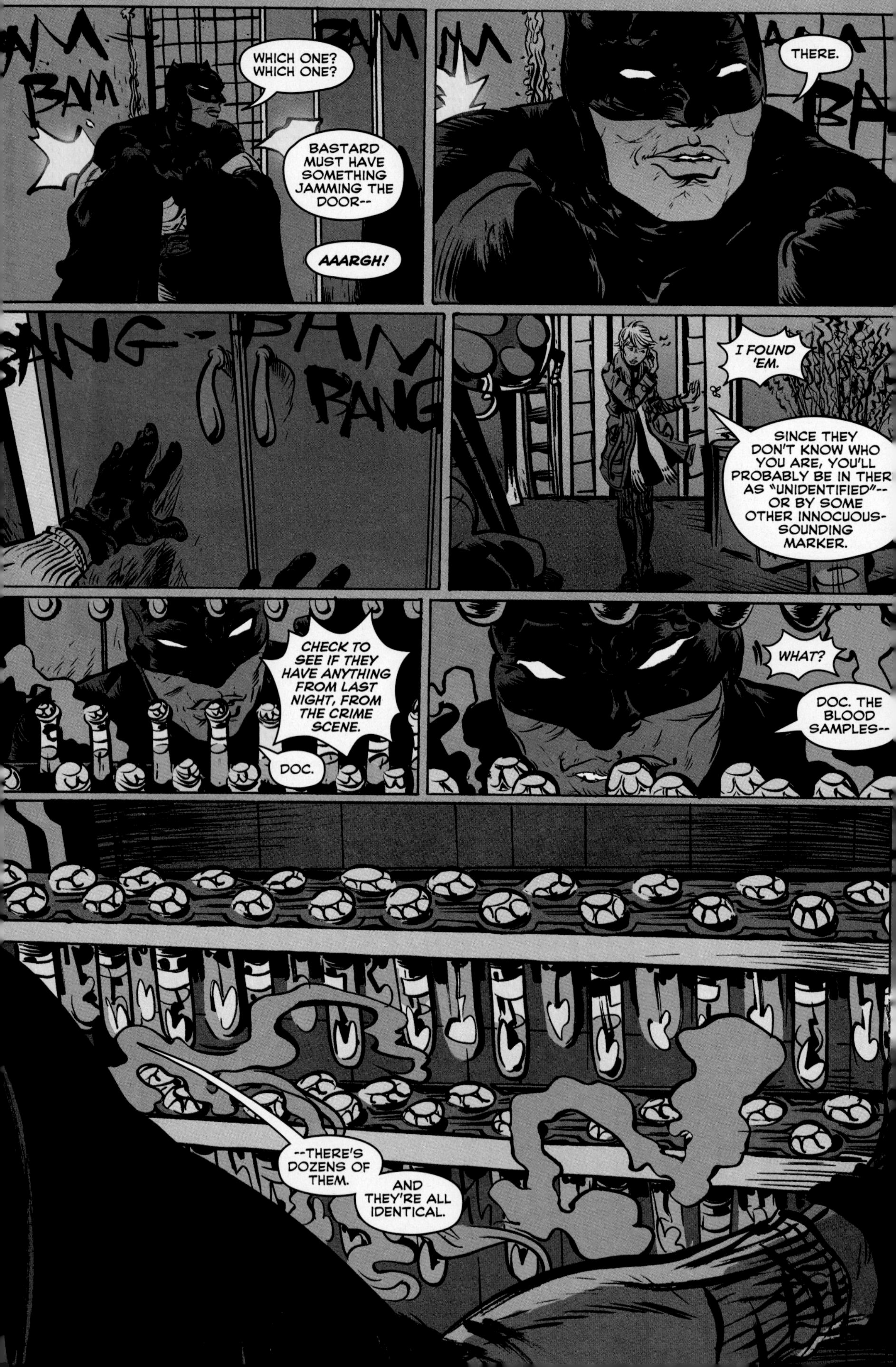
BAM
BAM
WHICH ONE? WHICH ONE?
BASTARD MUST HAVE SOMETHING JAMMING THE DOOR--
AAARGH!
BAM
THERE.
BANG--BAM
BANG
I FOUND 'EM.
SINCE THEY DON'T KNOW WHO YOU ARE, YOU'LL PROBABLY BE IN THER AS "UNIDENTIFIED"--OR BY SOME OTHER INNOCUOUS-SOUNDING MARKER.
CHECK TO SEE IF THEY HAVE ANYTHING FROM LAST NIGHT, FROM THE CRIME SCENE.
DOC.
WHAT?
DOC. THE BLOOD SAMPLES--
--THERE'S DOZENS OF THEM.
AND THEY'RE ALL IDENTICAL.

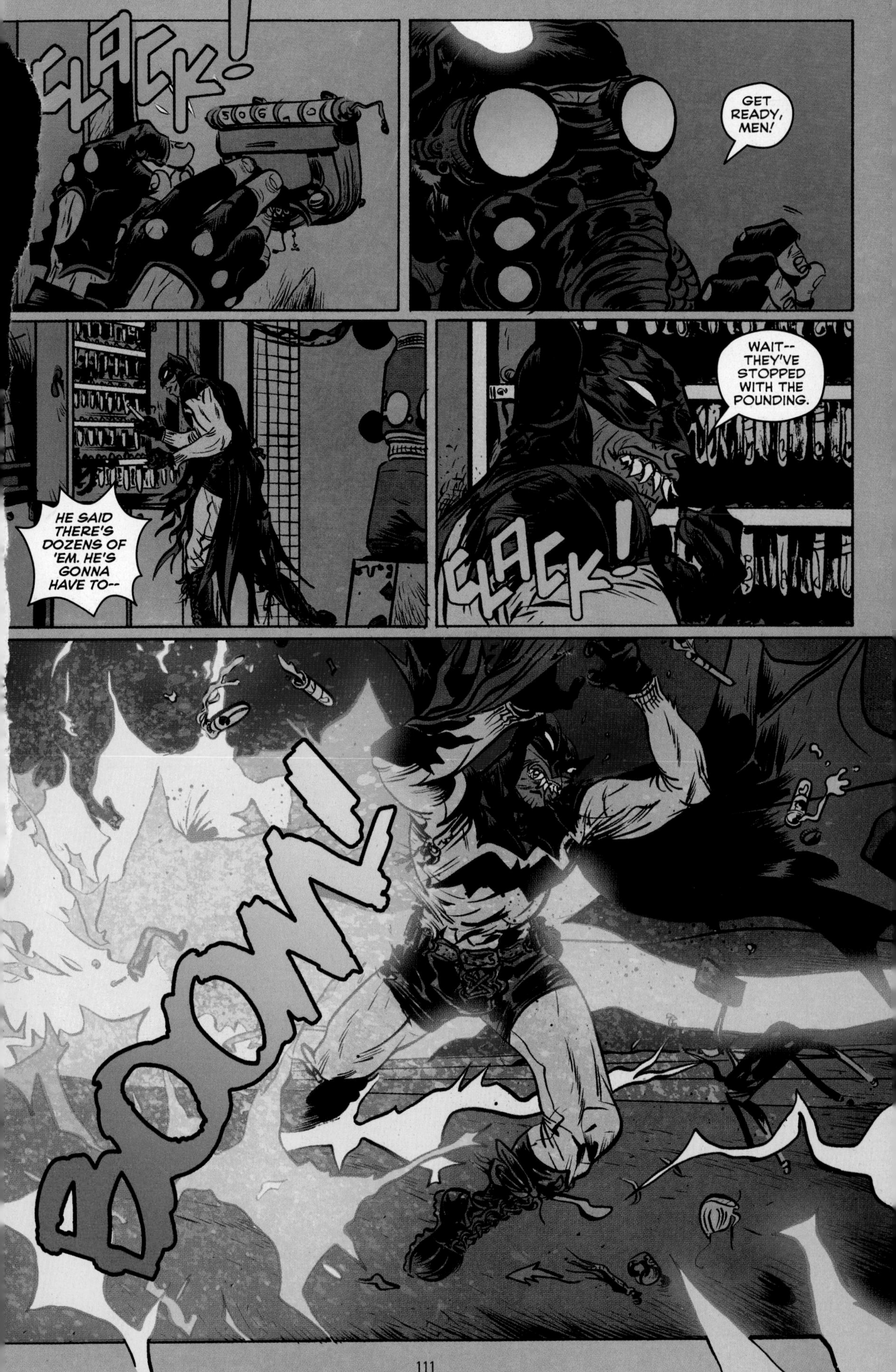
CLACK!
GET READY, MEN!
HE SAID THERE'S DOZENS OF 'EM. HE'S GONNA HAVE TO--
WAIT-- THEY'VE STOPPED WITH THE POUNDING.
CLACK!
BOOM!

≥PANT≤ ≥PANT≤ UGH!

≥PANT≤ ≥PANT≤ TORA--

TORA, FIND ME THE QUICKEST WAY OUT OF HERE. I'M SHUTTING THIS DOWN.

IT'S ABOUT TO GET UGLY.

BUT YOU KNOW THEY'RE GONNA HAVE EVERY EXIT UNDER LOCK AND KEY... BATMAN?

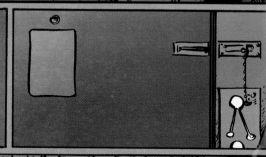

KNOCK-
-KNOCK-

KNOCK

KNOCK

?

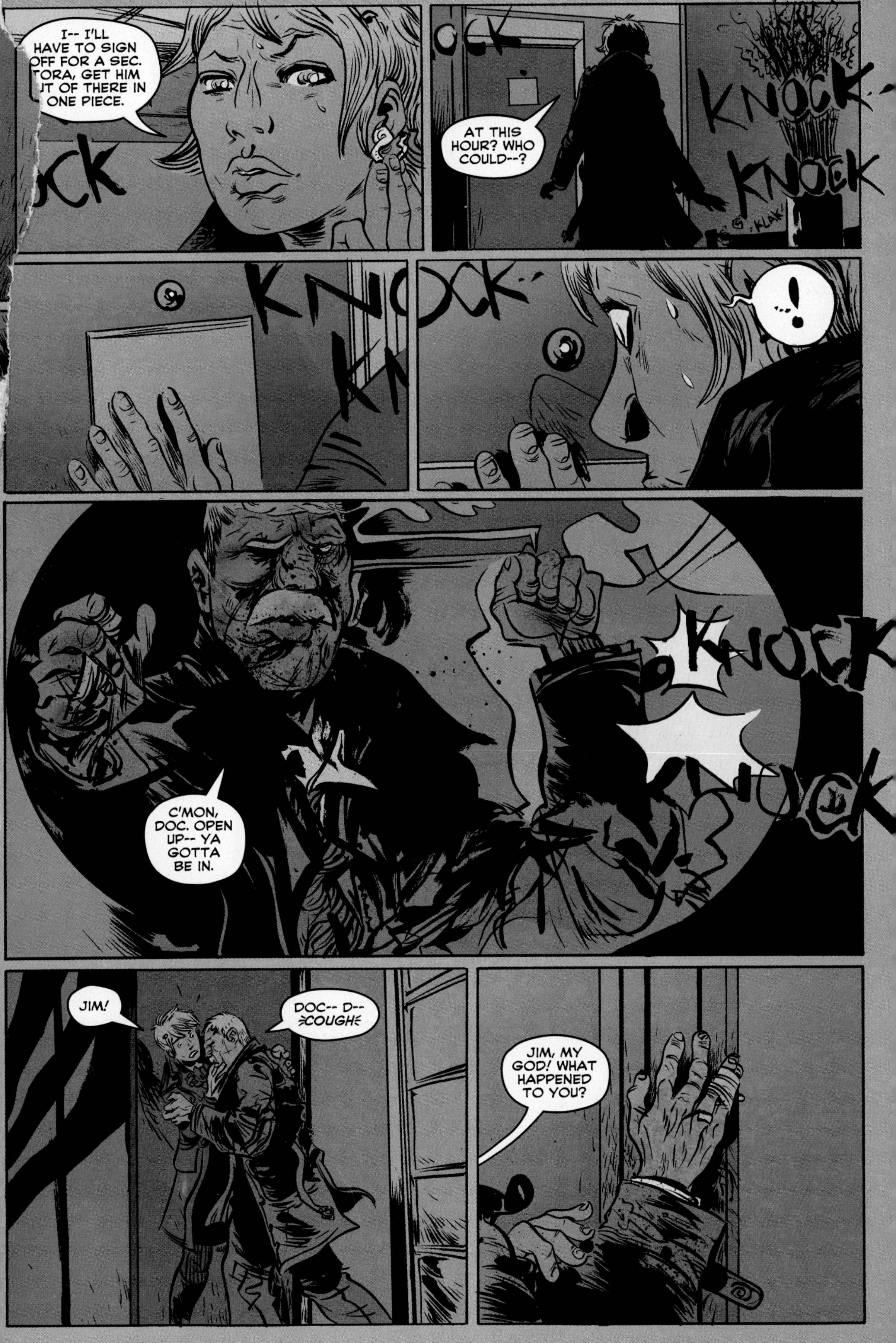

I-- I'LL HAVE TO SIGN OFF FOR A SEC. TORA, GET HIM UT OF THERE IN ONE PIECE.
OCK
OCK
AT THIS HOUR? WHO COULD--?
KNOCK
KNOCK
KLAK
KNOCK
!
C'MON, DOC. OPEN UP-- YA GOTTA BE IN.
KNOCK
KNOCK
JIM!
DOC-- D-- COUGH
JIM, MY GOD! WHAT HAPPENED TO YOU?

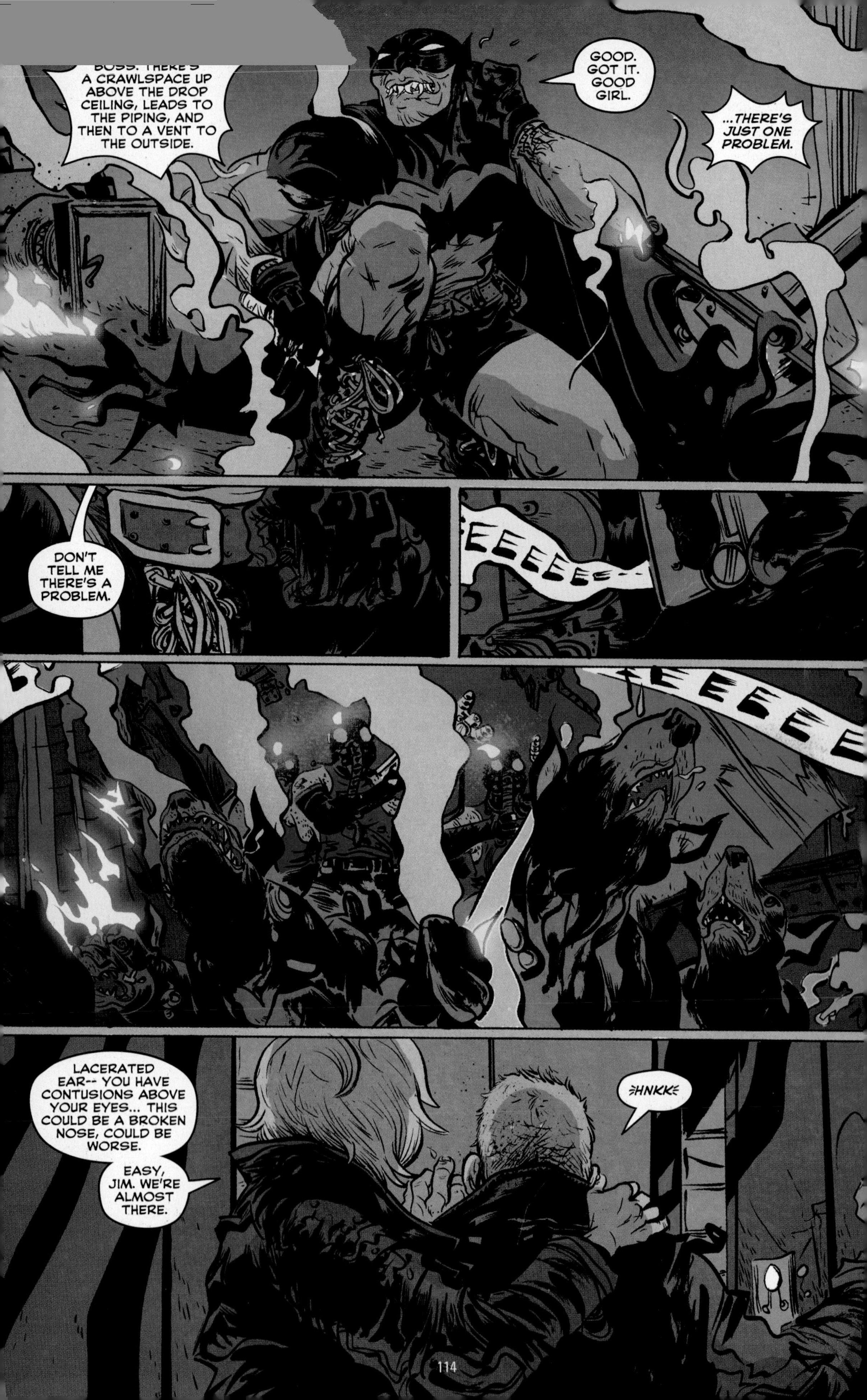
BOSS. THERE'S A CRAWLSPACE UP ABOVE THE DROP CEILING, LEADS TO THE PIPING, AND THEN TO A VENT TO THE OUTSIDE.
GOOD. GOT IT. GOOD GIRL.
...THERE'S JUST ONE PROBLEM.
DON'T TELL ME THERE'S A PROBLEM.
EEEEEEE--
EEEEEE
LACERATED EAR-- YOU HAVE CONTUSIONS ABOVE YOUR EYES... THIS COULD BE A BROKEN NOSE, COULD BE WORSE.
EASY, JIM. WE'RE ALMOST THERE.
HNKK

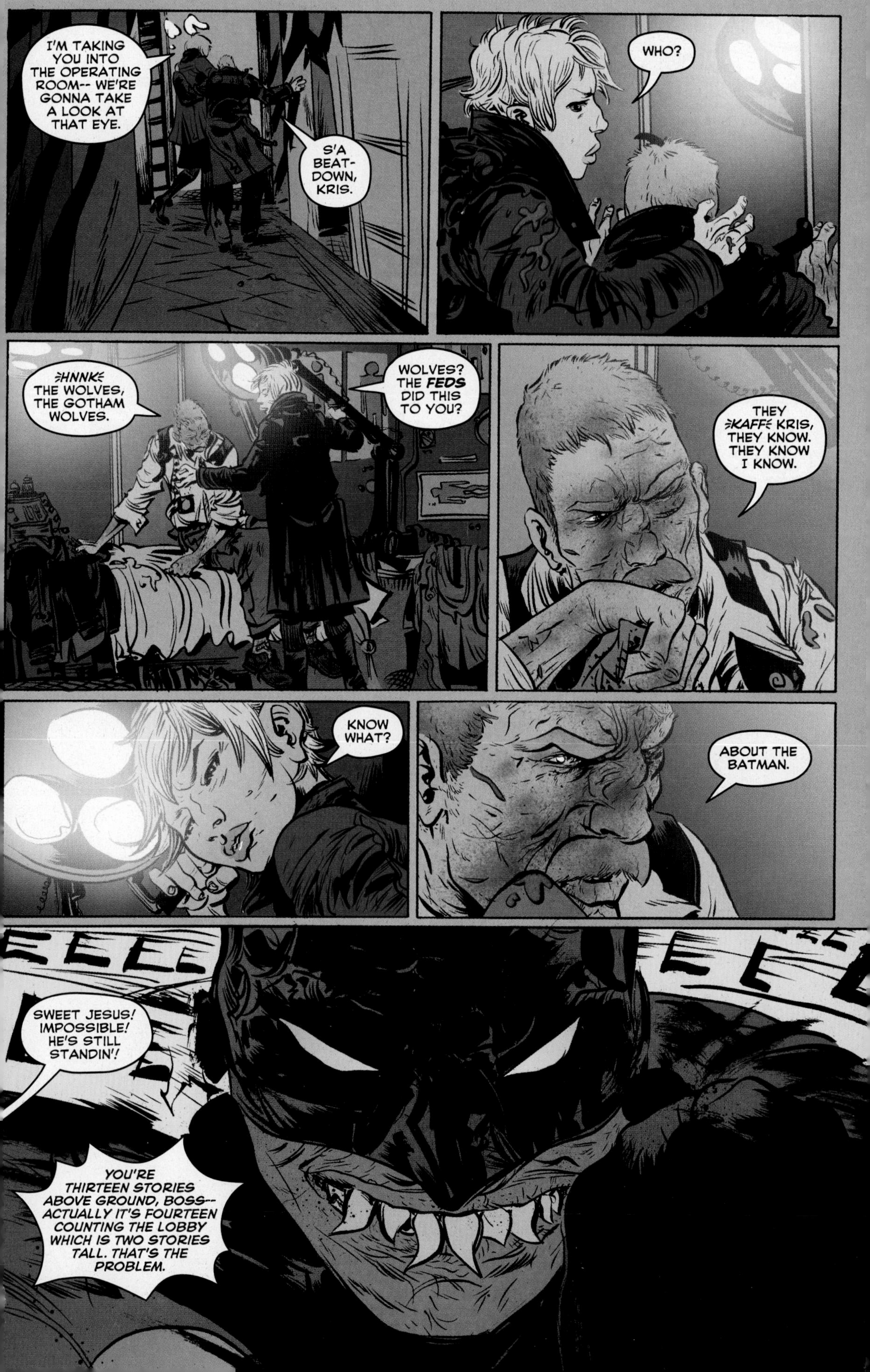
I'M TAKING YOU INTO THE OPERATING ROOM-- WE'RE GONNA TAKE A LOOK AT THAT EYE.
S'A BEAT-DOWN, KRIS.
WHO?
HNNK THE WOLVES, THE GOTHAM WOLVES.
WOLVES? THE *FEDS* DID THIS TO YOU?
THEY *KAFF* KRIS, THEY KNOW. THEY KNOW I KNOW.
KNOW WHAT?
ABOUT THE BATMAN.
EEEEE
EEE
SWEET JESUS! IMPOSSIBLE! HE'S STILL STANDIN'!
YOU'RE THIRTEEN STORIES ABOVE GROUND, BOSS-- ACTUALLY IT'S FOURTEEN COUNTING THE LOBBY WHICH IS TWO STORIES TALL. THAT'S THE PROBLEM.

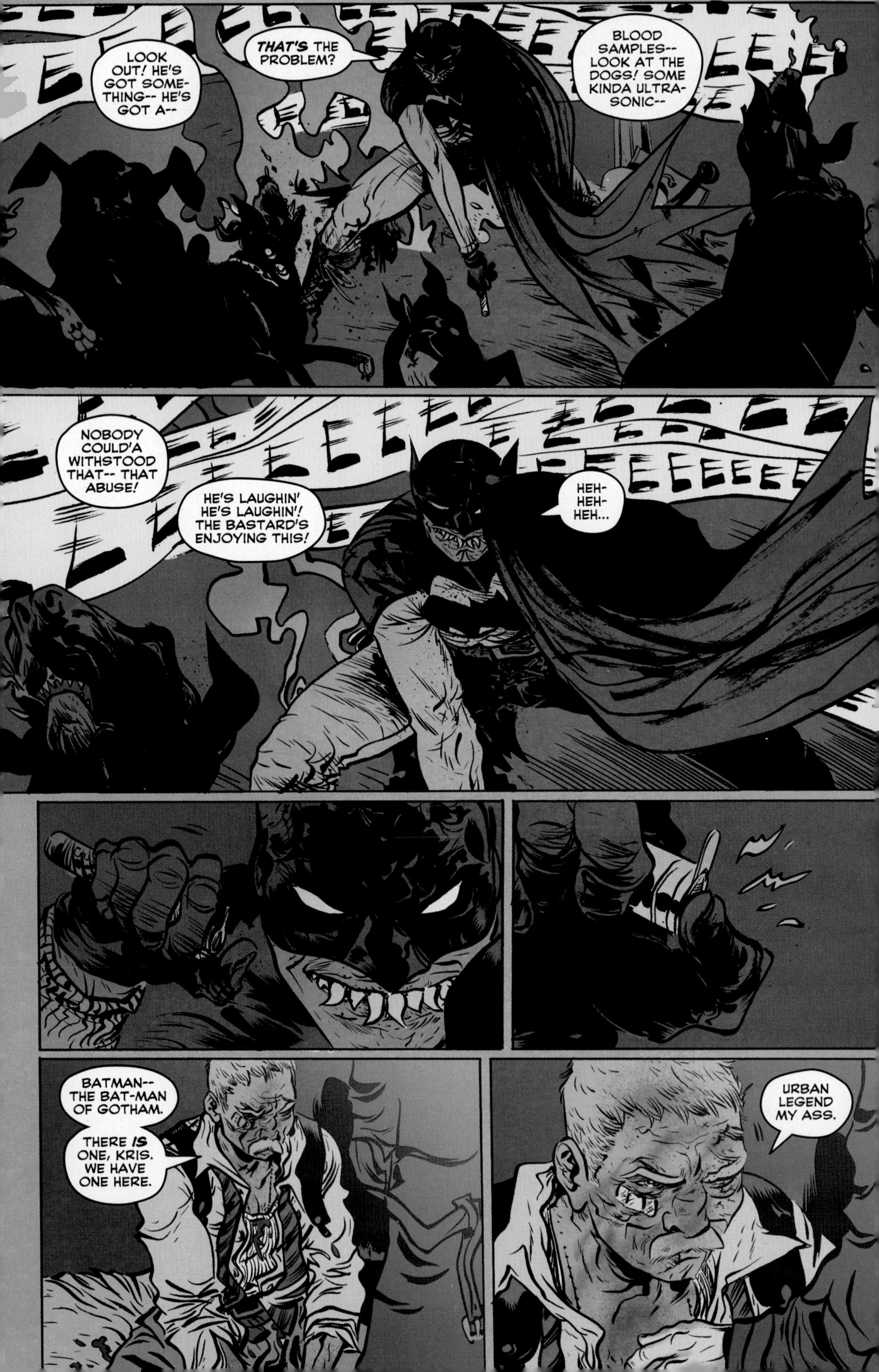
LOOK OUT! HE'S GOT SOME-THING-- HE'S GOT A--
THAT'S THE PROBLEM?
BLOOD SAMPLES-- LOOK AT THE DOGS! SOME KINDA ULTRA-SONIC--
NOBODY COULD'A WITHSTOOD THAT-- THAT ABUSE!
HE'S LAUGHIN' HE'S LAUGHIN'! THE BASTARD'S ENJOYING THIS!
HEH-HEH-HEH...
BATMAN-- THE BAT-MAN OF GOTHAM.
THERE IS ONE, KRIS. WE HAVE ONE HERE.
URBAN LEGEND MY ASS.

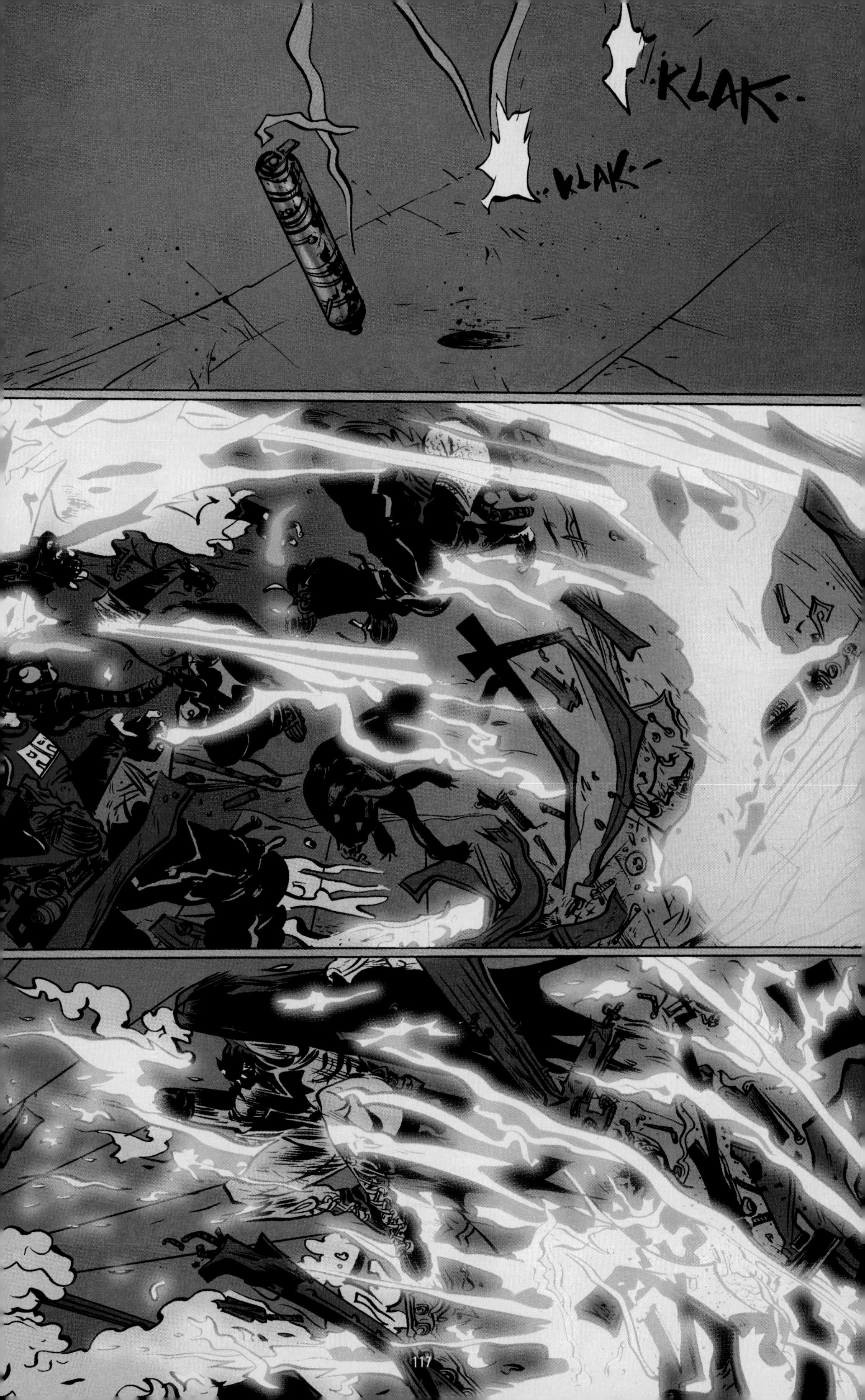
KLAK
KLAK

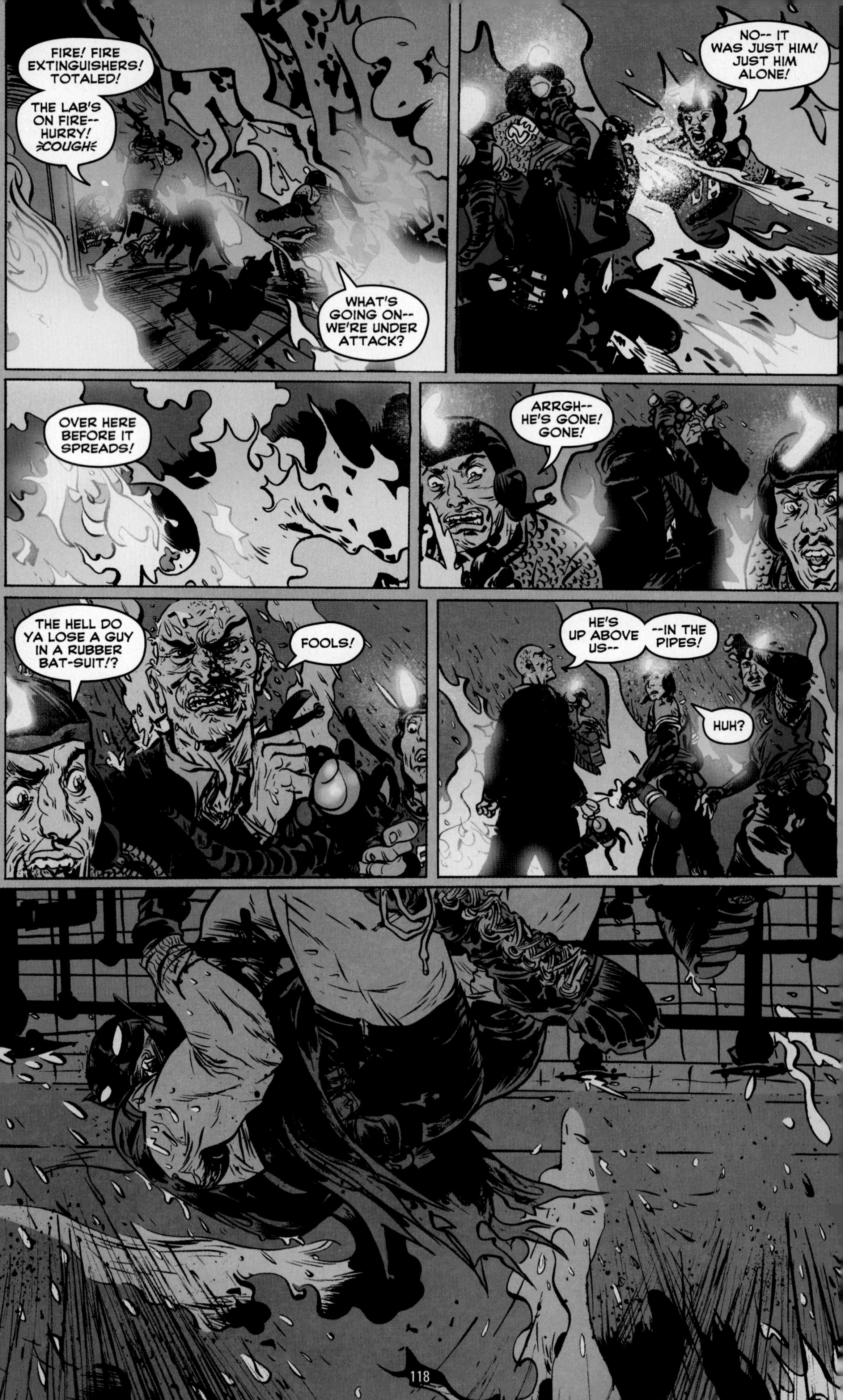
FIRE! FIRE EXTINGUISHERS! TOTALED!
THE LAB'S ON FIRE-- HURRY! COUGH
WHAT'S GOING ON-- WE'RE UNDER ATTACK?
NO-- IT WAS JUST HIM! JUST HIM ALONE!
OVER HERE BEFORE IT SPREADS!
ARRGH-- HE'S GONE! GONE!
THE HELL DO YA LOSE A GUY IN A RUBBER BAT-SUIT!?
FOOLS!
HE'S UP ABOVE US--
--IN THE PIPES!
HUH?

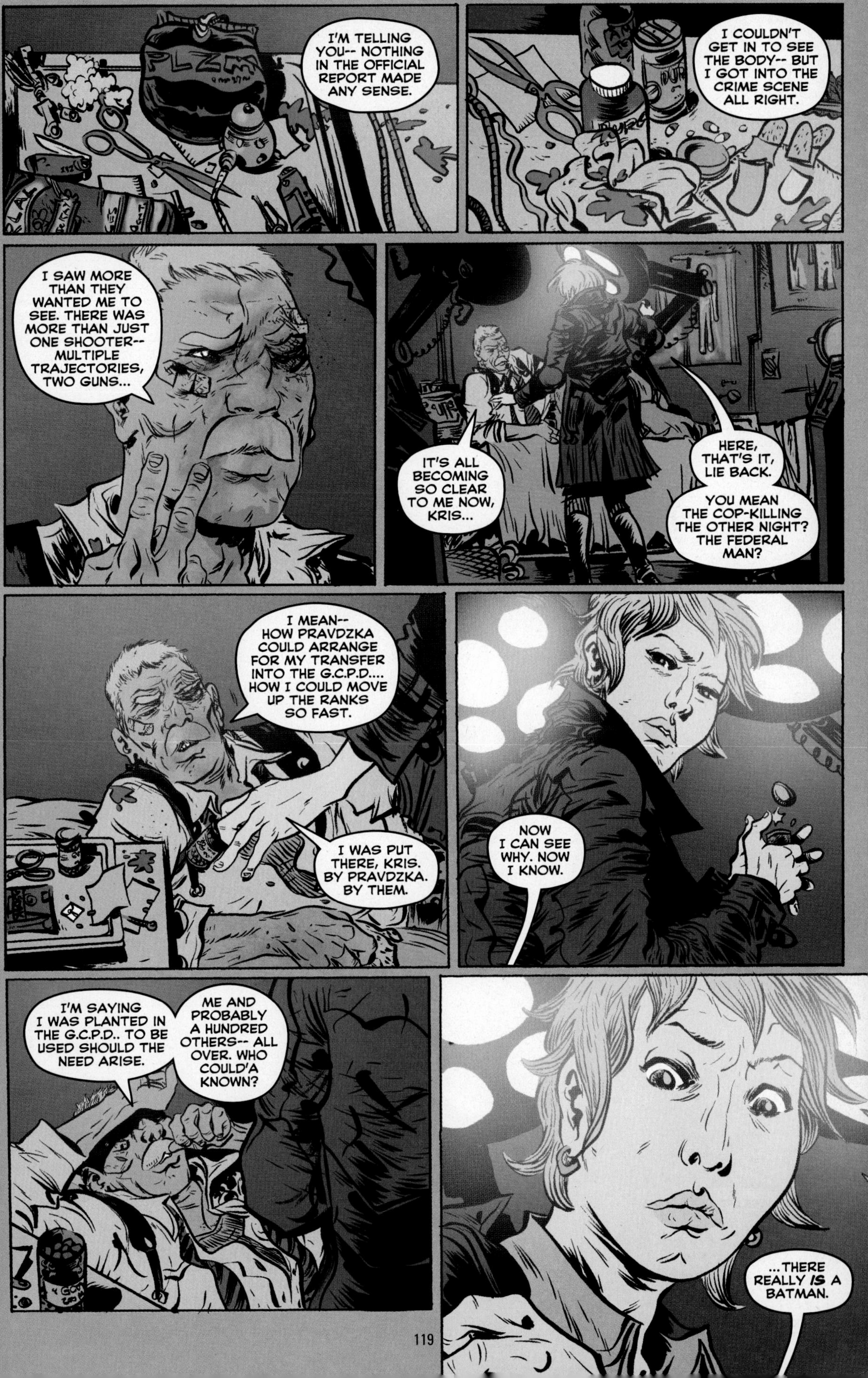
I'M TELLING YOU-- NOTHING IN THE OFFICIAL REPORT MADE ANY SENSE.
I COULDN'T GET IN TO SEE THE BODY-- BUT I GOT INTO THE CRIME SCENE ALL RIGHT.
I SAW MORE THAN THEY WANTED ME TO SEE. THERE WAS MORE THAN JUST ONE SHOOTER-- MULTIPLE TRAJECTORIES, TWO GUNS...
IT'S ALL BECOMING SO CLEAR TO ME NOW, KRIS...
HERE, THAT'S IT, LIE BACK.
YOU MEAN THE COP-KILLING THE OTHER NIGHT? THE FEDERAL MAN?
I MEAN-- HOW PRAVDZKA COULD ARRANGE FOR MY TRANSFER INTO THE G.C.P.D.... HOW I COULD MOVE UP THE RANKS SO FAST.
I WAS PUT THERE, KRIS. BY PRAVDZKA. BY THEM.
NOW I CAN SEE WHY. NOW I KNOW.
I'M SAYING I WAS PLANTED IN THE G.C.P.D.. TO BE USED SHOULD THE NEED ARISE.
ME AND PROBABLY A HUNDRED OTHERS-- ALL OVER. WHO COULD'A KNOWN?
...THERE REALLY *IS* A BATMAN.

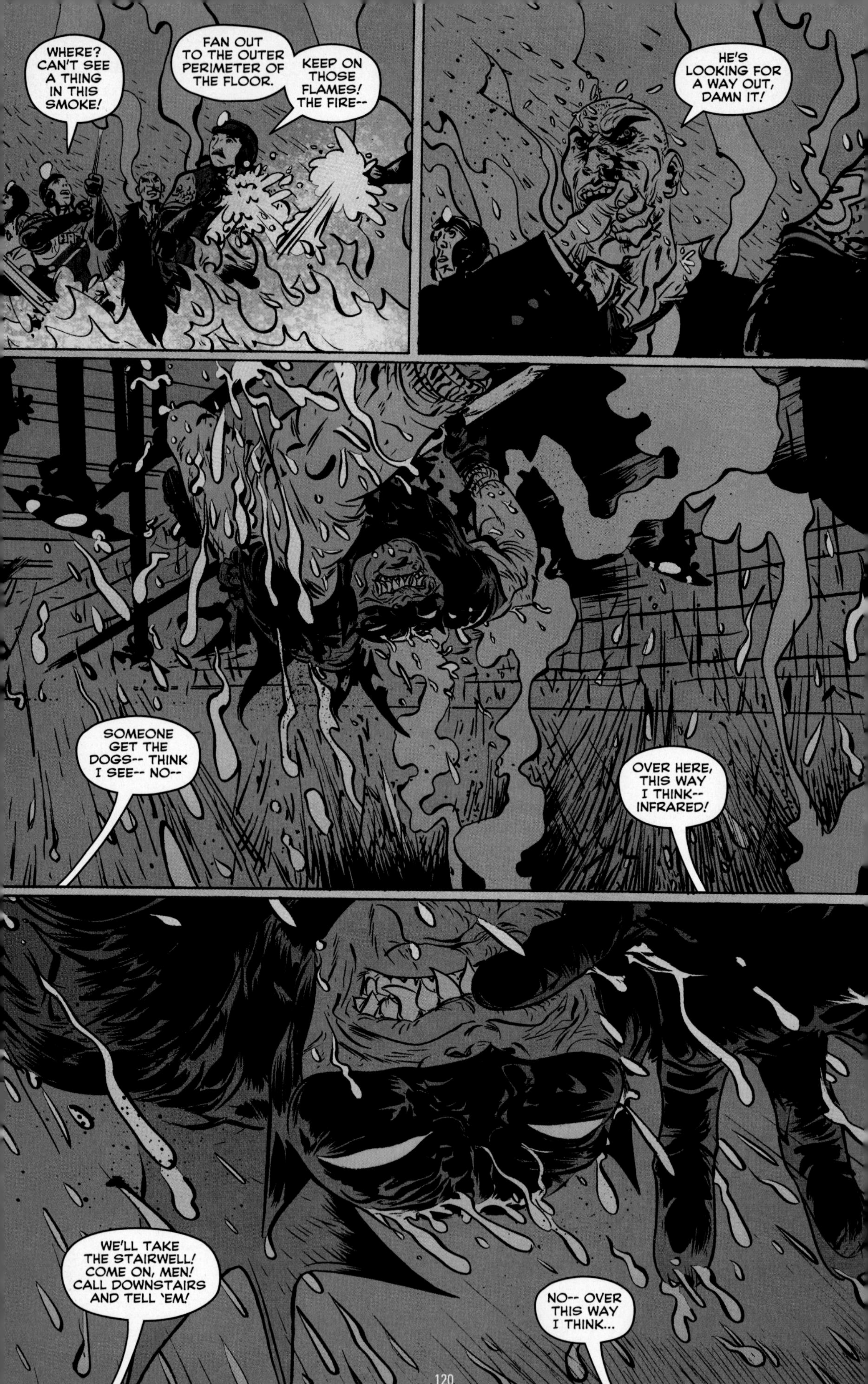
WHERE? CAN'T SEE A THING IN THIS SMOKE!
FAN OUT TO THE OUTER PERIMETER OF THE FLOOR.
KEEP ON THOSE FLAMES! THE FIRE--
HE'S LOOKING FOR A WAY OUT, DAMN IT!
SOMEONE GET THE DOGS-- THINK I SEE-- NO--
OVER HERE, THIS WAY I THINK-- INFRARED!
WE'LL TAKE THE STAIRWELL! COME ON, MEN! CALL DOWNSTAIRS AND TELL 'EM!
NO-- OVER THIS WAY I THINK...

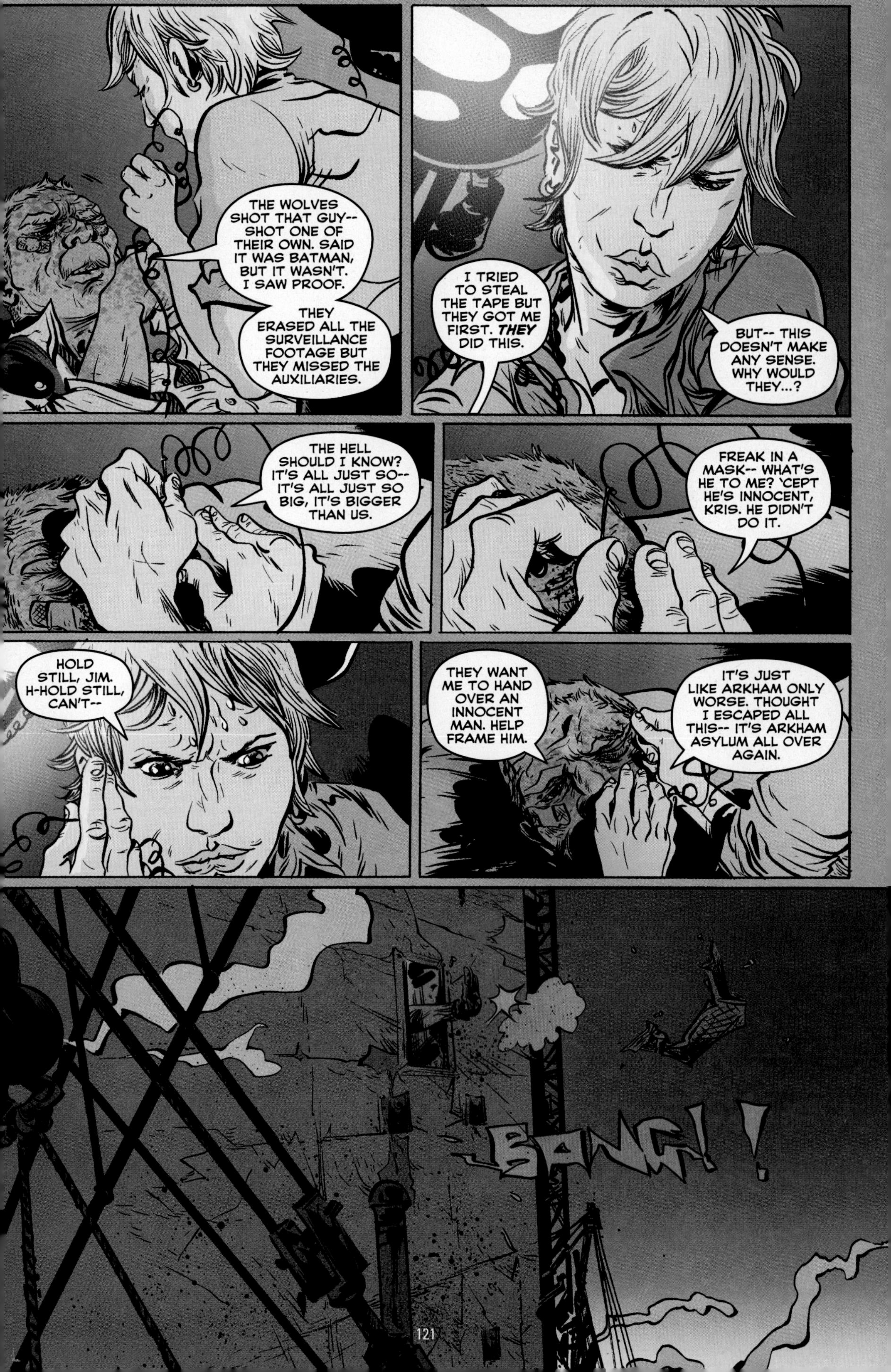
THE WOLVES SHOT THAT GUY-- SHOT ONE OF THEIR OWN. SAID IT WAS BATMAN, BUT IT WASN'T. I SAW PROOF.
THEY ERASED ALL THE SURVEILLANCE FOOTAGE BUT THEY MISSED THE AUXILIARIES.
I TRIED TO STEAL THE TAPE BUT THEY GOT ME FIRST. THEY DID THIS.
BUT-- THIS DOESN'T MAKE ANY SENSE. WHY WOULD THEY...?
THE HELL SHOULD I KNOW? IT'S ALL JUST SO-- IT'S ALL JUST SO BIG, IT'S BIGGER THAN US.
FREAK IN A MASK-- WHAT'S HE TO ME? 'CEPT HE'S INNOCENT, KRIS. HE DIDN'T DO IT.
HOLD STILL, JIM. H-HOLD STILL, CAN'T--
THEY WANT ME TO HAND OVER AN INNOCENT MAN. HELP FRAME HIM.
IT'S JUST LIKE ARKHAM ONLY WORSE. THOUGHT I ESCAPED ALL THIS-- IT'S ARKHAM ASYLUM ALL OVER AGAIN.
BANG! !

SKAKLANG

KLAANG...

ARKHAM?
I DON'T
UNDER-
STAND...

THERE'S
SOMETHING
YOU DON'T
KNOW ABOUT
ME, KRIS.

SOMETHING
BACK WHEN I
WAS STILL
WARDEN AT
ARKHAM.

ARKHAM
ASYLUM... WE
HAD ALL THOSE
NUTJOBS AND
CRIMINALS IN
THERE. ALL
THOSE SUPER-
VILLAINS.

HEH--
"SUPERVILLAINS."
REMEMBER
THAT? SUPER-
VILLAINS...

WE
HAD
SUPERVILLAINS
AT ARKHAM
ASYLUM...

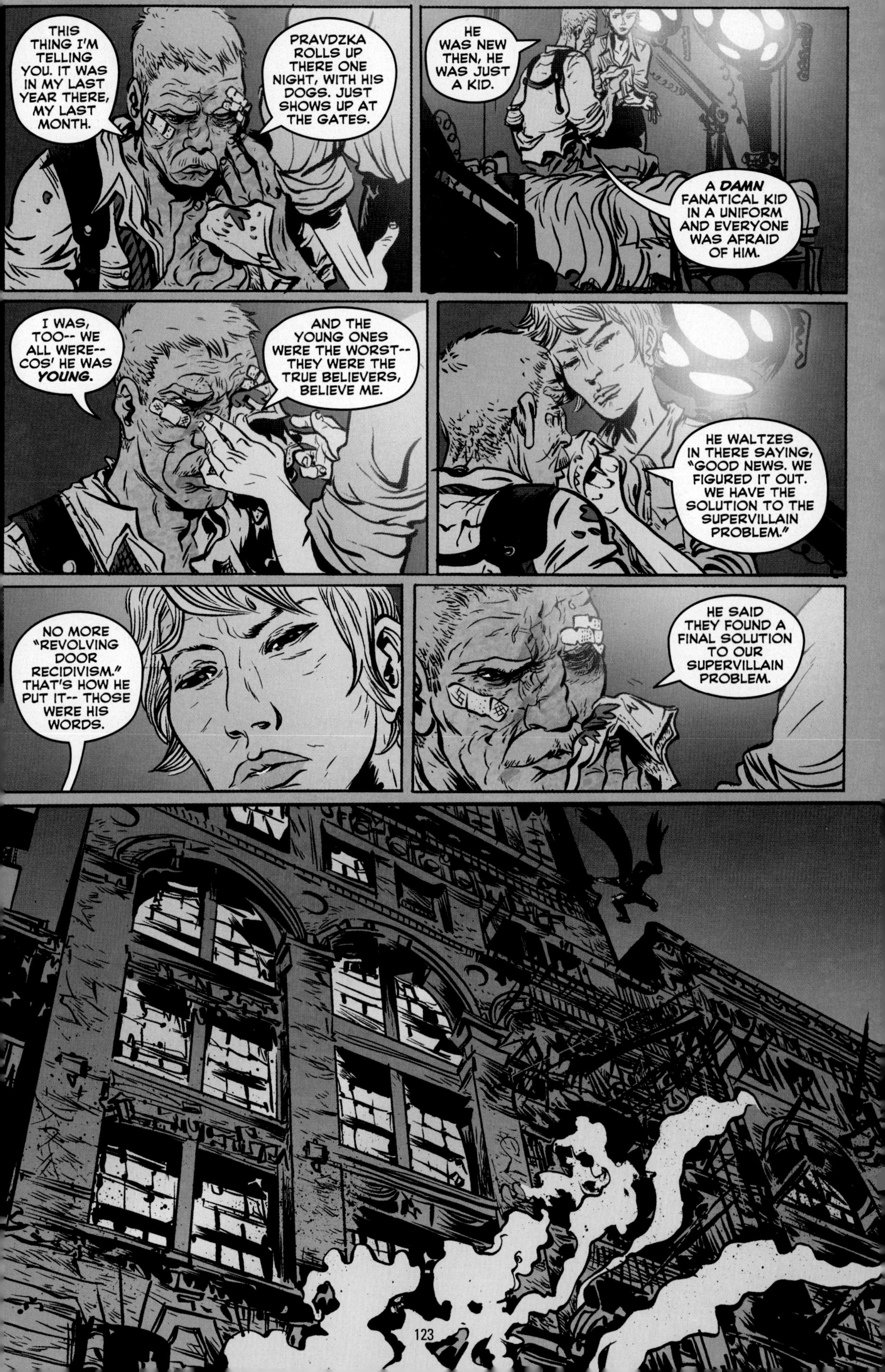
THIS THING I'M TELLING YOU. IT WAS IN MY LAST YEAR THERE, MY LAST MONTH.
PRAVDZKA ROLLS UP THERE ONE NIGHT, WITH HIS DOGS. JUST SHOWS UP AT THE GATES.
HE WAS NEW THEN, HE WAS JUST A KID.
A **DAMN** FANATICAL KID IN A UNIFORM AND EVERYONE WAS AFRAID OF HIM.
I WAS, TOO-- WE ALL WERE-- COS' HE WAS **YOUNG.**
AND THE YOUNG ONES WERE THE WORST-- THEY WERE THE TRUE BELIEVERS, BELIEVE ME.
HE WALTZES IN THERE SAYING, "GOOD NEWS. WE FIGURED IT OUT. WE HAVE THE SOLUTION TO THE SUPERVILLAIN PROBLEM."
NO MORE "REVOLVING DOOR RECIDIVISM." THAT'S HOW HE PUT IT-- THOSE WERE HIS WORDS.
HE SAID THEY FOUND A FINAL SOLUTION TO OUR SUPERVILLAIN PROBLEM.

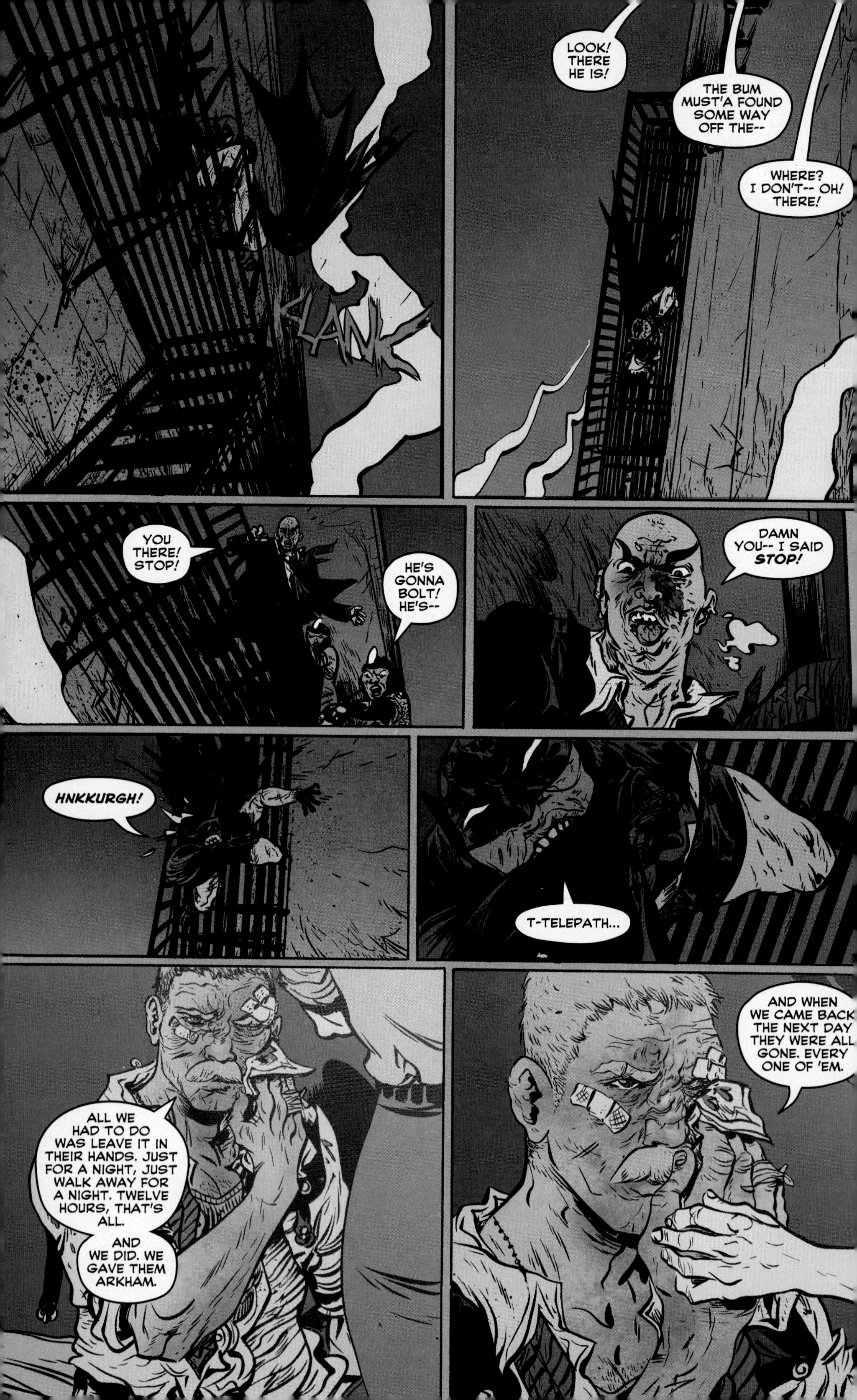
KLANK
LOOK! THERE HE IS!
THE BUM MUST'A FOUND SOME WAY OFF THE--
WHERE? I DON'T-- OH! THERE!
YOU THERE! STOP!
HE'S GONNA BOLT! HE'S--
DAMN YOU-- I SAID *STOP!*
HNKKURGH!
T-TELEPATH...
ALL WE HAD TO DO WAS LEAVE IT IN THEIR HANDS. JUST FOR A NIGHT, JUST WALK AWAY FOR A NIGHT. TWELVE HOURS, THAT'S ALL.
AND WE DID. WE GAVE THEM ARKHAM.
AND WHEN WE CAME BACK THE NEXT DAY THEY WERE ALL GONE. EVERY ONE OF 'EM.

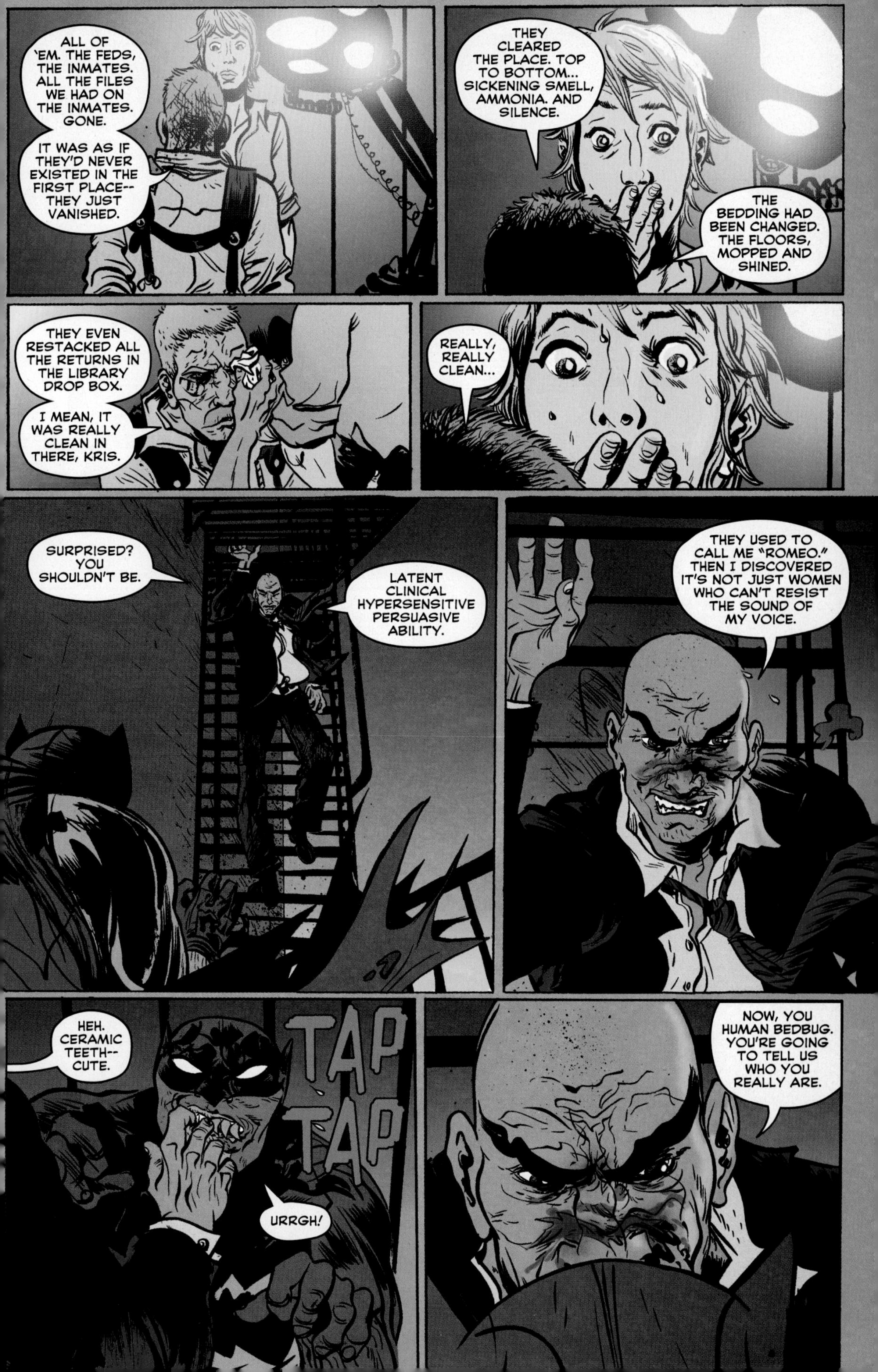
ALL OF 'EM. THE FEDS, THE INMATES. ALL THE FILES WE HAD ON THE INMATES. GONE.
IT WAS AS IF THEY'D NEVER EXISTED IN THE FIRST PLACE-- THEY JUST VANISHED.
THEY CLEARED THE PLACE. TOP TO BOTTOM... SICKENING SMELL, AMMONIA. AND SILENCE.
THE BEDDING HAD BEEN CHANGED. THE FLOORS, MOPPED AND SHINED.
THEY EVEN RESTACKED ALL THE RETURNS IN THE LIBRARY DROP BOX.
I MEAN, IT WAS REALLY CLEAN IN THERE, KRIS.
REALLY, REALLY CLEAN...
SURPRISED? YOU SHOULDN'T BE.
LATENT CLINICAL HYPERSENSITIVE PERSUASIVE ABILITY.
THEY USED TO CALL ME "ROMEO." THEN I DISCOVERED IT'S NOT JUST WOMEN WHO CAN'T RESIST THE SOUND OF MY VOICE.
HEH. CERAMIC TEETH-- CUTE.
TAP TAP
URRGH!
NOW, YOU HUMAN BEDBUG. YOU'RE GOING TO TELL US WHO YOU REALLY ARE.

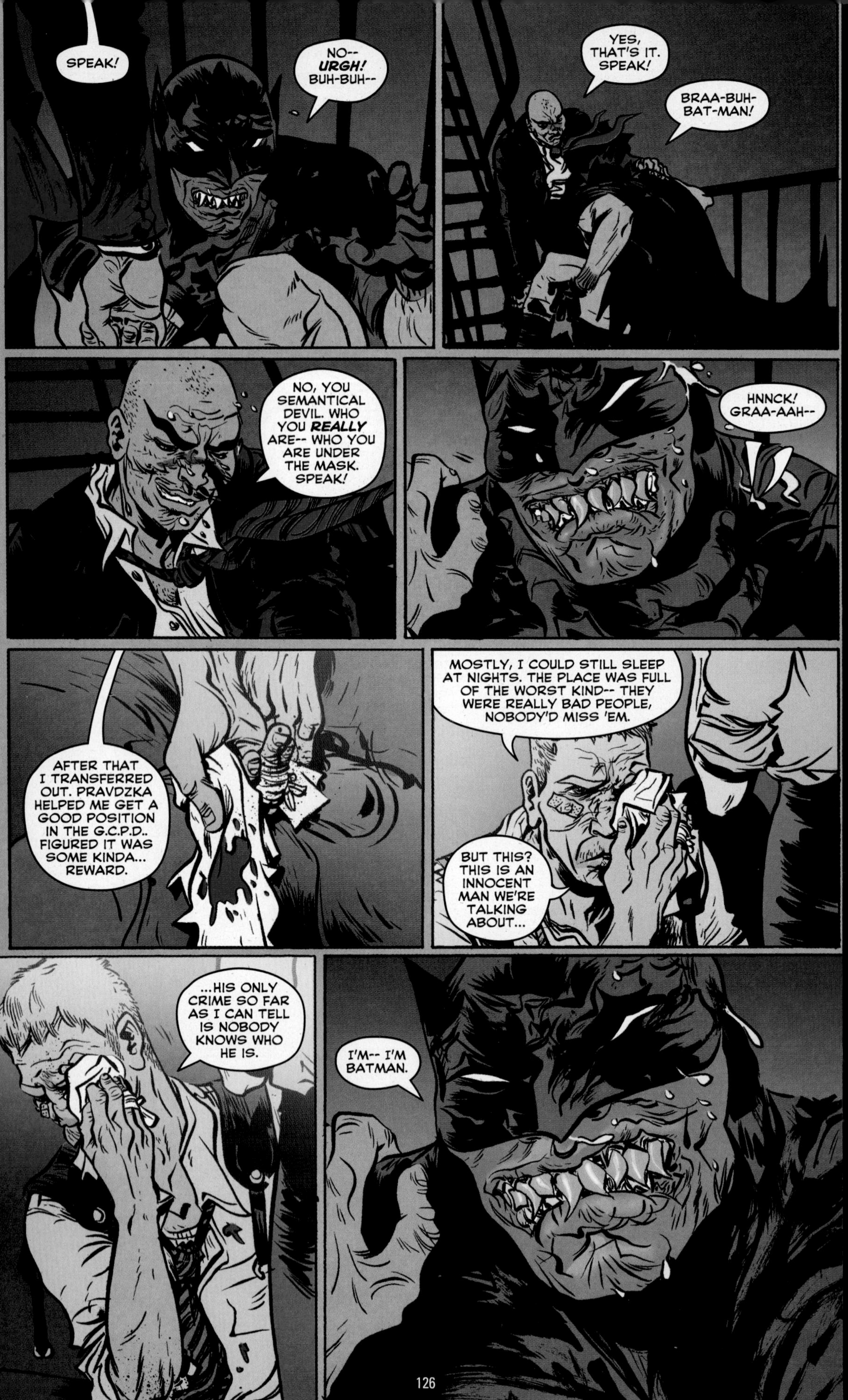
SPEAK!
NO-- URGH! BUH-BUH--
YES, THAT'S IT. SPEAK!
BRAA-BUH-BAT-MAN!
NO, YOU SEMANTICAL DEVIL. WHO YOU REALLY ARE-- WHO YOU ARE UNDER THE MASK. SPEAK!
HNNCK! GRAA-AAH--
AFTER THAT I TRANSFERRED OUT. PRAVDZKA HELPED ME GET A GOOD POSITION IN THE G.C.P.D.. FIGURED IT WAS SOME KINDA... REWARD.
MOSTLY, I COULD STILL SLEEP AT NIGHTS. THE PLACE WAS FULL OF THE WORST KIND-- THEY WERE REALLY BAD PEOPLE, NOBODY'D MISS 'EM.
BUT THIS? THIS IS AN INNOCENT MAN WE'RE TALKING ABOUT...
...HIS ONLY CRIME SO FAR AS I CAN TELL IS NOBODY KNOWS WHO HE IS.
I'M-- I'M BATMAN.

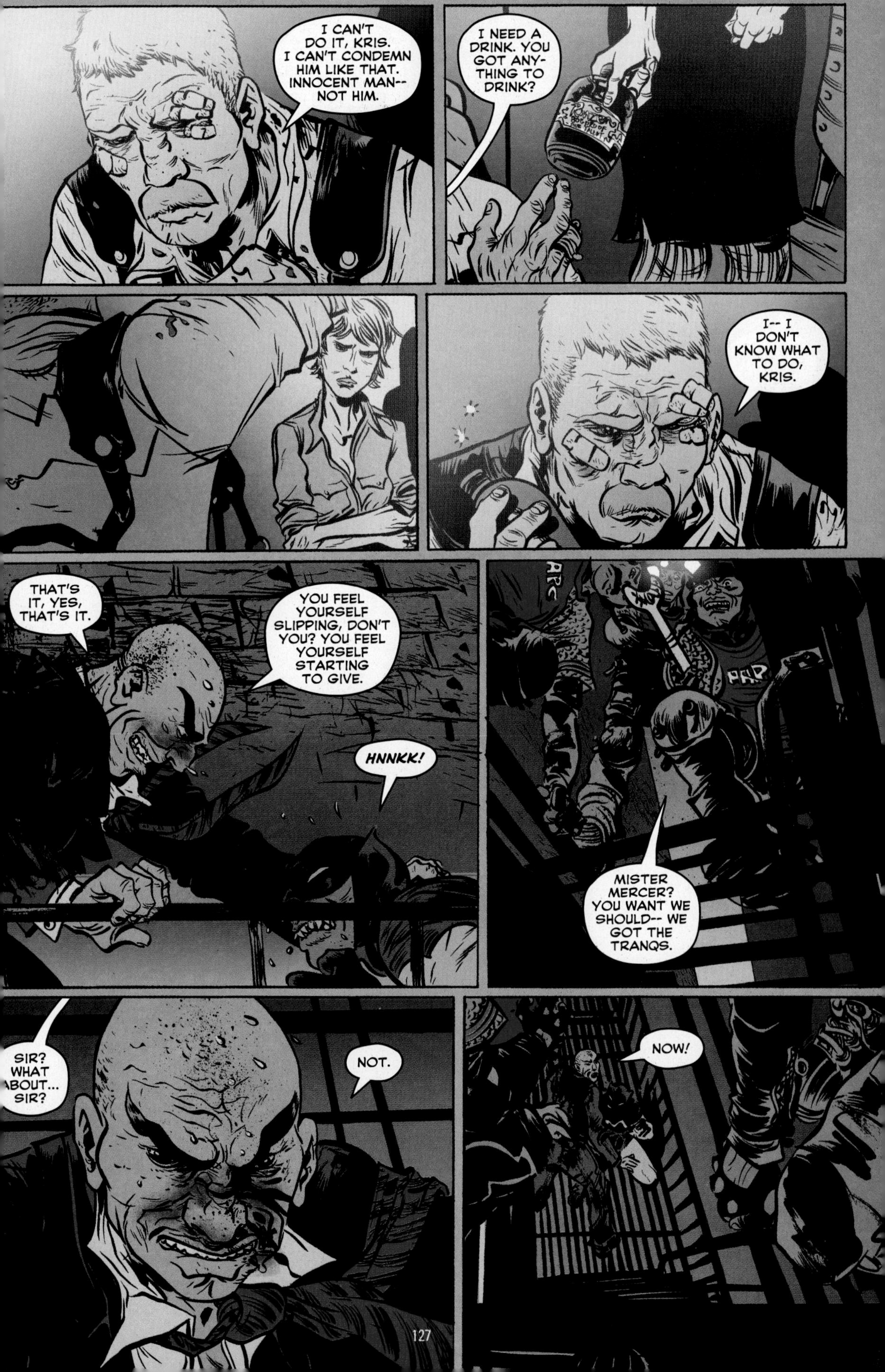
I CAN'T DO IT, KRIS. I CAN'T CONDEMN HIM LIKE THAT. INNOCENT MAN-- NOT HIM.
I NEED A DRINK. YOU GOT ANYTHING TO DRINK?
I-- I DON'T KNOW WHAT TO DO, KRIS.
THAT'S IT, YES, THAT'S IT.
YOU FEEL YOURSELF SLIPPING, DON'T YOU? YOU FEEL YOURSELF STARTING TO GIVE.
HNNKK!
MISTER MERCER? YOU WANT WE SHOULD-- WE GOT THE TRANQS.
SIR? WHAT ABOUT... SIR?
NOT.
NOW!

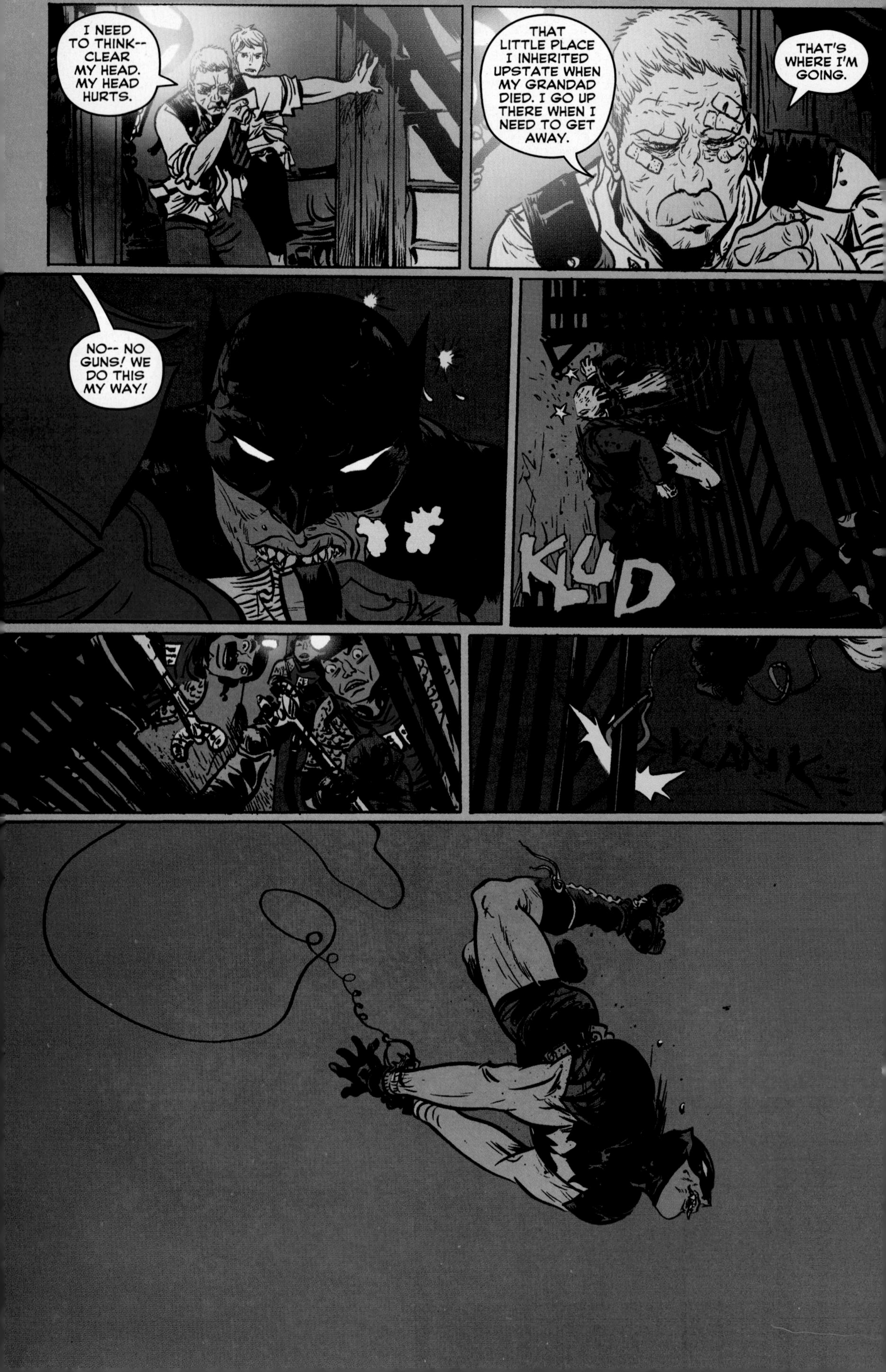
I NEED TO THINK-- CLEAR MY HEAD. MY HEAD HURTS.
THAT LITTLE PLACE I INHERITED UPSTATE WHEN MY GRANDAD DIED. I GO UP THERE WHEN I NEED TO GET AWAY.
THAT'S WHERE I'M GOING.
NO-- NO GUNS! WE DO THIS MY WAY!
KLUD

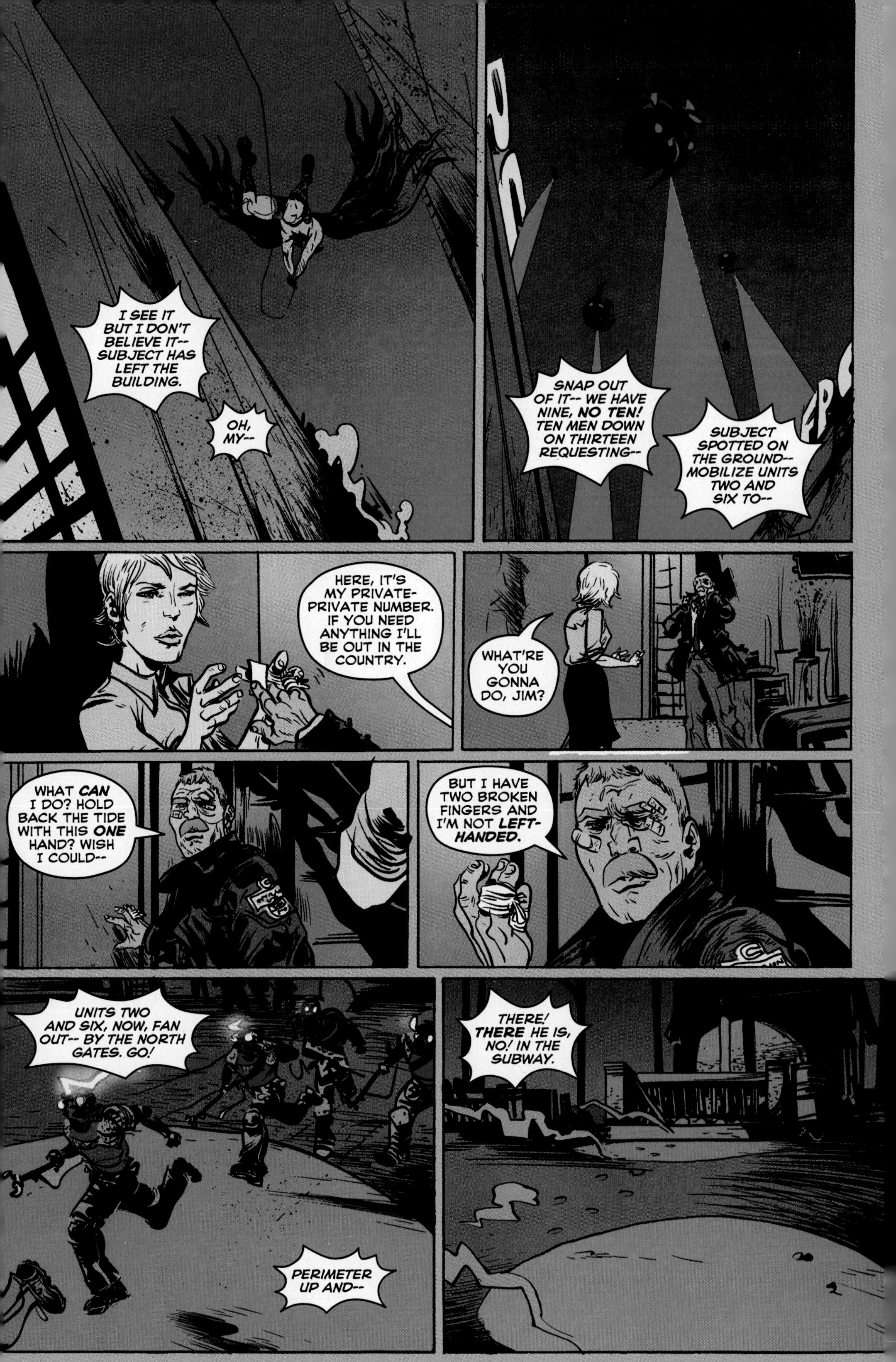
I SEE IT BUT I DON'T BELIEVE IT-- SUBJECT HAS LEFT THE BUILDING.
OH, MY--
SNAP OUT OF IT-- WE HAVE NINE, NO TEN! TEN MEN DOWN ON THIRTEEN REQUESTING--
SUBJECT SPOTTED ON THE GROUND-- MOBILIZE UNITS TWO AND SIX TO--
HERE, IT'S MY PRIVATE-PRIVATE NUMBER. IF YOU NEED ANYTHING I'LL BE OUT IN THE COUNTRY.
WHAT'RE YOU GONNA DO, JIM?
WHAT CAN I DO? HOLD BACK THE TIDE WITH THIS ONE HAND? WISH I COULD--
BUT I HAVE TWO BROKEN FINGERS AND I'M NOT LEFT-HANDED.
UNITS TWO AND SIX, NOW, FAN OUT-- BY THE NORTH GATES. GO!
PERIMETER UP AND--
THERE! THERE HE IS, NO! IN THE SUBWAY.

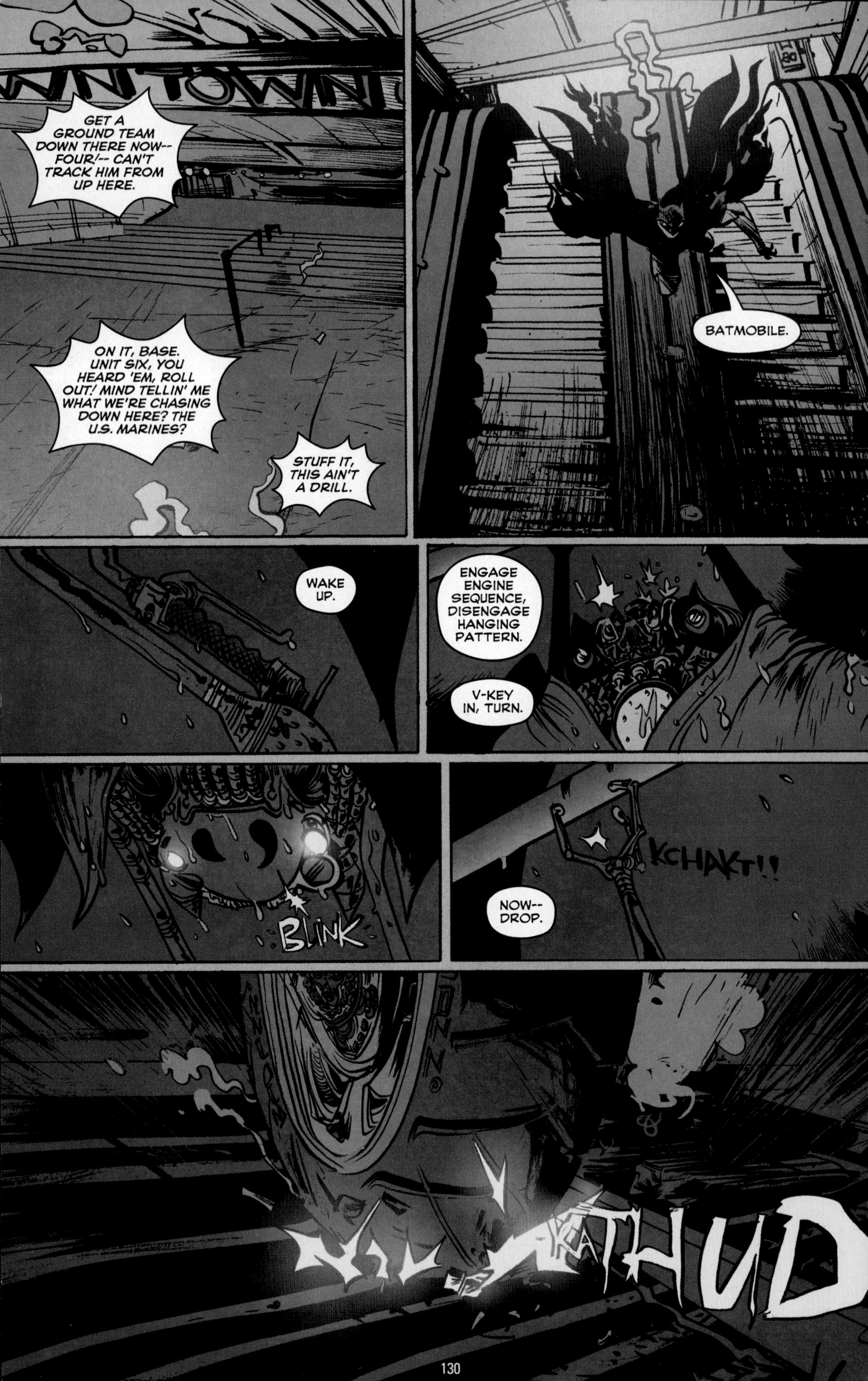
GET A GROUND TEAM DOWN THERE NOW-- FOUR!-- CAN'T TRACK HIM FROM UP HERE.
ON IT, BASE. UNIT SIX, YOU HEARD 'EM, ROLL OUT! MIND TELLIN' ME WHAT WE'RE CHASING DOWN HERE? THE U.S. MARINES?
STUFF IT, THIS AIN'T A DRILL.
BATMOBILE.
WAKE UP.
ENGAGE ENGINE SEQUENCE, DISENGAGE HANGING PATTERN.
V-KEY IN, TURN.
BLINK
KCHAKT!!
NOW-- DROP.
THUD

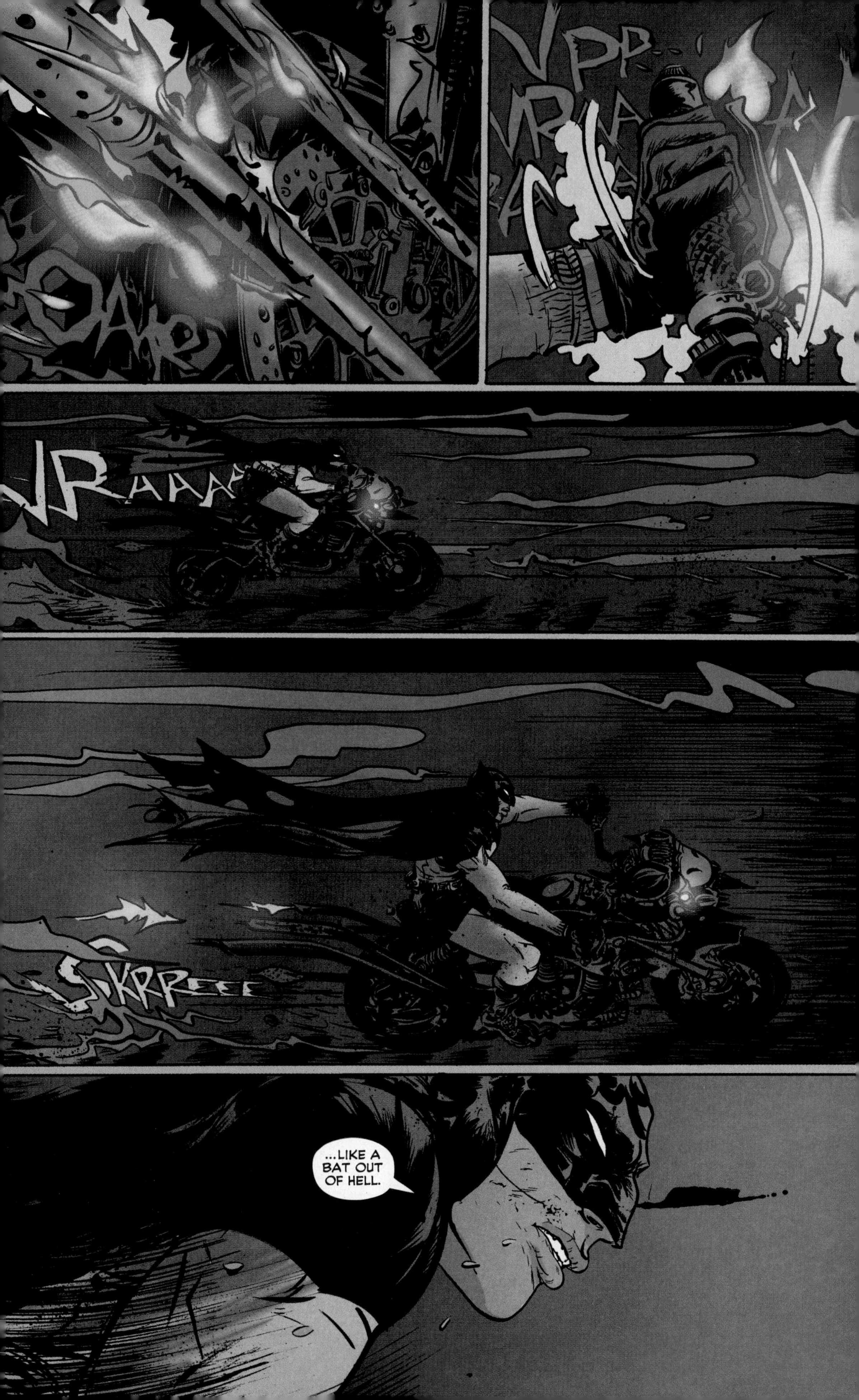
...LIKE A BAT OUT OF HELL.

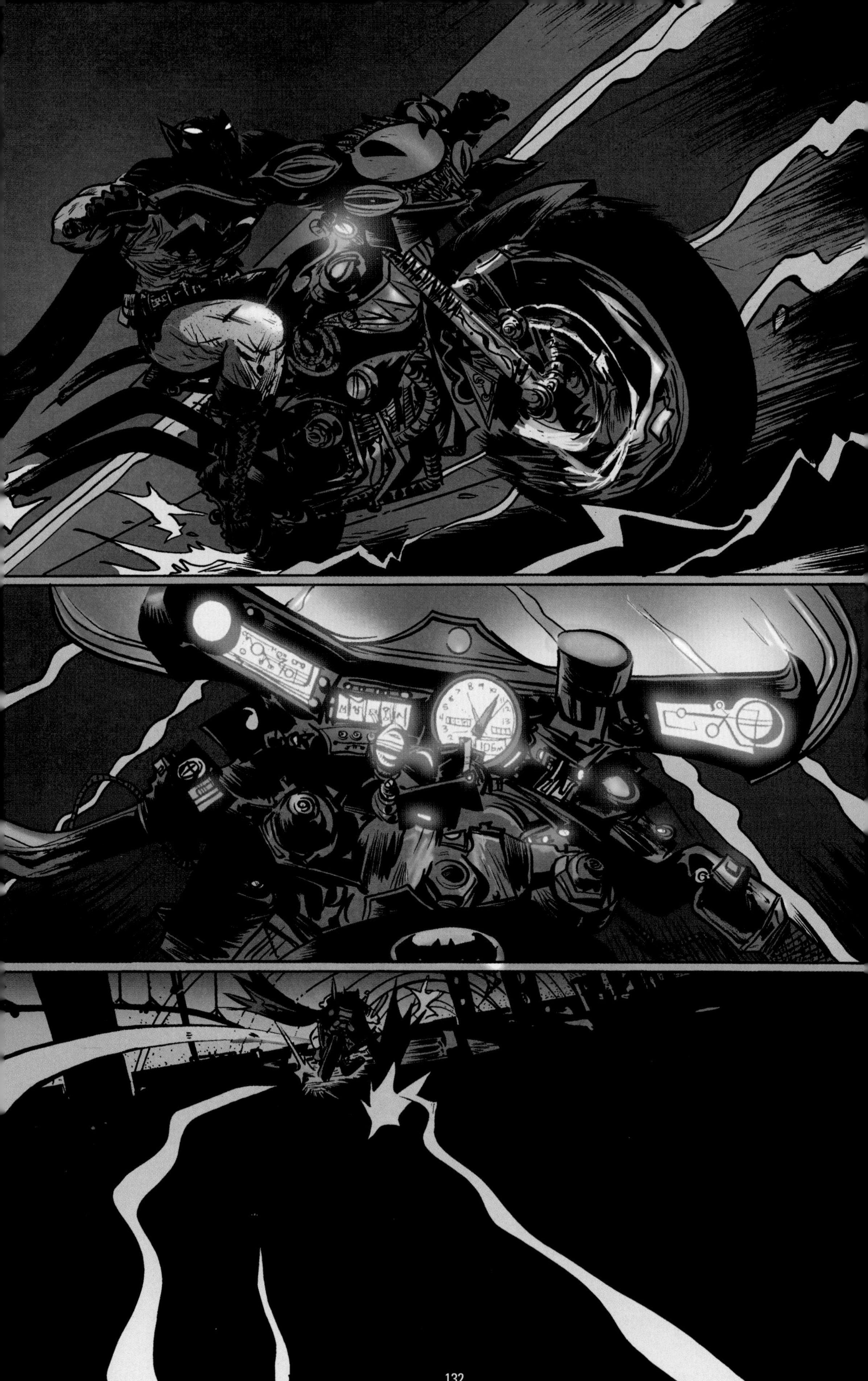

...ARE RELEASING NO FURTHER DETAILS REGARDING THIS ALARMING INCIDENT AT THIS TIME-- NO CASUALTIES.

...STAY WITH GOTHAM ONE FOR FULL--

...IMPOSED ON NEIGHBORHOODS IMMEDIATELY SURROUNDING THE F.P.C. PRECINCT BLOCK... CONFUSED AREA RESIDENTS ARE BEING TOLD TO--

...I MEAN I WAS *JUST* GOING OUT FOR MILK--

...CAN'T SEE WHY I OUGHTA BE DETAINED FOR TWO HOURS OVER A BOTTLE OF MILK.

...STREET-TO-STREET CURFEWS ARE BEING SET UP ACROSS LOWER GOTHAM IN RESPONSE TO THE BOMBING AT F.P.C. HEADQUARTERS TONIGHT.

...CONFIRMS REPORTS OF AN APPARENT *TERRORIST* ATTACK ON GOTHAM'S MAIN F.P.C. BUILDING EARLIER TONIGHT.

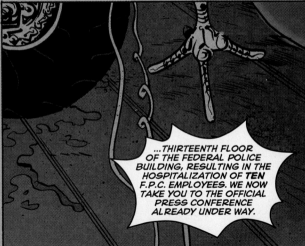

...THIRTEENTH FLOOR OF THE FEDERAL POLICE BUILDING, RESULTING IN THE HOSPITALIZATION OF *TEN* F.P.C. EMPLOYEES. WE NOW TAKE YOU TO THE OFFICIAL PRESS CONFERENCE ALREADY UNDER WAY.

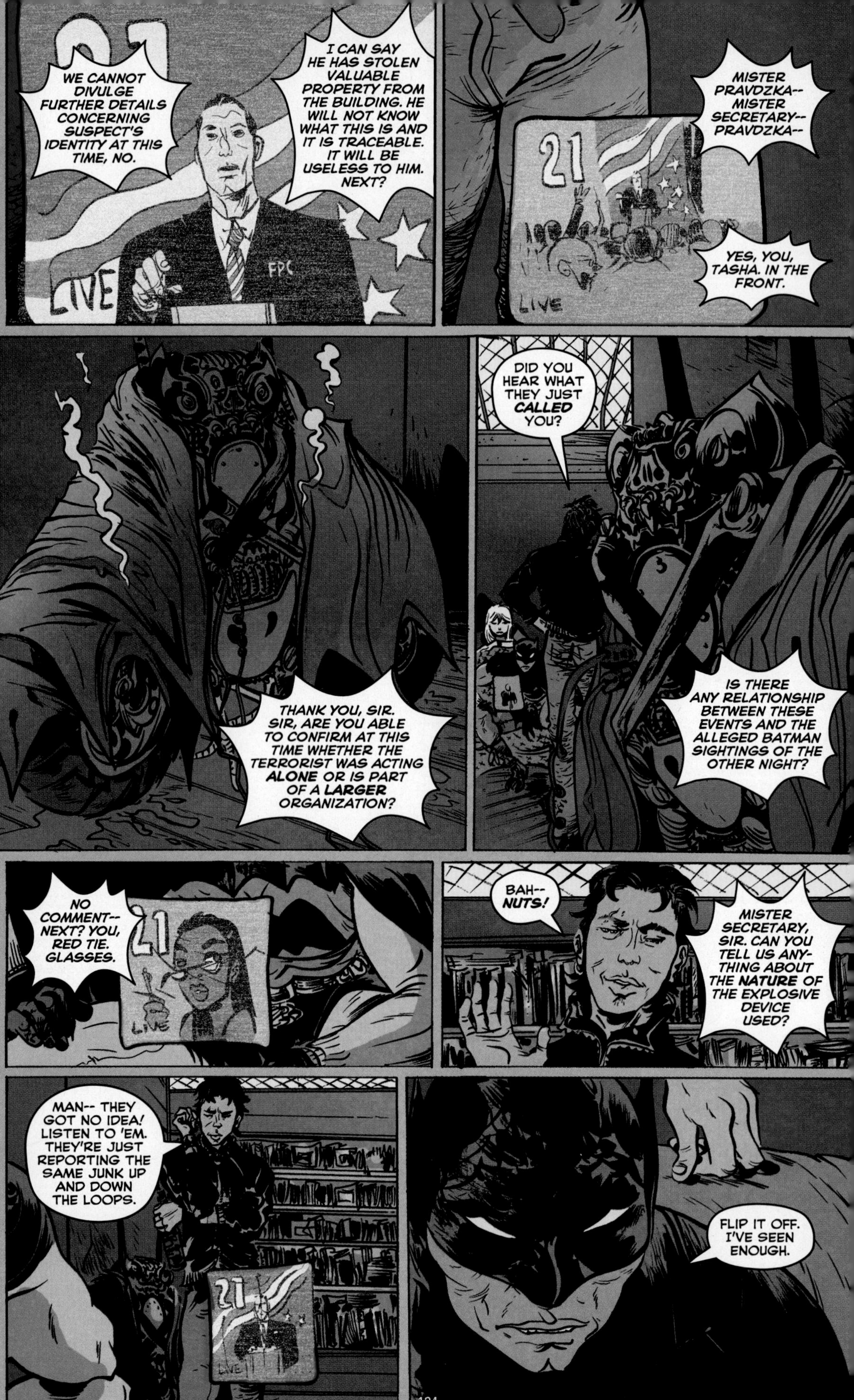

WE CANNOT DIVULGE FURTHER DETAILS CONCERNING SUSPECT'S IDENTITY AT THIS TIME, NO.
I CAN SAY HE HAS STOLEN VALUABLE PROPERTY FROM THE BUILDING. HE WILL NOT KNOW WHAT THIS IS AND IT IS TRACEABLE. IT WILL BE USELESS TO HIM. NEXT?
MISTER PRAVDZKA-- MISTER SECRETARY-- PRAVDZKA--
YES, YOU, TASHA. IN THE FRONT.
THANK YOU, SIR. SIR, ARE YOU ABLE TO CONFIRM AT THIS TIME WHETHER THE TERRORIST WAS ACTING ALONE OR IS PART OF A LARGER ORGANIZATION?
DID YOU HEAR WHAT THEY JUST CALLED YOU?
IS THERE ANY RELATIONSHIP BETWEEN THESE EVENTS AND THE ALLEGED BATMAN SIGHTINGS OF THE OTHER NIGHT?
NO COMMENT-- NEXT? YOU, RED TIE. GLASSES.
BAH-- NUTS!
MISTER SECRETARY, SIR. CAN YOU TELL US ANYTHING ABOUT THE NATURE OF THE EXPLOSIVE DEVICE USED?
MAN-- THEY GOT NO IDEA! LISTEN TO 'EM. THEY'RE JUST REPORTING THE SAME JUNK UP AND DOWN THE LOOPS.
FLIP IT OFF. I'VE SEEN ENOUGH.

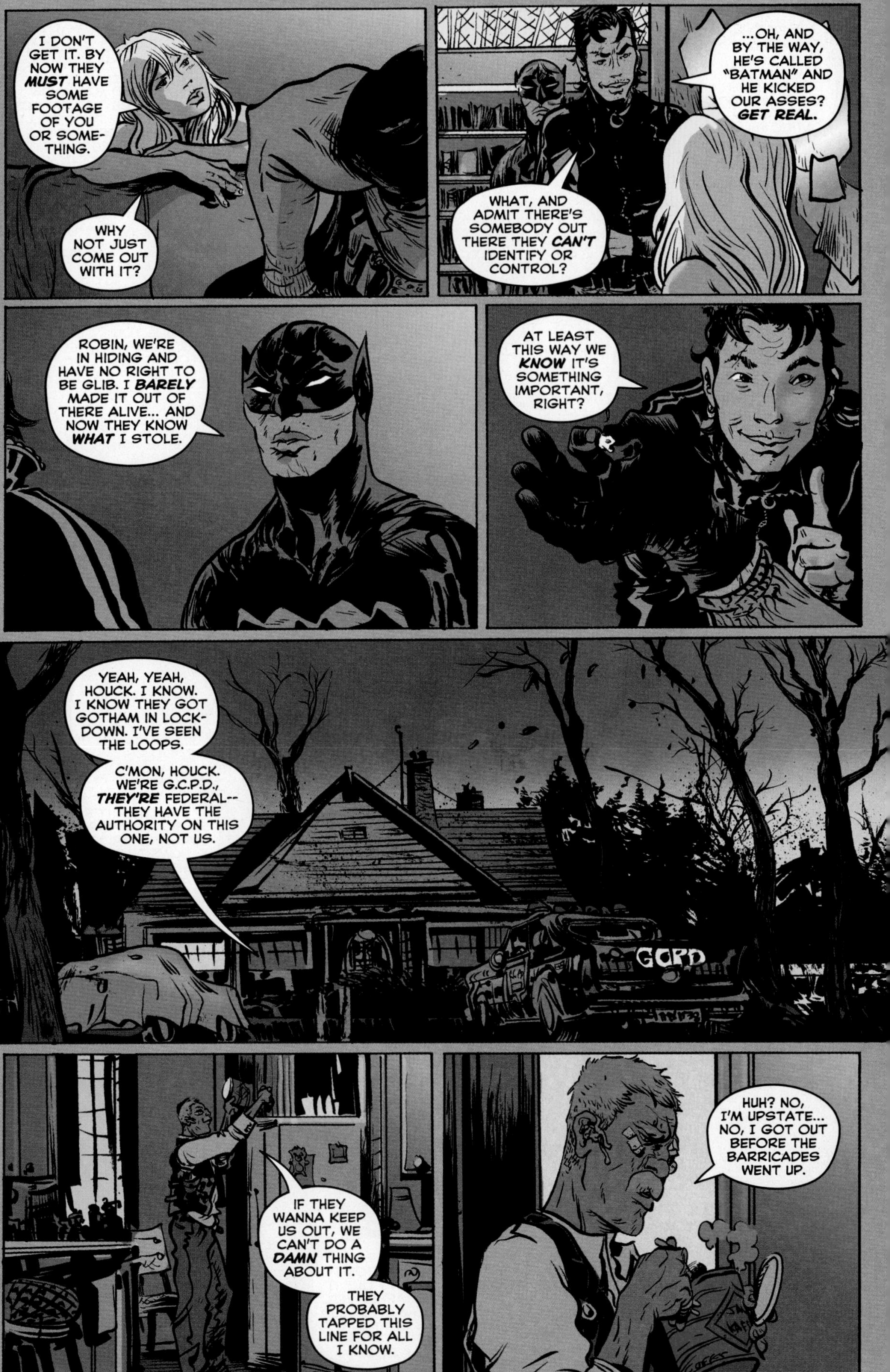
I DON'T GET IT. BY NOW THEY MUST HAVE SOME FOOTAGE OF YOU OR SOMETHING.
WHY NOT JUST COME OUT WITH IT?
WHAT, AND ADMIT THERE'S SOMEBODY OUT THERE THEY CAN'T IDENTIFY OR CONTROL?
...OH, AND BY THE WAY, HE'S CALLED "BATMAN" AND HE KICKED OUR ASSES? GET REAL.
ROBIN, WE'RE IN HIDING AND HAVE NO RIGHT TO BE GLIB. I BARELY MADE IT OUT OF THERE ALIVE... AND NOW THEY KNOW WHAT I STOLE.
AT LEAST THIS WAY WE KNOW IT'S SOMETHING IMPORTANT, RIGHT?
YEAH, YEAH, HOUCK. I KNOW. I KNOW THEY GOT GOTHAM IN LOCK-DOWN. I'VE SEEN THE LOOPS.
C'MON, HOUCK. WE'RE G.C.P.D., THEY'RE FEDERAL-- THEY HAVE THE AUTHORITY ON THIS ONE, NOT US.
GCPD
IF THEY WANNA KEEP US OUT, WE CAN'T DO A DAMN THING ABOUT IT.
THEY PROBABLY TAPPED THIS LINE FOR ALL I KNOW.
HUH? NO, I'M UPSTATE... NO, I GOT OUT BEFORE THE BARRICADES WENT UP.

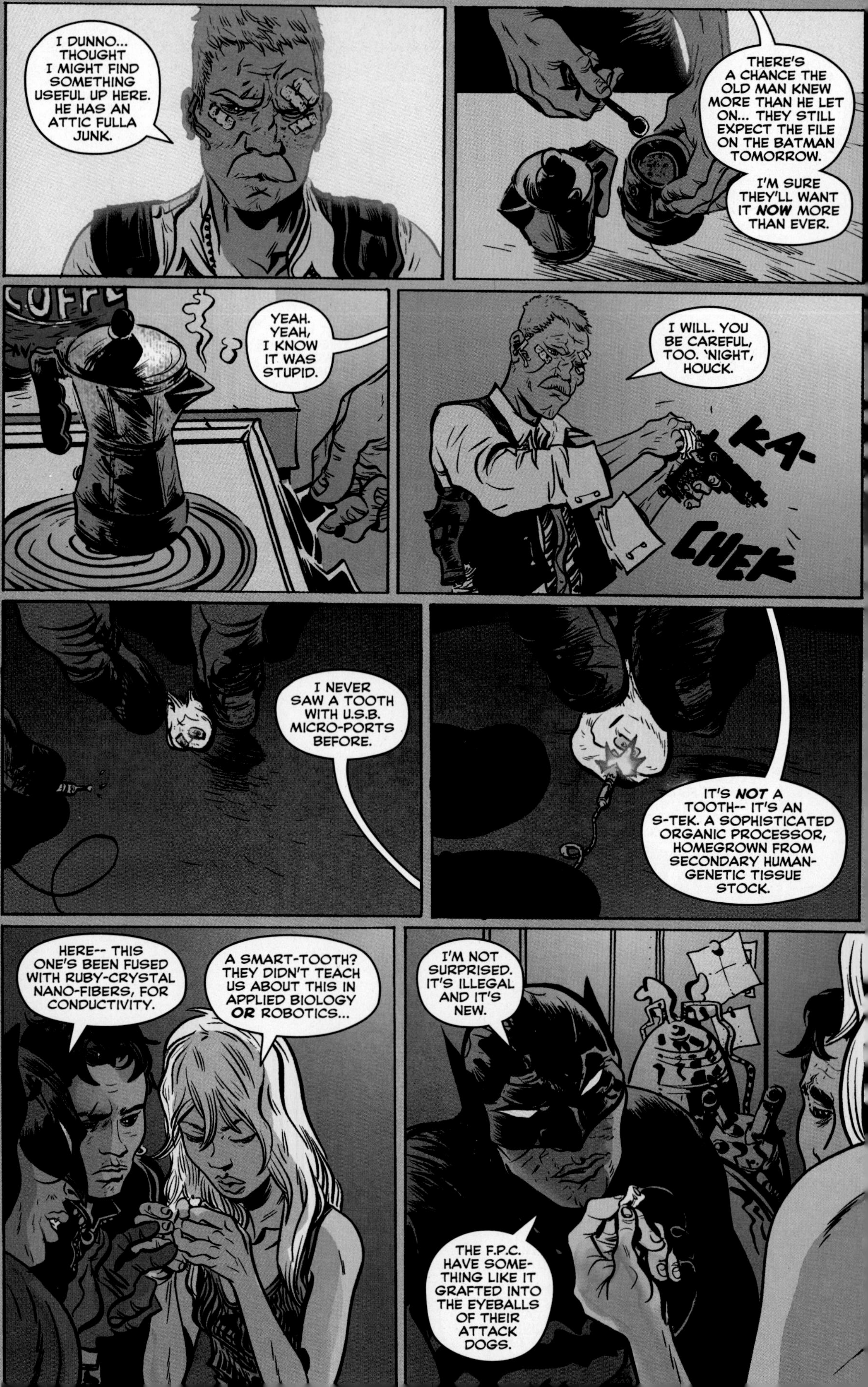
I DUNNO... THOUGHT I MIGHT FIND SOMETHING USEFUL UP HERE. HE HAS AN ATTIC FULLA JUNK.
THERE'S A CHANCE THE OLD MAN KNEW MORE THAN HE LET ON... THEY STILL EXPECT THE FILE ON THE BATMAN TOMORROW.
I'M SURE THEY'LL WANT IT *NOW* MORE THAN EVER.
YEAH. YEAH, I KNOW IT WAS STUPID.
I WILL. YOU BE CAREFUL, TOO. 'NIGHT, HOUCK.
KA-CHEK
I NEVER SAW A TOOTH WITH U.S.B. MICRO-PORTS BEFORE.
IT'S *NOT* A TOOTH-- IT'S AN S-TEK. A SOPHISTICATED ORGANIC PROCESSOR, HOMEGROWN FROM SECONDARY HUMAN-GENETIC TISSUE STOCK.
HERE-- THIS ONE'S BEEN FUSED WITH RUBY-CRYSTAL NANO-FIBERS, FOR CONDUCTIVITY.
A SMART-TOOTH? THEY DIDN'T TEACH US ABOUT THIS IN APPLIED BIOLOGY *OR* ROBOTICS...
I'M NOT SURPRISED. IT'S ILLEGAL AND IT'S NEW.
THE F.P.C. HAVE SOME-THING LIKE IT GRAFTED INTO THE EYEBALLS OF THEIR ATTACK DOGS.

SEEMS KINDA ELABORATE. COULDN'T JUST BE FOR STORAGE CAPACITY...?

VIRTUAL INVISIBILITY.

CONCEALED ORGANICS DON'T REGISTER UNDER SCANS LIKE METAL OR PLASTICS DO. THE VIC WAS A FED OR SOMEONE POSING AS ONE.

EVEN FEDS GET STOPPED SOMETIMES.

IF IT'S A SUPER-PROCESSOR, WHERE'S ITS COOLING UNIT?

YES, I WAS WONDERING THAT MYSELF. PLANTED IN THE JAWBONE IS MY GUESS, OR ON HIS BELT. OR THERE WAS AN R.C. REMOTE SOMEPLACE NEARBY...

HE WAS DEAD WHEN I FOUND HIM SO I DIDN'T THINK TO ASK.

MADE IT EASIER GETTING THE TOOTH, THOUGH.

WAIT-- HERE.

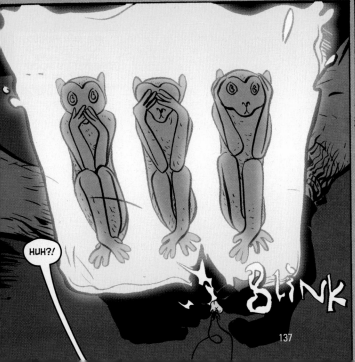

HUH?!

BLINK

THAT'S ODD--

CLIK!

LOOKS LIKE HE KEPT ABOUT EVERYTHING HE EVER OWNED.

PHOTOS...

THE OLD MAN. I REMEMBER HIM...

HIS JAW WOULD SOMETIMES GO POP WHEN HE CHEWED HIS FOOD-- *SCARED* ME SILLY.

TAUGHT ME TO PLAY *CHESS*, TAUGHT ME MY MULTIPLICATION TABLES *AND* LONG DIVISION.

I REMEMBER HOW HE BOILED DOWN LEAD SLUGS TO POUR INTO THE FRONT END OF MY SOAP-BOX DERBY RACER-- TO MAKE IT GO FASTER. I MUST'A BEEN EIGHT OR NINE WHEN WE DID THAT.

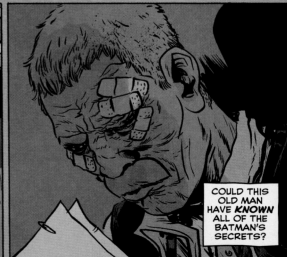

COULD THIS OLD MAN HAVE *KNOWN* ALL OF THE BATMAN'S SECRETS?

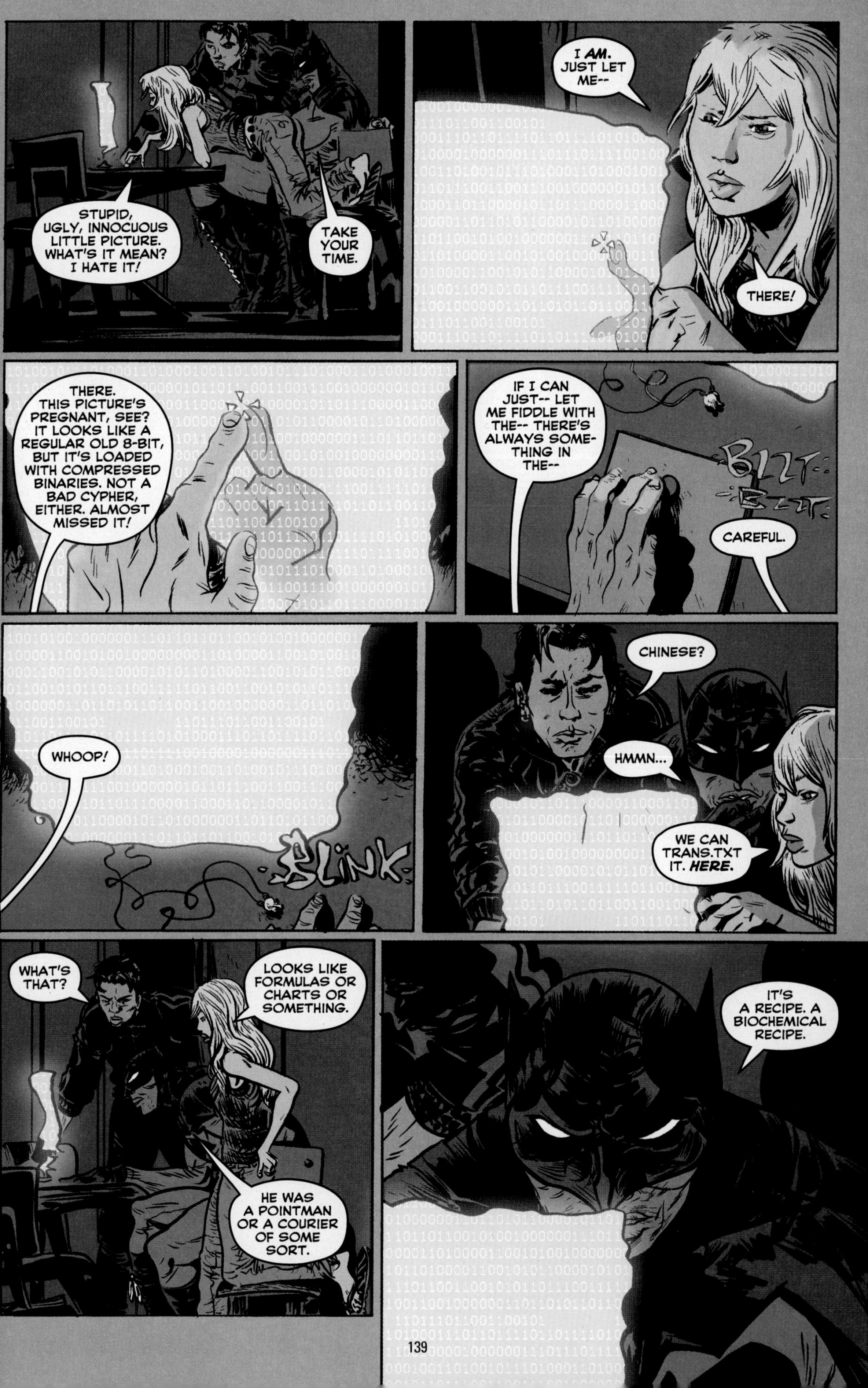
STUPID, UGLY, INNOCUOUS LITTLE PICTURE. WHAT'S IT MEAN? I HATE IT!
TAKE YOUR TIME.
I AM. JUST LET ME--
THERE!
THERE. THIS PICTURE'S PREGNANT, SEE? IT LOOKS LIKE A REGULAR OLD 8-BIT, BUT IT'S LOADED WITH COMPRESSED BINARIES. NOT A BAD CYPHER, EITHER. ALMOST MISSED IT!
IF I CAN JUST-- LET ME FIDDLE WITH THE-- THERE'S ALWAYS SOME-THING IN THE--
BZZT
BZZT
CAREFUL.
WHOOP!
BLINK
CHINESE?
HMMN...
WE CAN TRANS.TXT IT. HERE.
WHAT'S THAT?
LOOKS LIKE FORMULAS OR CHARTS OR SOMETHING.
HE WAS A POINTMAN OR A COURIER OF SOME SORT.
IT'S A RECIPE. A BIOCHEMICAL RECIPE.

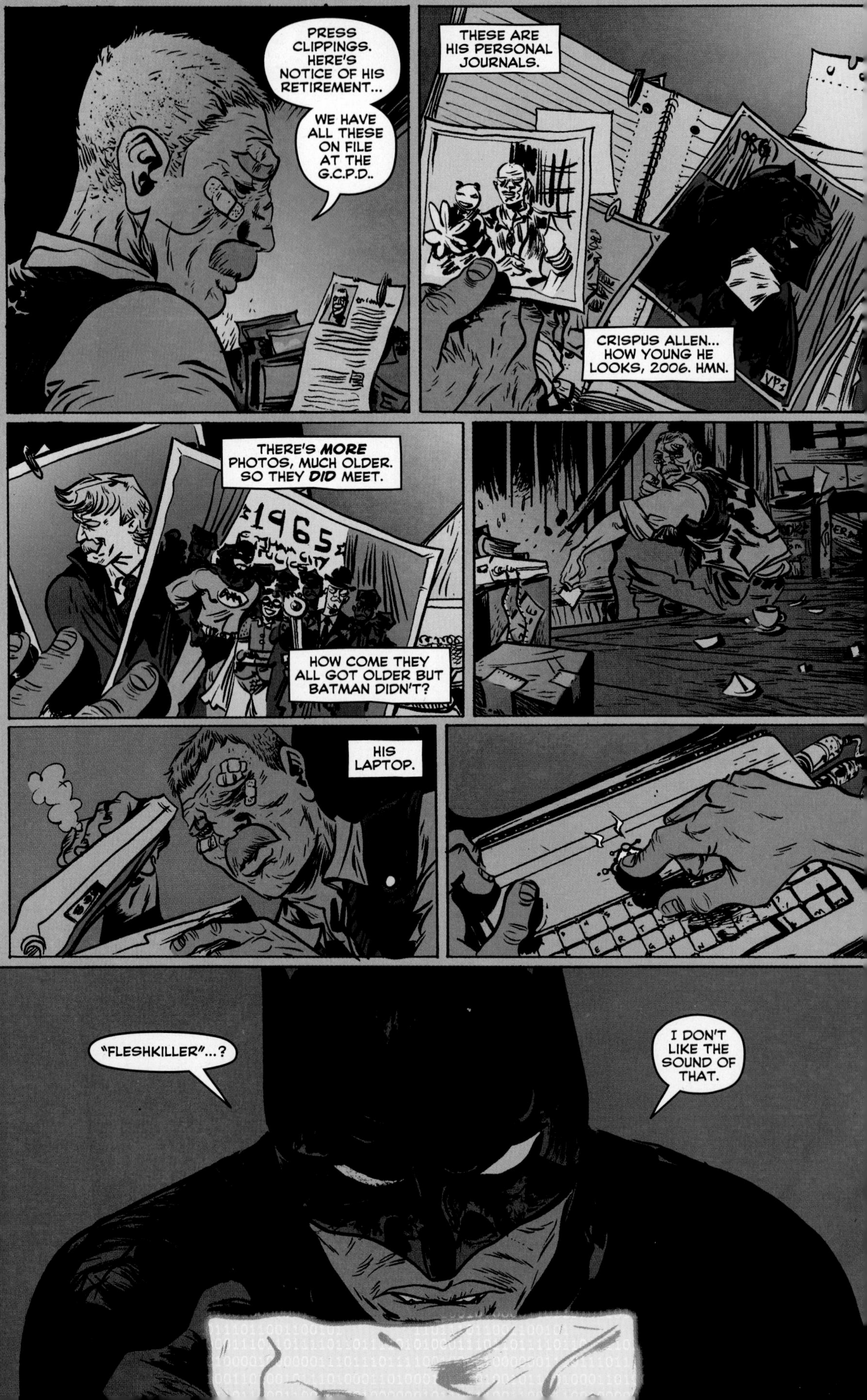
PRESS CLIPPINGS. HERE'S NOTICE OF HIS RETIREMENT...
WE HAVE ALL THESE ON FILE AT THE G.C.P.D..
THESE ARE HIS PERSONAL JOURNALS.
CRISPUS ALLEN... HOW YOUNG HE LOOKS, 2006. HMN.
THERE'S MORE PHOTOS, MUCH OLDER. SO THEY DID MEET.
1965
HOW COME THEY ALL GOT OLDER BUT BATMAN DIDN'T?
HIS LAPTOP.
"FLESHKILLER"...?
I DON'T LIKE THE SOUND OF THAT.

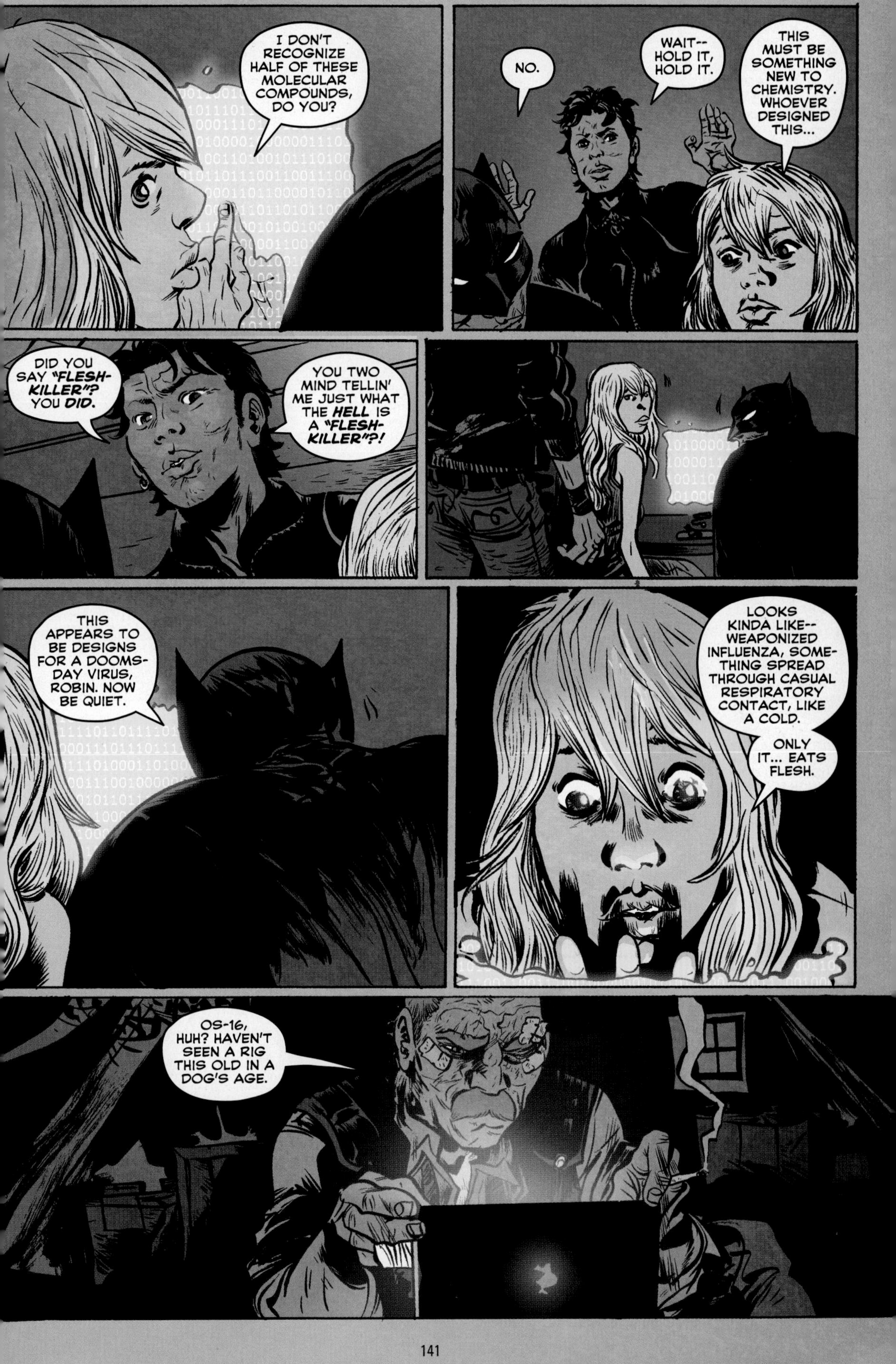

I DON'T RECOGNIZE HALF OF THESE MOLECULAR COMPOUNDS, DO YOU?
NO.
WAIT-- HOLD IT, HOLD IT.
THIS MUST BE SOMETHING NEW TO CHEMISTRY. WHOEVER DESIGNED THIS...
DID YOU SAY "FLESH-KILLER"? YOU DID.
YOU TWO MIND TELLIN' ME JUST WHAT THE HELL IS A "FLESH-KILLER"?!
THIS APPEARS TO BE DESIGNS FOR A DOOMSDAY VIRUS, ROBIN. NOW BE QUIET.
LOOKS KINDA LIKE-- WEAPONIZED INFLUENZA, SOMETHING SPREAD THROUGH CASUAL RESPIRATORY CONTACT, LIKE A COLD.
ONLY IT... EATS FLESH.
OS-16, HUH? HAVEN'T SEEN A RIG THIS OLD IN A DOG'S AGE.

NOTHING, THERE'S *NOTHING* SPECIAL HERE. *HANG ON...* THERE'S SOMETHING LOCKED AND HIDDEN ON THE HARDDRIVE HERE.

SAYS I NEED THE PASSWORD. WHAT'S THE PASSWORD?

IT-- STARTS IN THE LUNGS, IT SETTLES THERE. TWELVE HOURS AFTER INITIAL INCUBATION, THE VIRUS HATCHES, AND SPREADS...

...IT WORMS ITS WAY OUT, GOING FROM CELL TO CELL, INCH BY INCH. OH, MY GOD.

IT WON'T STOP 'TIL THERE'S *NOTHING*, NOT EVEN A *FINGERNAIL* OF YOU LEFT... FOUR DAYS.

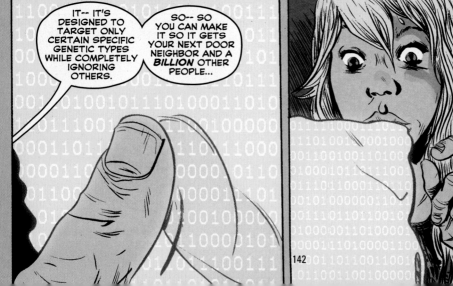

IT-- IT'S DESIGNED TO TARGET ONLY CERTAIN SPECIFIC GENETIC TYPES WHILE COMPLETELY IGNORING OTHERS.

SO-- SO YOU CAN MAKE IT SO IT GETS YOUR NEXT DOOR NEIGHBOR AND A *BILLION* OTHER PEOPLE...

...BUT NOT YOU.

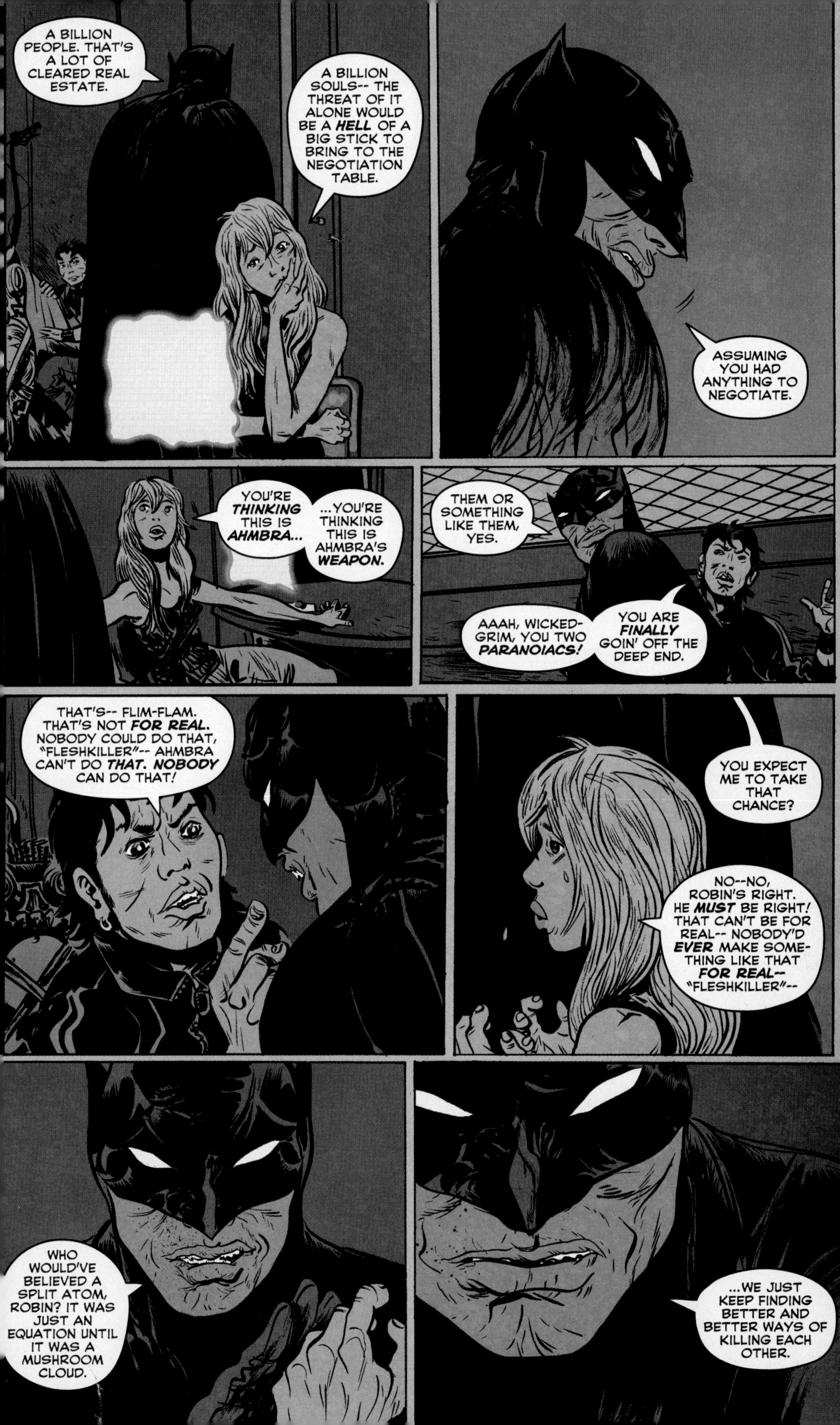
A BILLION PEOPLE. THAT'S A LOT OF CLEARED REAL ESTATE.
A BILLION SOULS-- THE THREAT OF IT ALONE WOULD BE A HELL OF A BIG STICK TO BRING TO THE NEGOTIATION TABLE.
ASSUMING YOU HAD ANYTHING TO NEGOTIATE.
YOU'RE THINKING THIS IS AHMBRA...
...YOU'RE THINKING THIS IS AHMBRA'S WEAPON.
THEM OR SOMETHING LIKE THEM, YES.
AAAH, WICKED-GRIM, YOU TWO PARANOIACS!
YOU ARE FINALLY GOIN' OFF THE DEEP END.
THAT'S-- FLIM-FLAM. THAT'S NOT FOR REAL. NOBODY COULD DO THAT, "FLESHKILLER"-- AHMBRA CAN'T DO THAT. NOBODY CAN DO THAT!
YOU EXPECT ME TO TAKE THAT CHANCE?
NO--NO, ROBIN'S RIGHT. HE MUST BE RIGHT! THAT CAN'T BE FOR REAL-- NOBODY'D EVER MAKE SOME-THING LIKE THAT FOR REAL-- "FLESHKILLER"--
WHO WOULD'VE BELIEVED A SPLIT ATOM, ROBIN? IT WAS JUST AN EQUATION UNTIL IT WAS A MUSHROOM CLOUD.
...WE JUST KEEP FINDING BETTER AND BETTER WAYS OF KILLING EACH OTHER.

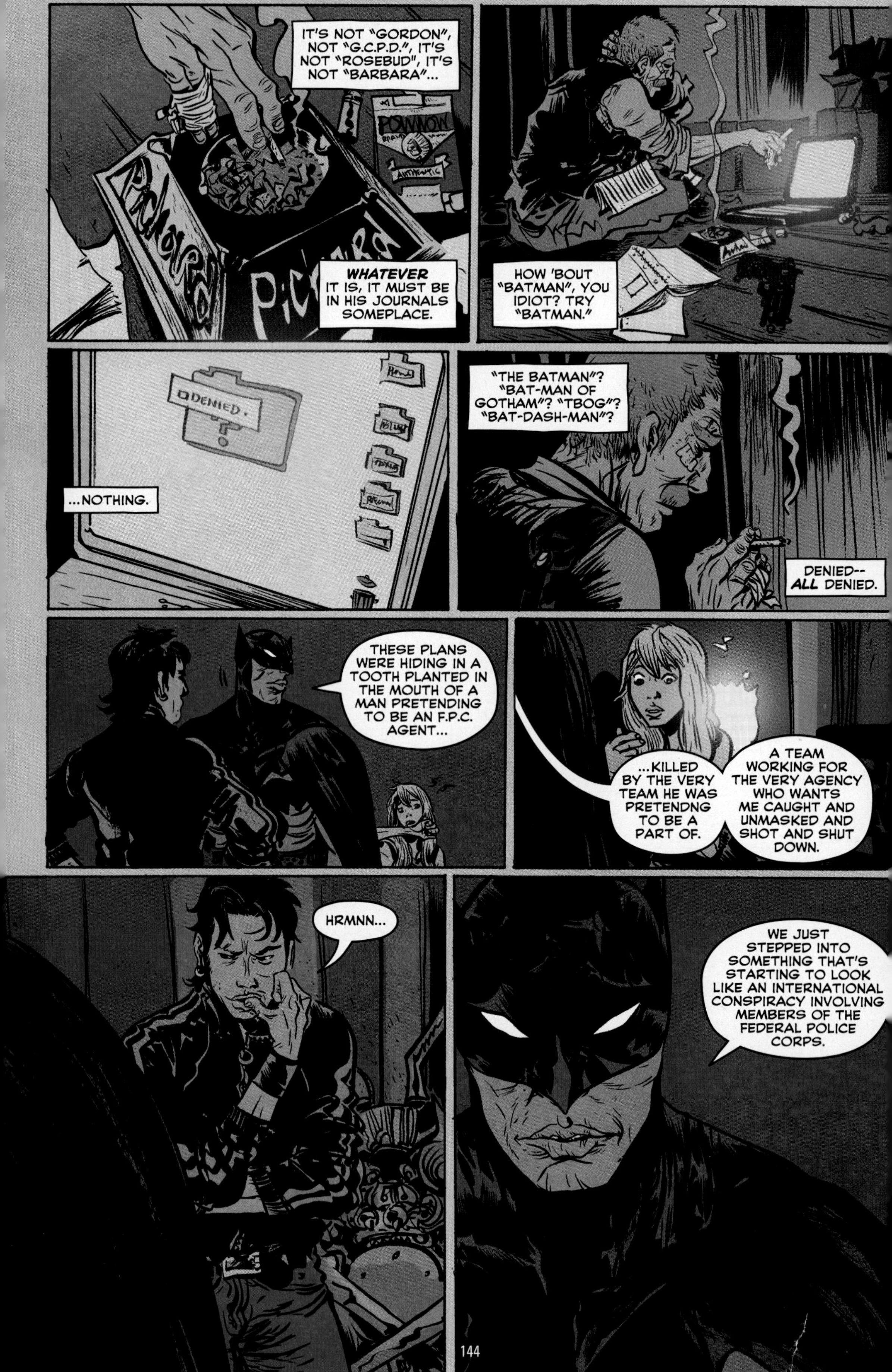
IT'S NOT "GORDON", NOT "G.C.P.D.", IT'S NOT "ROSEBUD", IT'S NOT "BARBARA"...
WHATEVER IT IS, IT MUST BE IN HIS JOURNALS SOMEPLACE.
HOW 'BOUT "BATMAN", YOU IDIOT? TRY "BATMAN."
DENIED.
...NOTHING.
"THE BATMAN"? "BAT-MAN OF GOTHAM"? "TBOG"? "BAT-DASH-MAN"?
DENIED-- ALL DENIED.
THESE PLANS WERE HIDING IN A TOOTH PLANTED IN THE MOUTH OF A MAN PRETENDING TO BE AN F.P.C. AGENT...
...KILLED BY THE VERY TEAM HE WAS PRETENDNG TO BE A PART OF.
A TEAM WORKING FOR THE VERY AGENCY WHO WANTS ME CAUGHT AND UNMASKED AND SHOT AND SHUT DOWN.
HRMNN...
WE JUST STEPPED INTO SOMETHING THAT'S STARTING TO LOOK LIKE AN INTERNATIONAL CONSPIRACY INVOLVING MEMBERS OF THE FEDERAL POLICE CORPS.

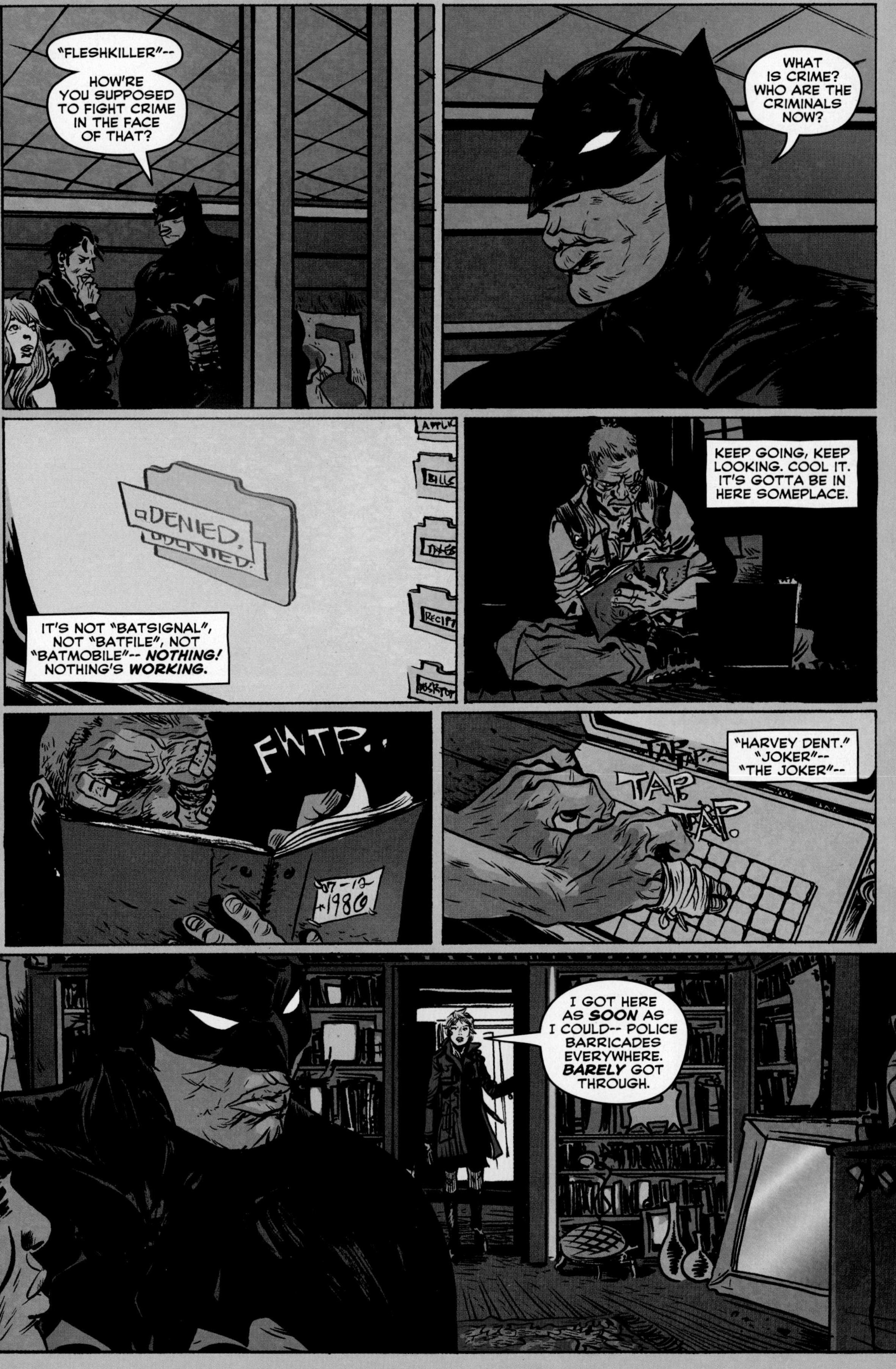

"FLESHKILLER"--
HOW'RE YOU SUPPOSED TO FIGHT CRIME IN THE FACE OF THAT?
WHAT IS CRIME? WHO ARE THE CRIMINALS NOW?
DENIED, DENIED.
IT'S NOT "BATSIGNAL", NOT "BATFILE", NOT "BATMOBILE"-- NOTHING! NOTHING'S WORKING.
KEEP GOING, KEEP LOOKING. COOL IT. IT'S GOTTA BE IN HERE SOMEPLACE.
FWTP..
"HARVEY DENT." "JOKER"-- "THE JOKER"--
TAP TAP TAP TAP.
I GOT HERE AS SOON AS I COULD-- POLICE BARRICADES EVERYWHERE. BARELY GOT THROUGH.

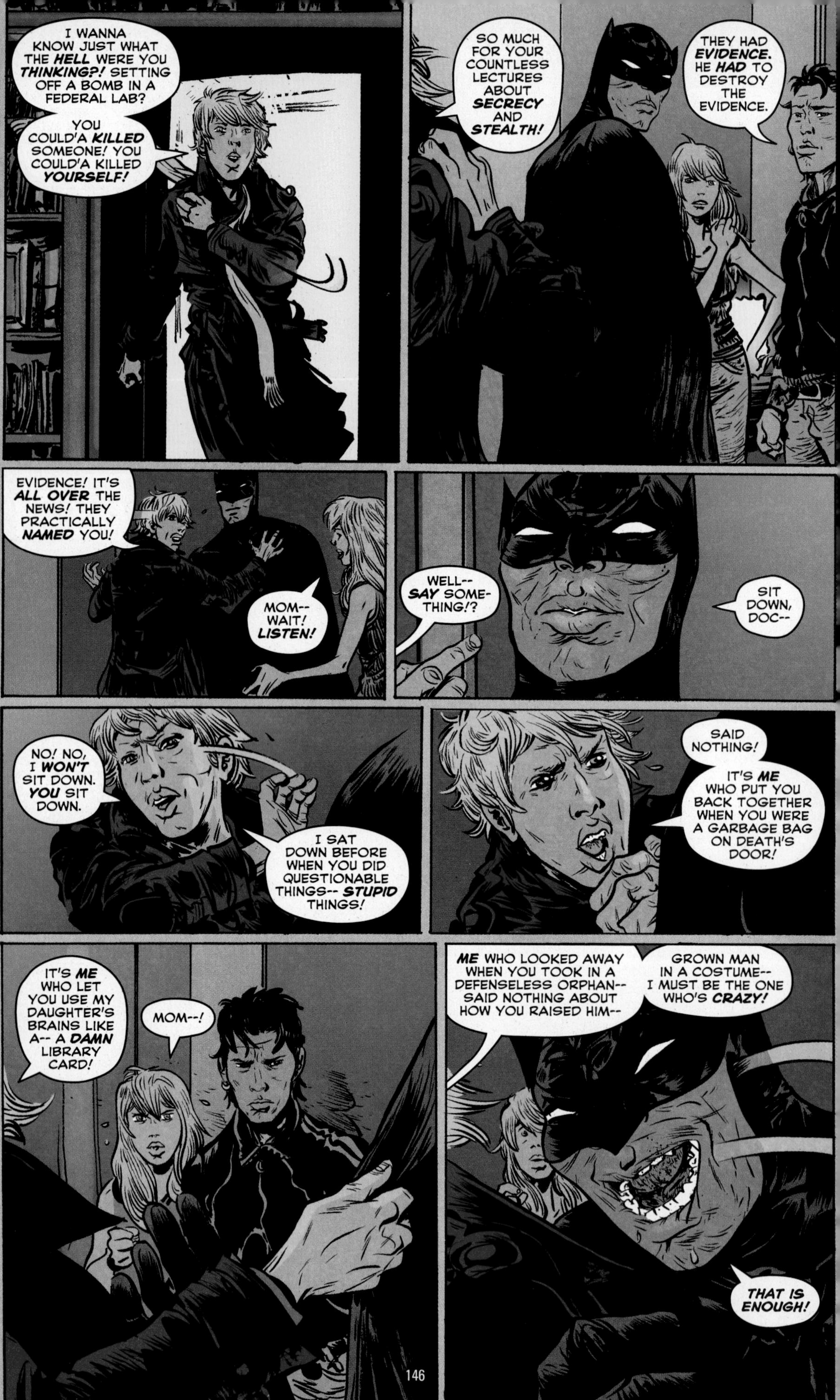

I WANNA KNOW JUST WHAT THE **HELL** WERE YOU **THINKING?!** SETTING OFF A BOMB IN A FEDERAL LAB?
YOU COULD'A **KILLED** SOMEONE! YOU COULD'A KILLED **YOURSELF!**
SO MUCH FOR YOUR COUNTLESS LECTURES ABOUT **SECRECY** AND **STEALTH!**
THEY HAD **EVIDENCE.** HE **HAD** TO DESTROY THE EVIDENCE.
EVIDENCE! IT'S **ALL OVER** THE NEWS! THEY PRACTICALLY **NAMED** YOU!
MOM-- WAIT! **LISTEN!**
WELL-- **SAY** SOME-THING!?
SIT DOWN, DOC--
NO! NO, I **WON'T** SIT DOWN. **YOU** SIT DOWN.
I SAT DOWN BEFORE WHEN YOU DID QUESTIONABLE THINGS-- **STUPID** THINGS!
SAID NOTHING!
IT'S **ME** WHO PUT YOU BACK TOGETHER WHEN YOU WERE A GARBAGE BAG ON DEATH'S DOOR!
IT'S **ME** WHO LET YOU USE MY DAUGHTER'S BRAINS LIKE A-- A **DAMN** LIBRARY CARD!
MOM--!
ME WHO LOOKED AWAY WHEN YOU TOOK IN A DEFENSELESS ORPHAN-- SAID NOTHING ABOUT HOW YOU RAISED HIM--
GROWN MAN IN A COSTUME-- I MUST BE THE ONE WHO'S **CRAZY!**
THAT IS ENOUGH!

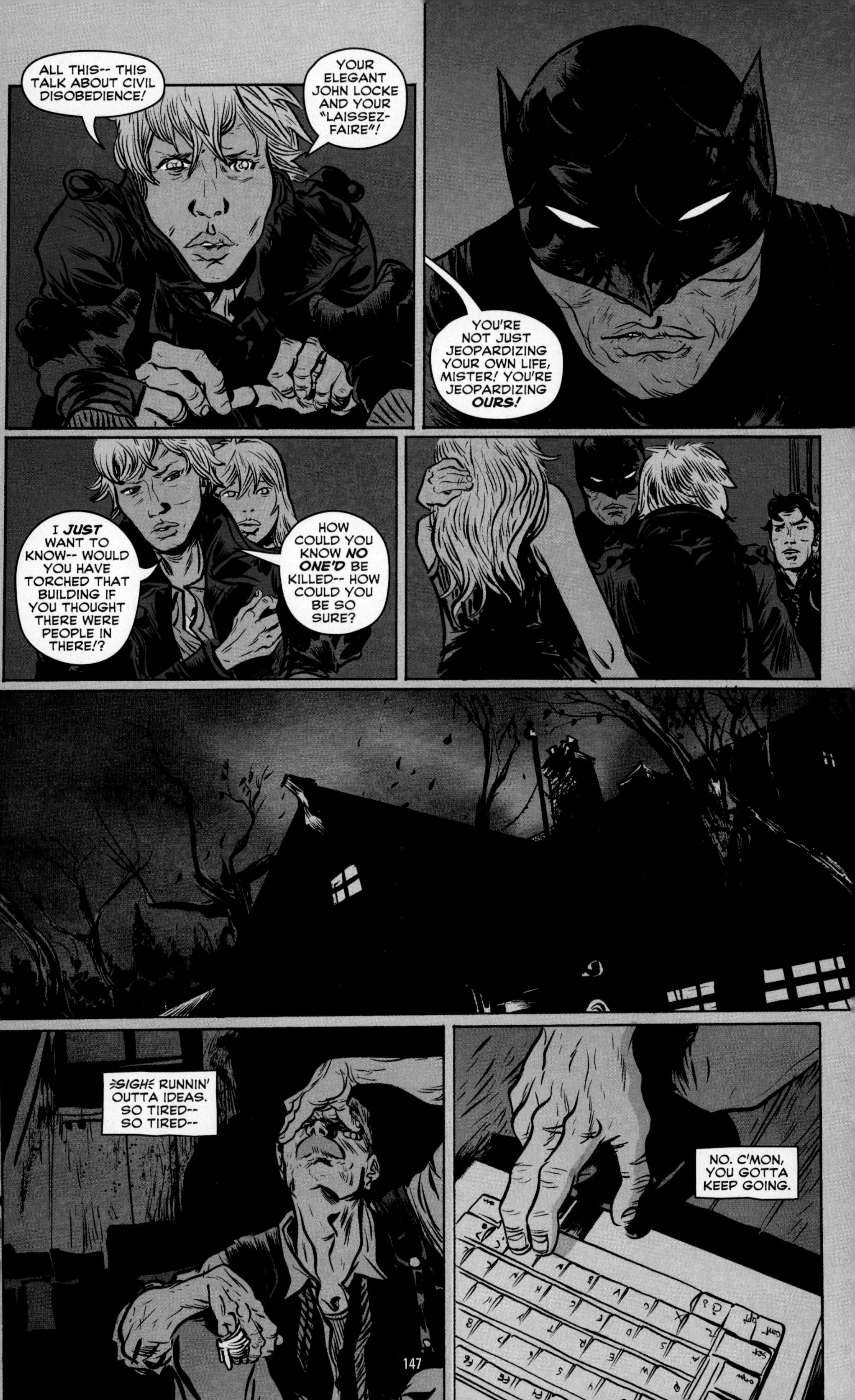
ALL THIS-- THIS TALK ABOUT CIVIL DISOBEDIENCE!
YOUR ELEGANT JOHN LOCKE AND YOUR "LAISSEZ-FAIRE"!
YOU'RE NOT JUST JEOPARDIZING YOUR OWN LIFE, MISTER! YOU'RE JEOPARDIZING OURS!
I JUST WANT TO KNOW-- WOULD YOU HAVE TORCHED THAT BUILDING IF YOU THOUGHT THERE WERE PEOPLE IN THERE!?
HOW COULD YOU KNOW NO ONE'D BE KILLED-- HOW COULD YOU BE SO SURE?
SIGH RUNNIN' OUTTA IDEAS. SO TIRED-- SO TIRED--
NO. C'MON, YOU GOTTA KEEP GOING.

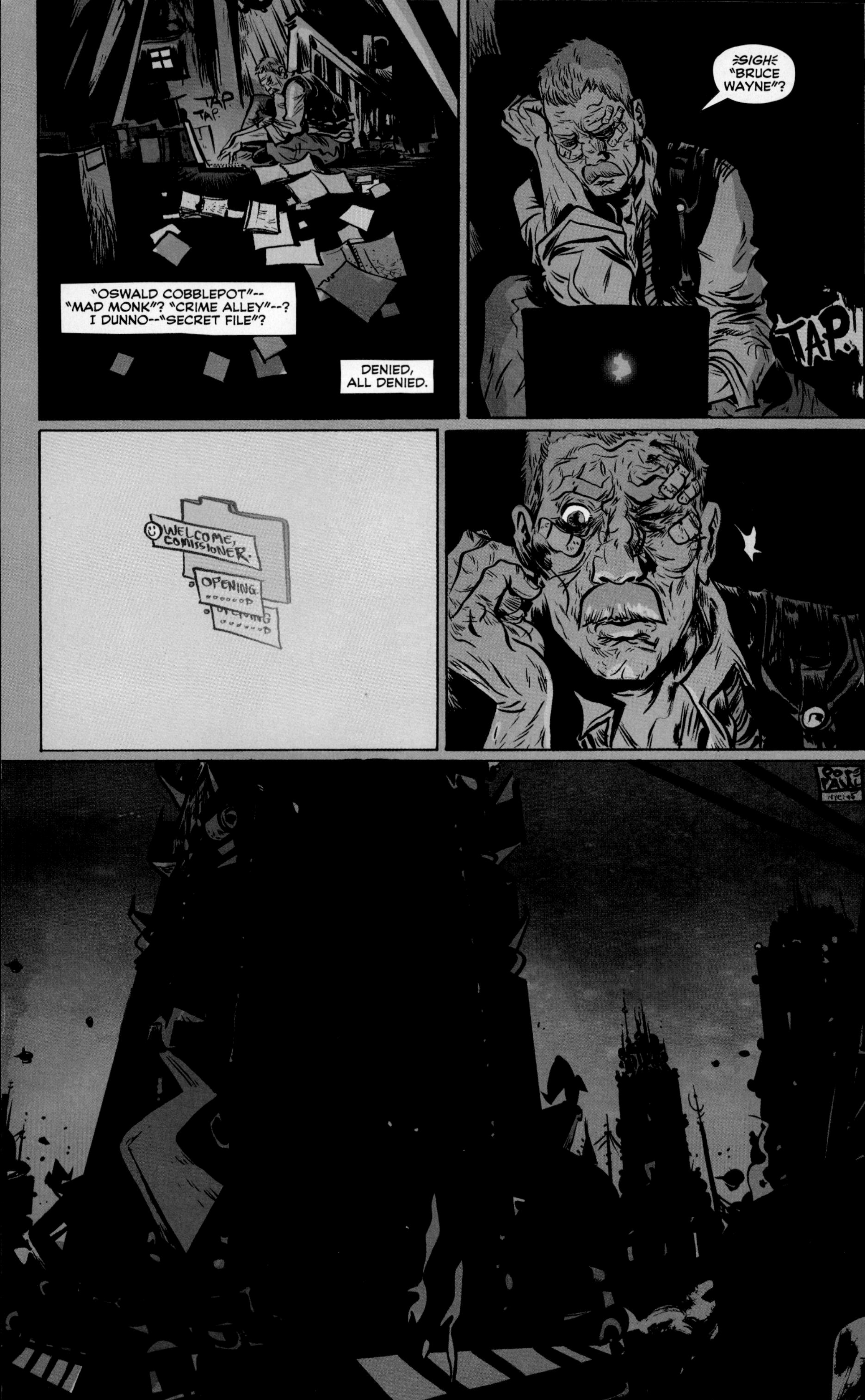
TAP TAP.
"OSWALD COBBLEPOT"-- "MAD MONK"? "CRIME ALLEY"--? I DUNNO--"SECRET FILE"?
DENIED, ALL DENIED.
SIGH "BRUCE WAYNE"?
TAP.
WELCOME, COMISSIONER.
OPENING.

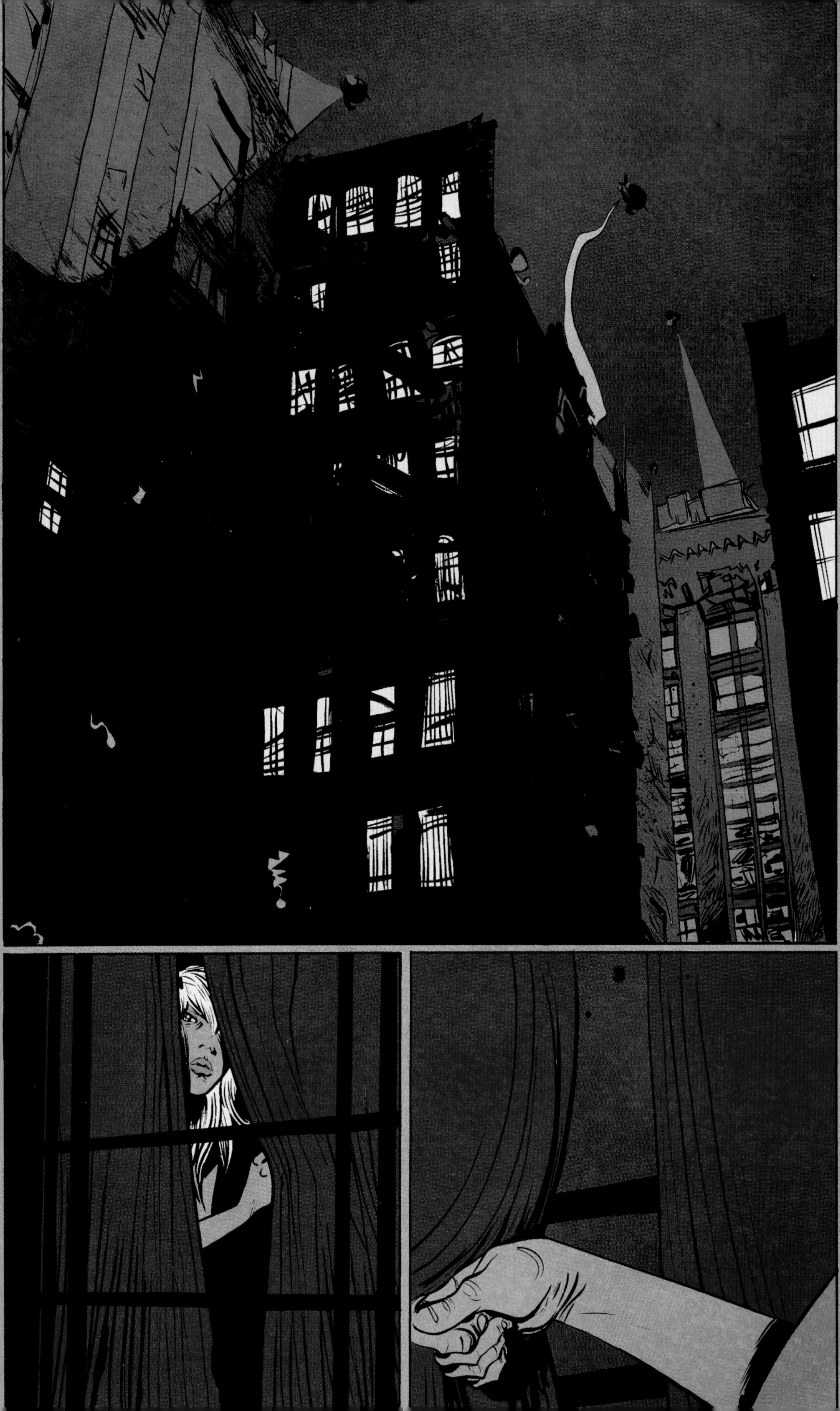

DOC, I KNOW IT'S HARD TO BELIEVE-- BUT YOU HAVE TO BELIEVE ME.

LET IT SINK IN.

BUT-- BUT WHERE'S IT FROM? WHOSE IS IT? *"FLESHKILLER..."*

WHO'D EVER MAKE SUCH A THING?

THOSE ARE THE THINGS WE *DON'T* KNOW. I'M NOT EVEN SO SURE THE COURIER KNEW...

...THOSE WEAPONS PLANS WERE IN CHINESE.

...*AND* LOCKED WITH A CYPHER.

"COURIER"-- YOU MEAN THE DEAD MAN. WASN'T HE A FED?

HE WAS A PLANT POSING AS ONE-- OR HE WAS A DOUBLE AGENT. HE MAY BE ONE OF MANY.

WHOEVER HE WAS, HE WAS KILLED BY THE F.P.C....

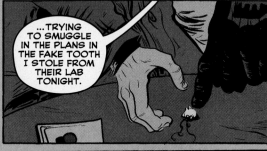

...TRYING TO SMUGGLE IN THE PLANS IN THE FAKE TOOTH I STOLE FROM THEIR LAB TONIGHT.

SMUGGLED? BUT--

IT'S A CONJECTURE BUT IT FITS. I DON'T THINK WE'RE DEALING WITH A LAUGHING SOCIOPATH IN PANCAKE MAKE-UP THIS TIME.

THIS IS STARTING TO LOOK LIKE A FULL-OUT MILITARY COUP.

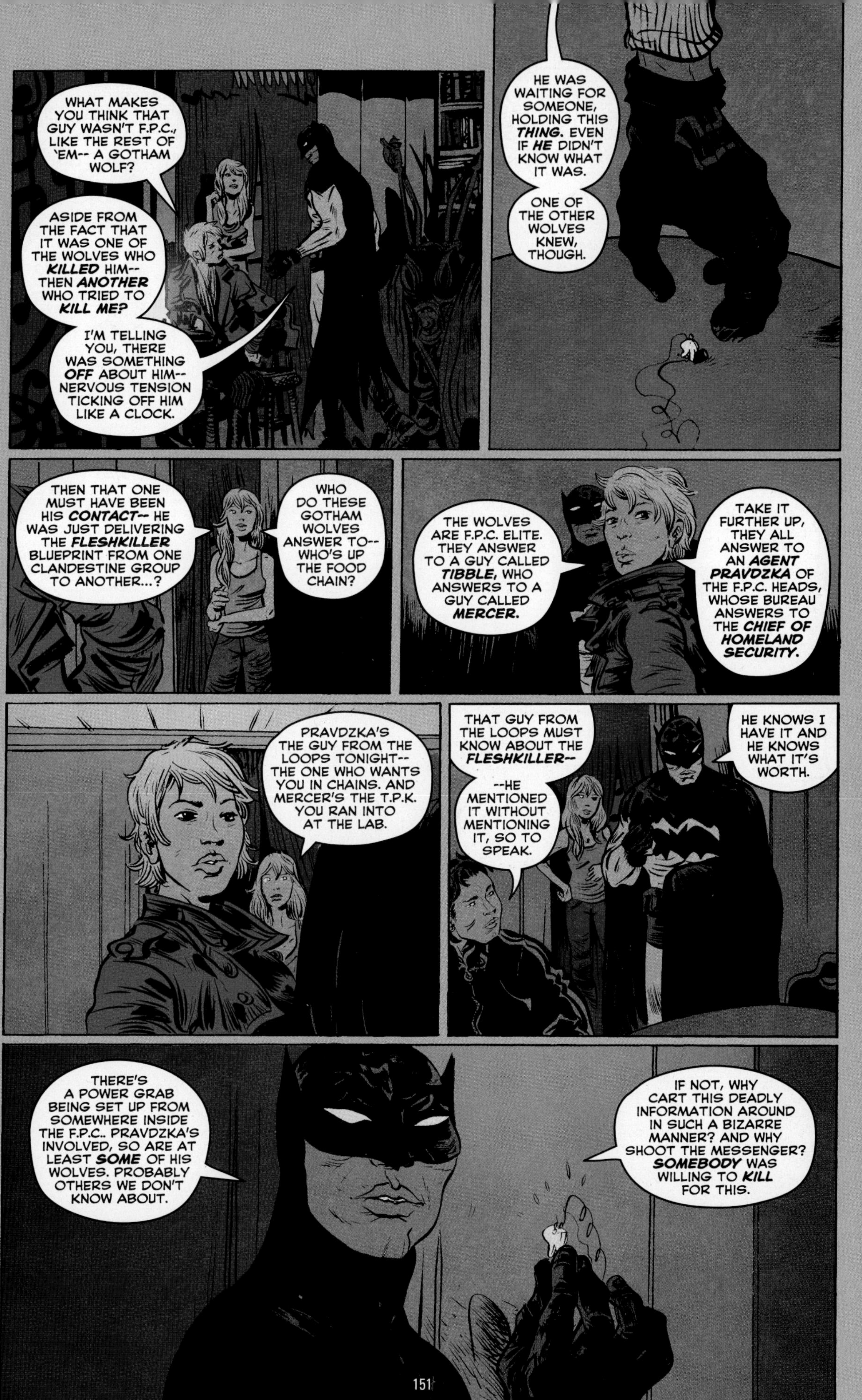
WHAT MAKES YOU THINK THAT GUY WASN'T F.P.C., LIKE THE REST OF 'EM-- A GOTHAM WOLF?
ASIDE FROM THE FACT THAT IT WAS ONE OF THE WOLVES WHO KILLED HIM-- THEN ANOTHER WHO TRIED TO KILL ME?
I'M TELLING YOU, THERE WAS SOMETHING OFF ABOUT HIM-- NERVOUS TENSION TICKING OFF HIM LIKE A CLOCK.
HE WAS WAITING FOR SOMEONE, HOLDING THIS THING. EVEN IF HE DIDN'T KNOW WHAT IT WAS.
ONE OF THE OTHER WOLVES KNEW, THOUGH.
THEN THAT ONE MUST HAVE BEEN HIS CONTACT-- HE WAS JUST DELIVERING THE FLESHKILLER BLUEPRINT FROM ONE CLANDESTINE GROUP TO ANOTHER...?
WHO DO THESE GOTHAM WOLVES ANSWER TO-- WHO'S UP THE FOOD CHAIN?
THE WOLVES ARE F.P.C. ELITE. THEY ANSWER TO A GUY CALLED TIBBLE, WHO ANSWERS TO A GUY CALLED MERCER.
TAKE IT FURTHER UP, THEY ALL ANSWER TO AN AGENT PRAVDZKA OF THE F.P.C. HEADS, WHOSE BUREAU ANSWERS TO THE CHIEF OF HOMELAND SECURITY.
PRAVDZKA'S THE GUY FROM THE LOOPS TONIGHT-- THE ONE WHO WANTS YOU IN CHAINS. AND MERCER'S THE T.P.K. YOU RAN INTO AT THE LAB.
THAT GUY FROM THE LOOPS MUST KNOW ABOUT THE FLESHKILLER--
--HE MENTIONED IT WITHOUT MENTIONING IT, SO TO SPEAK.
HE KNOWS I HAVE IT AND HE KNOWS WHAT IT'S WORTH.
THERE'S A POWER GRAB BEING SET UP FROM SOMEWHERE INSIDE THE F.P.C.. PRAVDZKA'S INVOLVED, SO ARE AT LEAST SOME OF HIS WOLVES. PROBABLY OTHERS WE DON'T KNOW ABOUT.
IF NOT, WHY CART THIS DEADLY INFORMATION AROUND IN SUCH A BIZARRE MANNER? AND WHY SHOOT THE MESSENGER? SOMEBODY WAS WILLING TO KILL FOR THIS.

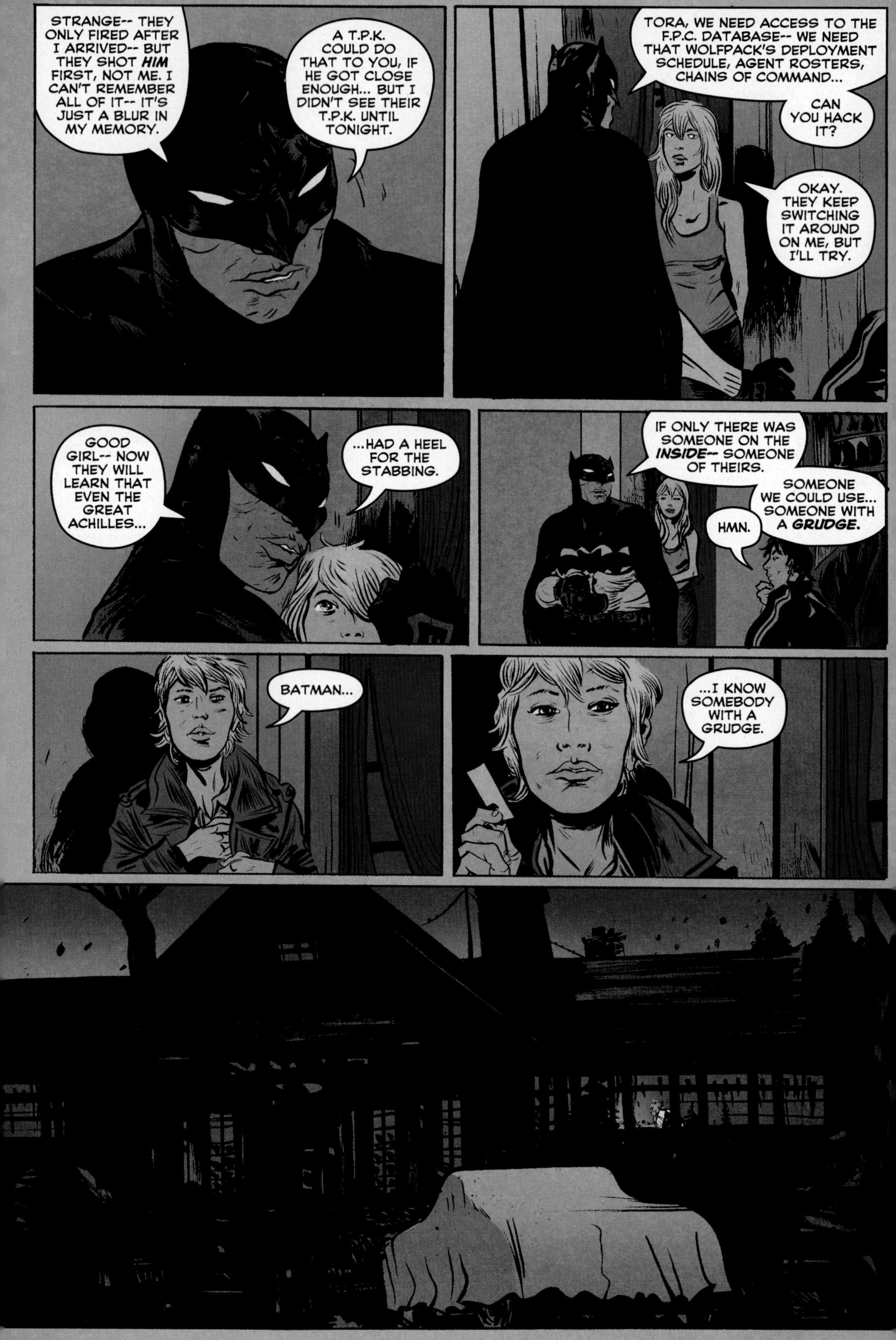
STRANGE-- THEY ONLY FIRED AFTER I ARRIVED-- BUT THEY SHOT HIM FIRST, NOT ME. I CAN'T REMEMBER ALL OF IT-- IT'S JUST A BLUR IN MY MEMORY.
A T.P.K. COULD DO THAT TO YOU, IF HE GOT CLOSE ENOUGH... BUT I DIDN'T SEE THEIR T.P.K. UNTIL TONIGHT.
TORA, WE NEED ACCESS TO THE F.P.C. DATABASE-- WE NEED THAT WOLFPACK'S DEPLOYMENT SCHEDULE, AGENT ROSTERS, CHAINS OF COMMAND...
CAN YOU HACK IT?
OKAY. THEY KEEP SWITCHING IT AROUND ON ME, BUT I'LL TRY.
GOOD GIRL-- NOW THEY WILL LEARN THAT EVEN THE GREAT ACHILLES...
...HAD A HEEL FOR THE STABBING.
IF ONLY THERE WAS SOMEONE ON THE INSIDE-- SOMEONE OF THEIRS.
SOMEONE WE COULD USE... SOMEONE WITH A GRUDGE.
HMN.
BATMAN...
...I KNOW SOMEBODY WITH A GRUDGE.

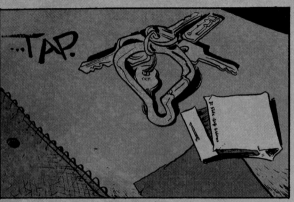

...TAP.

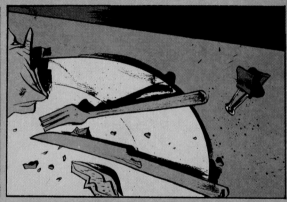

TAP...

TAP.
TAP.

INCREDIBLE-- ONE HUNDRED YEARS OF HISTORY, ALL THE **SECRETS** HE'S MANAGED TO KEEP UNDER THAT MASK ALL THIS TIME. IT'S ALL RIGHT HERE.

THE G.C.P.D.'S **REAL** BATMAN FILE. IT WAS HERE ALL THIS TIME.

BEEP. BEEP. BEEP.

YEAH?

GORDON, IT'S TIBBLE. HOW YA DOIN', OLD BUDDY? WHERE ARE YA? IN THE COUNTRY?

AAH. NO, I'M IN *YOUR* OFFICE. COMFORTABLE CHAIR YA HAVE HERE. HELPED MYSELF TO ONE OF YOUR *CASTROS*.

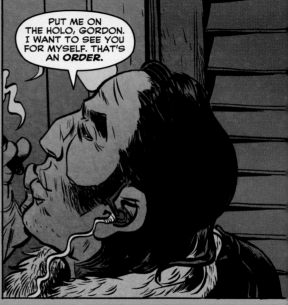

PUT ME ON THE HOLO, GORDON. I WANT TO SEE YOU FOR MYSELF. THAT'S AN *ORDER*.

≥GRUMBLE≥

JUST MAKE SURE YOU CLOSE THE LID TO THE HUMIDOR. THOSE THINGS GO STALE IF YOU LET 'EM.

CLICK

WELL, WHAT DO YOU WANT? IT'S LATE.

WHY, GORDON. YOU LOOK A WRECK. WHATEVER HAPPENED TO YOU?

I FELL DOWN SOME STAIRS. WHAT DO YOU THINK HAPPENED TO ME?

NOTHING, THAT'S WHAT I *THOUGHT* HAPPENED. REGRETTABLE...

...*SO*, TELL ME, GORDON. YOU HAVE THE FULL BATMAN FILE BY NOW?

SURE.

HAVE IT ON YOU?

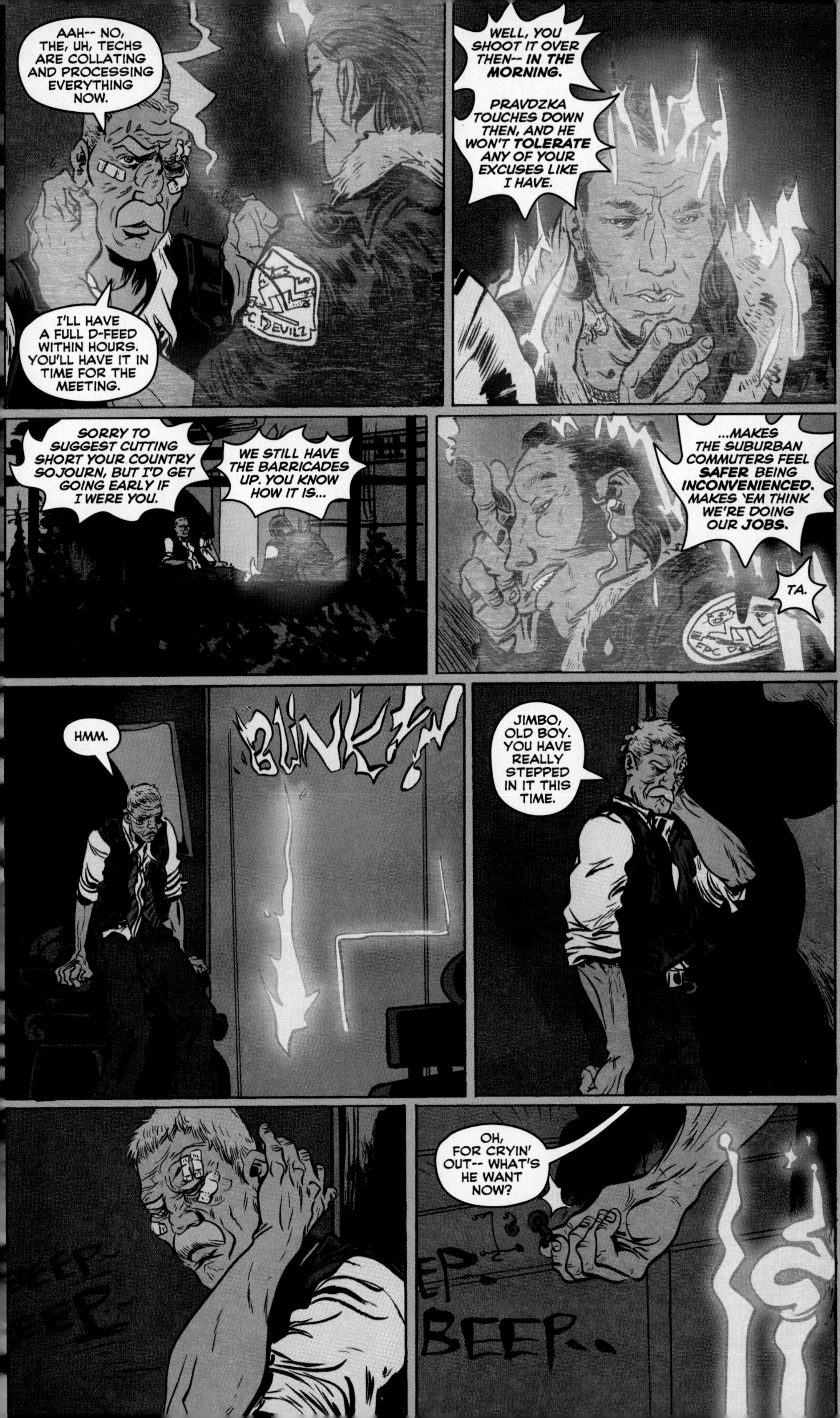
AAH-- NO, THE, UH, TECHS ARE COLLATING AND PROCESSING EVERYTHING NOW.
I'LL HAVE A FULL D-FEED WITHIN HOURS. YOU'LL HAVE IT IN TIME FOR THE MEETING.
FPC DEVILZ
WELL, YOU SHOOT IT OVER THEN-- IN THE MORNING.
PRAVDZKA TOUCHES DOWN THEN, AND HE WON'T TOLERATE ANY OF YOUR EXCUSES LIKE I HAVE.
SORRY TO SUGGEST CUTTING SHORT YOUR COUNTRY SOJOURN, BUT I'D GET GOING EARLY IF I WERE YOU.
WE STILL HAVE THE BARRICADES UP. YOU KNOW HOW IT IS...
...MAKES THE SUBURBAN COMMUTERS FEEL SAFER BEING INCONVENIENCED. MAKES 'EM THINK WE'RE DOING OUR JOBS.
TA.
HMM.
BLINK!
JIMBO, OLD BOY. YOU HAVE REALLY STEPPED IN IT THIS TIME.
BEEP-
BEEP-
OH, FOR CRYIN' OUT-- WHAT'S HE WANT NOW?
BEEP--

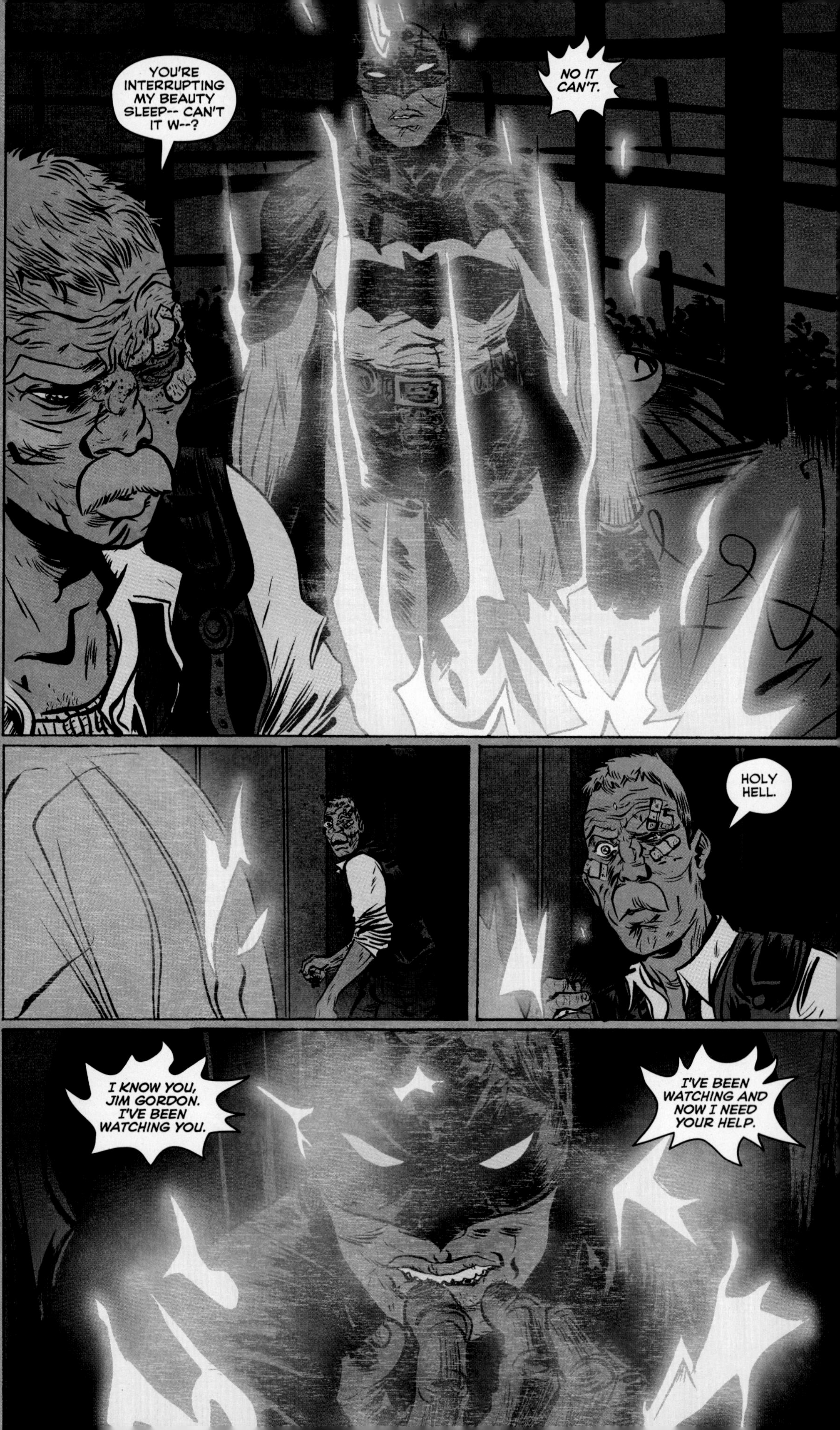
YOU'RE INTERRUPTING MY BEAUTY SLEEP-- CAN'T IT W--?
NO IT CAN'T.
HOLY HELL.
I KNOW YOU, JIM GORDON. I'VE BEEN WATCHING YOU.
I'VE BEEN WATCHING AND NOW I NEED YOUR HELP.

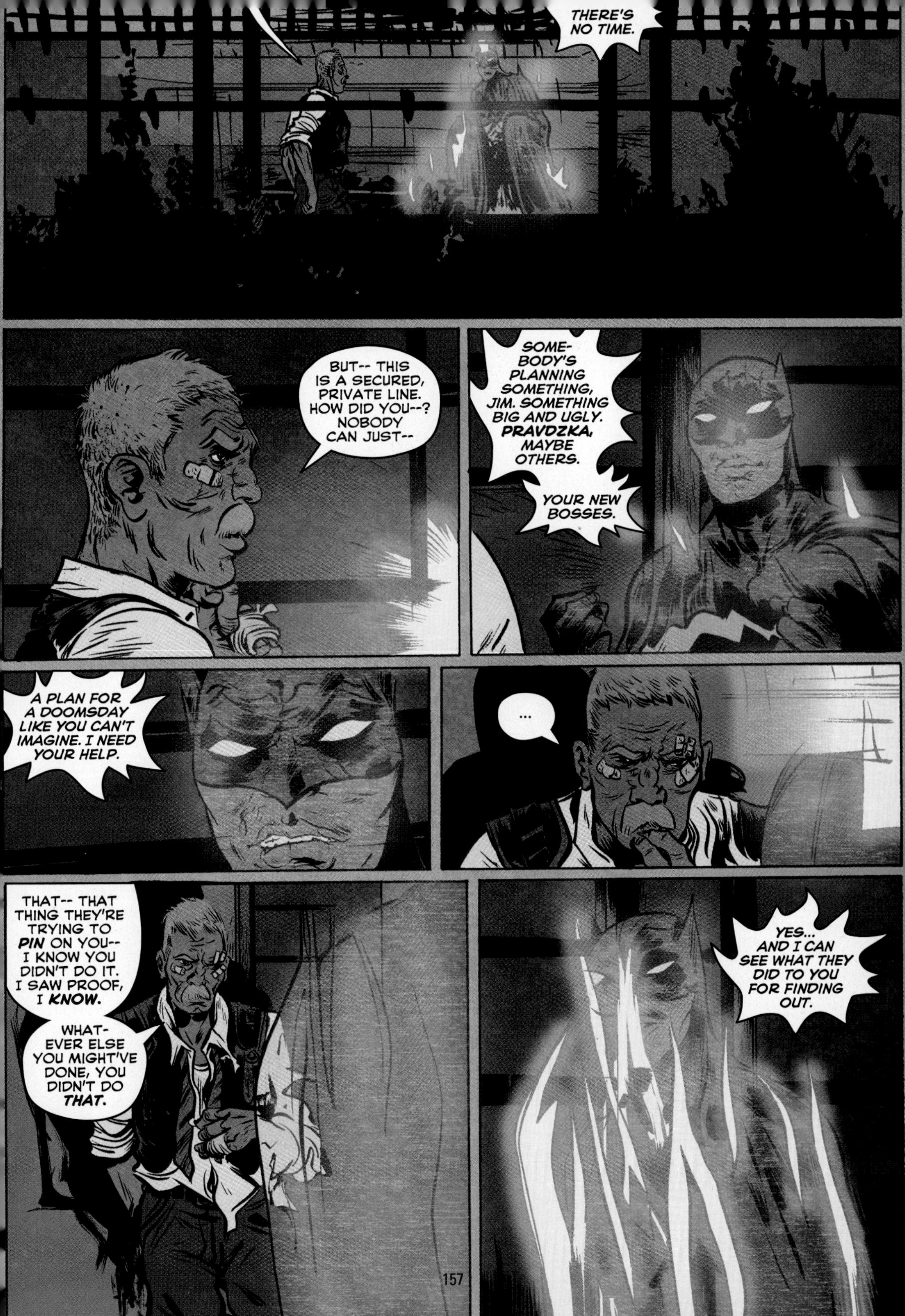

THERE'S NO TIME.
BUT-- THIS IS A SECURED, PRIVATE LINE. HOW DID YOU--? NOBODY CAN JUST--
SOME-BODY'S PLANNING SOMETHING, JIM. SOMETHING BIG AND UGLY. PRAVDZKA, MAYBE OTHERS.
YOUR NEW BOSSES.
A PLAN FOR A DOOMSDAY LIKE YOU CAN'T IMAGINE. I NEED YOUR HELP.
...
THAT-- THAT THING THEY'RE TRYING TO PIN ON YOU-- I KNOW YOU DIDN'T DO IT. I SAW PROOF, I KNOW.
WHAT-EVER ELSE YOU MIGHT'VE DONE, YOU DIDN'T DO THAT.
YES... AND I CAN SEE WHAT THEY DID TO YOU FOR FINDING OUT.

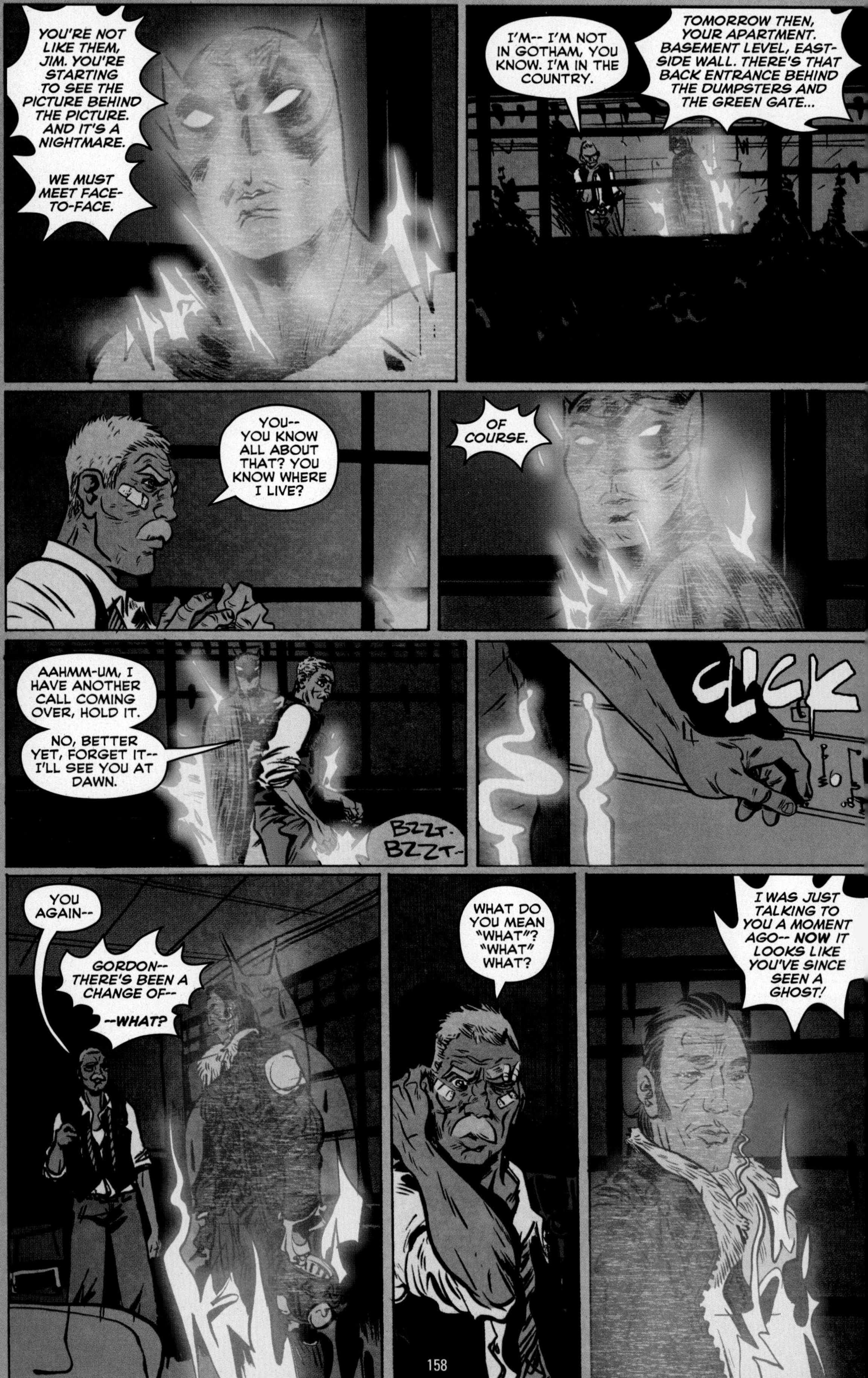
YOU'RE NOT LIKE THEM, JIM. YOU'RE STARTING TO SEE THE PICTURE BEHIND THE PICTURE. AND IT'S A NIGHTMARE.
WE MUST MEET FACE-TO-FACE.
I'M-- I'M NOT IN GOTHAM, YOU KNOW. I'M IN THE COUNTRY.
TOMORROW THEN, YOUR APARTMENT. BASEMENT LEVEL, EAST-SIDE WALL. THERE'S THAT BACK ENTRANCE BEHIND THE DUMPSTERS AND THE GREEN GATE...
YOU-- YOU KNOW ALL ABOUT THAT? YOU KNOW WHERE I LIVE?
OF COURSE.
AAHMM-UM, I HAVE ANOTHER CALL COMING OVER, HOLD IT.
NO, BETTER YET, FORGET IT-- I'LL SEE YOU AT DAWN.
BZZT. BZZT-
CLICK
YOU AGAIN--
GORDON-- THERE'S BEEN A CHANGE OF--
--WHAT?
WHAT DO YOU MEAN "WHAT"? "WHAT" WHAT?
I WAS JUST TALKING TO YOU A MOMENT AGO-- NOW IT LOOKS LIKE YOU'VE SINCE SEEN A GHOST!

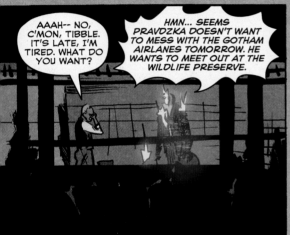

AAAH-- NO, C'MON, TIBBLE. IT'S LATE, I'M TIRED. WHAT DO YOU WANT?

HMN... SEEMS PRAVDZKA DOESN'T WANT TO MESS WITH THE GOTHAM AIRLANES TOMORROW. HE WANTS TO MEET OUT AT THE WILDLIFE PRESERVE.

THERE'S AN OLD HUNTING LODGE OUT THERE-- YOU KNOW IT?

YEAH, I KNOW THAT PLACE.

GOOD-- AND REMEMBER TO BRING THAT FILE. STATE PARK, DAWN. THAT'S ONLY IN A FEW HOURS.

THIS WAY IT'S EASIER FOR YOU, ANYHOW.

DON'T HAVE TO FACE THE PILE-UPS COMING BACK DURING THE MORNING RUSH. SEE YA.

...SEE YA.

WELL, CONSIDERING YOU JUST RODE HER OVER SIX MILES OF MESSED-UP SUBWAY TRACKS, BIKE'S LOOKIN' GOOD. SHE'S READY TO ROLL-- ENHANCEMENTS AND ALL.

HOW ABOUT THE OTHER ONE?

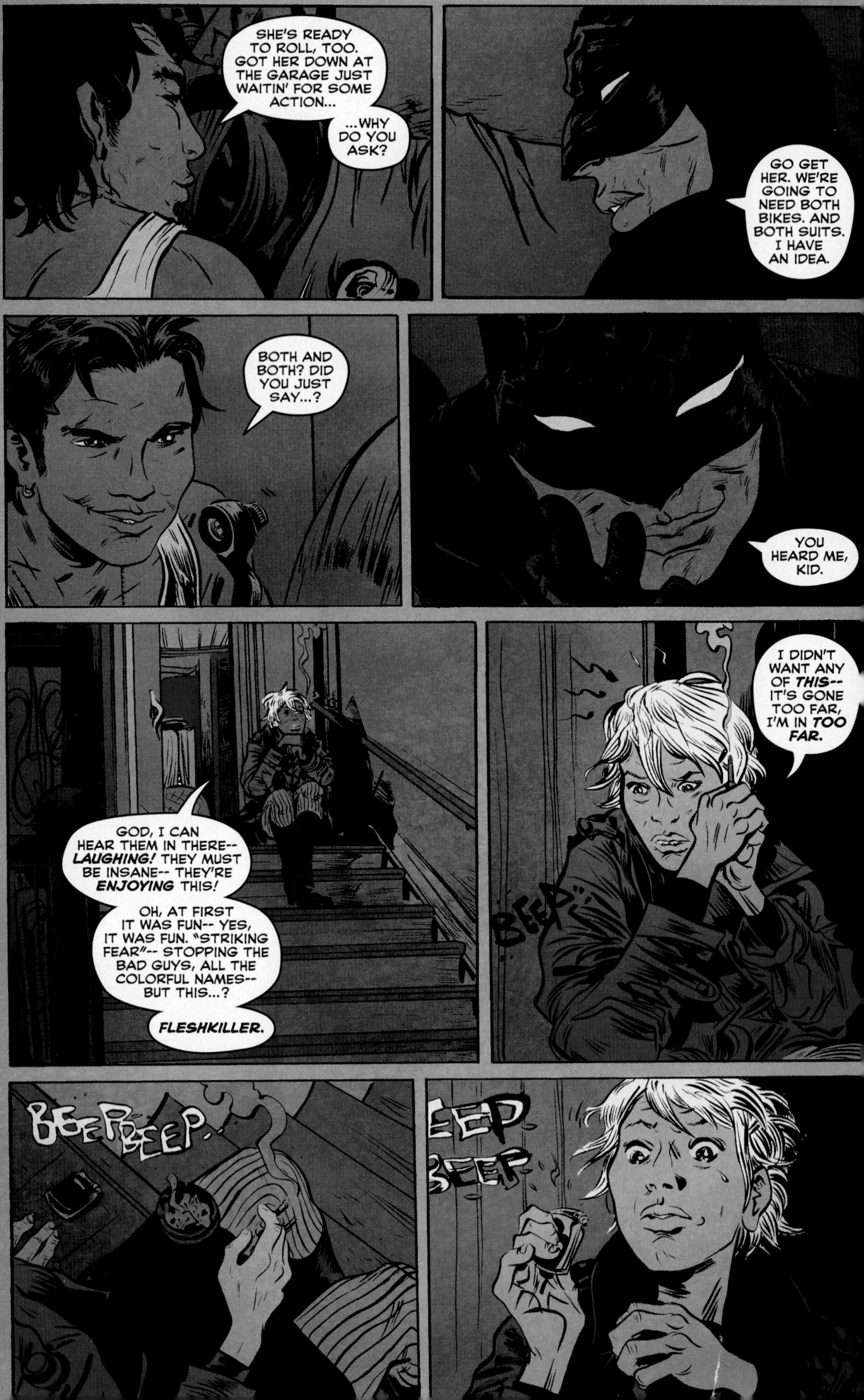
SHE'S READY TO ROLL, TOO. GOT HER DOWN AT THE GARAGE JUST WAITIN' FOR SOME ACTION...
...WHY DO YOU ASK?
GO GET HER. WE'RE GOING TO NEED BOTH BIKES. AND BOTH SUITS. I HAVE AN IDEA.
BOTH AND BOTH? DID YOU JUST SAY...?
YOU HEARD ME, KID.
GOD, I CAN HEAR THEM IN THERE-- *LAUGHING!* THEY MUST BE INSANE-- THEY'RE *ENJOYING* THIS!
OH, AT FIRST IT WAS FUN-- YES, IT WAS FUN. "STRIKING FEAR"-- STOPPING THE BAD GUYS, ALL THE COLORFUL NAMES-- BUT THIS...?
FLESHKILLER.
I DIDN'T WANT ANY OF ***THIS***-- IT'S GONE TOO FAR, I'M IN ***TOO FAR.***
BEEP...
BEEPBEEP...
EEP
BEEP

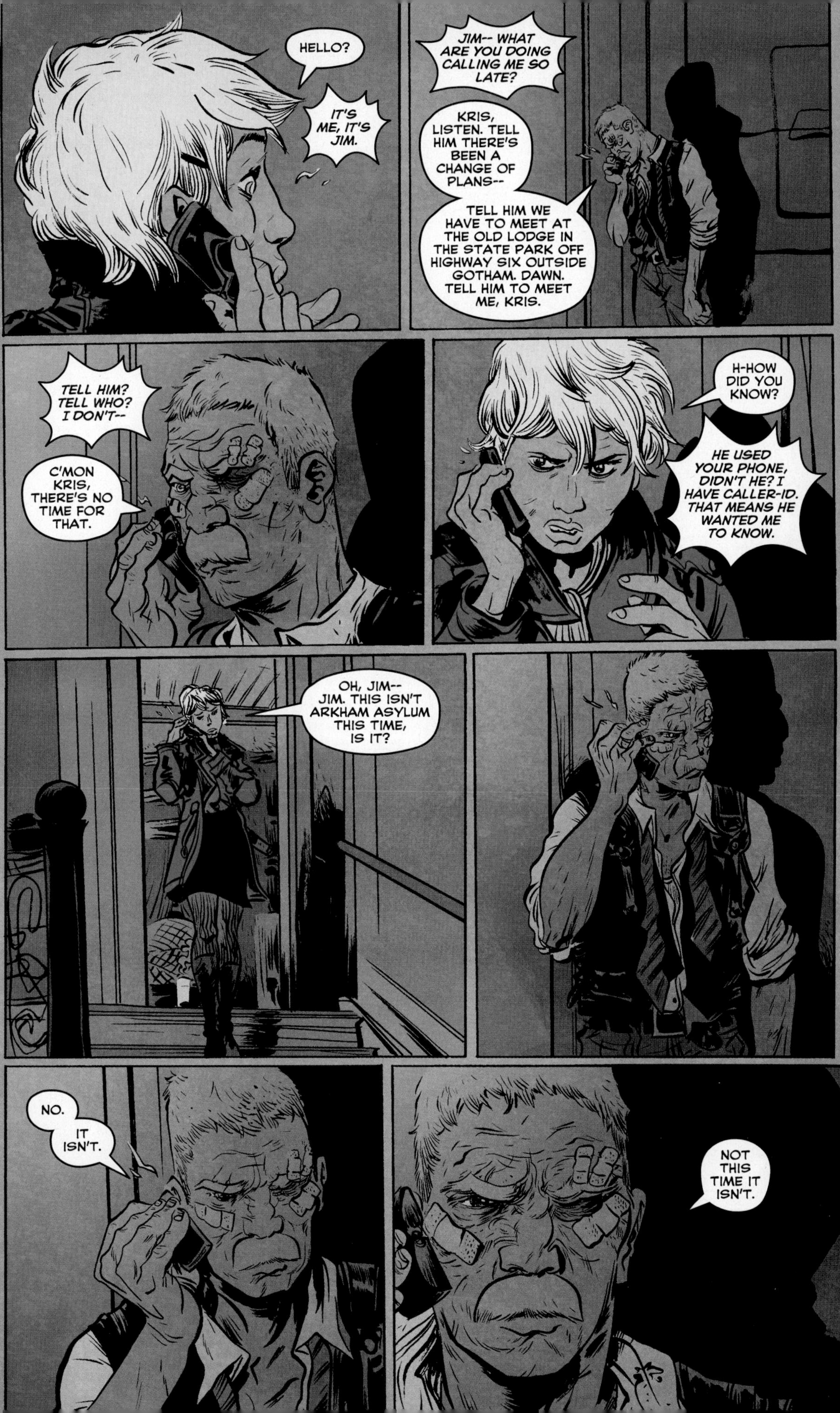
HELLO?
IT'S ME, IT'S JIM.
JIM-- WHAT ARE YOU DOING CALLING ME SO LATE?
KRIS, LISTEN. TELL HIM THERE'S BEEN A CHANGE OF PLANS--
TELL HIM WE HAVE TO MEET AT THE OLD LODGE IN THE STATE PARK OFF HIGHWAY SIX OUTSIDE GOTHAM. DAWN. TELL HIM TO MEET ME, KRIS.
TELL HIM? TELL WHO? I DON'T--
C'MON KRIS, THERE'S NO TIME FOR THAT.
H-HOW DID YOU KNOW?
HE USED YOUR PHONE, DIDN'T HE? I HAVE CALLER-ID. THAT MEANS HE WANTED ME TO KNOW.
OH, JIM-- JIM. THIS ISN'T ARKHAM ASYLUM THIS TIME, IS IT?
NO.
IT ISN'T.
NOT THIS TIME IT ISN'T.

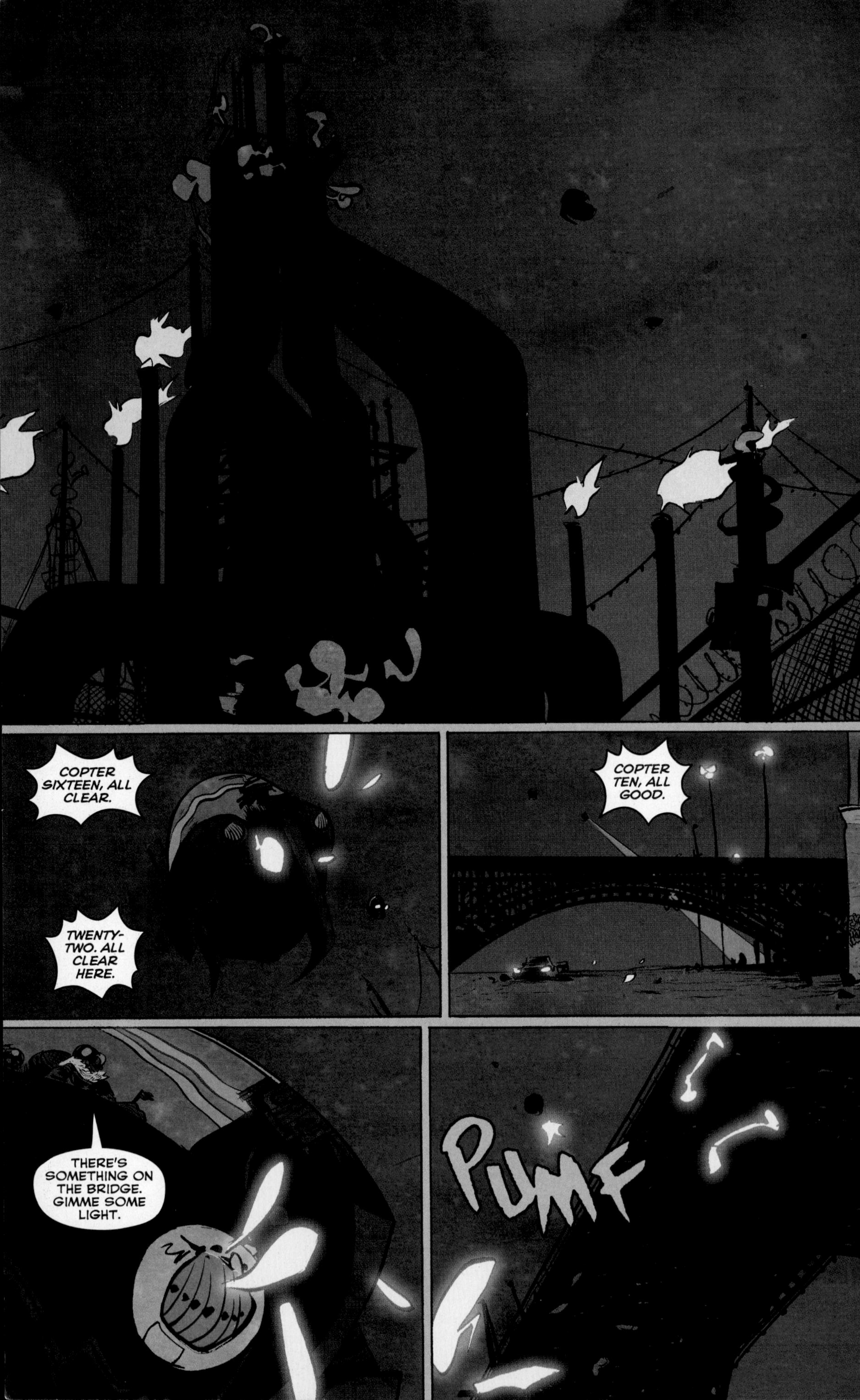
COPTER SIXTEEN, ALL CLEAR.
TWENTY-TWO. ALL CLEAR HERE.
COPTER TEN, ALL GOOD.
THERE'S SOMETHING ON THE BRIDGE. GIMME SOME LIGHT.
PUMF

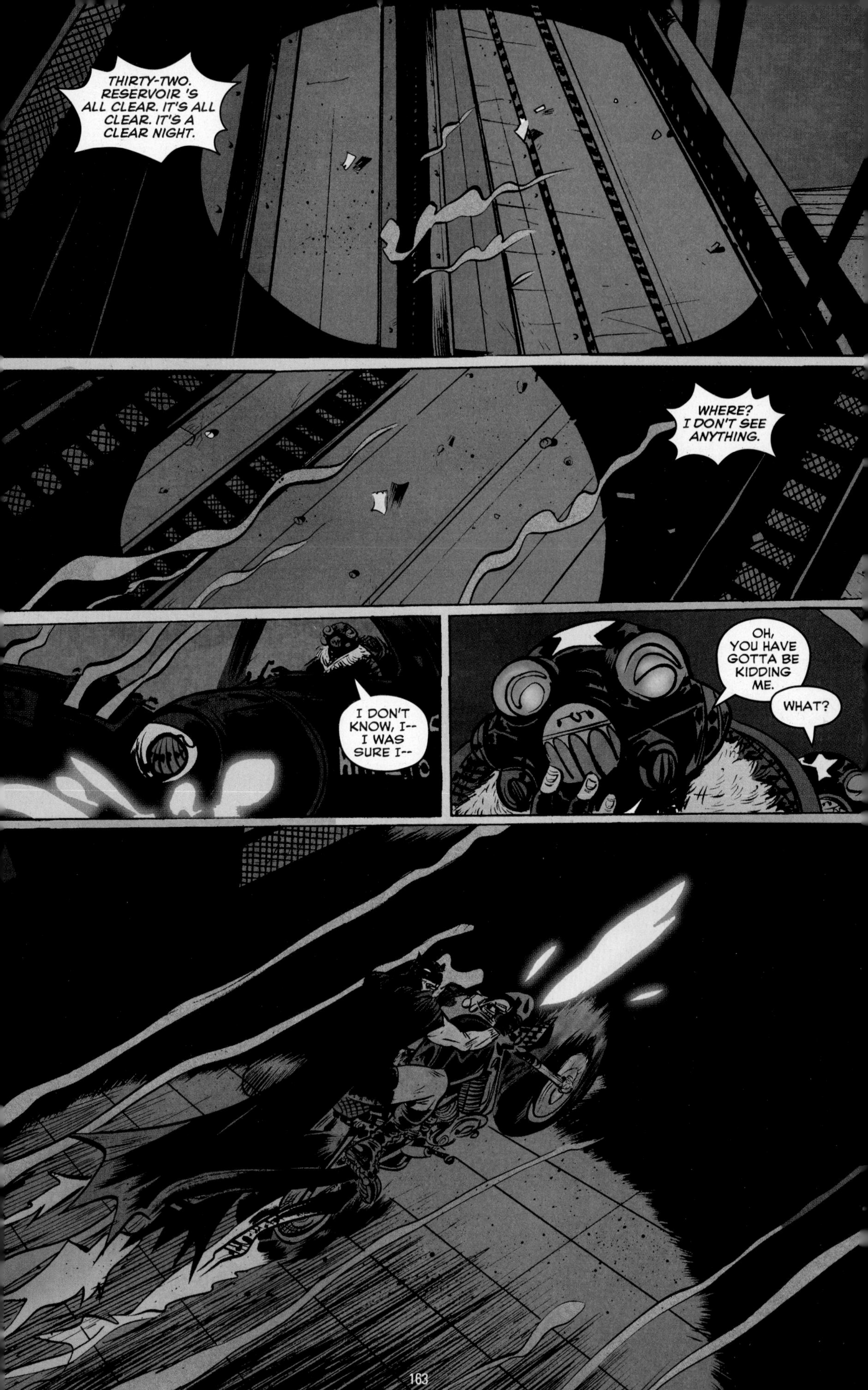
THIRTY-TWO. RESERVOIR 'S ALL CLEAR. IT'S ALL CLEAR. IT'S A CLEAR NIGHT.
WHERE? I DON'T SEE ANYTHING.
I DON'T KNOW, I-- I WAS SURE I--
OH, YOU HAVE GOTTA BE KIDDING ME.
WHAT?

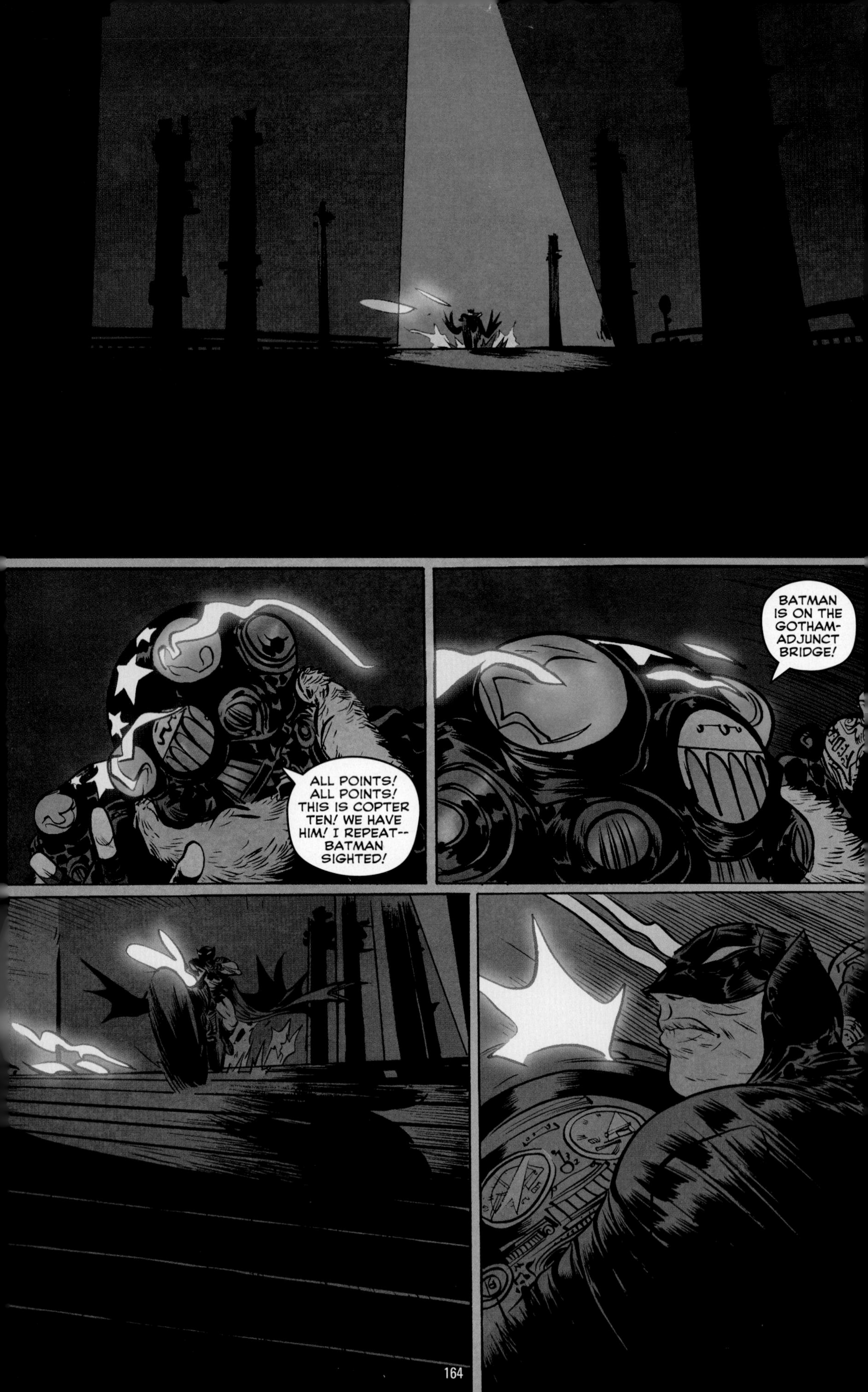
ALL POINTS! ALL POINTS! THIS IS COPTER TEN! WE HAVE HIM! I REPEAT-- BATMAN SIGHTED!
BATMAN IS ON THE GOTHAM-ADJUNCT BRIDGE!

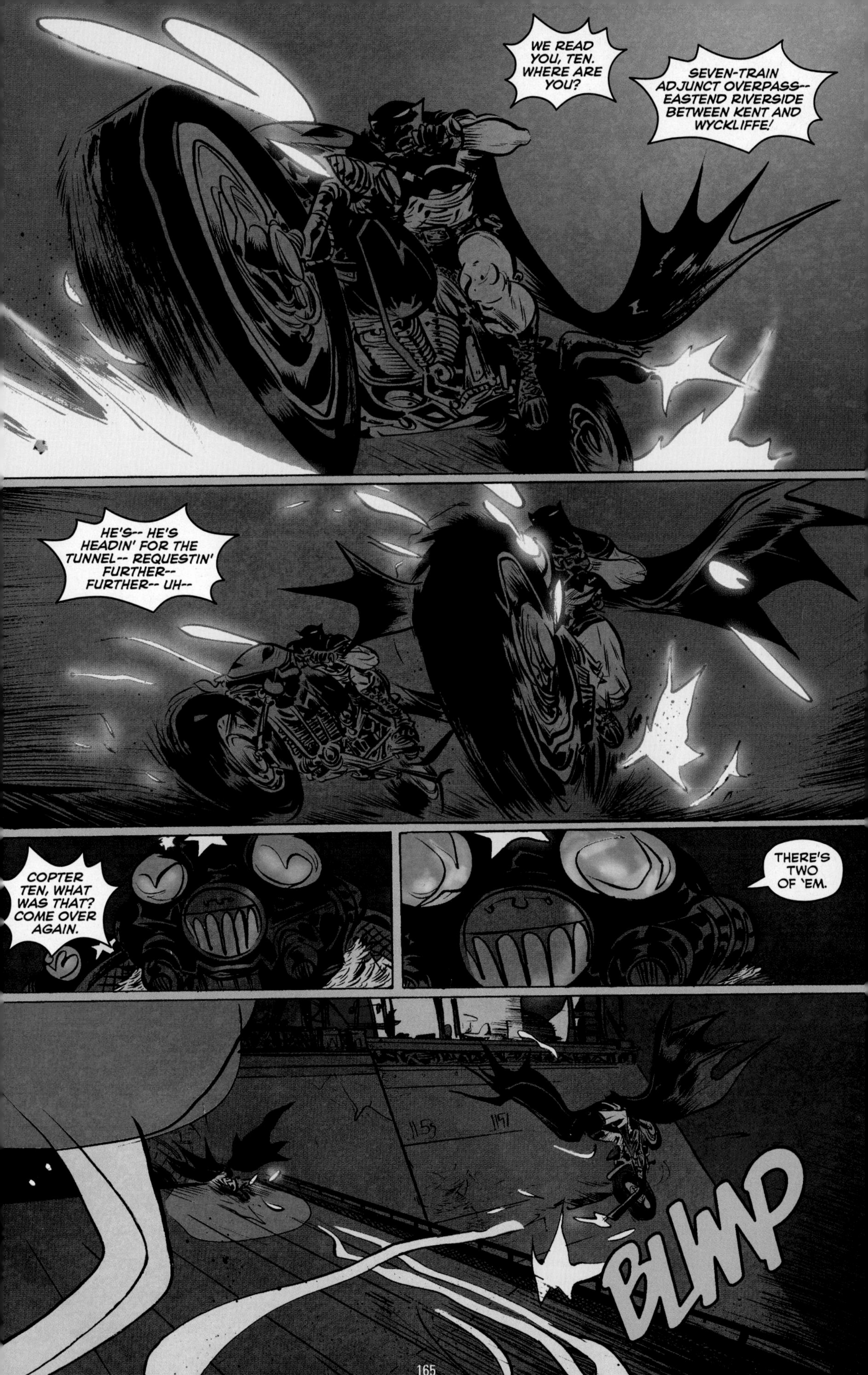
WE READ YOU, TEN. WHERE ARE YOU?
SEVEN-TRAIN ADJUNCT OVERPASS-- EASTEND RIVERSIDE BETWEEN KENT AND WYCKLIFFE!
HE'S-- HE'S HEADIN' FOR THE TUNNEL-- REQUESTIN' FURTHER-- FURTHER-- UH--
COPTER TEN, WHAT WAS THAT? COME OVER AGAIN.
THERE'S TWO OF 'EM.
BLMP

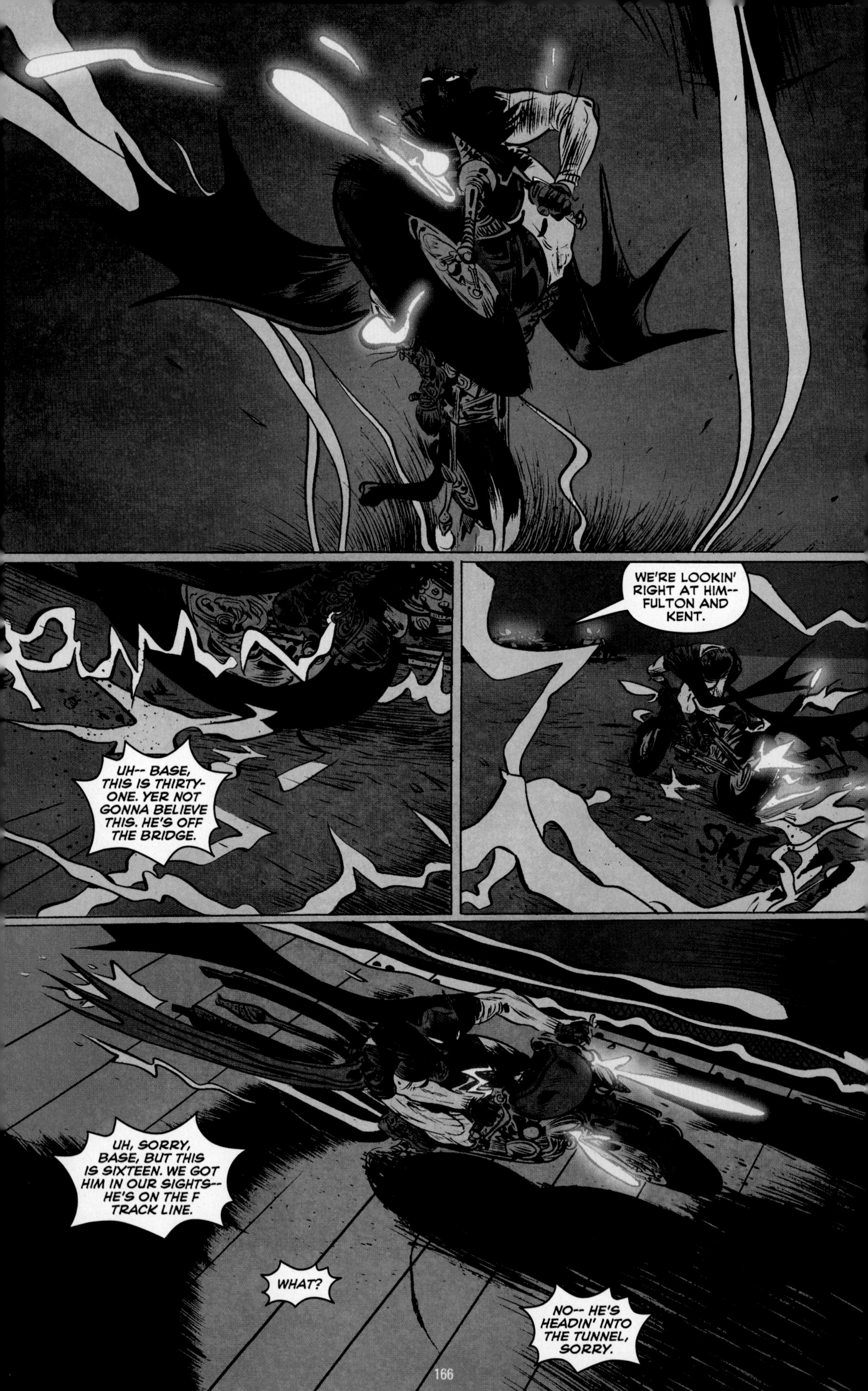
UH-- BASE, THIS IS THIRTY-ONE. YER NOT GONNA BELIEVE THIS. HE'S OFF THE BRIDGE.
WE'RE LOOKIN' RIGHT AT HIM-- FULTON AND KENT.
UH, SORRY, BASE, BUT THIS IS SIXTEEN. WE GOT HIM IN OUR SIGHTS-- HE'S ON THE F TRACK LINE.
WHAT?
NO-- HE'S HEADIN' INTO THE TUNNEL, SORRY.

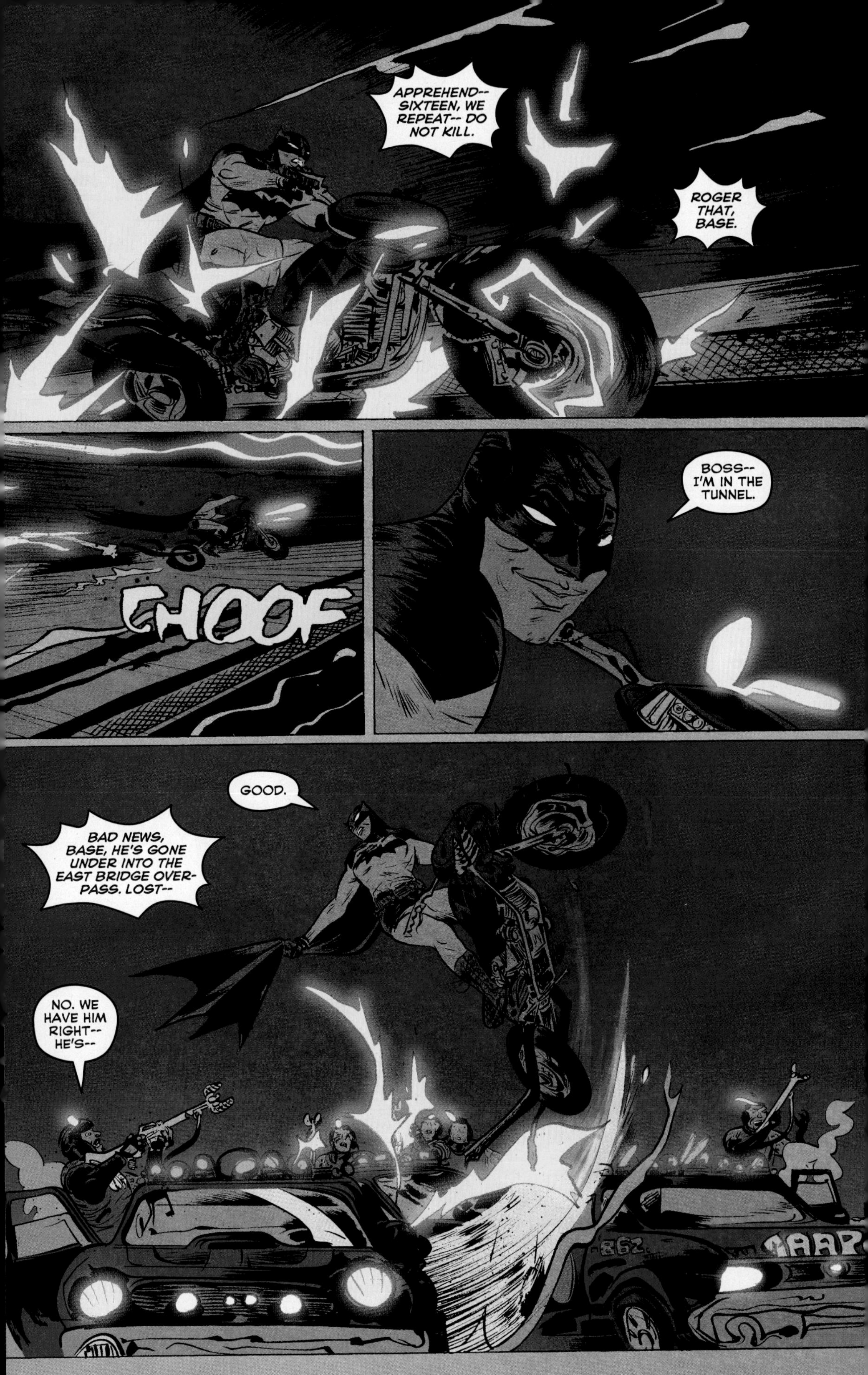
APPREHEND-- SIXTEEN, WE REPEAT-- DO NOT KILL.
ROGER THAT, BASE.
CHOOF
BOSS-- I'M IN THE TUNNEL.
GOOD.
BAD NEWS, BASE, HE'S GONE UNDER INTO THE EAST BRIDGE OVER-PASS. LOST--
NO. WE HAVE HIM RIGHT-- HE'S--

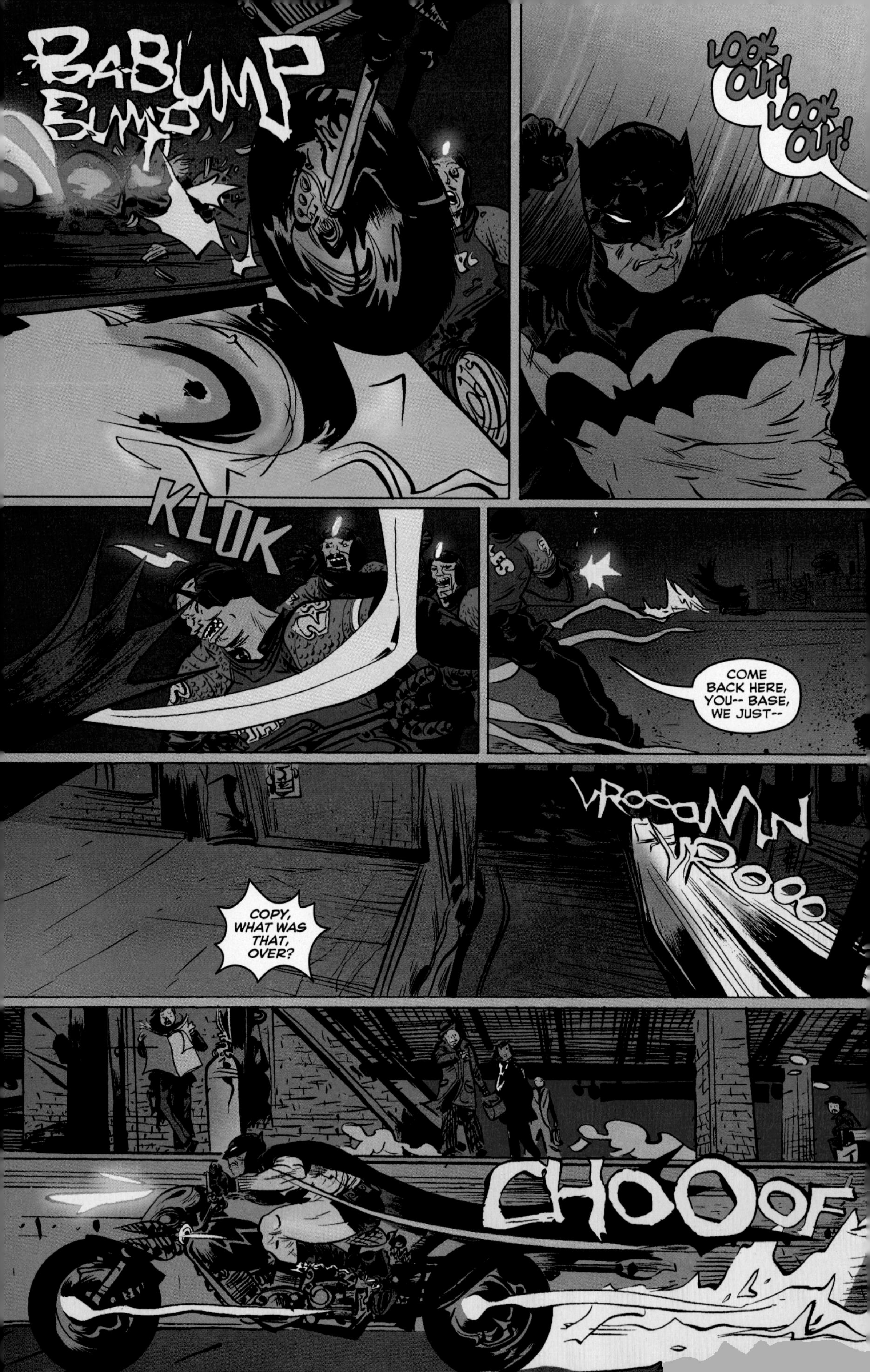
BABUMP BUMP
LOOK OUT! LOOK OUT!
KLOK
COME BACK HERE, YOU-- BASE, WE JUST--
VROOMMN
COPY, WHAT WAS THAT, OVER?
CHOOOF

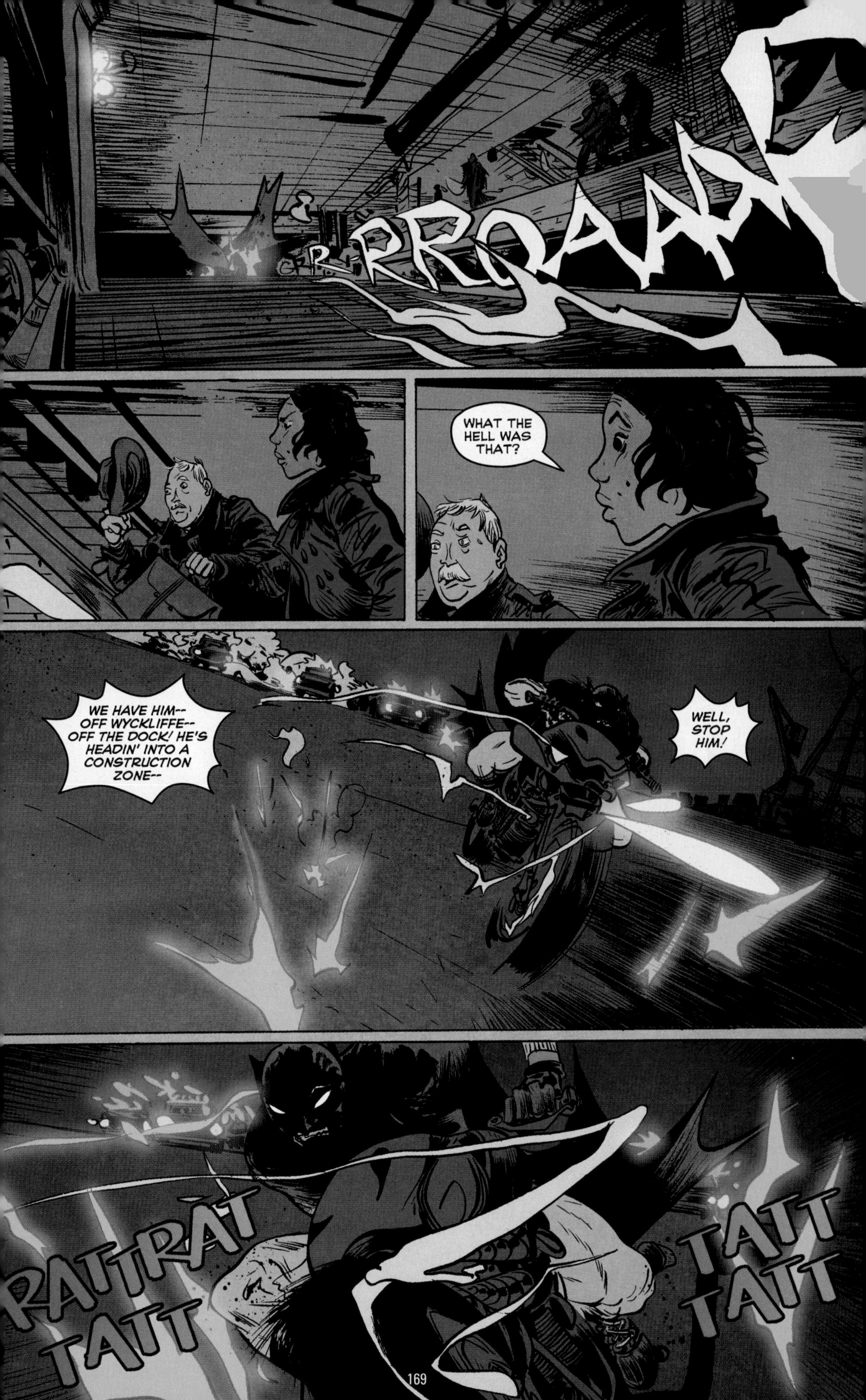
GRRRROAAAR
WHAT THE HELL WAS THAT?
WE HAVE HIM-- OFF WYCKLIFFE-- OFF THE DOCK! HE'S HEADIN' INTO A CONSTRUCTION ZONE--
WELL, STOP HIM!
RATTRAT TATT
TATT TATT

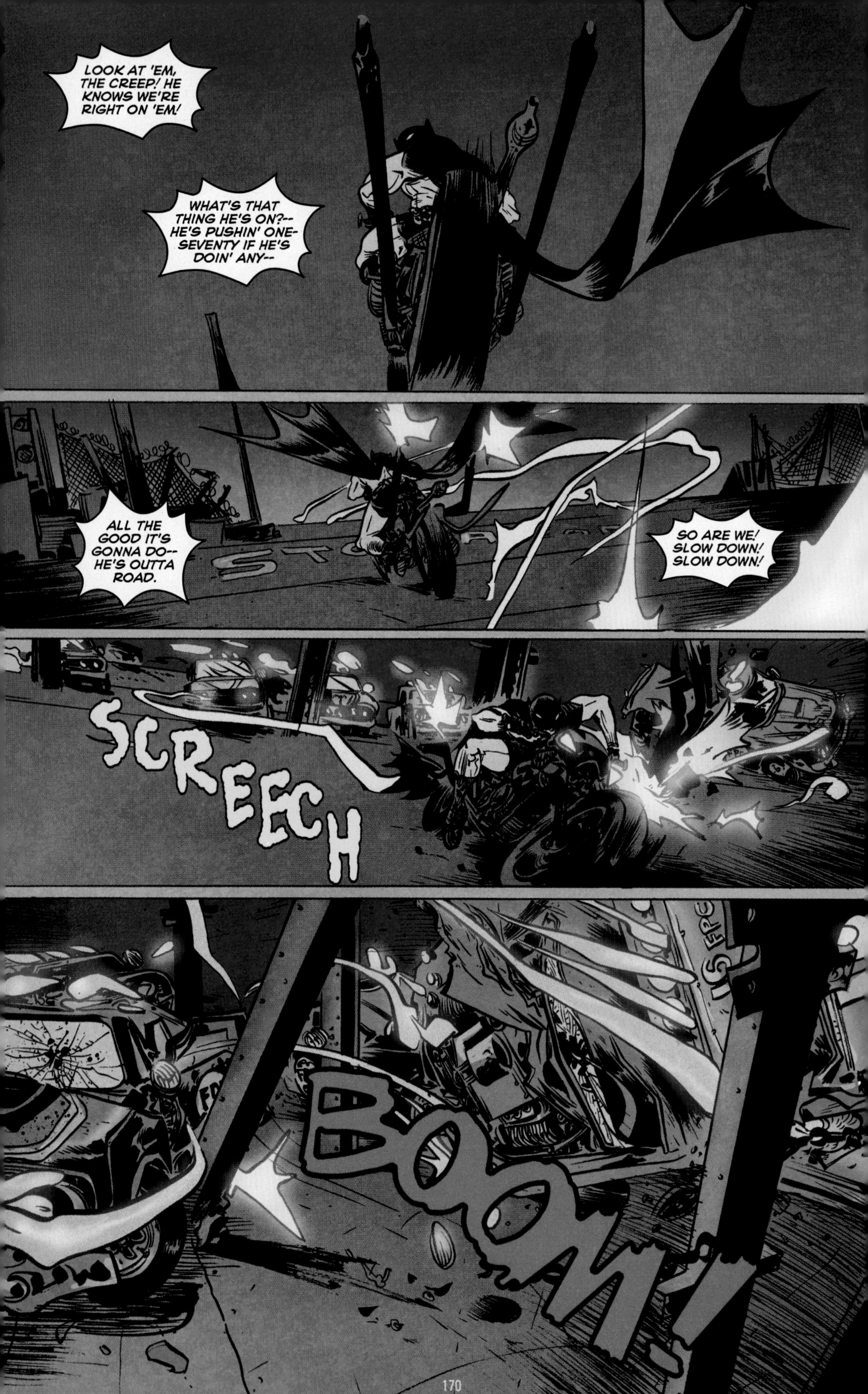
LOOK AT 'EM, THE CREEP! HE KNOWS WE'RE RIGHT ON 'EM!
WHAT'S THAT THING HE'S ON?-- HE'S PUSHIN' ONE-SEVENTY IF HE'S DOIN' ANY--
ALL THE GOOD IT'S GONNA DO-- HE'S OUTTA ROAD.
SO ARE WE! SLOW DOWN! SLOW DOWN!
SCREECH
BOOM!

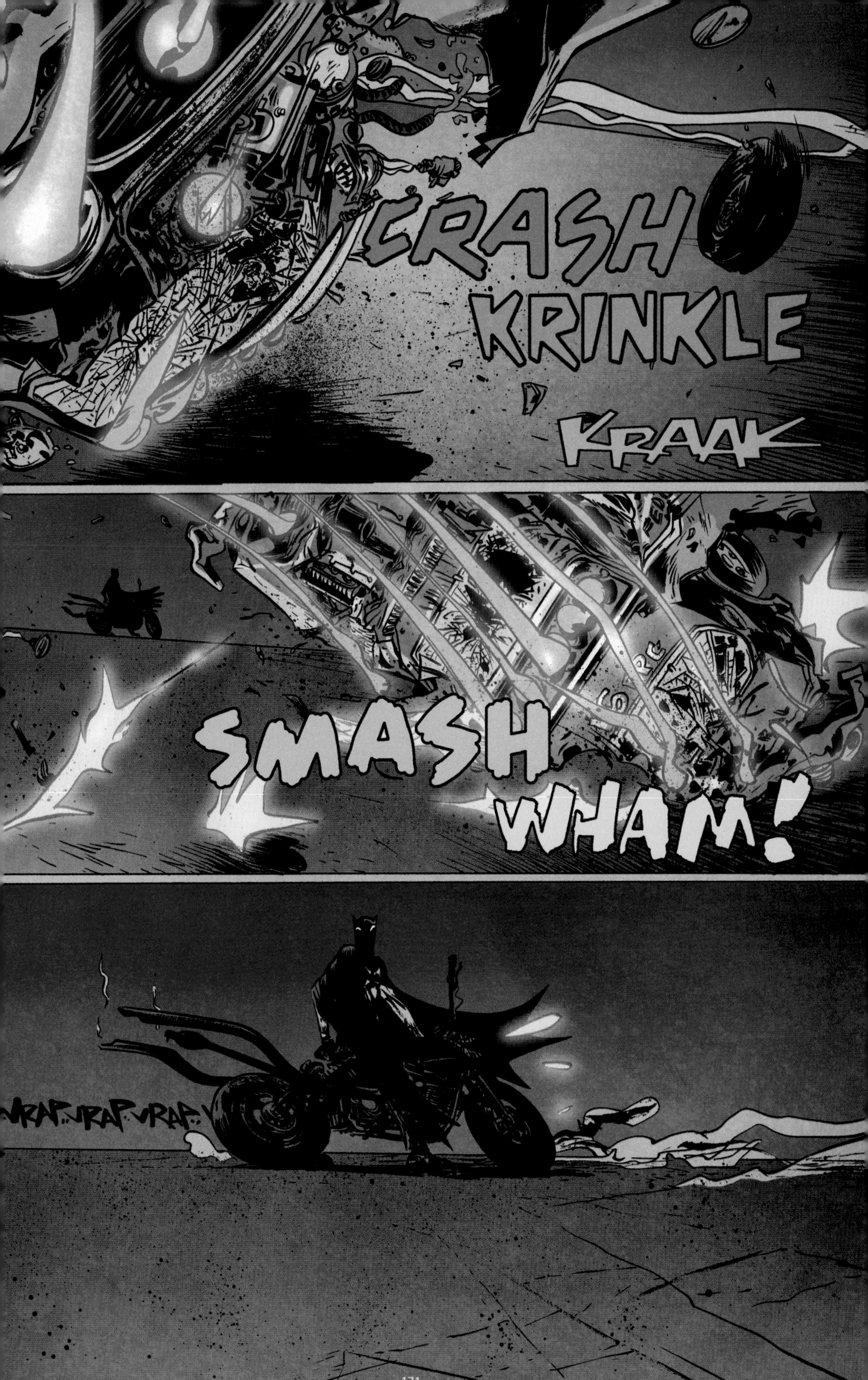
CRASH
KRINKLE
KRAAK
SMASH
WHAM!
VRAP.. VRAP.. VRAP..

CLICK!!

RRRRAAA

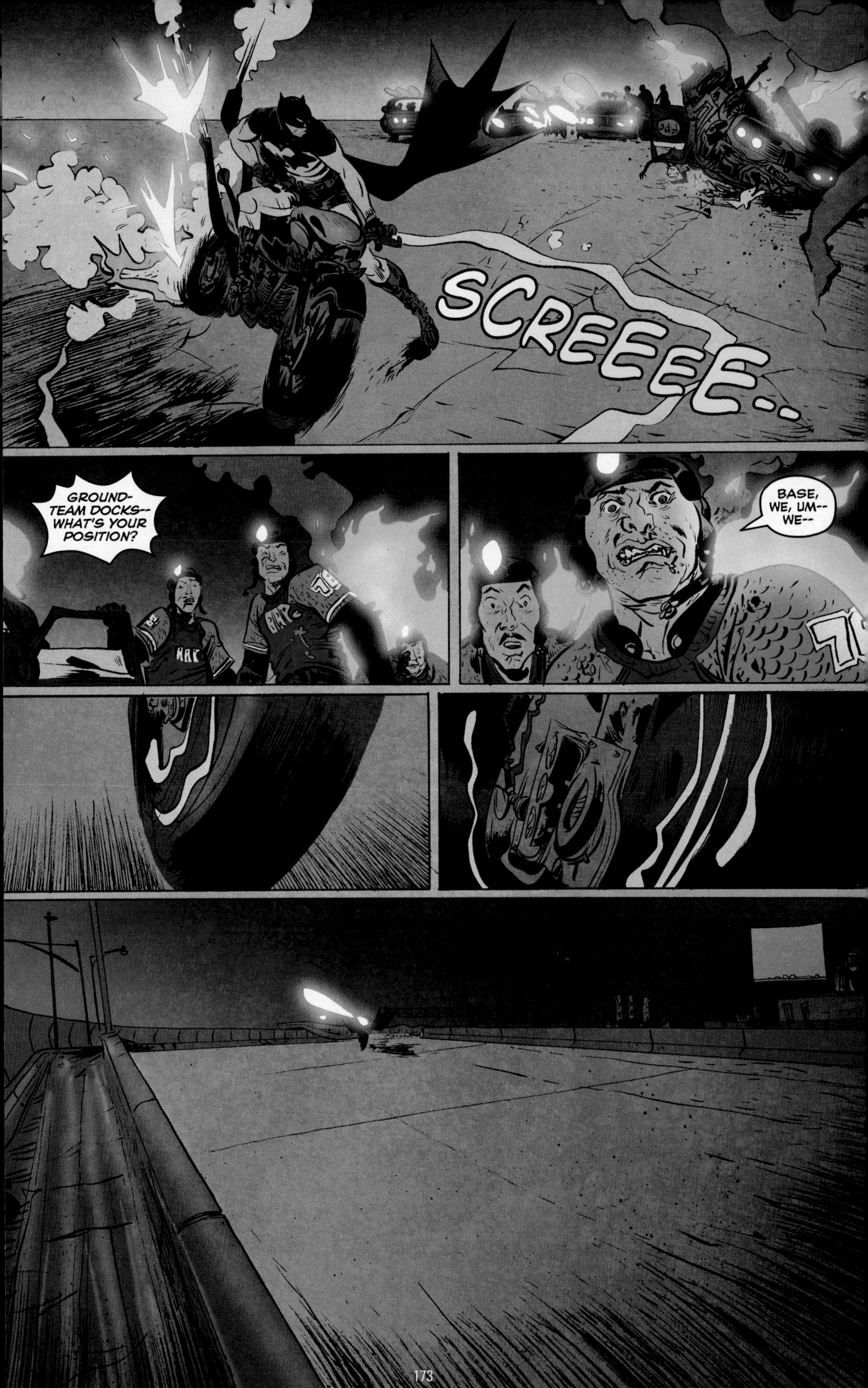
SCREEEEE...
GROUND-TEAM DOCKS--WHAT'S YOUR POSITION?
BASE, WE, UM--WE--

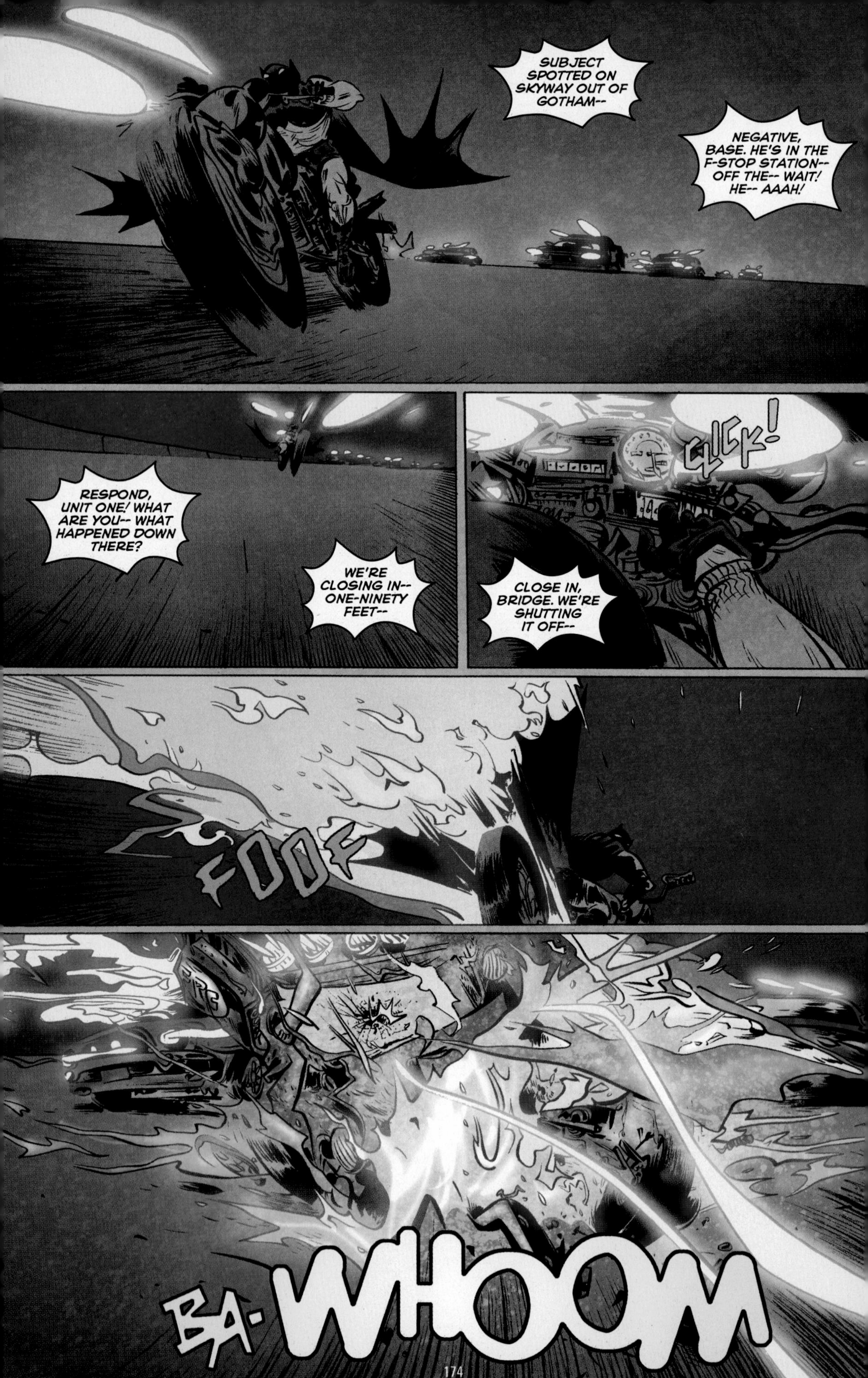
SUBJECT SPOTTED ON SKYWAY OUT OF GOTHAM--
NEGATIVE, BASE. HE'S IN THE F-STOP STATION-- OFF THE-- WAIT! HE-- AAAH!
RESPOND, UNIT ONE! WHAT ARE YOU-- WHAT HAPPENED DOWN THERE?
WE'RE CLOSING IN-- ONE-NINETY FEET--
CLICK!
CLOSE IN, BRIDGE. WE'RE SHUTTING IT OFF--
FOOF
BA-WHOOM

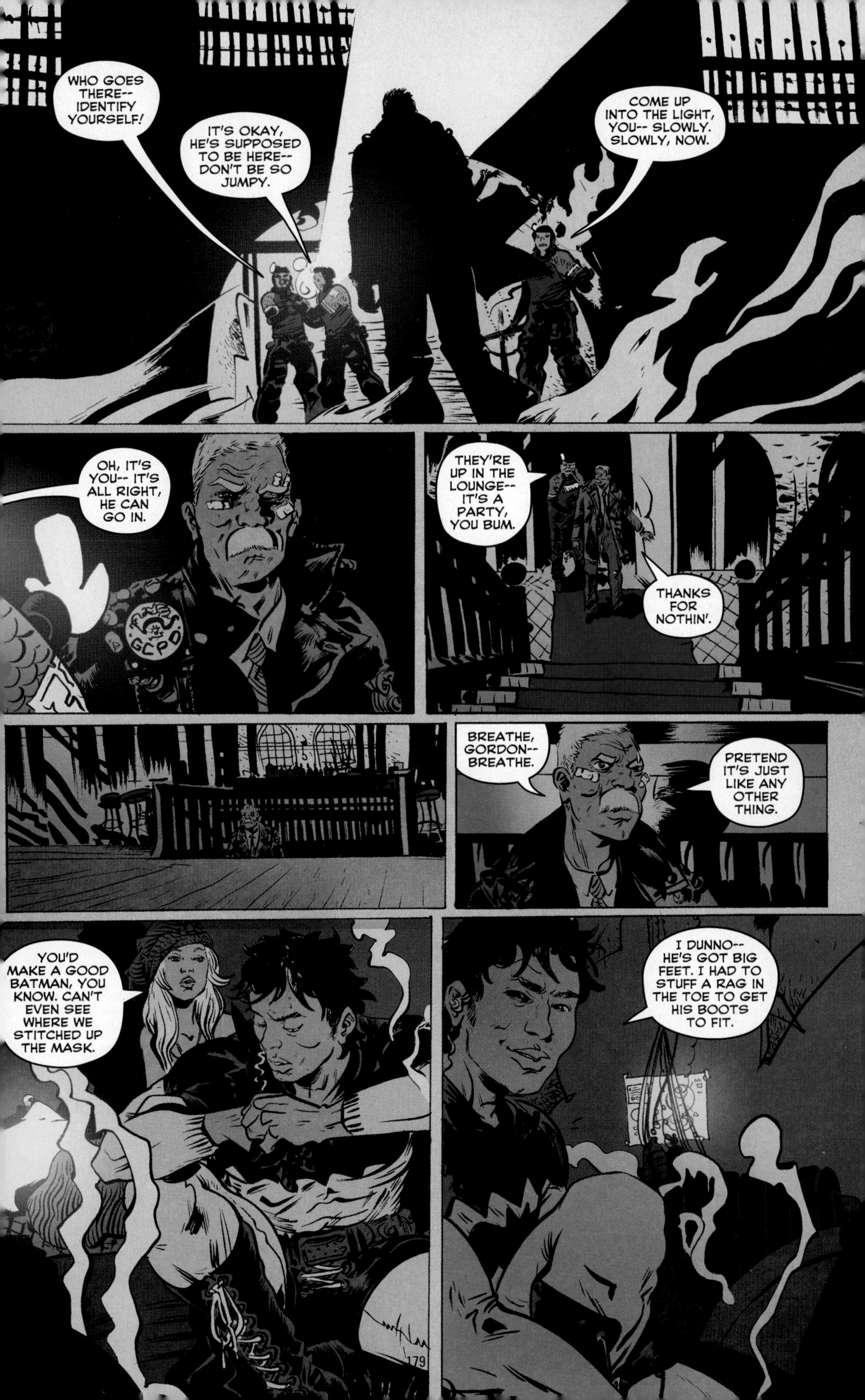
WHO GOES THERE-- IDENTIFY YOURSELF!
IT'S OKAY, HE'S SUPPOSED TO BE HERE-- DON'T BE SO JUMPY.
COME UP INTO THE LIGHT, YOU-- SLOWLY. SLOWLY, NOW.
OH, IT'S YOU-- IT'S ALL RIGHT, HE CAN GO IN.
GCPD
THEY'RE UP IN THE LOUNGE-- IT'S A PARTY, YOU BUM.
THANKS FOR NOTHIN'.
BREATHE, GORDON-- BREATHE.
PRETEND IT'S JUST LIKE ANY OTHER THING.
YOU'D MAKE A GOOD BATMAN, YOU KNOW. CAN'T EVEN SEE WHERE WE STITCHED UP THE MASK.
I DUNNO-- HE'S GOT BIG FEET. I HAD TO STUFF A RAG IN THE TOE TO GET HIS BOOTS TO FIT.

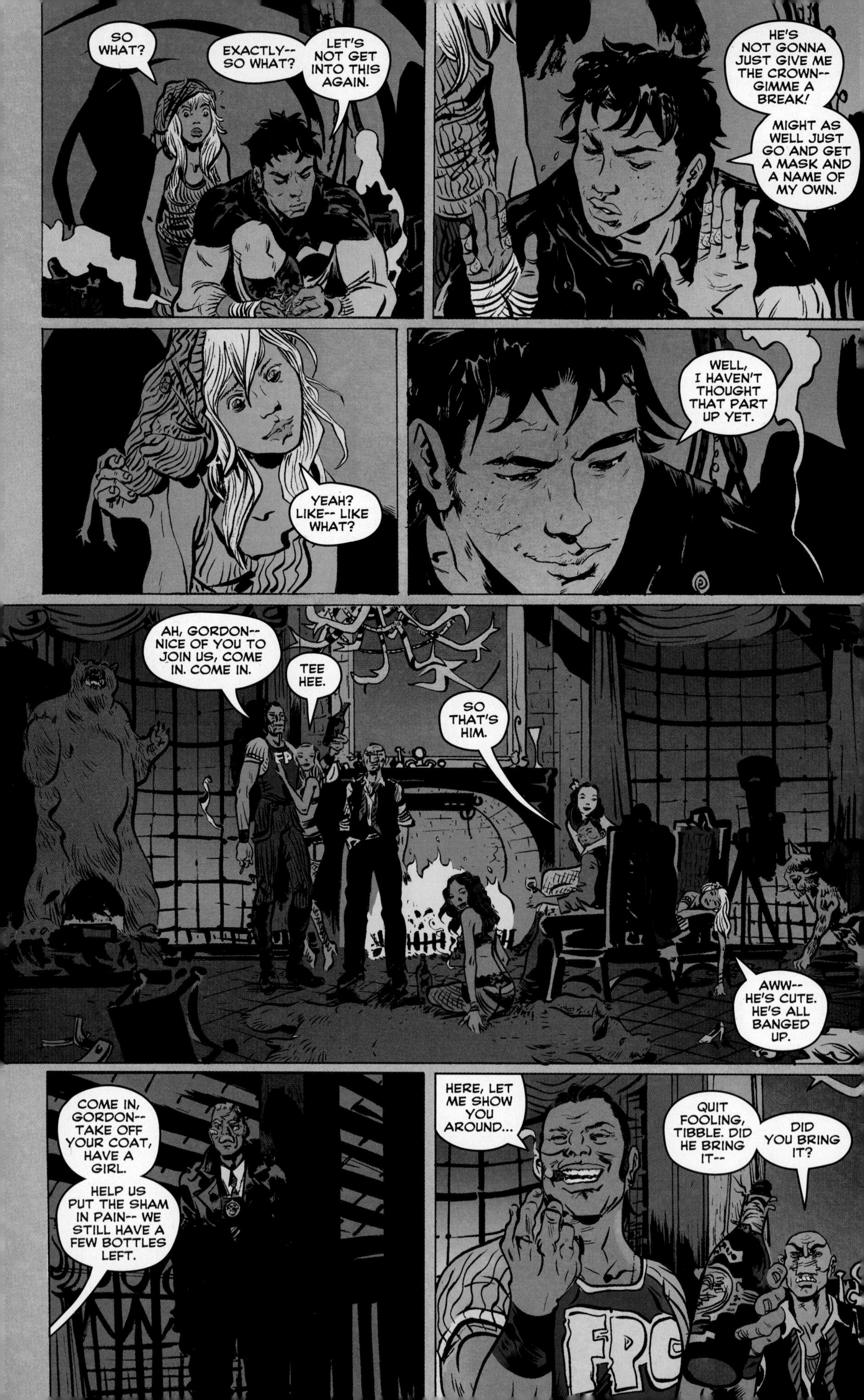
SO WHAT?
EXACTLY-- SO WHAT?
LET'S NOT GET INTO THIS AGAIN.
HE'S NOT GONNA JUST GIVE ME THE CROWN-- GIMME A BREAK!
MIGHT AS WELL JUST GO AND GET A MASK AND A NAME OF MY OWN.
YEAH? LIKE-- LIKE WHAT?
WELL, I HAVEN'T THOUGHT THAT PART UP YET.
AH, GORDON-- NICE OF YOU TO JOIN US, COME IN. COME IN.
TEE HEE.
SO THAT'S HIM.
AWW-- HE'S CUTE. HE'S ALL BANGED UP.
COME IN, GORDON-- TAKE OFF YOUR COAT, HAVE A GIRL.
HELP US PUT THE SHAM IN PAIN-- WE STILL HAVE A FEW BOTTLES LEFT.
HERE, LET ME SHOW YOU AROUND...
QUIT FOOLING, TIBBLE. DID HE BRING IT--
DID YOU BRING IT?

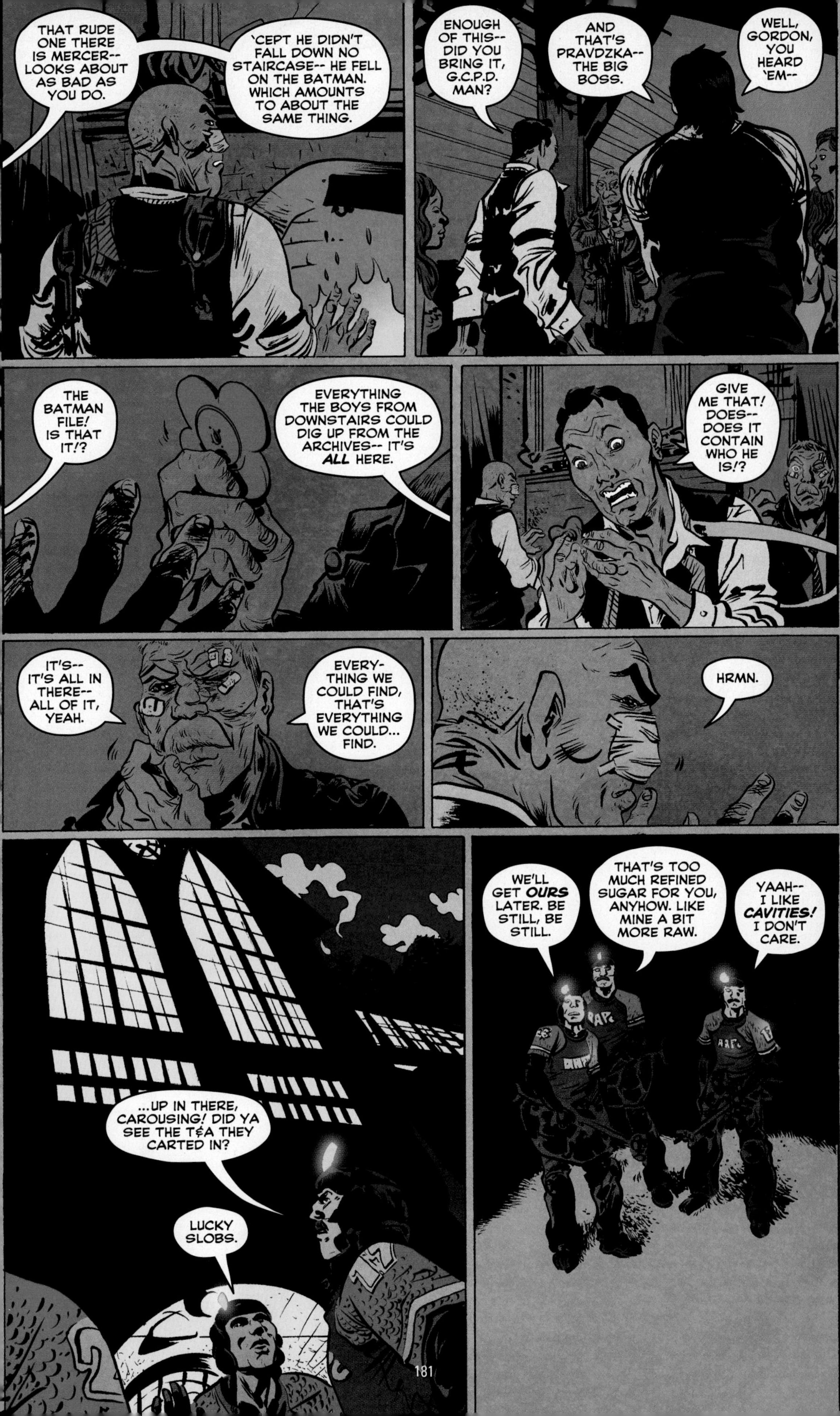
THAT RUDE ONE THERE IS MERCER-- LOOKS ABOUT AS BAD AS YOU DO.
`CEPT HE DIDN'T FALL DOWN NO STAIRCASE-- HE FELL ON THE BATMAN. WHICH AMOUNTS TO ABOUT THE SAME THING.
ENOUGH OF THIS-- DID YOU BRING IT, G.C.P.D. MAN?
AND THAT'S PRAVDZKA-- THE BIG BOSS.
WELL, GORDON, YOU HEARD 'EM--
THE BATMAN FILE! IS THAT IT!?
EVERYTHING THE BOYS FROM DOWNSTAIRS COULD DIG UP FROM THE ARCHIVES-- IT'S ALL HERE.
GIVE ME THAT! DOES-- DOES IT CONTAIN WHO HE IS!?
IT'S-- IT'S ALL IN THERE-- ALL OF IT, YEAH.
EVERY-THING WE COULD FIND, THAT'S EVERYTHING WE COULD... FIND.
HRMN.
...UP IN THERE, CAROUSING! DID YA SEE THE T&A THEY CARTED IN?
LUCKY SLOBS.
WE'LL GET OURS LATER. BE STILL, BE STILL.
THAT'S TOO MUCH REFINED SUGAR FOR YOU, ANYHOW. LIKE MINE A BIT MORE RAW.
YAAH-- I LIKE CAVITIES! I DON'T CARE.

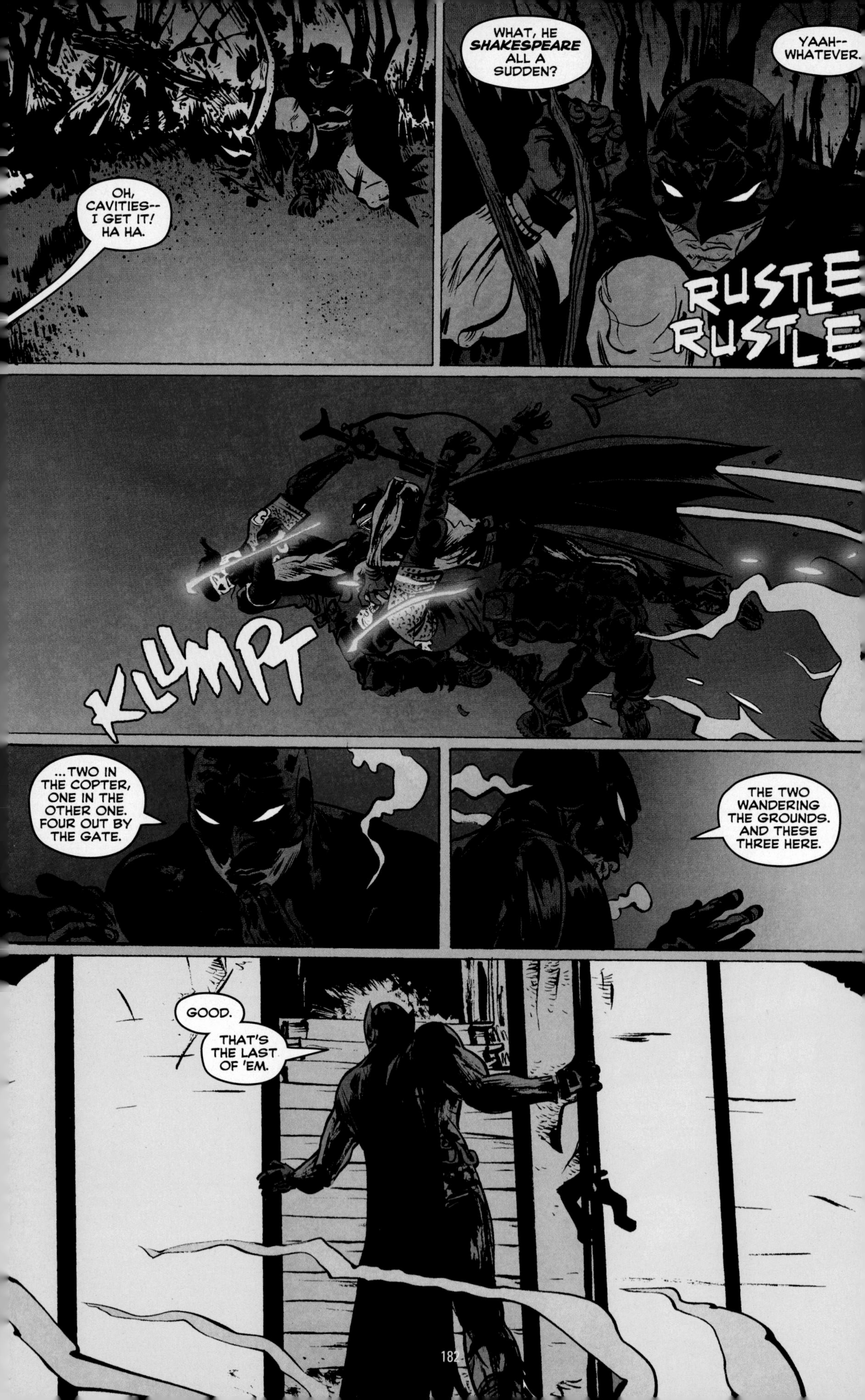

OH, CAVITIES-- I GET IT! HA HA.
WHAT, HE SHAKESPEARE ALL A SUDDEN?
YAAH-- WHATEVER.
RUSTLE RUSTLE
KLUMPT
...TWO IN THE COPTER, ONE IN THE OTHER ONE. FOUR OUT BY THE GATE.
THE TWO WANDERING THE GROUNDS. AND THESE THREE HERE.
GOOD.
THAT'S THE LAST OF 'EM.

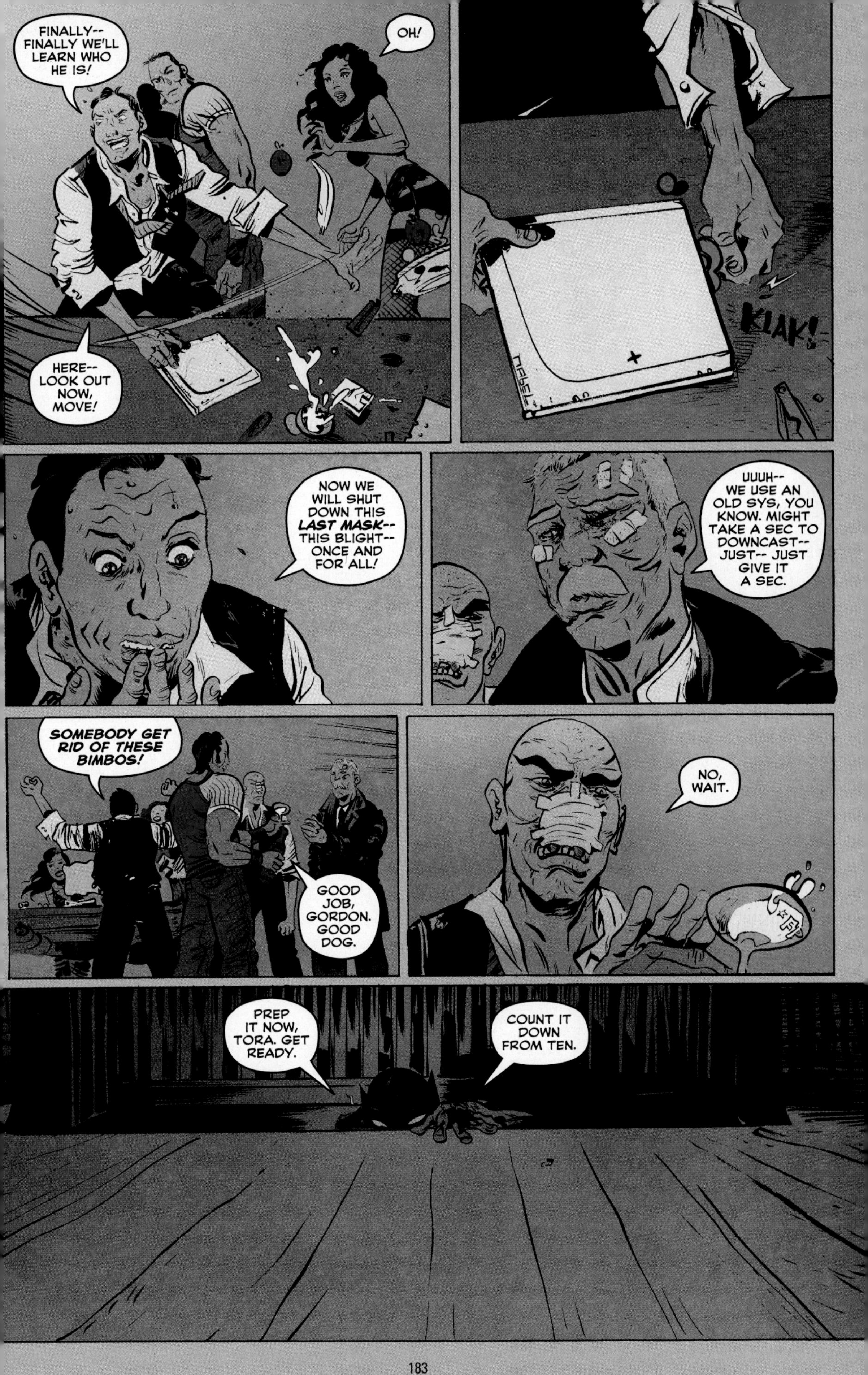
FINALLY--
FINALLY WE'LL LEARN WHO HE IS!
OH!
HERE-- LOOK OUT NOW, MOVE!
KLAK!
NOW WE WILL SHUT DOWN THIS LAST MASK-- THIS BLIGHT-- ONCE AND FOR ALL!
UUUH-- WE USE AN OLD SYS, YOU KNOW. MIGHT TAKE A SEC TO DOWNCAST-- JUST-- JUST GIVE IT A SEC.
SOMEBODY GET RID OF THESE BIMBOS!
GOOD JOB, GORDON. GOOD DOG.
NO, WAIT.
PREP IT NOW, TORA. GET READY.
COUNT IT DOWN FROM TEN.

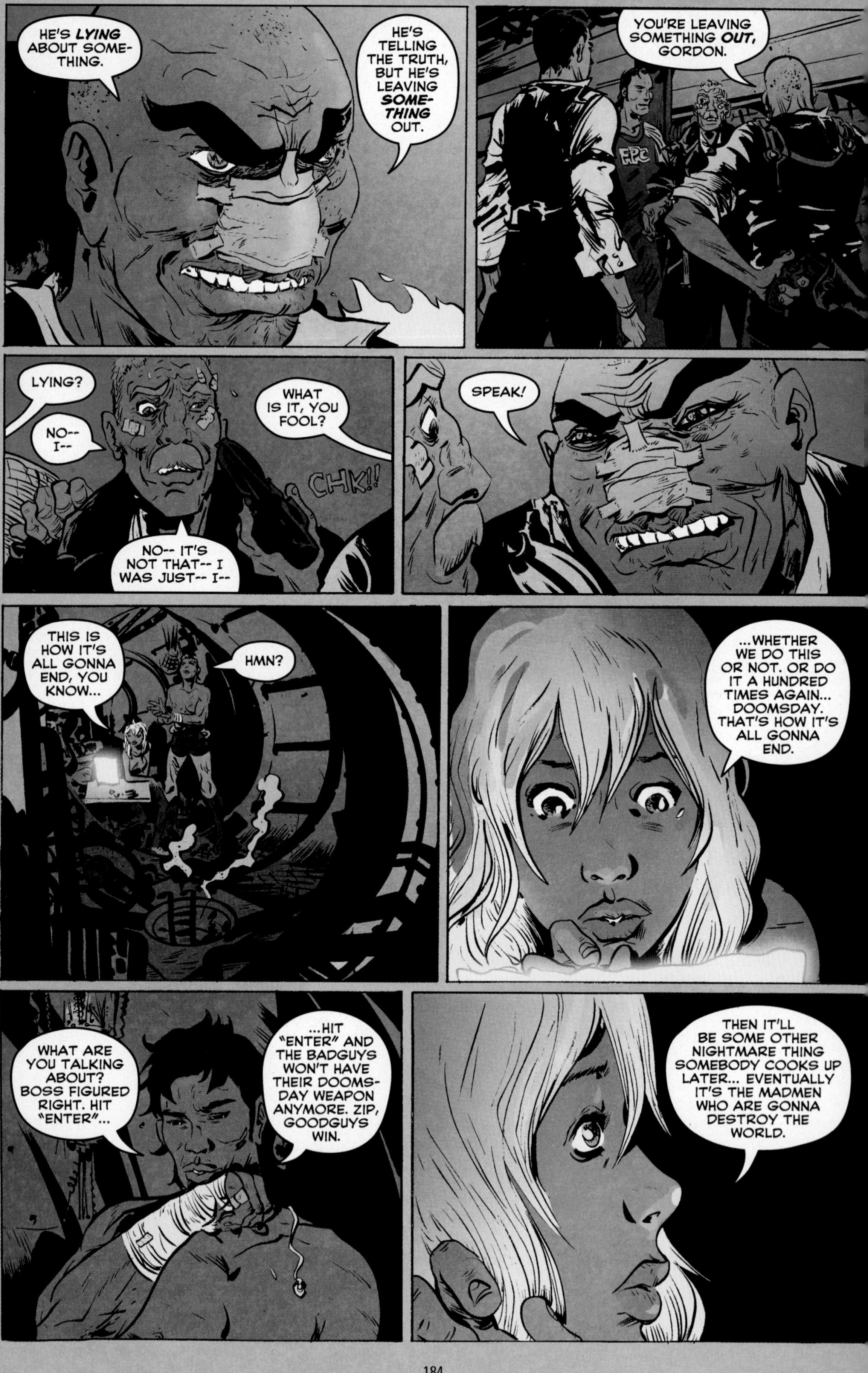
HE'S **LYING** ABOUT SOMETHING.
HE'S TELLING THE TRUTH, BUT HE'S LEAVING **SOMETHING** OUT.
YOU'RE LEAVING SOMETHING **OUT,** GORDON.
LYING?
NO-- I--
WHAT IS IT, YOU FOOL?
CHK!!
NO-- IT'S NOT THAT-- I WAS JUST-- I--
SPEAK!
THIS IS HOW IT'S ALL GONNA END, YOU KNOW...
HMN?
...WHETHER WE DO THIS OR NOT. OR DO IT A HUNDRED TIMES AGAIN... DOOMSDAY. THAT'S HOW IT'S ALL GONNA END.
WHAT ARE YOU TALKING ABOUT? BOSS FIGURED RIGHT. HIT "ENTER"...
...HIT "ENTER" AND THE BADGUYS WON'T HAVE THEIR DOOMSDAY WEAPON ANYMORE. ZIP, GOODGUYS WIN.
THEN IT'LL BE SOME OTHER NIGHTMARE THING SOMEBODY COOKS UP LATER... EVENTUALLY IT'S THE MADMEN WHO ARE GONNA DESTROY THE WORLD.

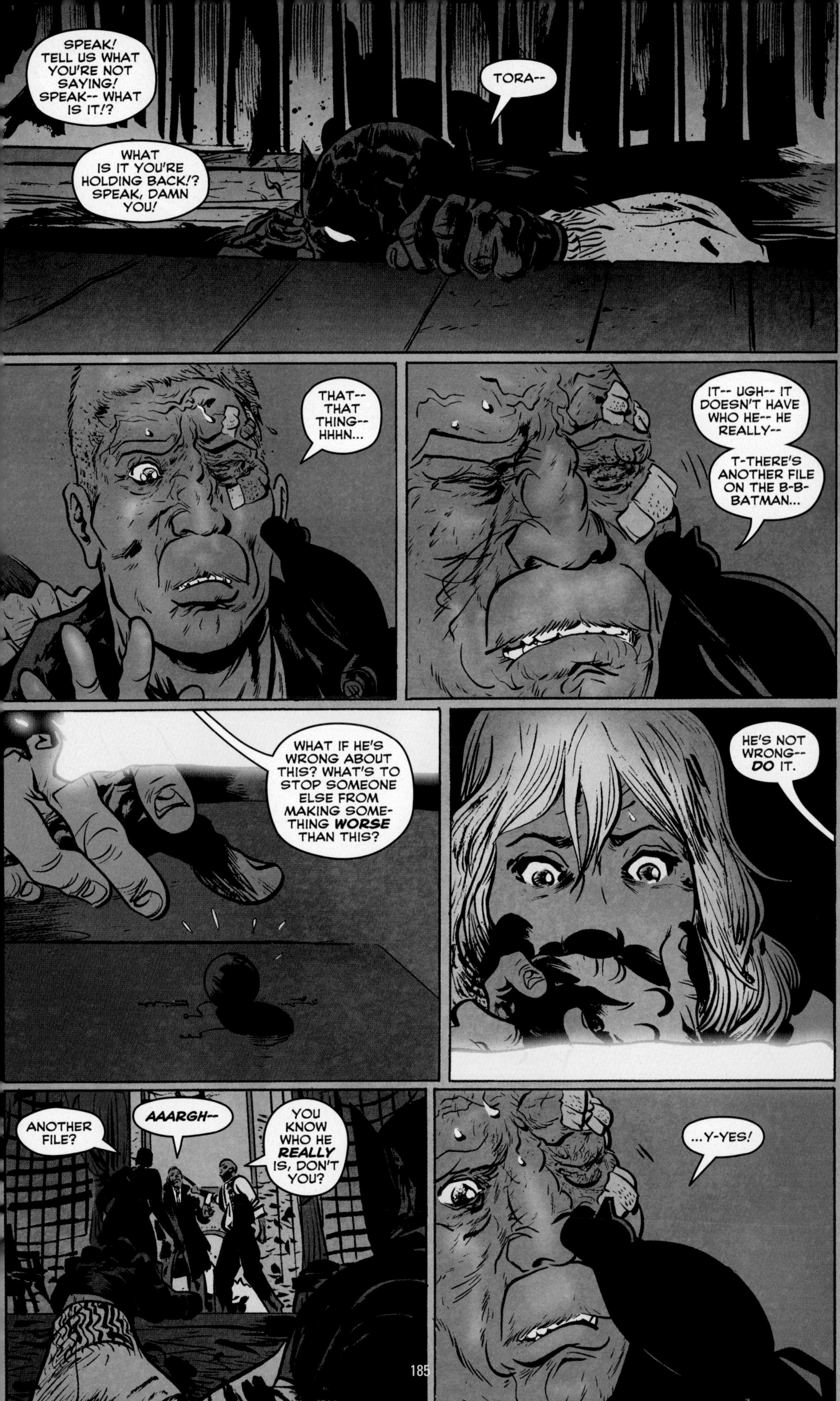
SPEAK! TELL US WHAT YOU'RE NOT SAYING! SPEAK-- WHAT IS IT!?
WHAT IS IT YOU'RE HOLDING BACK!? SPEAK, DAMN YOU!
TORA--
THAT-- THAT THING-- HHHN...
IT-- UGH-- IT DOESN'T HAVE WHO HE-- HE REALLY--
T-THERE'S ANOTHER FILE ON THE B-B-BATMAN...
WHAT IF HE'S WRONG ABOUT THIS? WHAT'S TO STOP SOMEONE ELSE FROM MAKING SOMETHING WORSE THAN THIS?
HE'S NOT WRONG-- DO IT.
ANOTHER FILE?
AAARGH--
YOU KNOW WHO HE REALLY IS, DON'T YOU?
...Y-YES!

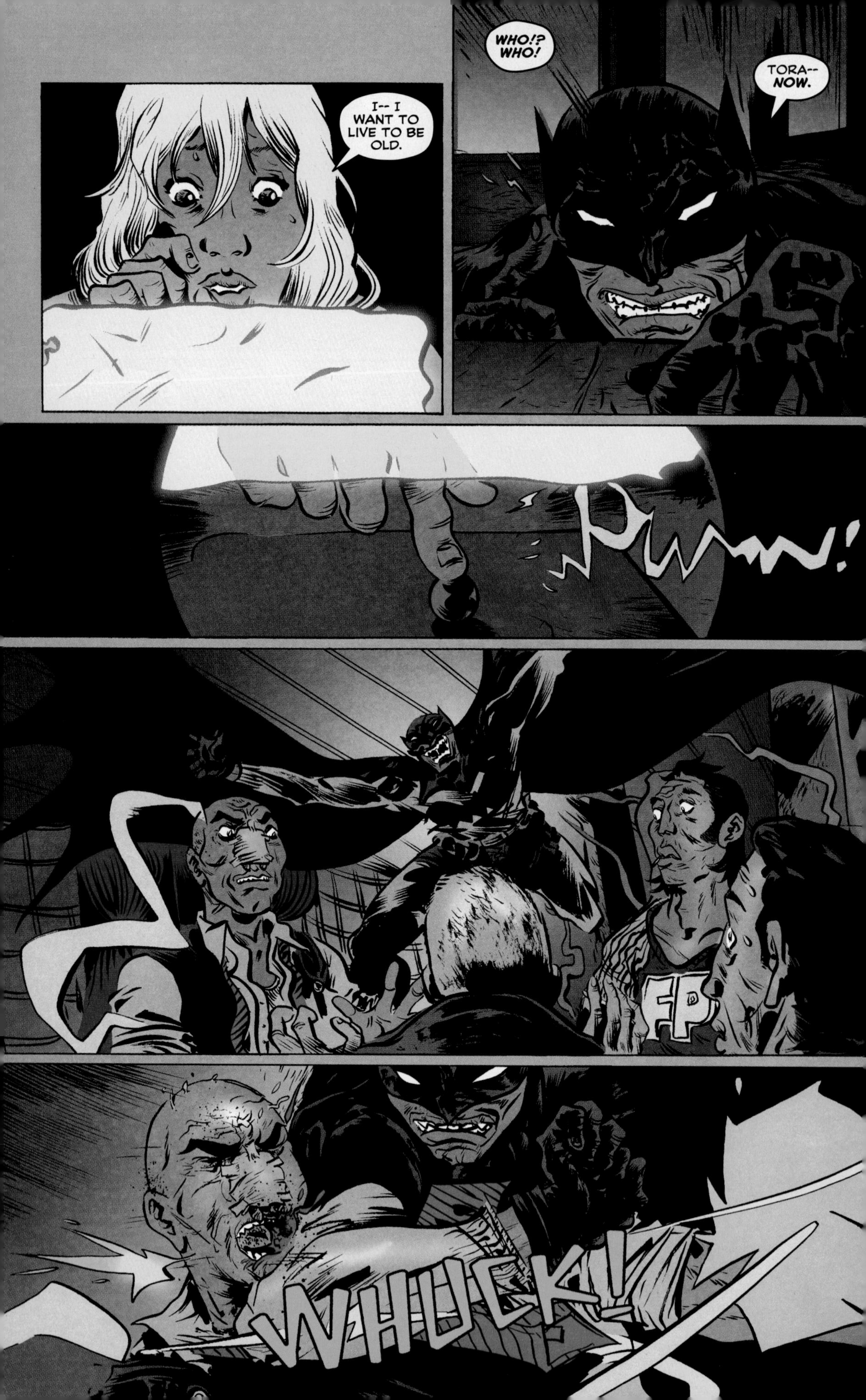
I-- I WANT TO LIVE TO BE OLD.
WHO!? WHO!
TORA-- NOW.
PWWW!
FP
WHUCK!

WHOMP!

CLICK!

CLICK! CLICK!

CLICK! CLICK! CLI-

AAAAH! AAA!

SNATCH

HLAK KLa

⋶KAFF⋶
⋶KAFF⋶
WHERE-- ARE YOU HIDING IT?

WHERE'S THE FLESHKILLER?

AAAA AAH!

001001
101111
00000111
101

WHERE? WHY NOT TAKE A LOOK OVER THE ETHER.

I JUST CAST IT ACROSS THE WORLD-WIDE, UP ON!

WHAA--? YOU'RE LYING!

TAK
TAK
TAK

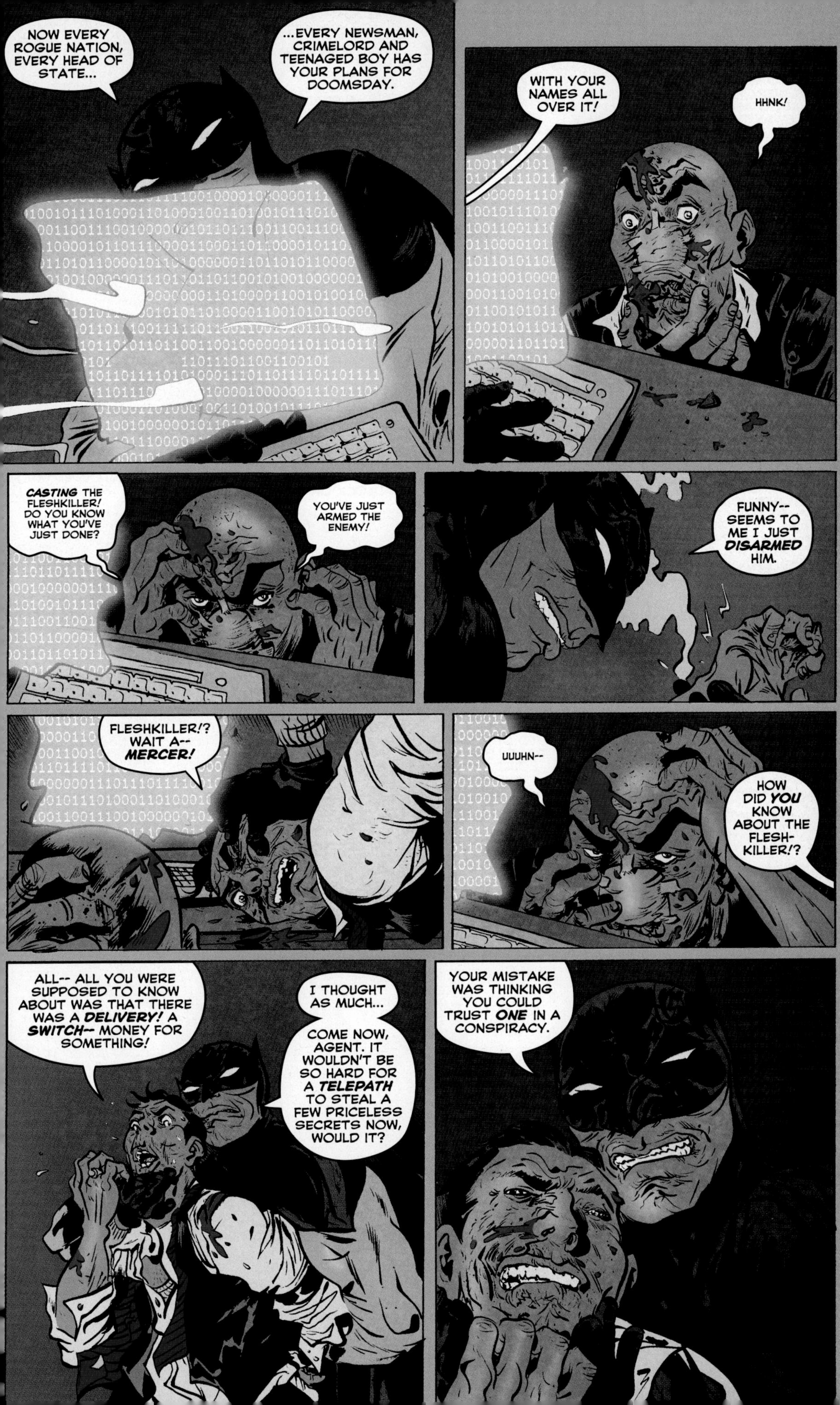

NOW EVERY ROGUE NATION, EVERY HEAD OF STATE...
...EVERY NEWSMAN, CRIMELORD AND TEENAGED BOY HAS YOUR PLANS FOR DOOMSDAY.
WITH YOUR NAMES ALL OVER IT!
HHNK!
CASTING THE FLESHKILLER! DO YOU KNOW WHAT YOU'VE JUST DONE?
YOU'VE JUST ARMED THE ENEMY!
FUNNY-- SEEMS TO ME I JUST DISARMED HIM.
FLESHKILLER!? WAIT A-- MERCER!
UUUHN--
HOW DID YOU KNOW ABOUT THE FLESH-KILLER!?
ALL-- ALL YOU WERE SUPPOSED TO KNOW ABOUT WAS THAT THERE WAS A DELIVERY! A SWITCH-- MONEY FOR SOMETHING!
I THOUGHT AS MUCH...
COME NOW, AGENT. IT WOULDN'T BE SO HARD FOR A TELEPATH TO STEAL A FEW PRICELESS SECRETS NOW, WOULD IT?
YOUR MISTAKE WAS THINKING YOU COULD TRUST ONE IN A CONSPIRACY.

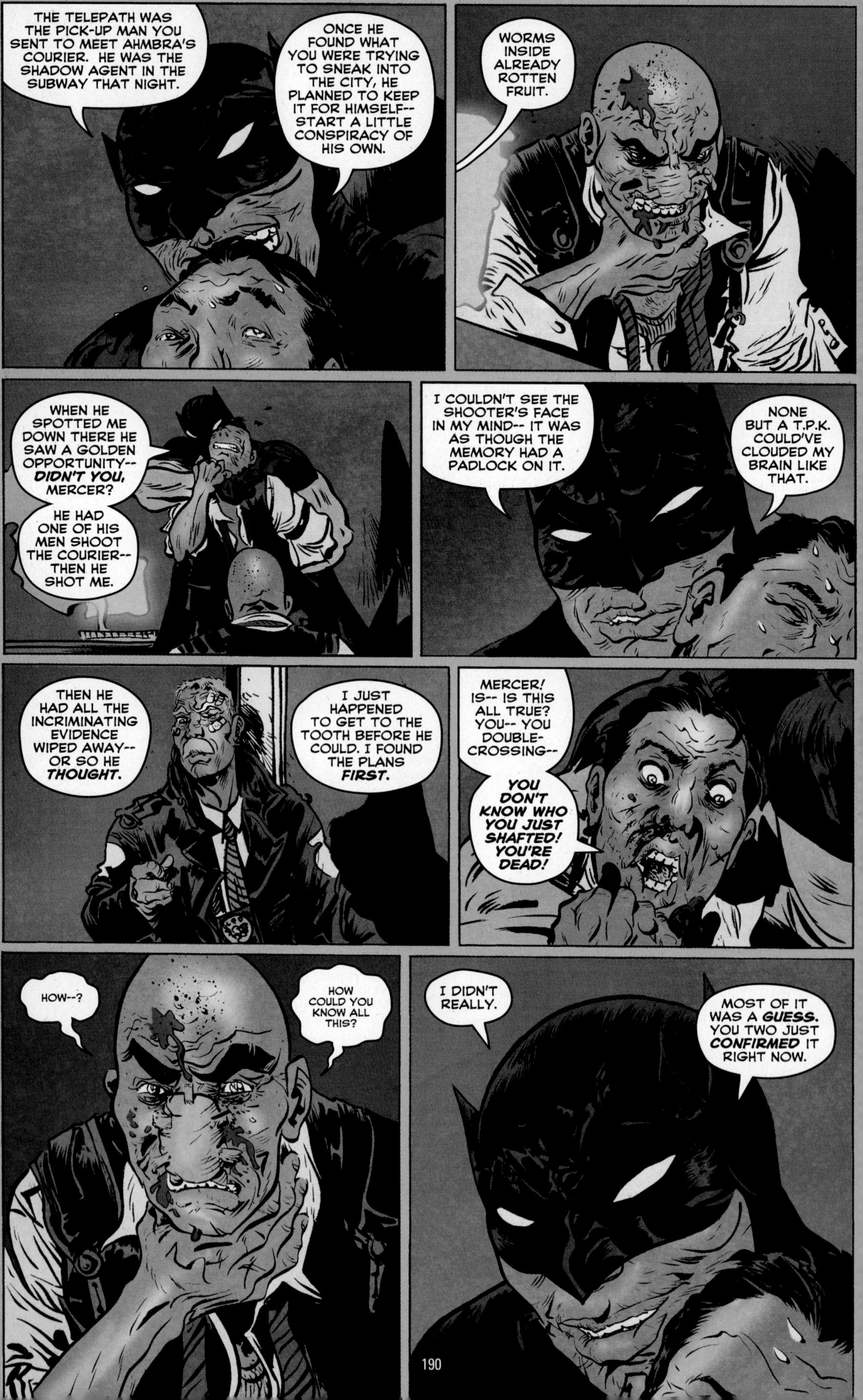
THE TELEPATH WAS THE PICK-UP MAN YOU SENT TO MEET AHMBRA'S COURIER. HE WAS THE SHADOW AGENT IN THE SUBWAY THAT NIGHT.
ONCE HE FOUND WHAT YOU WERE TRYING TO SNEAK INTO THE CITY, HE PLANNED TO KEEP IT FOR HIMSELF-- START A LITTLE CONSPIRACY OF HIS OWN.
WORMS INSIDE ALREADY ROTTEN FRUIT.
WHEN HE SPOTTED ME DOWN THERE HE SAW A GOLDEN OPPORTUNITY-- ***DIDN'T YOU,*** MERCER?
HE HAD ONE OF HIS MEN SHOOT THE COURIER-- THEN HE SHOT ME.
I COULDN'T SEE THE SHOOTER'S FACE IN MY MIND-- IT WAS AS THOUGH THE MEMORY HAD A PADLOCK ON IT.
NONE BUT A T.P.K. COULD'VE CLOUDED MY BRAIN LIKE THAT.
THEN HE HAD ALL THE INCRIMINATING EVIDENCE WIPED AWAY-- OR SO HE ***THOUGHT***.
I JUST HAPPENED TO GET TO THE TOOTH BEFORE HE COULD. I FOUND THE PLANS ***FIRST***.
MERCER! IS-- IS THIS ALL TRUE? YOU-- YOU DOUBLE-CROSSING--
YOU DON'T KNOW WHO YOU JUST SHAFTED! YOU'RE DEAD!
HOW--?
HOW COULD YOU KNOW ALL THIS?
I DIDN'T REALLY.
MOST OF IT WAS A ***GUESS.*** YOU TWO JUST ***CONFIRMED*** IT RIGHT NOW.

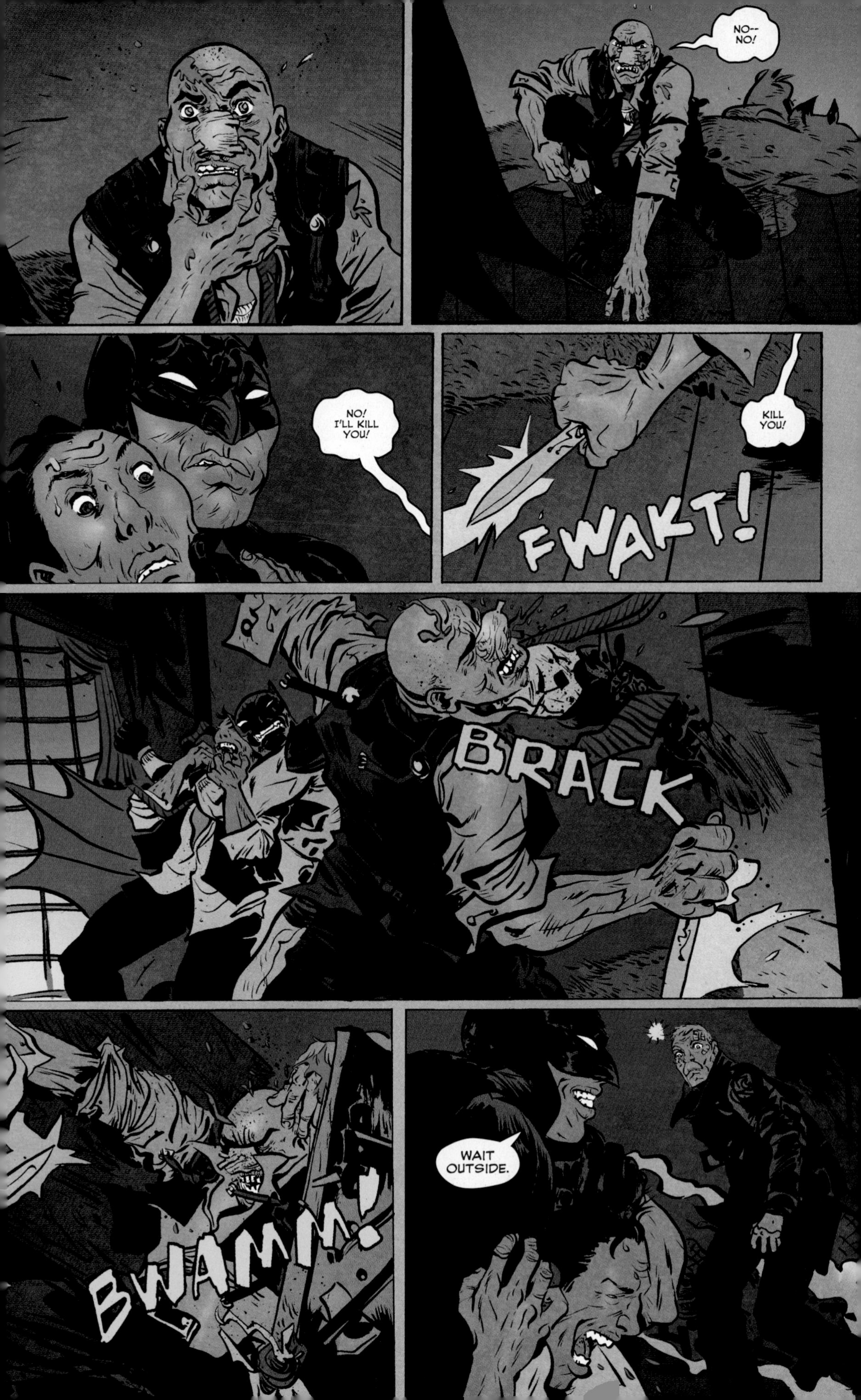
NO--
NO!
NO!
I'LL KILL
YOU!
KILL
YOU!
FWAKT!
BRACK
BWAMM!
WAIT
OUTSIDE.

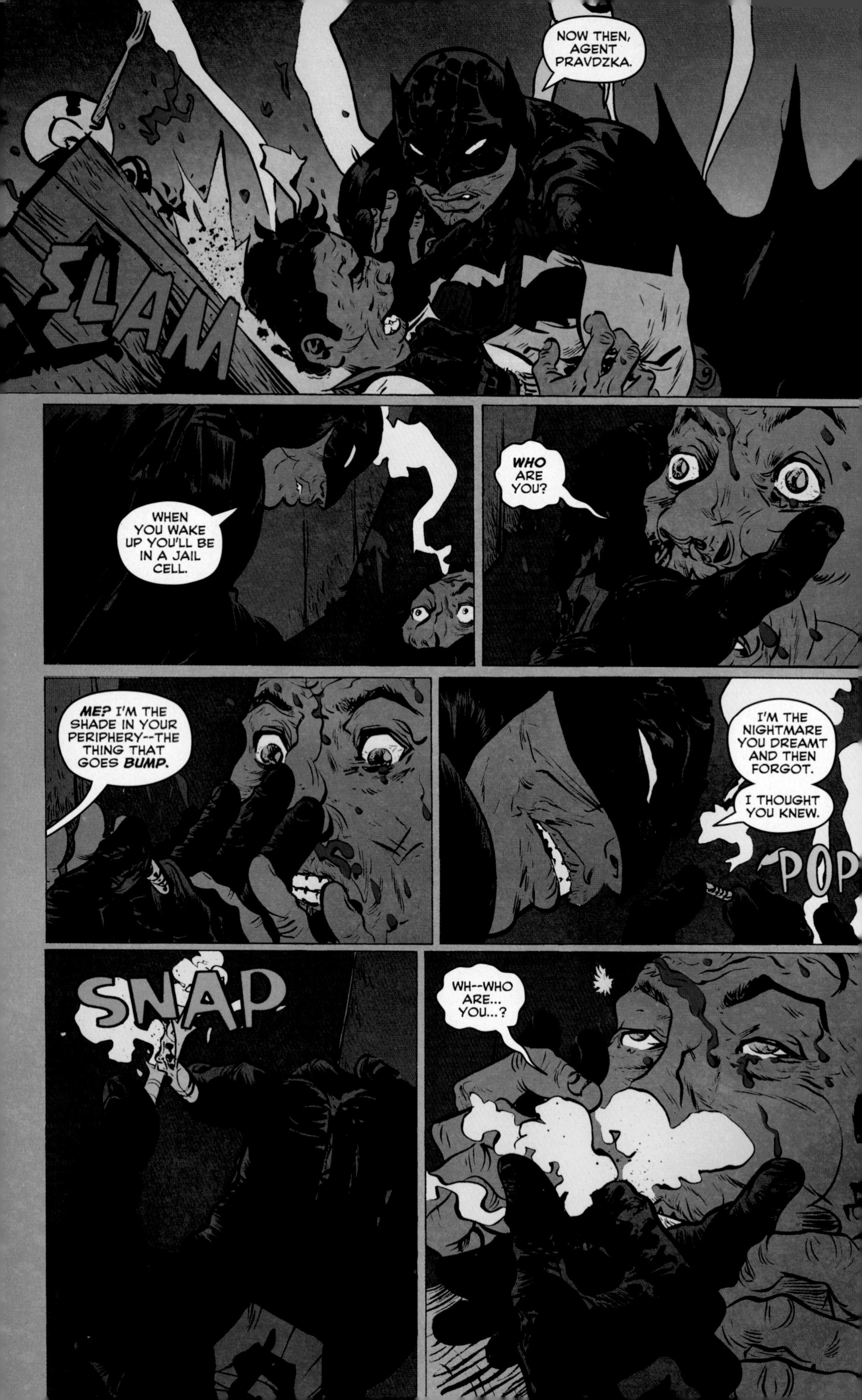
NOW THEN, AGENT PRAVDZKA.
SLAM
WHEN YOU WAKE UP YOU'LL BE IN A JAIL CELL.
WHO ARE YOU?
ME? I'M THE SHADE IN YOUR PERIPHERY--THE THING THAT GOES BUMP.
I'M THE NIGHTMARE YOU DREAMT AND THEN FORGOT.
I THOUGHT YOU KNEW.
POP
SNAP
WH--WHO ARE... YOU...?

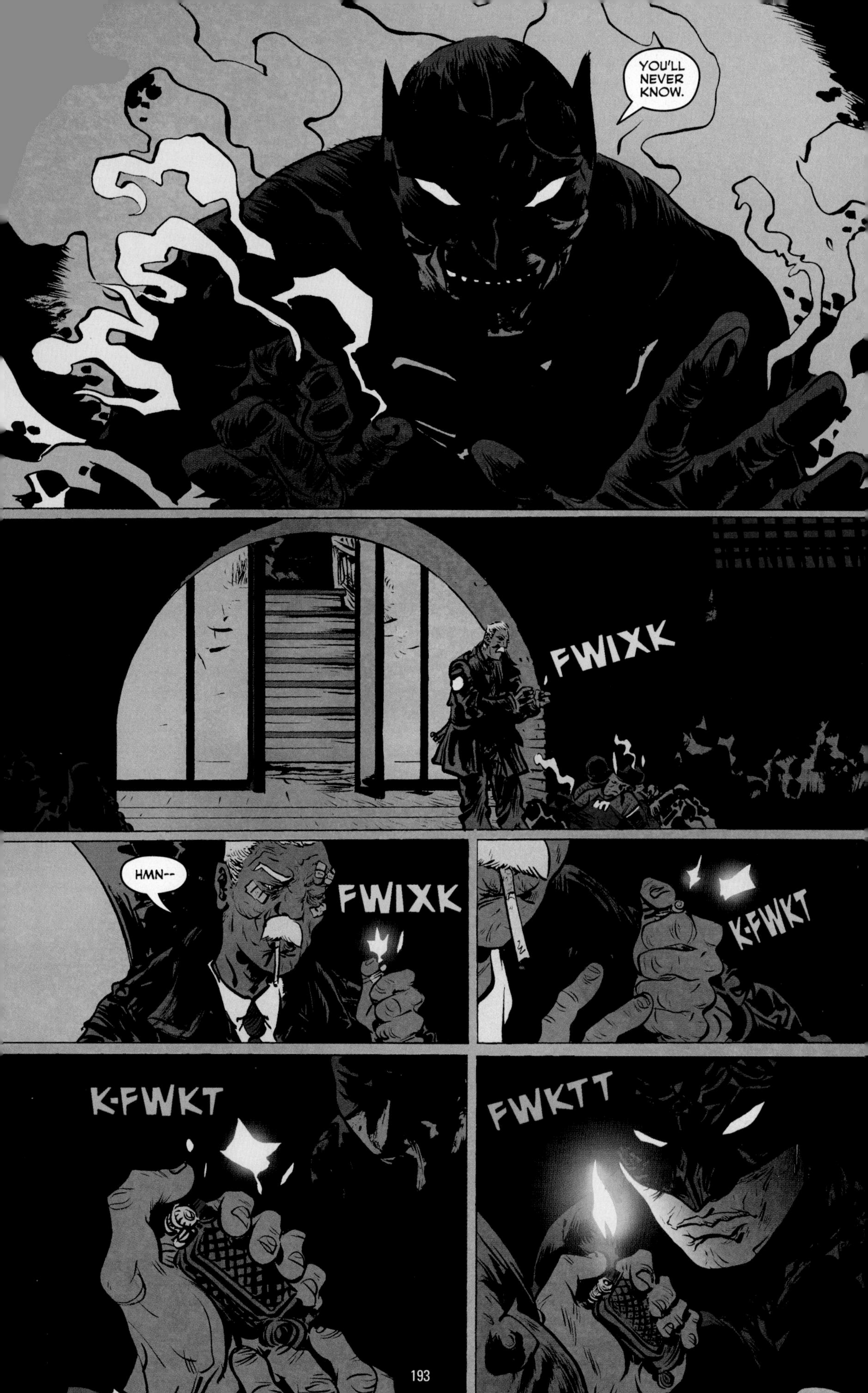
YOU'LL NEVER KNOW.
FWIXK
HMN--
FWIXK
K-FWKT
K-FWKT
FWKTT

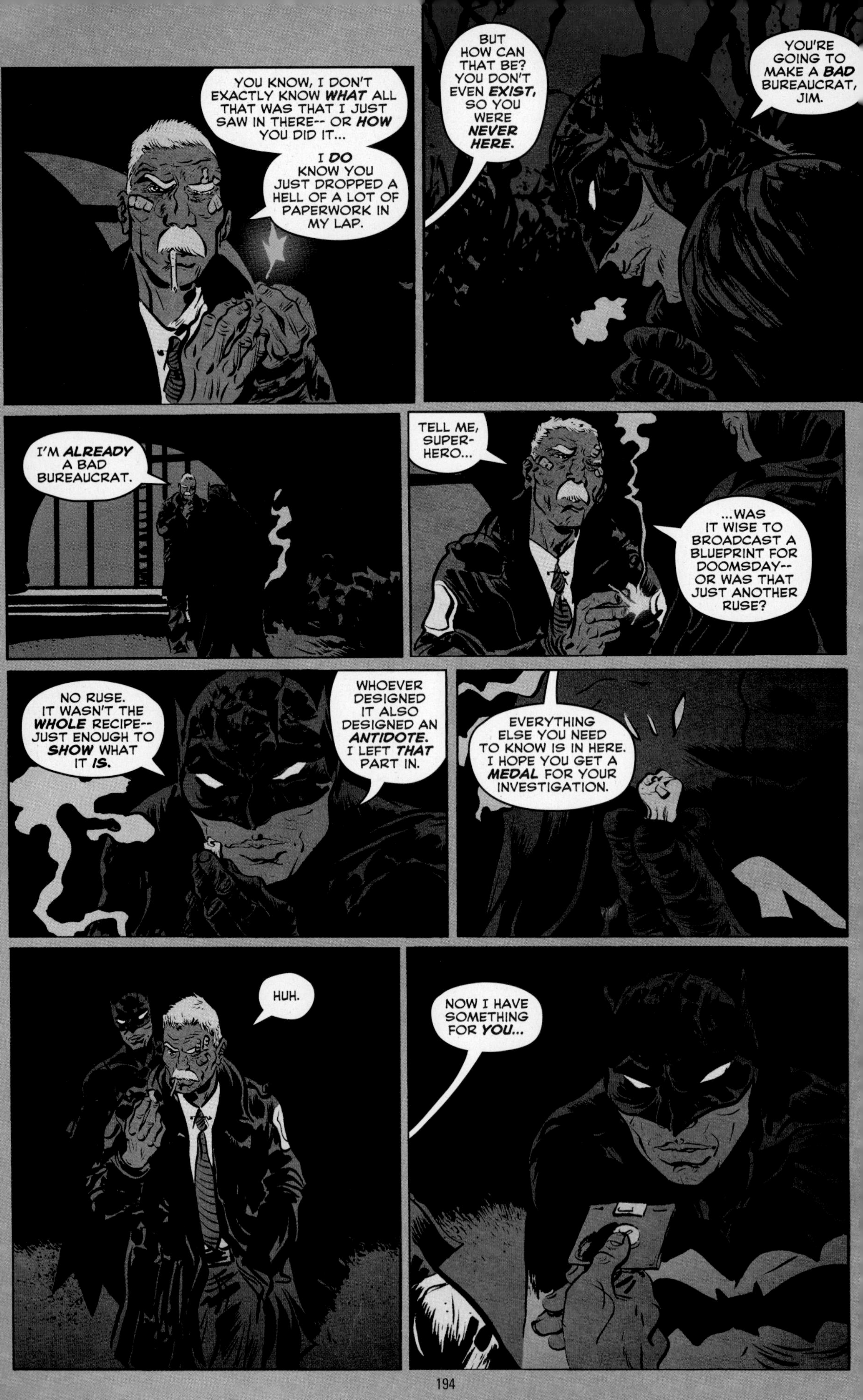
YOU KNOW, I DON'T EXACTLY KNOW WHAT ALL THAT WAS THAT I JUST SAW IN THERE-- OR HOW YOU DID IT...
I DO KNOW YOU JUST DROPPED A HELL OF A LOT OF PAPERWORK IN MY LAP.
BUT HOW CAN THAT BE? YOU DON'T EVEN EXIST, SO YOU WERE NEVER HERE.
YOU'RE GOING TO MAKE A BAD BUREAUCRAT, JIM.
I'M ALREADY A BAD BUREAUCRAT.
TELL ME, SUPER-HERO...
...WAS IT WISE TO BROADCAST A BLUEPRINT FOR DOOMSDAY-- OR WAS THAT JUST ANOTHER RUSE?
NO RUSE. IT WASN'T THE WHOLE RECIPE-- JUST ENOUGH TO SHOW WHAT IT IS.
WHOEVER DESIGNED IT ALSO DESIGNED AN ANTIDOTE. I LEFT THAT PART IN.
EVERYTHING ELSE YOU NEED TO KNOW IS IN HERE. I HOPE YOU GET A MEDAL FOR YOUR INVESTIGATION.
HUH.
NOW I HAVE SOMETHING FOR YOU...

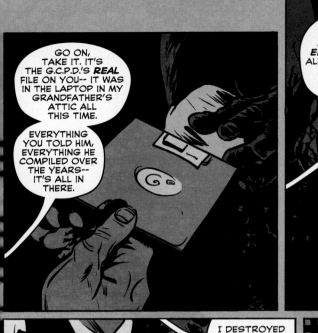

GO ON, TAKE IT. IT'S THE G.C.P.D.'S **REAL** FILE ON YOU-- IT WAS IN THE LAPTOP IN MY GRANDFATHER'S ATTIC ALL THIS TIME.

EVERYTHING YOU TOLD HIM, EVERYTHING HE COMPILED OVER THE YEARS-- IT'S ALL IN THERE.

YOU KNOW, HE SOMEHOW MANAGED TO **ERASE** ALMOST ALL THE RELEVANT DATA IN THE OFFICIAL FILE DOWNTOWN?

WELL, HE **DID.**

I DESTROYED THE ORIGINAL. THAT'S THE ONLY SOURCE COPY THERE IS. NOW **NOBODY** KNOWS WHO YOU ARE.

EXCEPT FOR YOUR DOCTOR. AND YOUR LITTLE SET-UP/CLEAN-UP CREW.

AND NOW ME.

BUT I'M NOT GONNA SAY A WORD OF IT TO ANYONE... **BRUCE.**

WHY ARE YOU--?

WHY? FOR THE SAME REASON YOU ARE.

NOW YOU BETTER DISAPPEAR BEFORE MY MEN AND THE CAMERAS ARRIVE.

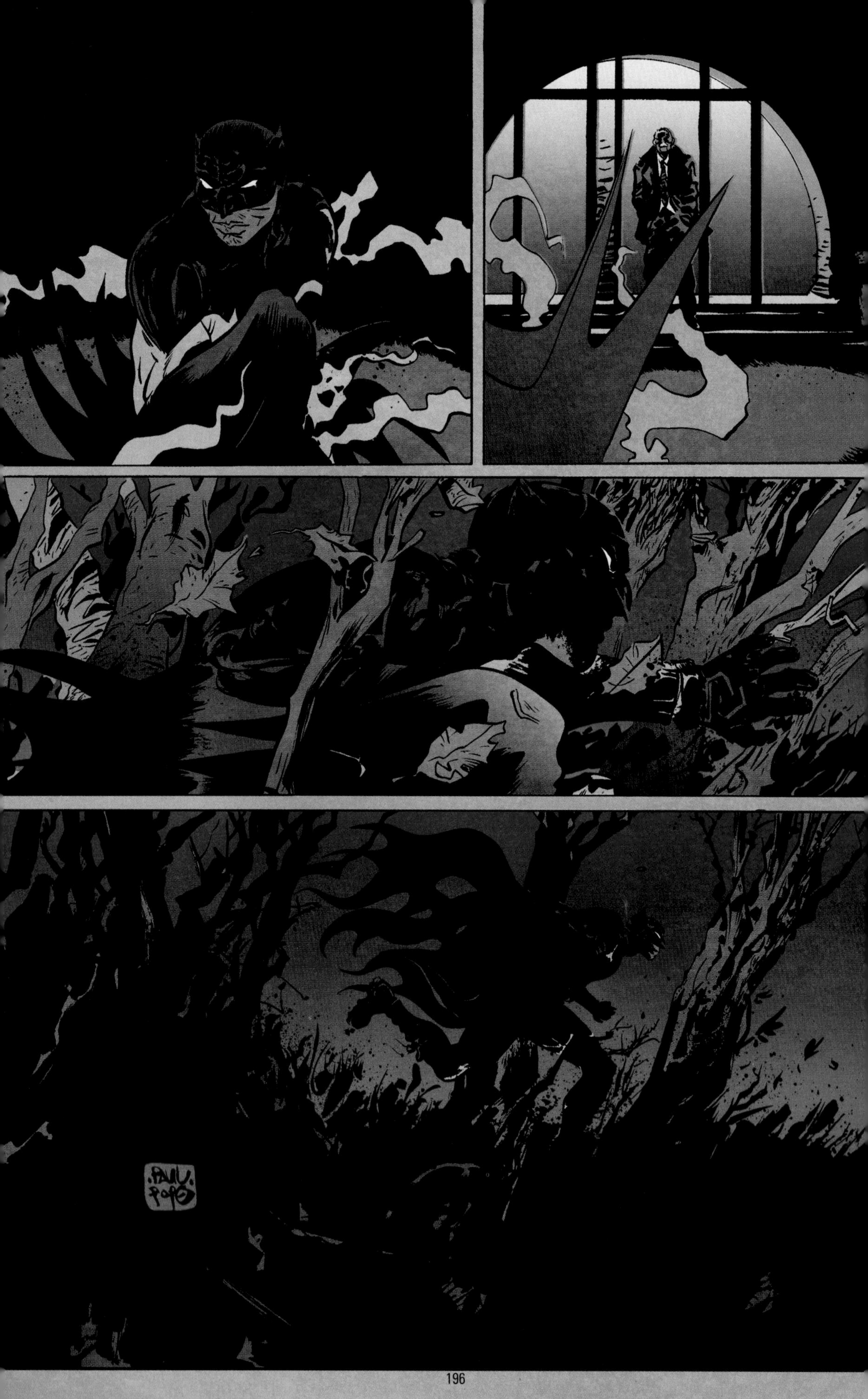
PAUL POPE

BATMAN: YEAR 100
NEWS ARCHIVES

 collected from BATMAN YEAR 100 #1-4 | design by RINZEN

"BATMAN" FEARS AFTER ALLEGED CREATURE SIGHTINGS

GOTHAM CITY: 11:29:39: FEAR GRIPS GOTHAM NEIGHBORHOOD AFTER DOZENS OF CITIZENS REPORT SEEING BAT-LIKE CREATURE LEAPING FROM ROOF TO ROOF. (SEE RELATED: MORE NEWS AT GCDAY.WEB)

GOTHAM METRO POLICE RECEIVED ABOUT 20 REPORTS OF A MYSTERIOUS CREATURE WITH A BAT-LIKE FACE, IN AND AROUND HUDSON AND KANE AVENUES, A SENIOR OFFICIAL WITH GCPD TOLD REUTERS EARLIER TONIGHT. GOTHAM POLICE LIEUTENANT CAPTAIN THOMAS HOUCK TOLD REPORTERS THEY HAD FOUND NO CLUES OR PHYSICAL EVIDENCE THAT WOULD EXPLAIN THE PHENOMENA. "TONIGHT WE RECEIVED ABOUT A DOZEN CALLS REPORTING CREATURE SIGHTINGS BY RESIDENTS OF APARTMENT BUILDINGS ON CYPRESS STREET," HOUCK SAID. "OF THESE, NINE HAVE BEEN SHOWN TO HAVE NO VERIFIABILITY. THE OTHER REPORTS INVOLVED SOME EVIDENCE OF MINOR WOUNDS AND WE ARE TRYING TO CONFIRM THE CAUSES OF THOSE INJURIES WITH BOTH GOTHAM MERCY AND GOTHAM CENTRAL HOSPITAL," HE SAID. HE HAD NO FURTHER COMMENTS AS OF THIS LATEST REPORT FILING.

NEWS ONE REPORTERS REVEALED THAT THEY MANAGED TO INTERVIEW A HANDFUL OF CYPRESS STREET RESIDENTS IN THE GOTHAM NEIGHBORHOOD OF EASTEND BEFORE FEDERAL POLICE CORPS AGENTS QUARANTINED THE AREA AS PART OF A SEPARATE, UNRELATED POLICE INVESTIGATION. ALLEGED EYEWITNESSES CLAIMED TO HAVE SEEN AN ANIMAL-LIKE CREATURE WITH A BAT'S FACE AND HUMAN BODY LEAPING BETWEEN BUILDING ROOFTOPS. ONE MAN REPORTED SPECIFICALLY SEEING "A LARGE MAN WITHOUT ARMS, RUNNING UNDER WHAT LOOKED LIKE A HEAVY, BLACK SHEET, LIKE A BLACK GHOST." FPC AGENTS QUELLED HYSTERIA BY POSTING STREET-TO-STREET ROADBLOCKS AND IMPOSING AN IMMEDIATE CURFEW ON THE EASTEND NEIGHBORHOOD SOUTH OF DELANY STREET AND EAST OF BROAD, STRETCHING ALL THE WAY TO THE RIVER. POLICE VEHICLES PATROLLED THE AREA OVERHEAD AS RESIDENTS SPENT THE REST OF THE NIGHT ON THEIR ROOFTOPS OR IN THEIR HOMES, ARMED WITH STICKS AND LEAD PIPES. NO FURTHER INJURIES OR SIGHTINGS WERE REPORTED.

FPC AGENT BARUCH MERCER ADMITTED DURING AN UNRELATED, OFFICIAL NEWS CONFERENCE LATE LAST NIGHT THAT WHILE THERE ARE ABOUT 1,000 FPC PERSONNEL CURRENTLY STATIONED IN AND AROUND GOTHAM, IT HAS NOTHING TO DO WITH THIS EVENT. FURTHER, AGENT MERCER STRESSED THAT THE FPC POLICE ACTIVITY IN THE SAME EASTEND NEIGHBORHOOD IS RELATED TO A SEPARATE INVESTIGATION. HE WOULD NEITHER CONFIRM NOR DENY REPORTS OF THE SO-CALLED "BAT-MAN OF GOTHAM".(REUTERS CONTRIBUTED TO THIS REPORT)∎

PANIC AS GOTHAM GCPD HUNT "BAT-LIKE" CREATURE

CMN.WEB/NEWS/N.29.39 PM

GOTHAM POLICE HAVE RECEIVED NUMEROUS REPORTS LATE THURSDAY NIGHT OF A MYSTERIOUS CREATURE WITH BAT-LIKE FEATURES AND A HUMAN BODY. THE SIGHTINGS OCCURRED IN THE CITY BLOCK OF 200-300 CYPRESS STREET, NOW UNDER FPC SURVEILLANCE DUE TO A SEPARATE, UNRELATED POLICE INVESTIGATION. GOTHAM ONE HAS REPORTED THAT A SMALL NUMBER OF RESIDENTS OF THE CYPRESS STREET MISSION BUILDING AND ADJOINING RESIDENCY HILL APARTMENT COMPLEX HAVE SUSTAINED INJURIES RELATED TO THE ALLEGED CREATURE SIGHTINGS. EYEWITNESS ACCOUNTS VARY AS TO THE APPEARANCE AND NATURE OF THE ALLEGED CREATURE SOME RESIDENTS ARE CALLING "THE BAT-MAN OF GOTHAM." ONE MAN SHOWED GOTHAM ONE REPORTERS WHAT APPEARED TO BE BITE WOUNDS, CLAIMING HE HAD BEEN ATTACKED BY THIS CREATURE. DOCTORS AT GOTHAM MERCY HAVE VERIFIED THAT THE MAN HAD BEEN ATTACKED BY SOMETHING, ALTHOUGH THEY WOULD NOT AT THIS TIME SPECULATE AS TO WHAT MAY HAVE ATTACKED HIM. CONFIDENTIALLY, ONE ORDERLY AT THE HOSPITAL TOLD REPORTERS IT WAS LIKELY THE RESULT OF DOG BITES. THIS MAN IS NOW BEING HELD FOR FURTHER TESTING AND WAS NOT AVAILABLE FOR ADDITIONAL QUESTIONING BY THE MEDIA.

"THE BAT-MAN OF GOTHAM" WAS THE NAME GIVEN TO A MYTHICAL URBAN MONSTER OF POPULAR LEGEND IN THE LAST CENTURY.

GCPD OFFICIALS HAVE VERIFIED THE SIGHTING REPORTS AND SAY AN INVESTIGATION IS NOW UNDER WAY, ALTHOUGH THEY WOULD NOT SPECULATE AS TO THE NATURE OF THE MYSTERIOUS FIGURE RESIDENTS ALLEGEDLY SAW. ONE OFFICER HAS BLAMED THE PANIC ON UNEDUCATED POOR PEOPLE, MANY OF THEM SUPERSTITIOUS AND STRONG BELIEVERS IN THE SUPERNATURAL. "WE'VE SEEN THINGS LIKE THIS BEFORE. IT'S LIKELY A GANG OF TEENAGERS IN MASKS, OUT TO SCARE PEOPLE," SAID THE OFFICER. "THERE IS NO SUCH THING AS A BAT-MAN OF GOTHAM."

THE STATE POWER COMPANY HAS ASSURED RESIDENTS THERE WILL BE NO INTERRUPTION IN THE GOTHAM POWER SUPPLY TONIGHT, SO THAT WORRIED TENANTS COULD FEEL SAFER KNOWING MAGNETIC LOCKS AND HOME LIGHTS WILL FUNCTION PROPERLY. WITH THE HOLIDAY SEASON APPROACHING AND HOME HEATING DEMANDS ON THE RISE, GOTHAM'S STATE-OWNED POWER SUPPLIER HAS EXPERIENCED A NUMBER OF UNFORTUNATE ROLLING BROWNOUTS.∎

TO: ALL AGENTS CONNECTED TO CASE #312163221-A

FROM: FPC HEAD DIVISION, WASHINGTON DC
CLASSIFIED/INTERNAL BRANCH MEMO ONLY/DO NOT CIRCULATE
REPORT CONCERNING CASE #312163221-A (SO-CALLED "BAT-MAN OF GOTHAM")

GOTHAM CITY 11-28-39

CLASSIFIED DOCUMENT: DO NOT CIRCULATE

NOTICE TO ALL AGENTS—FOLLOWING THE UNAVOIDABLE PUBLIC RELEASE OF 911-THREADS TO GCPD DISPATCH BRANCH #15 (CONCERNING INITIAL SIGHTINGS OF SO-CALLED "BAT-MAN OF GOTHAM" BY RESIDENTS OF THE 200-300 BLOCK CYPRESS AVE., GOTHAM CITY, 11-28-39), THE FOLLOWING ORDERS ARE NOW ISSUED:

1.1— NO AGENT(S) CONNECTED TO CASE #312163221-A WILL BE AUTHORIZED TO ISSUE PUBLIC STATEMENTS REGARDING ANY DETAIL(S) OF THIS ONGOING INVESTIGATION, NOR ARE AGENTS AUTHORIZED TO ISSUE STATEMENTS EITHER CONFIRMING OR DENYING EXISTENCE OF SO-CALLED "BAT-MAN OF GOTHAM." NO EXCEPTIONS. PLEASE REFER ALL FURTHER PUBLIC OR MEDIA-SOURCE INQUIRIES TO THE FPC OFFICE OF MEDIA RELATIONS.

2.1— AGENTS ARE ORDERED TO PRIVATELY MAINTAIN AN ABSOLUTE STANDARD OF STRICT CONFIDENTIALITY REGARDING ANY AND ALL ASPECTS OF THE ONGOING CASE INVESTIGATION. AGENTS ARE EXPRESSLY FORBIDDEN IN ANY WAY TO SPEAK, WRITE, OR OTHERWISE TRANSMIT ANY INFORMATION CONCERNING CASE SPECIFICS, TO INSINUATE, OR TO OTHERWISE SPECULATE ON ANY ASPECT OF THIS INVESTIGATION WITH ANY PERSON OR PERSONS NOT DIRECTLY CONNECTED TO THE ONGOING FPC INVESTIGATION. AGENTS MAY ONLY DISCUSS THE DETAILS OF THIS CASE WITH OTHER MEMBERS OF THE INVESTIGATION TEAM. ANY VIOLATION OF THESE EDICTS WILL BE PUNISHED TO THE FULLEST EXTENT OF THE LAW.

THESE POLICY ORDERS SHALL REMAIN IN PLACE UNTIL OR UNLESS OTHERWISE INDICATED OFFICIALLY BY FPC HEAD DIVISION.

PRIORITY NOTICE TO ALL AGENTS
CONNECTED TO CASE #312163221-A

FROM: FPC HEAD DIVSION. WASH. DC
CLASSIFIED/INTERNAL BRANCH MEMO ONLY/DO NOT CIRCULATE

REPORT CONCERNING CASE #312163221-A (SO-CALLED "BAT-MAN OF GOTHAM." GOTHAM CITY. 11-28-39)
NOTICE TO ALL AGENTS–FOLLOWING THE UNAVOIDABLE PUBLIC RELEASE OF 911-THREADS CALLED IN TO
GCPD DISPATCH BRANCH #15 (CONCERNING INITIAL SIGHTINGS OF SO-CALLED "BAT-MAN OF GOTHAM" BY
RESIDENTS OF THE 200-300 BLOCK CYPRESS AVE.. GOTHAM CITY. 11-28-39). THE FOLLOWING ORDERS
ARE NOW ISSUED:

1.1– NO AGENT(S) CONNECTED TO CASE #312163221-A WILL BE AUTHORIZED TO ISSUE PUBLIC STATEMENTS
REGARDING ANY DETAIL(S) OF THIS ONGOING INVESTIGATION, NOR ARE AGENTS AUTHORIZED TO ISSUE
STATEMENTS EITHER CONFIRMING OR DENYING EXISTENCE OF SO-CALLED "BAT-MAN OF GOTHAM."
NO EXCEPTIONS. PLEASE REFER ALL FURTHER PUBLIC OR MEDIA-SOURCE INQUIRIES TO THE FPC OFFICE
OF MEDIA RELATIONS.

2.1– AGENTS ARE ORDERED TO PRIVATELY MAINTAIN AN ABSOLUTE STANDARD OF STRICT CONFIDENTIALITY
REGARDING ANY AND ALL ASPECTS OF THE ONGOING CASE INVESTIGATION. AGENTS ARE EXPRESSLY FORBIDDEN
IN ANY WAY TO SPEAK, WRITE, OR OTHERWISE TRANSMIT ANY INFORMATION CONCERNING CASE SPECIFICS, TO
INSINUATE, OR TO OTHERWISE SPECULATE ON ANY ASPECT OF THIS INVESTIGATION WITH ANY PERSON OR
PERSONS NOT DIRECTLY CONNECTED TO THE ONGOING FPC INVESTIGATION. AGENTS MAY ONLY DISCUSS THE
DETAILS OF THIS CASE WITH OTHER MEMBERS OF THE INVESTIGATION TEAM. ANY VIOLATION OF THESE EDICTS
WILL BE PUNISHED TO THE FULLEST EXTENT OF THE LAW.

**THESE POLICY ORDERS SHALL REMAIN IN PLACE UNTIL OR UNLESS OTHERWISE
INDICATED OFFICIALLY BY FPC HEAD DIVISION.**

THE FOLLOWING IS THE OFFICIAL SUMMATION
OF MINUTES OF CASE #312163221-A, 11-28-39
--DO NOT CIRCULATE--

THE FOLLOWING OFFICIAL POST-ANALYSIS STATEMENT OF THE MINUTES OF CASE #312163221-A (AS PROVIDED
BY FPC HEAD DIV., WASH. DC) IS ISSUED DIRECTLY AND CONFIDENTIALLY TO ALL AGENTS ACTING ON CASE
#312163221-A ONLY. PLEASE DISREGARD ALL MEDIA REPORTS REGARDING THIS CASE. ALL FURTHER
CONFIDENTIAL INQUIRIES ARE TO BE DIRECTED TO THE OFFICES OF FPC AGENT MERCER OR FPC AGENT TIBBLE.

1.1– FOLLOWING THE INITIAL 11:12 PM CONFRONTATION BETWEEN AGENTS OF THE GOTHAM FPC WOLVES POLICE
TEAM AND SO-CALLED BAT-MAN OF GOTHAM (HEREAFTER REFERRED TO AS "SUSPECT") IN ADAMS STREET
SUBWAY STATION, SUSPECT WAS LAST SEEN FLEEING FROM STATION ON FOOT VIA THE NW END OF TRACK 6
ON THE F-LINE TRAIN. ONE FPC AGENT (#34112) WAS REPORTED AS DEAD ON THE SCENE, VICTIM OF GUNFIRE–
CAUSE OF DEATH: MULTIPLE GUNSHOT WOUNDS (SEE ATTACHED REPORT FROM FPC MEDICAL EXAMINER'S
OFFICE). FOR THE FOLLOWING TEN MINUTES, SUSPECT WAS UNDETECTED BY AGENTS ON THE GROUND.

DISPATCH COPTERS WERE DEPLOYED, PATROLLING A ONE-HALF-MILE RADIUS AROUND THE SIX NEAREST SUBWAY
EXITS, ORDERED TO SPREAD OUT IN A QUARTER-MILE RADIUS FROM EACH F-LINE SUBWAY EXIT FOR EVERY
ENSUING INTERVAL OF ONE MINUTE. DOGTEAMS AND GROUND TROOPS WERE AIRLIFTED TO SELECT AREA
STRATEGIC POINTS, FOLLOWING ABELL-WORONORVIK PROCEDURAL FORMATION MODELS.

2.1– AT 11:22 PM, DOGTEAM-ALPHA DETECTED SUSPECT ON BUILDING ROOFTOP OF 200-300 CYPRESS AVE.
BLOCK. SUSPECT WAS CHASED OVER ADJOINING ROOFTOPS OF BUILDINGS A AND B (SEE ATTACHED: MAP) BY
DOGTEAM-ALPHA, THEN WAS SEEN TO CLEAR A 23-FOOT LEAP BETWEEN ROOFTOPS (EVENT RECORDED ON DOG-
RETINA REMOTES, SEE ATTACHED FILE #21121-DTR) OF BUILDINGS B AND C). **CONTINUED...**

PROVISIONAL CONCLUSIONS DRAWN FROM RELEVANT FACTS CONCERNING CASE #312163221-A:

1.1– SUSPECT IS BELIEVED TO BE A CAUCASIAN MALE BETWEEN 24 AND 60 YEARS OF AGE, PROJECTED TO BE WELL OVER 6 FEET TALL, WEIGHING BETWEEN 225 AND 250 LBS. SUSPECT EXHIBITED SIGNS OF BEING WELL TRAINED IN MARTIAL COMBAT TECHNIQUES, DISPLAYING AN ALMOST OLYMPIAN DEGREE OF ATHLETIC PROWESS, AND IS TO BE CONSIDERED DANGEROUS. IT IS STRONGLY BELIEVED SUSPECT WAS WEARING AN EXO-ENHANCEMENT SUIT DURING THIS ENTIRE EVENT. NO DISTINGUISHING FACIAL FEATURES HAVE BEEN RECORDED, OWING TO THE FACT THAT SUSPECT WAS OBSERVED TO BE WEARING A DARK MASK AND CLOAK THROUGHOUT THIS ENTIRE INCIDENT.

2.1– SUSPECT IS BEING CALLED "BAT-MAN OF GOTHAM" BASED ON THE OBSCURE CHARACTER OF GOTHAM URBAN LEGEND. HE IS WANTED FOR QUESTIONING REGARDING THE MURDER OF FPC AGENT #34112. IT IS BELIEVED SUSPECT WAS ACTING ALONE THROUGHOUT THIS ENTIRE EVENT. IT IS UNKNOWN WHETHER SUSPECT HAS ANY GROUP AFFILIATION. AT THIS TIME, SUSPECT'S MOTIVES REMAIN UNKNOWN. THROUGHOUT THIS EVENT, SUSPECT SAID NOTHING AND ISSUED NO DEMANDS, PLEAS, STATEMENTS OF INTENT, OR COMMUNICATIONS OF ANY KIND.

3.1– SUSPECT REMAINS AN UNCLASSIFIED, UNDOCUMENTED INDIVIDUAL KNOWN TO BE IN POSSESSION OF DANGEROUS, POSSIBLY ILLEGAL TACTICAL WEAPONRY. APPROACH ONLY WITH THE HIGHEST LEVEL OF CAUTION.

SUSPECT IS WANTED FOR FURTHER QUESTIONING.

WE STRESS TO ALL AGENTS: THE "BAT-MAN OF GOTHAM" IS TO BE CONSIDERED ARMED AND DANGEROUS, A LEVEL-SIX CRIMINAL. ORDERS ARE TO APPREHEND ALIVE. REPEAT—SUBJECT IS TO BE APPREHENDED ALIVE. UNDER NO CIRCUMSTANCES IS LETHAL FORCE AUTHORIZED.

ADDENDUM: THE FOLLOWING ARE THE TWO INITIAL POLICE TRANSCRIPTS OF GOTHAM "BAT-MAN" SIGHTING INCIDENT, RELEASED TO THE MEDIA, 11-28-39.

GOTHAM NEWS ONE HAS OBTAINED, THROUGH THE OFFICE OF BUREAU CHIEF WALLIS GRATCH, OFFICIAL GCPD TRANSCRIPTS OF INITIAL CALLS TO THE DISTRICT DISPATCHER RELATING TO THE "BAT-MAN" SIGHTINGS FROM LATE THURSDAY NIGHT. NOTE: TAPE TRANSCRIPTS HAVE BEEN PRE-EDITED BY GCPD TO PROTECT THE PRIVACY OF INDIVIDUALS INVOLVED.

DISPATCH #1 COMMUNICATIONS DISPATCHER #62155: TWO-BRAVO-SIX, TWO-BRAVO-SIX. COPY.
GCPD VEHICLE 2-B-6: GO AHEAD.
COMMUNICATIONS DISPATCHER #62155: PLEASE PROCEED TO XXXX CYPRESS STREET. A COMPLAINANT IS ADVISING OF A LARGE WILD ANIMAL ON THE ROOF OF A BUILDING. THE ADDRESS IS XXXX CYPRESS.
GCPD VEHICLE 2-B-6: WHAT KIND OF ANIMAL?
COMMUNICATIONS DISPATCHER #62155: SHE COULDN'T SAY. SHE SAID IT WAS A LARGE ANIMAL. SHE WASN'T SURE. SHE SAID IT WAS A LARGE MONKEY OR A MAN WITH A DOG'S FACE OR A BAT'S FACE.
GCPD VEHICLE 2-B-6: A BAT'S FACE?
COMMUNICATIONS DISPATCHER #62155: YES.
GCPD VEHICLE 2-B-6: (AUDIBLE LAUGHTER IN BACKGROUND) CLEAR.
COMMUNICATIONS DISPATCHER #62155: YOU'RE CLEAR.
GCPD VEHICLE 2-B-6: TWO-BRAVO-SIX. WHAT WAS THE ADDRESS ON THAT DOG-FACED MAN AGAIN?
COMMUNICATIONS DISPATCHER #62155: XXXX CYPRESS.
GCPD VEHICLE 2-B-6: CHECK. IS THIS A JOKE?
COMMUNICATIONS DISPATCHER #62155: I DON'T KNOW. PROCEED WITH AN EIGHT-TWELVE (POLICE CODE: CAUTION, UNKNOWN AND POTENTIALLY DANGEROUS SITUATION INVOLVING AN ANIMAL).
GCPD VEHICLE 2-B-6: CHECK. AN EIGHT-TWELVE. TWO-BRAVO-SIX, RESPONDING. OVER.
COMMUNICATIONS DISPATCHER #62155: OVER.

DISPATCH #2
GCPD VEHICLE 2-C-7: PRECINCT 15, THIS IS VEHICLE TWO-CHARLIE-SEVEN. WE'RE IN THE AREA AND WE OVERHEARD THAT LAST REPORT. WANT US TO GO OVER THERE?
COMMUNICATIONS DISPATCHER #62155: HELLO, TWO-CHARLIE-SEVEN, YES. ALL RIGHT, THAT MIGHT BE A GOOD IDEA.
GCPD VEHICLE 2-C-7: ROGER.

MINUTES OF CASE #312163221-A, 11-28-39 CONTINUED

3.1– AT 11:24 PM, A CIVILIAN CALL THREADED INTO 911-LINE OF GCPD PRECINCT #15, DISPATCHER #6. A CITIZEN OF THE 200-300 CYPRESS AVE. BLOCK REPORTED SIGHTING OF MYSTERIOUS FIGURE ON ROOFTOP OF BUILDING C. A SECOND CALL THREADED INTO 911-LINE OF THE GCPD PRECINCT #15, DISPATCHER #3 AT 11:28 PM, WITH A CITIZEN SIGHTING-REPORT ALMOST IDENTICAL TO THE FIRST. ALL SUBSEQUENT SIGHTING-REPORTS (SEVEN IN ALL) VARIED IN DESCRIPTIVE DETAILS, ALTHOUGH ALL TESTIFY TO THE THREATENING PRESENCE OF EITHER A MAN OR A LARGE ANIMAL ON THE BUILDING ROOFTOPS OF BUILDINGS C AND/OR D OF THE 200-300 CYPRESS AVE. BLOCK.

REPORT CONCERNING ANALYSIS OF ITEMS RECOVERED FROM F.P.C. BUILDING FOLLOWING SO-CALLED "BATMAN" INCIDENT IN THE GOTHAM F.P.C. HEADQUARTERS BUILDING, 11:30:39.

THE FOLLOWING IS A LIST OF ITEMS RECOVERED FROM THE CRIME SCENE AS WELL AS THE LOCATION OF SAID DISCOVERY:

1. CASING REMNANTS BELIEVED TO HAVE BEEN PART OF SMOKE BOMB, ANOTHER BELIEVED TO HAVE BEEN FROM NERVE-AGENT DISPERSAL WEAPON (ALSO CALLED "NERVE BOMB")-BASEMENT
2. CASINGS BELIEVED TO HAVE ONCE BEEN PART OF SMOKE BOMB, ANOTHER BELIEVED TO HAVE BEEN FROM THERMITE BOMB-13TH FLOOR
3. ONE CLOTHESPIN SWITCH, VARIOUS D-CLIPS DESIGNED TO SUPPORT WEIGHTS UP TO 500 LBS., HIGH-TENSION RAPPELLING ROPE CONSISTING OF A NETWORK OF 50 LB. STEEL WIRE THREADS INTERMESHED, 200 FT. IN LENGTH-VENTILATION SHAFT NORTH SIDE #4B
4. SUSPENSION APPARATUS AND HAND-HELD GRIP DEVICE OF UNKNOWN ORIGIN; CLIMBING TOOLS-VENTILATION SHAFT NORTH SIDE #4B. NOTE: THESE ITEMS WERE LEFT HANGING AT THE 13TH FLOOR LEVEL
5. CHEMICAL CORROSION SAMPLES SUGGESTING THE PRESENCE OF A SECOND THERMITE BOMB (NO ADDITIONAL CASINGS DISCOVERED AT THIS SITE)-13TH FLOOR
6. CAPE SAMPLE-BASEMENT, 13TH FLOOR (SEE BELOW)
7. SYNTHETIC CRYSTAL SAMPLE-BASEMENT (SEE BELOW)

CLASSIFIED INTERDEPARTMENTAL REPORT CONCERNING "BATMAN" INCIDENT AT F.P.C. HEADQUARTERS (GOTHAM CITY), 11-30-39

TO: F.P.C. HEAD DIVISION, WASHINGTON, DC
FROM: F.P.C. KINEMATICS DEPARTMENT, GOTHAM DIVISION

SIRS,
WE HAVE ANALYZED THE ENTIRE CONTENTS OF RECOVERED EVIDENCE FROM CRIME SCENE #1. WE REGRET TO INFORM THERE ARE NO IDENTIFYING FINGERPRINTS, HAIR SAMPLES, BLOOD OR SALIVA SAMPLES RECOVERED FROM VARIOUS LOCATIONS COMPRISING CRIME SCENE #1 AS OF THIS DATE. ADDITIONALLY, WITH THE EXCEPTION OF THE ITEMS CALLED "CAPE SAMPLES" AND "SYNTHETIC CRYSTAL SAMPLE," NONE OF THE RECOVERED ITEMS DISPLAYED ANY SPECIAL OR UNIQUE CHARACTERISTICS. ALL ITEMS, EXCEPT SO-CALLED "CAPE SAMPLES" AND "SYNTHETIC CRYSTAL SAMPLE," ARE CONSTRUCTED OF MATERIALS EASILY OBTAINED FROM ANY COMMON HARDWARE STORE OR ARMY SURPLUS OUTLET.

MORE THAN ANYTHING, THE BOMB-OBJECTS LISTED ABOVE RESEMBLE COMMON, ORDINARY GOLF BALLS MADE OF A DULL GREY METAL. THE CASINGS OF THE VARIOUS SO-CALLED BOMBS (INCLUDING "SMOKE BOMBS" AND THE SINGLE "NERVE BOMB") RECOVERED FROM THE BASEMENT AND 13TH FLOOR HAVE SHOWN TO BE OTHERWISE UNREMARKABLE HOLLOWED METAL SPHERES WITH TWO SCREW-TOP VALVES ON EITHER END. EACH EXHIBITED A SIMPLE "PINEAPPLE RING" TRIGGER-DEVICE WHICH UNDOUBTEDLY WORKED AS THE UNIT IGNITER. THE OBJECTS APPEAR TO HAVE BEEN MADE SPECIFICALLY FOR THE PURPOSE OF HOLDING THE MATERIALS CONTAINED IN EACH OF THE SO-CALLED BOMBS LISTED. EVIDENCE OF WELDING AND CLOSURE SEAMS IS VISIBLE ALONG THE DIAMETERS OF EACH OBJECT. THE OBJECTS ARE EACH ROUGHLY THE SAME SIZE AND WEIGHT AND HAVE BEEN FOUND TO BE COMPOSED OF A COMMON ALUMINUM ALLOY APPROXIMATELY 1/8 INCH THICKNESS. INSIDE EACH "SMOKE BOMB" WERE RECOVERED TRACINGS OF CONCENTRATED POTASSIUM NITRATE POWDER MIXED WITH COMMON HOUSEHOLD SUGAR (SINCE CARBONIZED) IN A 3:2 RATIO. THIS CHEMICAL MIXTURE UNDOUBTEDLY WAS THE SOURCE OF THE THICK SMOKE REPORTED BY AGENTS ON THE SCENE. AN ADDITIONAL BOMB ALSO RECOVERED FROM CRIME SCENE #1 INCLUDED THE SAME CHEMICAL MIXTURE WITH THE ADDITION OF A HIGHLY POTENT, NON-LETHAL NERVE AGENT WHICH HAS BEEN IDENTIFIED AS MILITARY-GRADE NEROXIN. IT WAS THIS SECOND TYPE OF BOMB WHICH RENDERED UNCONSCIOUS THE F.P.C. AGENTS AT THE 13TH FLOOR SITE. ALL OBJECTS DESCRIBED AS "SMOKE BOMBS" AND THE SINGLE OBJECT DESCRIBED AS "NERVE AGENT BOMB" APPEAR TO BE DESIGNED AND MANUFACTURED IN THE SAME WAY, LIKELY BY THE SAME PERSON.

THE ABOVE-LISTED CLOTHESPIN SWITCH AND OTHER CLIMBING APPARATUS ARE NO DIFFERENT FROM OTHER COMMON ITEMS FOUND IN ANY SPORTING GOODS STORE OR ARMY SURPLUS OUTLET AND DISPLAY NO UNIQUE CHARACTERISTICS. THE UNKNOWN OBJECTS LISTED AS "CLIMBING TOOLS" ARE UNIQUE ONLY INSOMUCH AS THEY HAVE BEEN DESIGNED AND MANUFACTURED BY SOMEONE INDIVIDUALLY AND DO NOT BELONG TO ANY LINE OR BRAND OF SPORTING OR MILITARY CONSUMABLE. CLOSE EXAMINATION OF THESE TOOLS SUGGESTS ALL WERE MADE USING NO LESS THAN TWO DIFFERENT METALWORK BAND SAWS, POLISHED AND SMOOTHED ON WHAT APPEARS TO BE A SINGLE MACHINE. EACH OBJECT IS MADE OF COMMON AND UNREMARKABLE MATERIALS AVAILABLE TO ANY METALWORKING SHOP AND DISPLAY NO BRAND NAMES OR OTHERWISE AUTHENTICATING DESIGN SIGNATURES.

THE CASINGS OF THE SO-CALLED "THERMITE BOMB" RECOVERED FROM THE 13TH FLOOR OF CRIME SCENE #1 ARE COMPOSED OF AN ALUMINUM ALLOY IDENTICAL TO THOSE DESCRIBED ABOVE. RESIDUE OF IRON OXIDE AND PURE ALUMINUM IN AN 8:3 RATIO HAVE BEEN FOUND IN REMNANTS OF THE EXPLOSIVE MIXTURE ISSUED FORTH FROM THIS ITEM. ADDITIONALLY, THERE WERE DISCOVERED ON THE SCENE A SOLID COPPER WIRE 2MM THICK AND A SPRING-TYPE CLOTHESPIN SWITCH.

TRACE DEPOSITS OF MAGNESIUM OXIDE WERE FOUND NEAR THE OBJECT AND MAY SUGGEST THE MEANS OF IGNITION. IT IS BELIEVED THE CLOTHESPIN SWITCHES WERE USED AS ACTIVATORS FOR THE EXPLOSIVE CHARGES INSIDE THE VARIOUS BOMBS.

INVESTIGATION OF THE NORTH VENTILATION SHAFT #4B SUGGESTS THE SUSPECT ENTERED THE BUILDING FROM THE ROOF. ALTHOUGH THE COVERING TO THE VENTILATION SHAFT WAS FOUND TO BE CLOSED AND LOCKED IN PLACE, THERE WAS EVIDENCE OF TAMPERING WITH THE SHAFT'S FACEPLATE. THE SCREWS WERE LOOSENED AND COULD BE EASILY REMOVED FROM WITHIN THE SHAFT. IT IS BELIEVED THAT FROM THIS ROOFTOP VANTAGE POINT, THE SUSPECT DESCENDED TO THE BASEMENT LEVEL WHERE HE ENTERED THE FLOOR THROUGH A DROP-PANEL HANGING FROM THE CEILING. FOUR SCREWS WERE FOUND ON THE FLOOR BENEATH THE PANEL. ALL SURVEILLANCE CAMERAS ON THIS LEVEL WERE FOUND TO BE DEACTIVATED (A DETAIL WHICH INITIALLY ALERTED AGENTS IN THE BUILDING TO THE PRESENCE OF THE INTRUDER). THE THREE F.P.C. EMPLOYEES ON STAFF AT THIS LOCATION WERE FOUND TO HAVE BEEN RENDERED UNCONSCIOUS AT THIS TIME. RESPIRATORY SAMPLES TAKEN FROM THESE VICTIMS SHOWED THEY HAD EACH INHALED A CONCENTRATED DOSE OF NEROXIN SPRAY. EACH WAS QUESTIONED BUT COULD REMEMBER NOTHING SIGNIFICANT OF THE EVENT AND HAD NO RECOLLECTION OF SENSING AN INTRUDER ON THE FLOOR PRIOR TO THE ATTACKS. EACH VICTIM WAS RENDERED UNCONSCIOUS FOR A PERIOD OF UP TO ONE HOUR FOLLOWING THE ATTACK.

FROM HERE, THE SUSPECT ENTERED THE COLD STORAGE MORGUE AND TAMPERED WITH THE CORPSE OF THE INDIVIDUAL KNOWN AS JOHN DOE. SOMETHING WAS REMOVED FROM THE BODY AT THIS TIME (SEE ATTACHED REPORT FILED BY AGENT MERCER FOR F.P.C. HEADS DIVISION MARKED TOP SECRET). GIVEN THAT IT TOOK AN ESTIMATED 1.3 MINUTES FOR THE SUSPECT TO GO FROM THE ROOF TO THE BASEMENT MORGUE, IT IS BELIEVED THIS INDIVIDUAL HAD A WORKING MAP OF THE BUILDING'S FLOOR PLAN. UPON ENGAGEMENT WITH F.P.C. AGENTS DISPATCHED TO THE BASEMENT LEVEL, A FIREFIGHT ENSUED. SUSPECT DISABLED ALL EIGHT MEMBERS OF THE GOTHAM TIGERS TEAM AFTER A FIERCE FIGHT AT THIS LOCATION. EYEWITNESS ACCOUNTS SUGGEST THE SUSPECT LEFT THE FLOOR THROUGH THE VENTILATION SHAFT USING A MECHANIZED PULLEY-AND-WIRE SYSTEM TO LIFT HIM BODILY OUT OF THE BASEMENT AND INTO THE SHAFT ABOVE. THE SUSPECT THEN ASCENDED TO THE 13TH FLOOR WHERE HE WAS ENGAGED BY AGENT MERCER AND ADDITIONAL MEMBERS OF THE TIGERS GROUND TEAM. A FIREFIGHT ENSUED, RESULTING IN MASSIVE EXPLOSIONS AND BUILDING DAMAGE CAUSED BY SUSPECT. AFTER THIS, THE SUSPECT LEFT THE BUILDING THROUGH AN AIRSHAFT ON THE NE CORNER OF THE 13TH FLOOR WHERE HE WAS CONFRONTED FOR A FINAL TIME BY AGENT MERCER AND MEMBERS OF THE GOTHAM TIGERS. SUSPECT DISAPPEARED AT THIS POINT AND REMAINS AT LARGE.

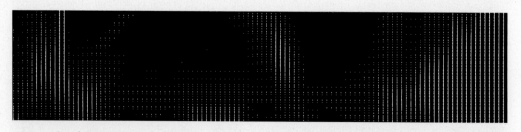

BATMAN: YEAR 100

BOB SHRECK

SIX PAGES (NINE ROUGHS)

HEY, HEY, SHRECK:

GOOD MORNING, BOBS!

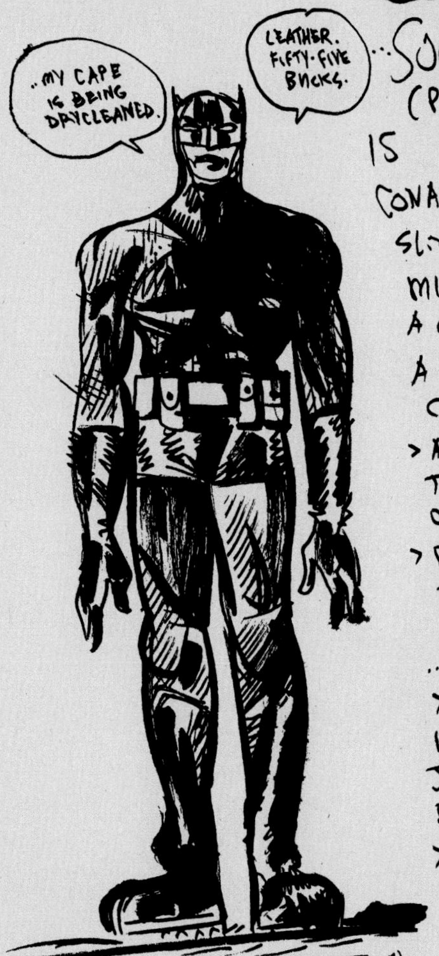

..MY CAPE IS BEING DRYCLEANED.
LEATHER. FIFTY-FIVE BUCKS.

...SOME QUESTIONS...
(PLEASE ANSWER FOR ME):

IS BATMAN BUILT LIKE CONAN? I SEE HIM A little slimmer... LIKE NURYEV OR MICHAEL JORDAN. MORE OF A GRACEFUL ATHLETE THAN A PRO WRESTLER. IS THAT COOL WITH YOU? NO?

> ALSO: NO BELT BUCKLE? ARE THOSE UTILITY POUCHES SOFT LEATHER OR HARD/MOLDED PLASTIC?

> DOES HIS COSTUME GATHER AT THE JOINTS + KNEES, OR IS IT SPANDEX-STRETCH MATERIAL? ... PVC OR WOOL? LEATHER? VYNYL?

> CAN HE HAVE SQUARE TRUNKS LIKE AN OLYMPIC SWIMMER? JOHNSON'S MODEL IS MORE LIKE BIKINI BRIEFS/UNDERWEAR.

> HOW TALL IS THIS DUDE?

> IS HIS MASK A SINGLE MOLD OR STITCHED PIECES OF LEATHER? IS IT HARD LIKE A FOOTBALL HELMET, OR IS IT PLIANT?

☆ PAUL POPE, pretender to the throne

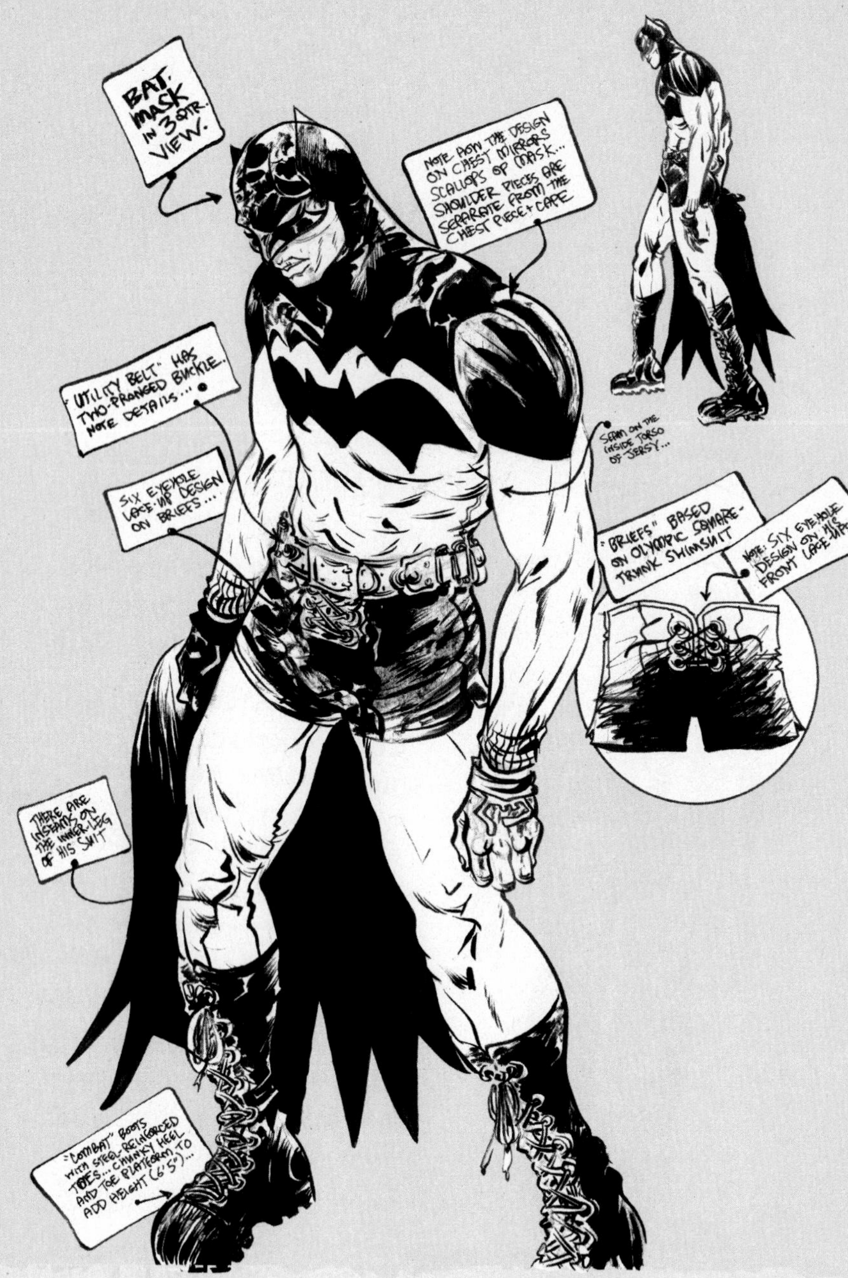
BAT-MASK IN 3 QTR. VIEW.
NOTE HOW THE DESIGN ON CHEST MIRRORS SCALLOPS OF MASK... SHOULDER PIECES ARE SEPARATE FROM THE CHEST PIECE + CAPE
"UTILITY BELT" HAS TWO-PRONGED BUCKLE. NOTE DETAILS...
SEAM ON THE INSIDE TORSO OF JERSY...
SIX EYEHOLE LACE-UP DESIGN ON BRIEFS...
"BRIEFS" BASED ON OLYMPIC SQUARE-TRUNK SWIMSUIT
NOTE: SIX EYEHOLE DESIGN ON HIS FRONT LACE-UPS...
THERE ARE INSEAMS ON THE INNER-LEG OF HIS SUIT
"COMBAT" BOOTS WITH STEEL-REINFORCED TOES... CHUNKY HEEL AND TOE PLATFORM TO ADD HEIGHT (6'5")...

Before starting work on BATMAN YEAR 100 I had a lot of time to think about what I wanted to do with both the story and the character. My preference is to work on stories where I am free to completely design a fictional world—literally from the ground up. Take Batman's boots for example. This guy would need a good, sturdy pair of boots. He'd need some serious footwear for all the trouble he'd be seeing. I imagine he'd prefer military combat boots, like the kind Airborne Rangers wear when they go leaping out of airplanes and helicopters; something steel-toed, lightweight, offering durability and support. That's an obvious choice, isn't it? You'd think it would be...

It's long been a pet peeve of mine when you come across comic book artists who insist on drawing generic, featureless boot-like shapes beneath the ankles of their superheroes, as if boots were just vague, foot-shaped stumps molded out of colorful plastic blobs, resembling something you'd get out of a toy box at a dentist's office. Even as a kid that irked me to no end. Same goes with artists who don't draw seams and wrinkles on fabrics. They ought to be there—and so should sweat and dirt, for that matter—otherwise, your characters will look like window display dummies with costumes spray-painted on. I made the sleeves on Batman's costume deliberately too short so we would constantly see his wrists poking out, just above the gloves. Something about that suggests, to me at least, a sense of his concealed human vulnerability.

His mask would probably have to be made out of hand-tooled leather, like a well-made Mexican wrestling mask.

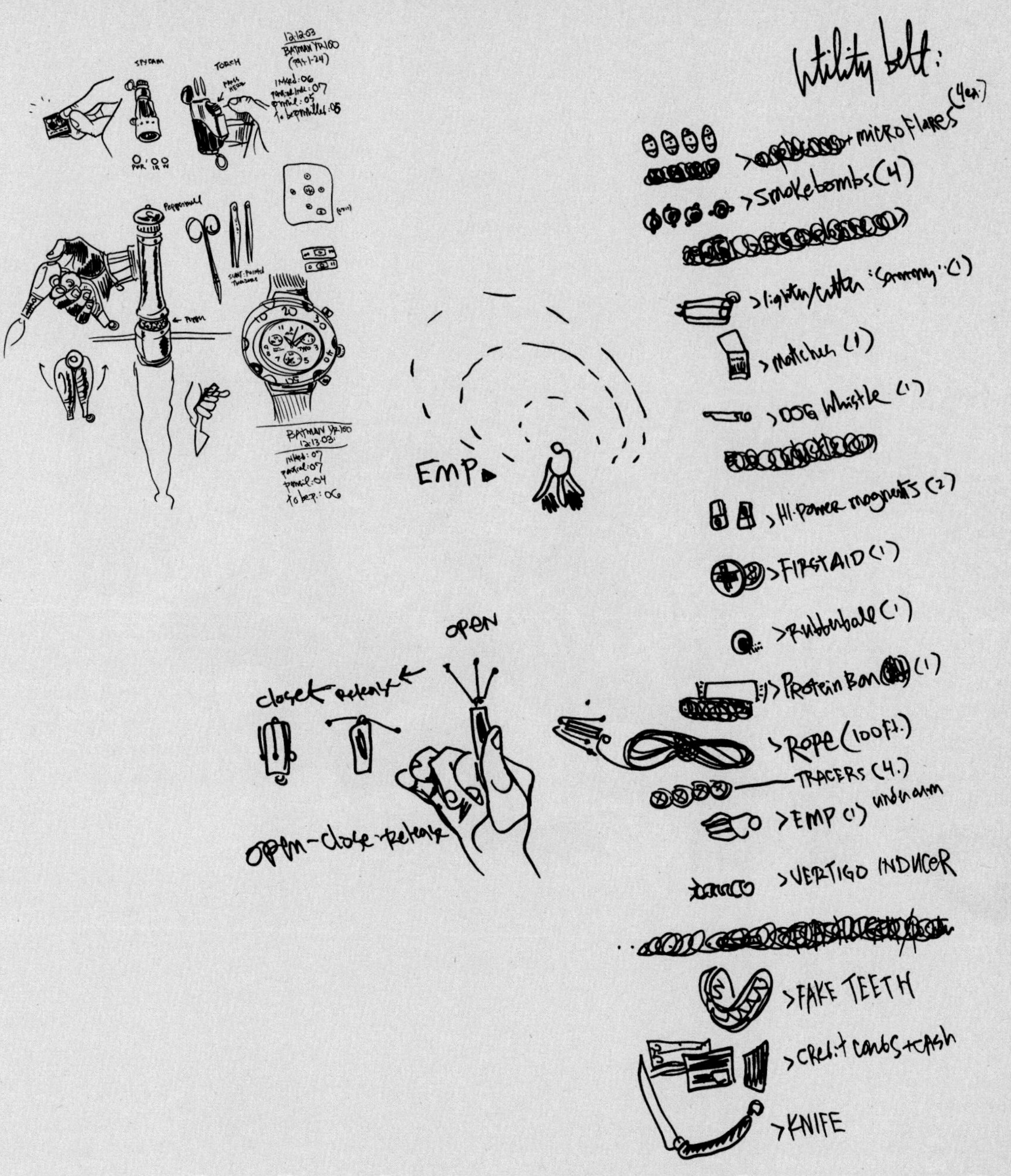

SPYCAM
TORCH
Utility belt:
microflares (4ea.)
smokebombs (4)
lighter/cutter (1)
matches (1)
DOG whistle (1)
HI-power magnets (2)
FIRSTAID (1)
Rubberball (1)
Protein Bar (1)
Rope (100ft.)
TRACERS (4.)
EMP (1) underarm
VERTIGO INDUCER
FAKE TEETH
Credit cards+cash
KNIFE
EMP
OPEN
close-release
open-close-release

Maybe it would have cleverly padded shapes sewn in, further disguising his true identity. Add to this the fake vampire teeth and a motorcycle which can fold in half and hang upside down like a bat and you have a pretty scary character.

His utility belt suggests an interesting challenge to a writer and a designer. You don't want to just use the belt as a lazy story device, a cheap *deus ex machina* which gets him out of tight spots like a rich uncle's inheritance. I mean—Bat-Shark Repellant? Give me a break.

I tried to select the belt contents based on what Batman himself would likely think he'd need before setting out for battle. How much weight would he want to carry around on him? How and where would he organize the utilities in order to best...utilize them? How would he keep all the little metal things from rattling around and making noise when he needs perfect stealth? If you notice, on page one we see some sort of little under-the-shoulder harness designed on the costume. Originally, I imagined Batman would naturally keep longer tools (such as rope or a knife) under his arm, although I had to drop this soon after I started drawing it since it actually interfered with the costume design in most cases. Too many pouches and belts and he stops looking like Batman and more like a mailman.

Because BATMAN YEAR 100 is a science-fiction story, we do see a couple of strangely futuristic devices in his arsenal, but I largely tried to keep this kind of thing to a minimum. Most of the ideas that went into designing the

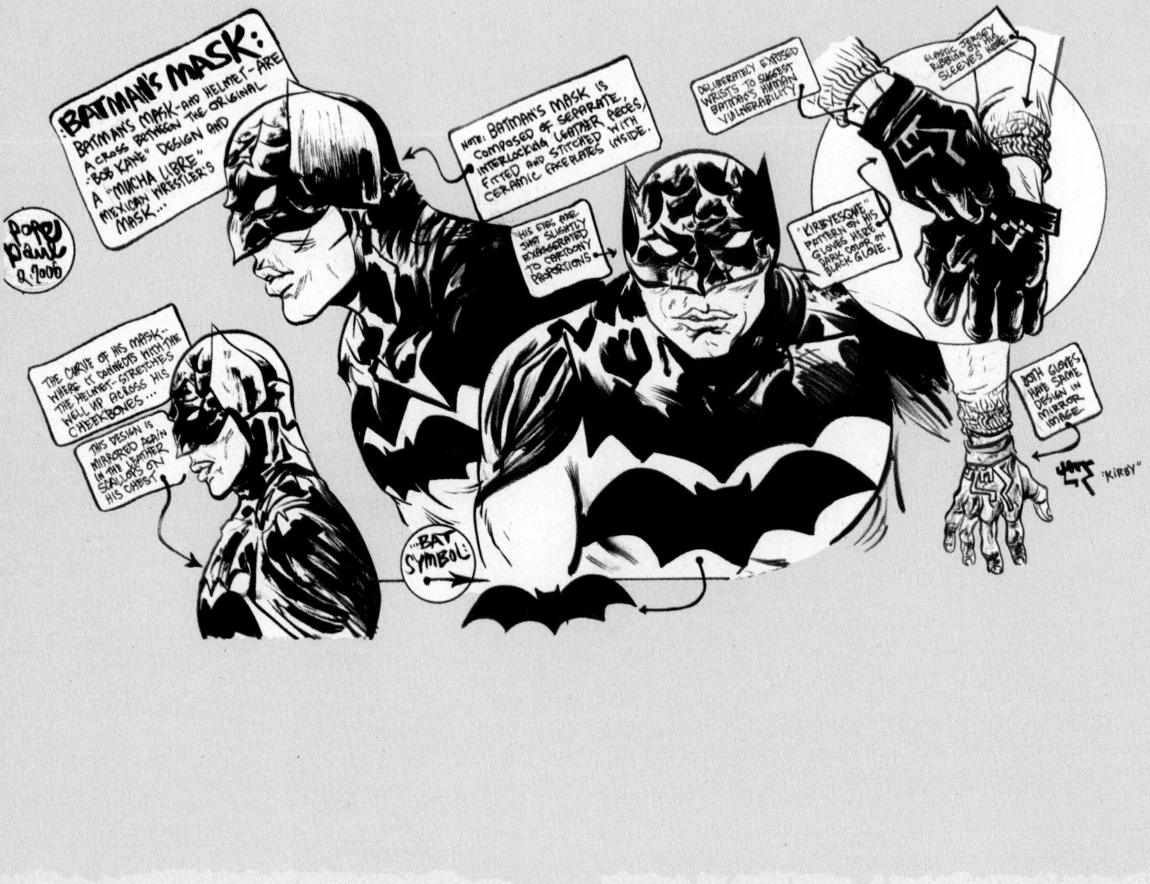
BATMAN'S MASK:
BATMAN'S MASK-AND HELMET-ARE A CROSS BETWEEN THE ORIGINAL "BOB KANE" DESIGN AND A "LUCHA LIBRE" MEXICAN WRESTLER'S MASK...
NOTE: BATMAN'S MASK IS COMPOSED OF SEPARATE, INTERLOCKING LEATHER PIECES, FITTED AND STITCHED WITH CERAMIC FACEPLATES INSIDE.
POPE PAUL 2.2006
HIS EYES ARE JUST SLIGHTLY EXAGGERATED TO CARTOONY PROPORTIONS
DELIBERATELY EXPOSED WRISTS TO SUGGEST BATMAN'S HUMAN VULNERABILITY
ELASTIC JERSEY RIBBING ON HIS SLEEVES HERE
"KIRBYESQUE" PATTERN ON HIS GLOVES HERE: DARK COLOR ON BLACK GLOVE.
THE CURVE OF HIS MASK... WHERE IT CONNECTS WITH THE HELMET- STRETCHES WELL UP ACROSS HIS CHEEKBONES...
THIS DESIGN IS MIRRORED AGAIN IN THE LEATHER SCALLOPS ON HIS CHEST
BOTH GLOVES HAVE SAME DESIGN IN MIRROR IMAGE
"KIRBY"
...BAT SYMBOL:

belt hardware came from a visit to the M.I.T Media Lab, researching military websites, and a quick pass through *The Anarchist Cookbook*. I didn't want Batman to have a thousand little super-spy gadgets that did all the work for him. Regardless of what's in his utility belt, Batman has to be believable, relying on muscle, brains, and will power more than anything else.

He would, however, need some room on the belt for some kind of high protein power bar, I knew that for sure. This is a very physical superhero we're talking about; he's bound to get hungry. It's another pet peeve of mine how little the question of hunger or the need to eat is addressed in comics. I wish it was something we saw more often. As infrequently as the subject is addressed, when we finally do get to see superheroes eating, they are almost always shown to be eating while wearing gloves. Have you ever tried to eat Thanksgiving dinner while wearing a pair of leather gloves?

PAUL POPE NYC 11.12.06

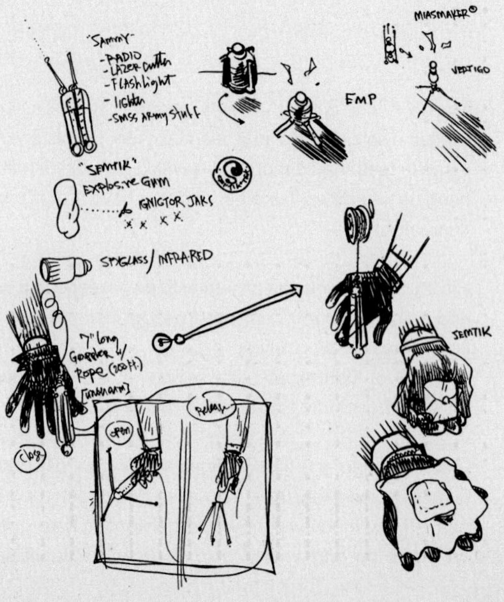
"Sammy"
-RADIO
-LAZER cutter
-FLASHlight
-lighter
-SWISS Army Stuff
EMP
MIASMAKER®
VERTIGO
"SEMTIK"
Explosive Gum
IGNITOR JAKS
SPYGLASS/INFRARED
SEMTIK

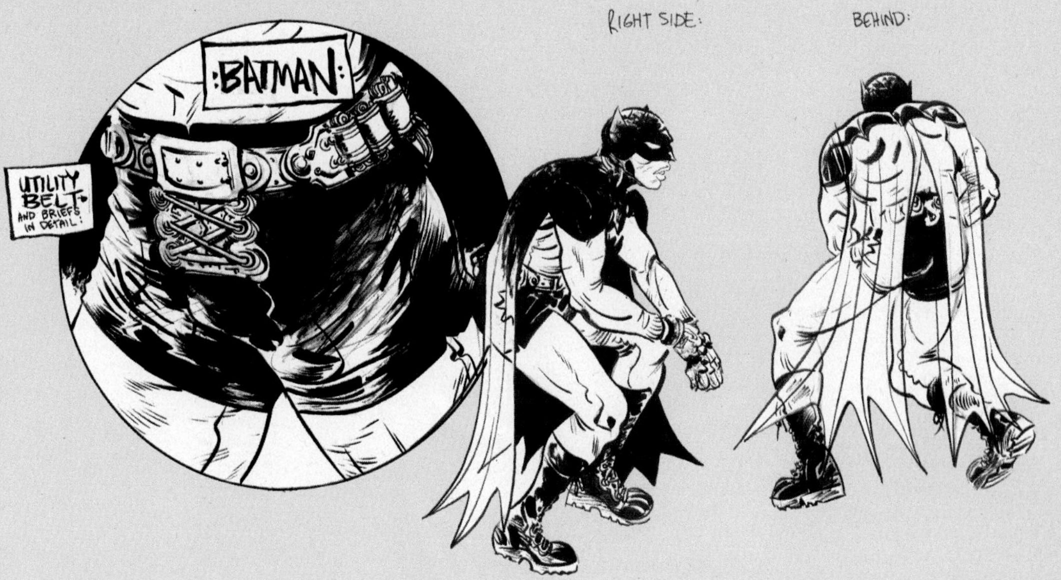
RIGHT SIDE:
BEHIND:
BATMAN
UTILITY BELT AND BRIEFS IN DETAIL:

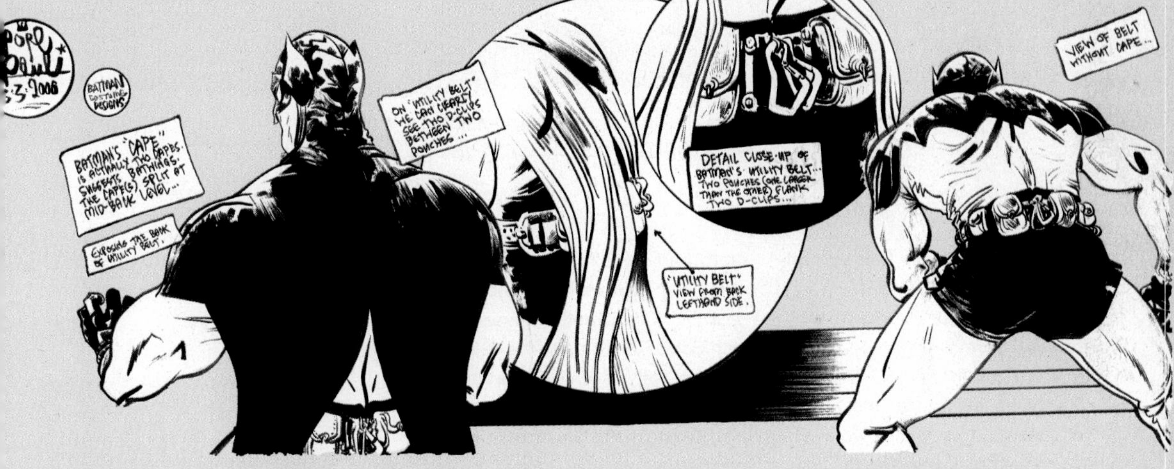
BATMAN COSTUME DESIGNS
BATMAN'S "CAPE" IS ACTUALLY TWO CAPES. SUGGESTS BATWINGS. THE CAPE(S) SPLIT AT MID-BACK LEVEL...
EXPOSING THE BACK OF UTILITY BELT.
ON "UTILITY BELT" WE CAN CLEARLY SEE TWO D-CLIPS BETWEEN TWO POUCHES...
DETAIL CLOSE-UP OF BATMAN'S UTILITY BELT... TWO POUCHES (ONE LARGER THAN THE OTHER) FLANK TWO D-CLIPS...
"UTILITY BELT" VIEW FROM BACK LEFTHAND SIDE.
VIEW OF BELT WITHOUT CAPE...

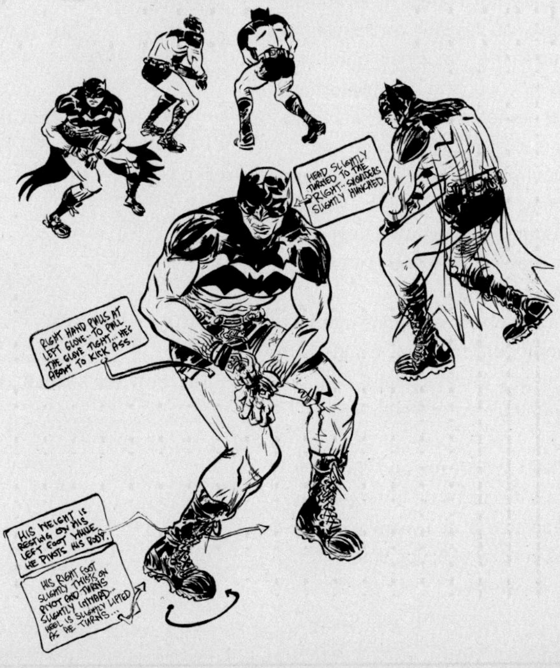
HEAD SLIGHTLY TURNED TO THE RIGHT.. SHOULDERS SLIGHTLY HUNCHED.
RIGHT HAND PULLS AT LEFT GLOVE.. TO PULL THE GLOVE TIGHT... HE'S ABOUT TO KICK ASS.
HIS WEIGHT IS RESTING ON HIS LEFT FOOT WHILE HE PIVOTS HIS BODY.
HIS RIGHT FOOT SLIGHTLY TWISTS ON PIVOT AND TURNS SLIGHTLY INWARD.. HEEL IS SLIGHTLY LIFTED AS HE TURNS...

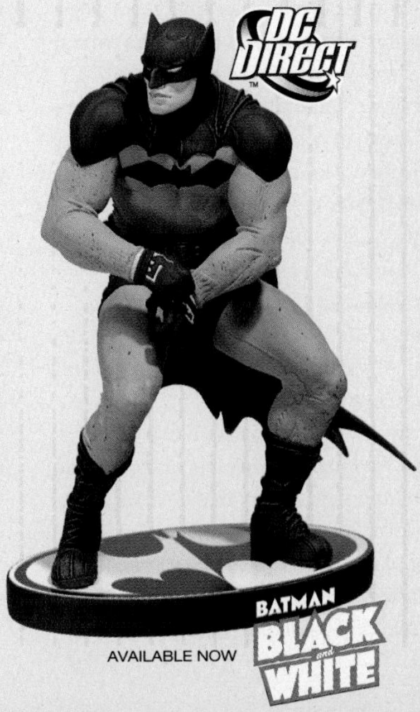
DC DIRECT
BATMAN BLACK and WHITE
AVAILABLE NOW

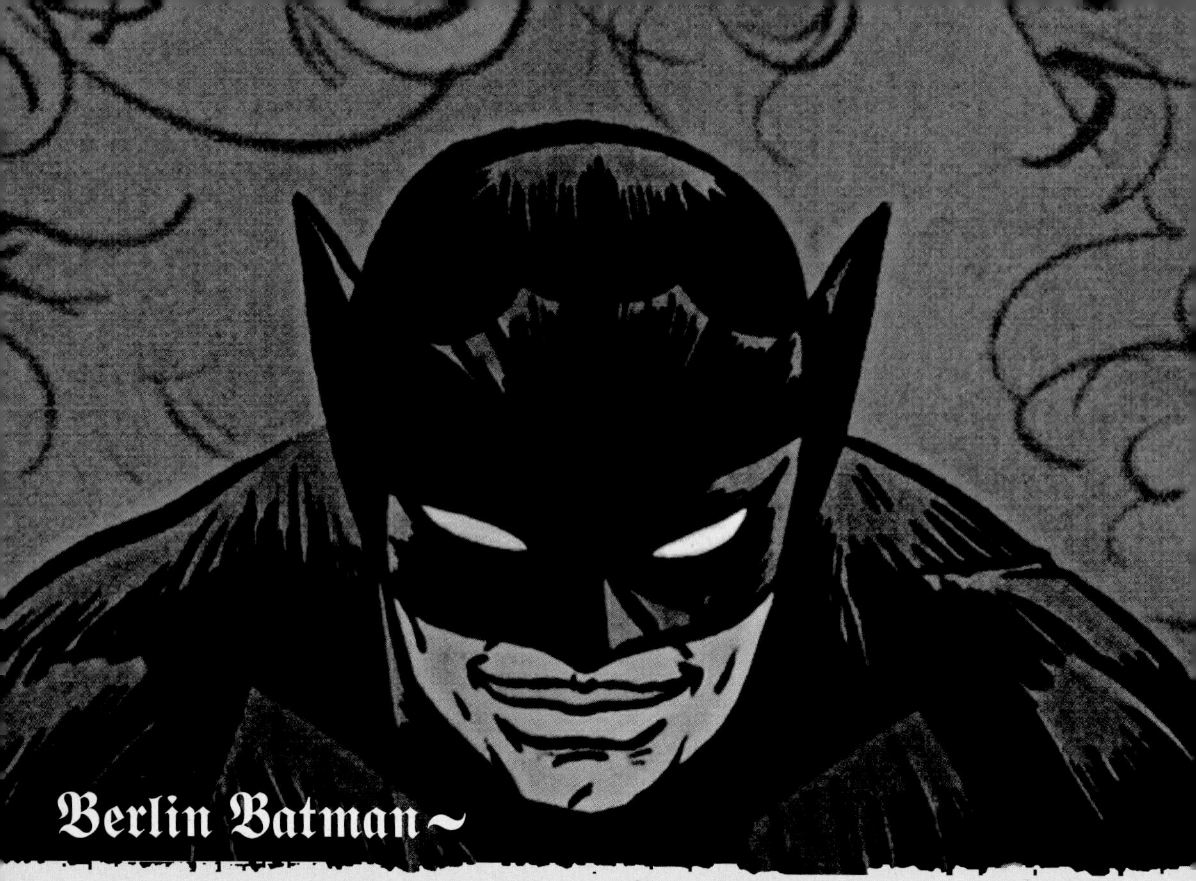

Berlin Batman~

THE FOLLOWING STORY WAS ORIGINALLY PRESENTED IN **THE BATMAN CHRONICLES #11**, AND IS SET IN 1939—THE SAME YEAR BATMAN DEBUTED IN COMICS.

To date, I've done six major Batman projects, including the Eisner Award-winning "Teenage Sidekick" (from SOLO #3) and "Broken Nose" (from BATMAN BLACK AND WHITE VOL. 2). "Berlin Batman" was not only the first Batman story I wrote and drew, it was my first work in mainstream comics. It was also my first big comics job published in full color. It's hard to believe it's been ten years since I did this story—it feels like it was almost yesterday—but it was done in 1997. I had just read of the real-world discovery of Austrian economist Ludwig Von Mises' private notebooks and papers, which had inexplicably resurfaced in Russia decades after having been confiscated by Hitler during World War II. It suggested a strange idea to me—What if Batman were a Jew, and, instead of Gotham City, he appeared in Berlin in 1939 under Nazi dictatorship? Hmn...

Frank Miller says that as a character, Batman is an unbreakable diamond—no matter how hard you throw him against the wall he won't shatter (and Frank should know). When he saw Year 100 for the first time his only comment was, "Man, and I thought I beat this guy up pretty bad — you're really working him over here!" And we had a good laugh over that. On down the years, beginning with Bob's Kane's definitive 1939 Batman, we've seen endless variations on the theme— and incredibly they are all glittering, reflective facets of the original, unbreakable, unshatterable pure diamond character. I guess mine would be the dystopian variation on Batman.

If it's left up to me, I imagine a good superhero story ought to combine all the best visual elements of an old Fritz Lang silent film (such as *Die Nibelungen* or *Die Spinnen*) with the best of Hong Kong action cinema (*Crouching Tiger, Hidden Dragon*). Somewhere between those two polar extremes exists BATMAN YEAR 100 and "Berlin Batman."

Plotwise, I can't help seeing the mask as a metaphor for privacy. Does a superhero have a right to a secret identity? In a police state, the answer would have to be NO.

Both BATMAN YEAR 100 and "Berlin Batman" are variations on this dystopian theme, separated by ten years' working time and a century of fiction time.

"Freedom is Slavery..."

PAUL POPE NYC 11.12.06

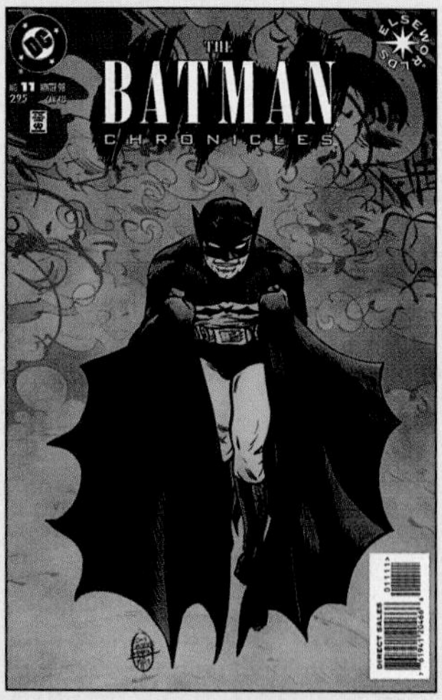
THE
BATMAN
CHRONICLES
ELSEWORLDS

THE BATMAN CHRONICLES #11

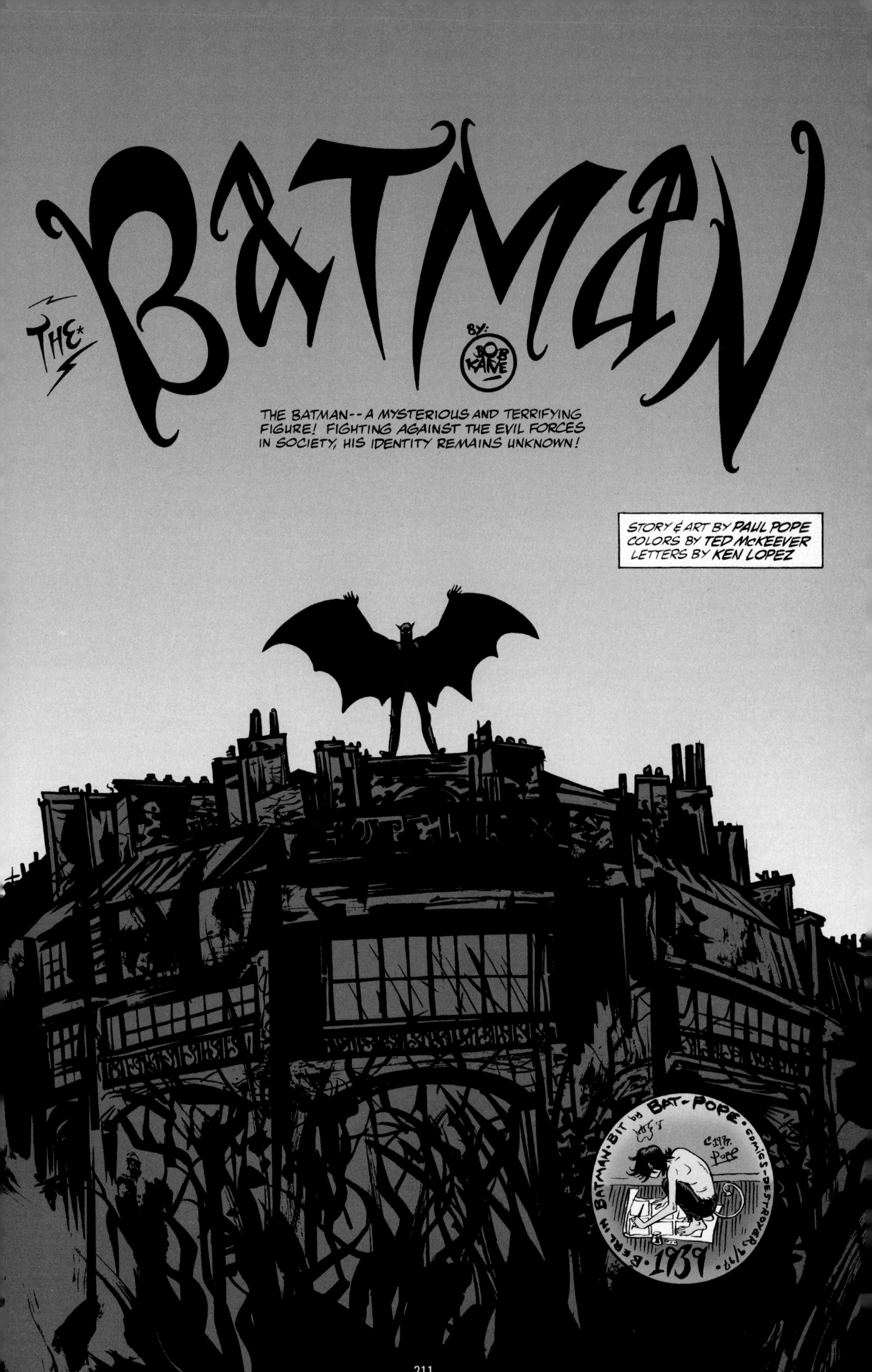
THE BATMAN
BY: BOB KANE
THE BATMAN--A MYSTERIOUS AND TERRIFYING FIGURE! FIGHTING AGAINST THE EVIL FORCES IN SOCIETY, HIS IDENTITY REMAINS UNKNOWN!
STORY & ART BY PAUL POPE
COLORS BY TED McKEEVER
LETTERS BY KEN LOPEZ
HOTEL
BERL IN BATMAN·BIT by BAT-POPE·COMICS-DESTROYER, 9/97·1939
©1997 POPE

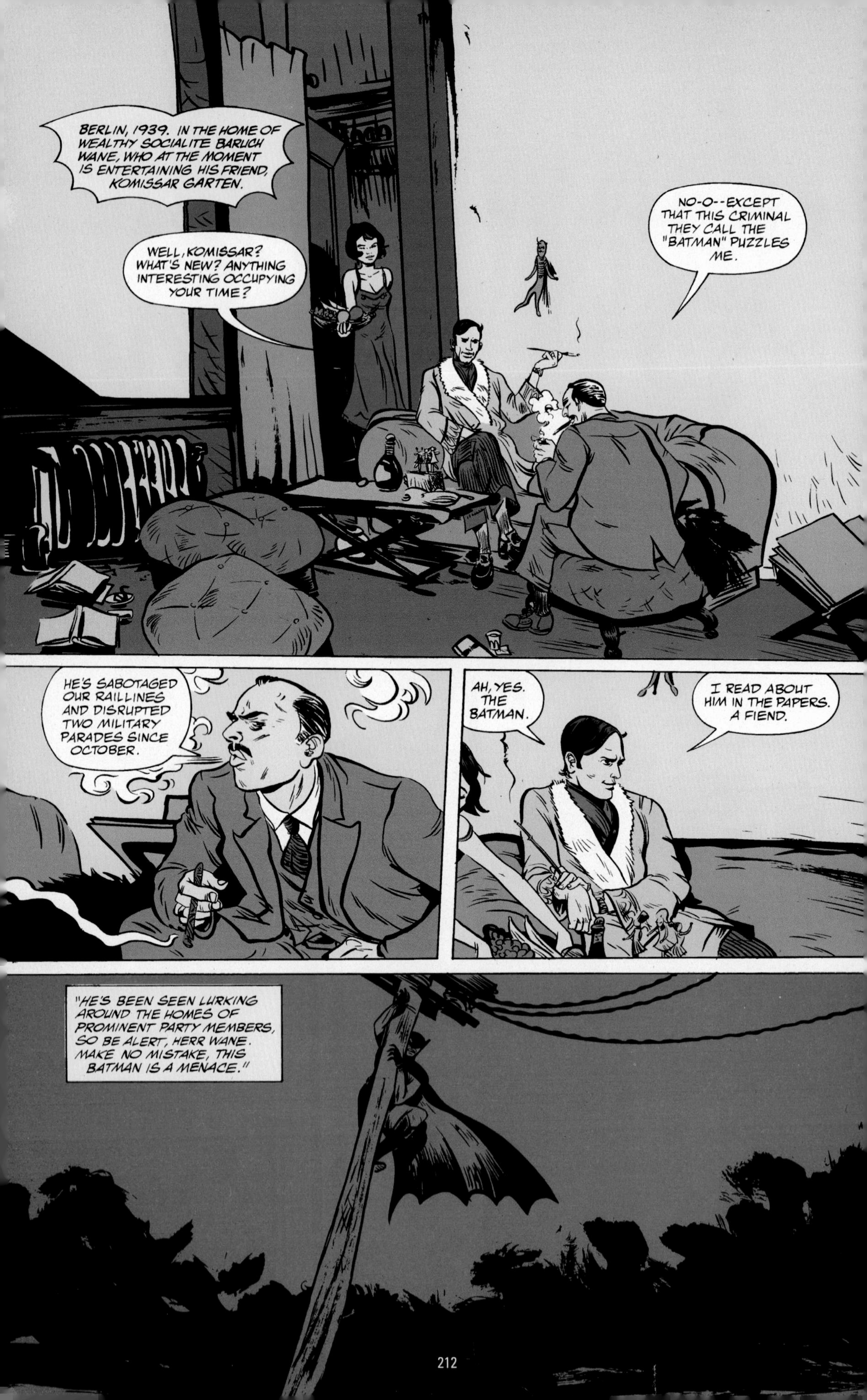
BERLIN, 1939. IN THE HOME OF WEALTHY SOCIALITE BARUCH WANE, WHO AT THE MOMENT IS ENTERTAINING HIS FRIEND, KOMISSAR GARTEN.
WELL, KOMISSAR? WHAT'S NEW? ANYTHING INTERESTING OCCUPYING YOUR TIME?
NO-O--EXCEPT THAT THIS CRIMINAL THEY CALL THE "BATMAN" PUZZLES ME.
HE'S SABOTAGED OUR RAILLINES AND DISRUPTED TWO MILITARY PARADES SINCE OCTOBER.
AH, YES. THE BATMAN.
I READ ABOUT HIM IN THE PAPERS. A FIEND.
"HE'S BEEN SEEN LURKING AROUND THE HOMES OF PROMINENT PARTY MEMBERS, SO BE ALERT, HERR WANE. MAKE NO MISTAKE, THIS BATMAN IS A MENACE."

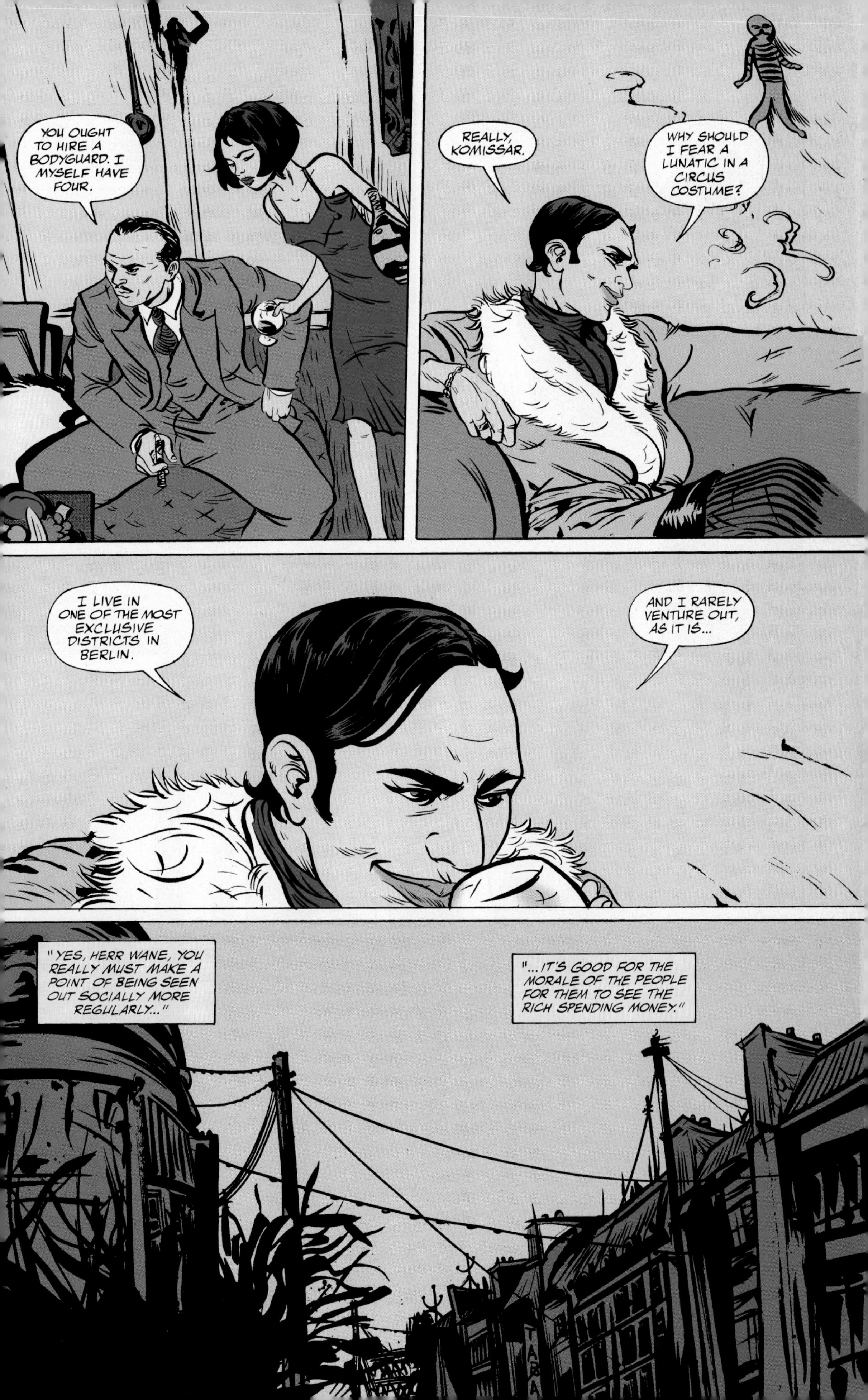
YOU OUGHT TO HIRE A BODYGUARD. I MYSELF HAVE FOUR.
REALLY, KOMISSAR.
WHY SHOULD I FEAR A LUNATIC IN A CIRCUS COSTUME?
I LIVE IN ONE OF THE MOST EXCLUSIVE DISTRICTS IN BERLIN.
AND I RARELY VENTURE OUT, AS IT IS...
"YES, HERR WANE, YOU REALLY MUST MAKE A POINT OF BEING SEEN OUT SOCIALLY MORE REGULARLY..."
"...IT'S GOOD FOR THE MORALE OF THE PEOPLE FOR THEM TO SEE THE RICH SPENDING MONEY."

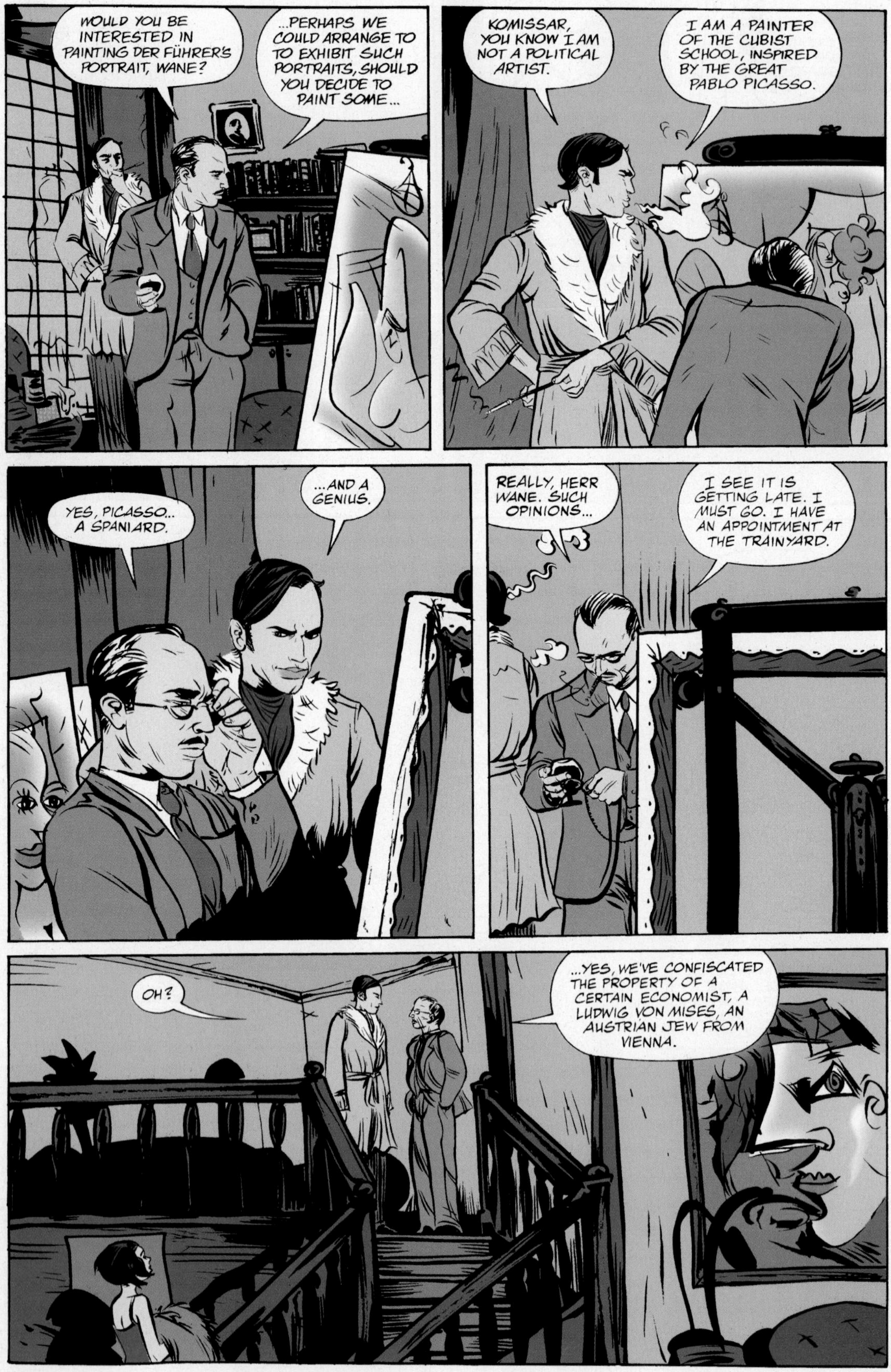
WOULD YOU BE INTERESTED IN PAINTING DER FÜHRER'S PORTRAIT, WANE?
...PERHAPS WE COULD ARRANGE TO TO EXHIBIT SUCH PORTRAITS, SHOULD YOU DECIDE TO PAINT SOME...
KOMISSAR, YOU KNOW I AM NOT A POLITICAL ARTIST.
I AM A PAINTER OF THE CUBIST SCHOOL, INSPIRED BY THE GREAT PABLO PICASSO.
YES, PICASSO... A SPANIARD.
...AND A GENIUS.
REALLY, HERR WANE. SUCH OPINIONS...
I SEE IT IS GETTING LATE. I MUST GO. I HAVE AN APPOINTMENT AT THE TRAINYARD.
OH?
...YES, WE'VE CONFISCATED THE PROPERTY OF A CERTAIN ECONOMIST, A LUDWIG VON MISES, AN AUSTRIAN JEW FROM VIENNA.

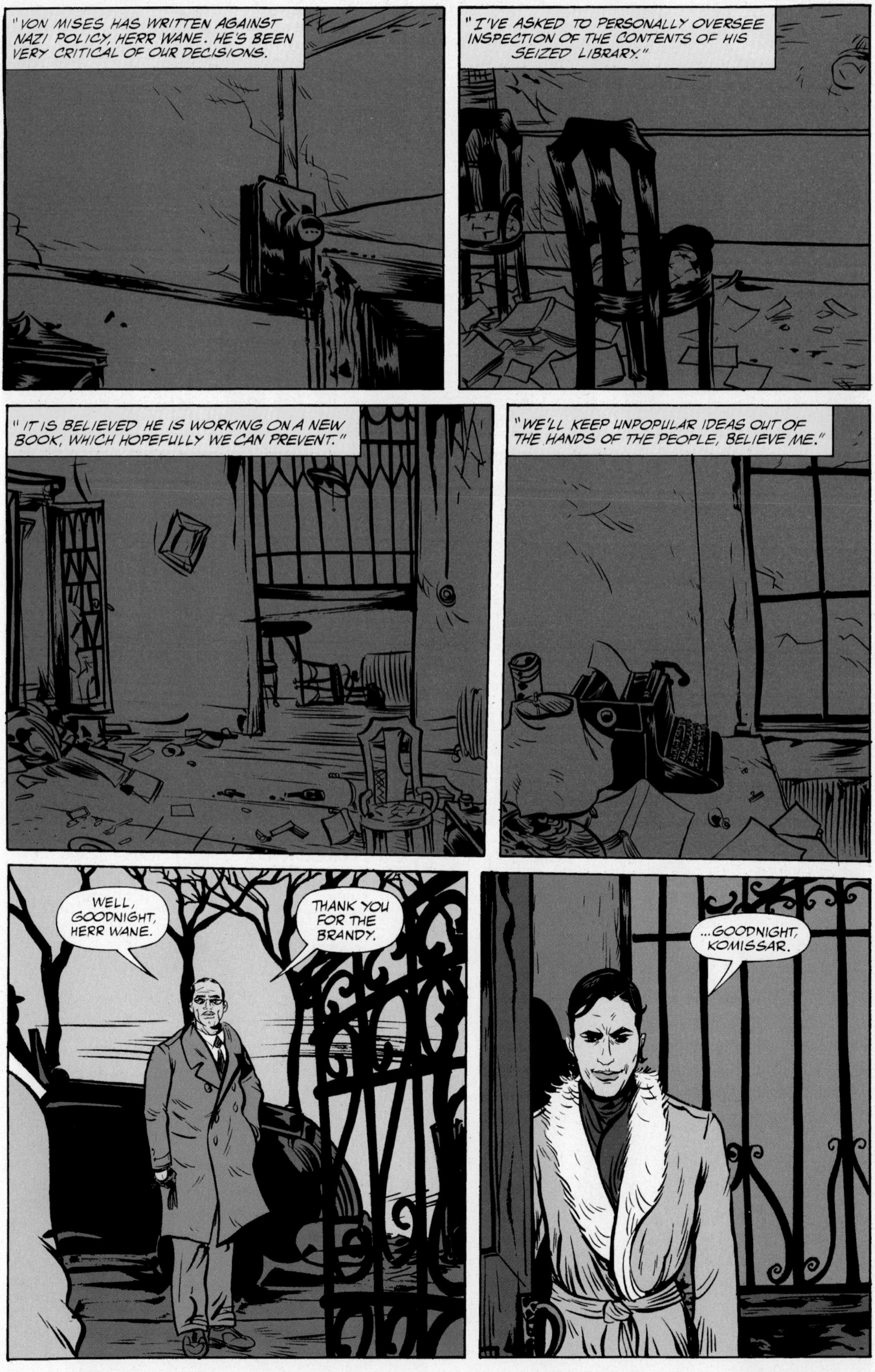
"VON MISES HAS WRITTEN AGAINST NAZI POLICY, HERR WANE. HE'S BEEN VERY CRITICAL OF OUR DECISIONS.
"I'VE ASKED TO PERSONALLY OVERSEE INSPECTION OF THE CONTENTS OF HIS SEIZED LIBRARY."
"IT IS BELIEVED HE IS WORKING ON A NEW BOOK, WHICH HOPEFULLY WE CAN PREVENT."
"WE'LL KEEP UNPOPULAR IDEAS OUT OF THE HANDS OF THE PEOPLE, BELIEVE ME."
WELL, GOODNIGHT, HERR WANE.
THANK YOU FOR THE BRANDY.
...GOODNIGHT, KOMISSAR.

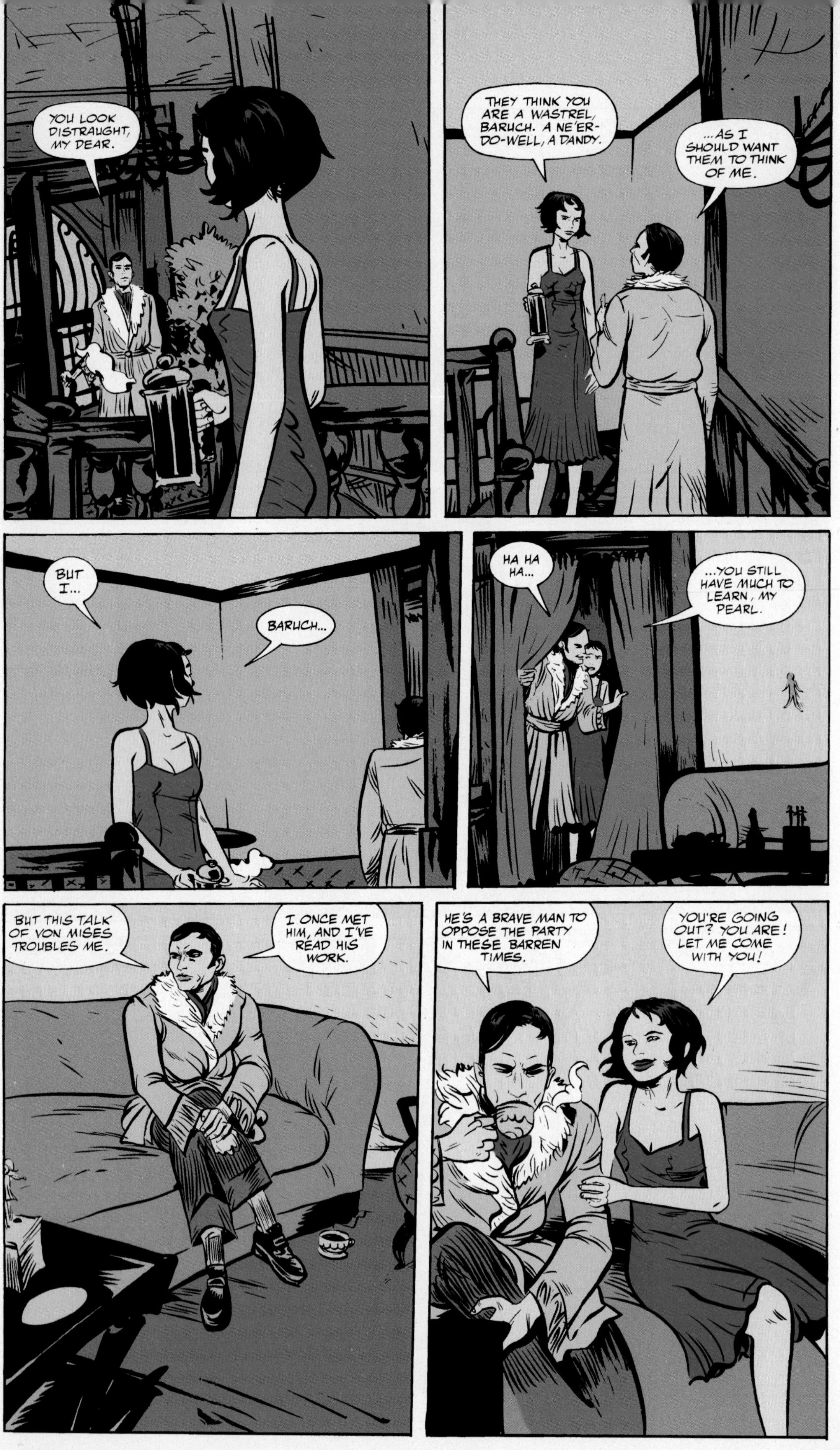
YOU LOOK DISTRAUGHT, MY DEAR.
THEY THINK YOU ARE A WASTREL, BARUCH. A NE'ER-DO-WELL, A DANDY.
...AS I SHOULD WANT THEM TO THINK OF ME.
BUT I...
BARUCH...
HA HA HA...
...YOU STILL HAVE MUCH TO LEARN, MY PEARL.
BUT THIS TALK OF VON MISES TROUBLES ME.
I ONCE MET HIM, AND I'VE READ HIS WORK.
HE'S A BRAVE MAN TO OPPOSE THE PARTY IN THESE BARREN TIMES.
YOU'RE GOING OUT? YOU ARE! LET ME COME WITH YOU!

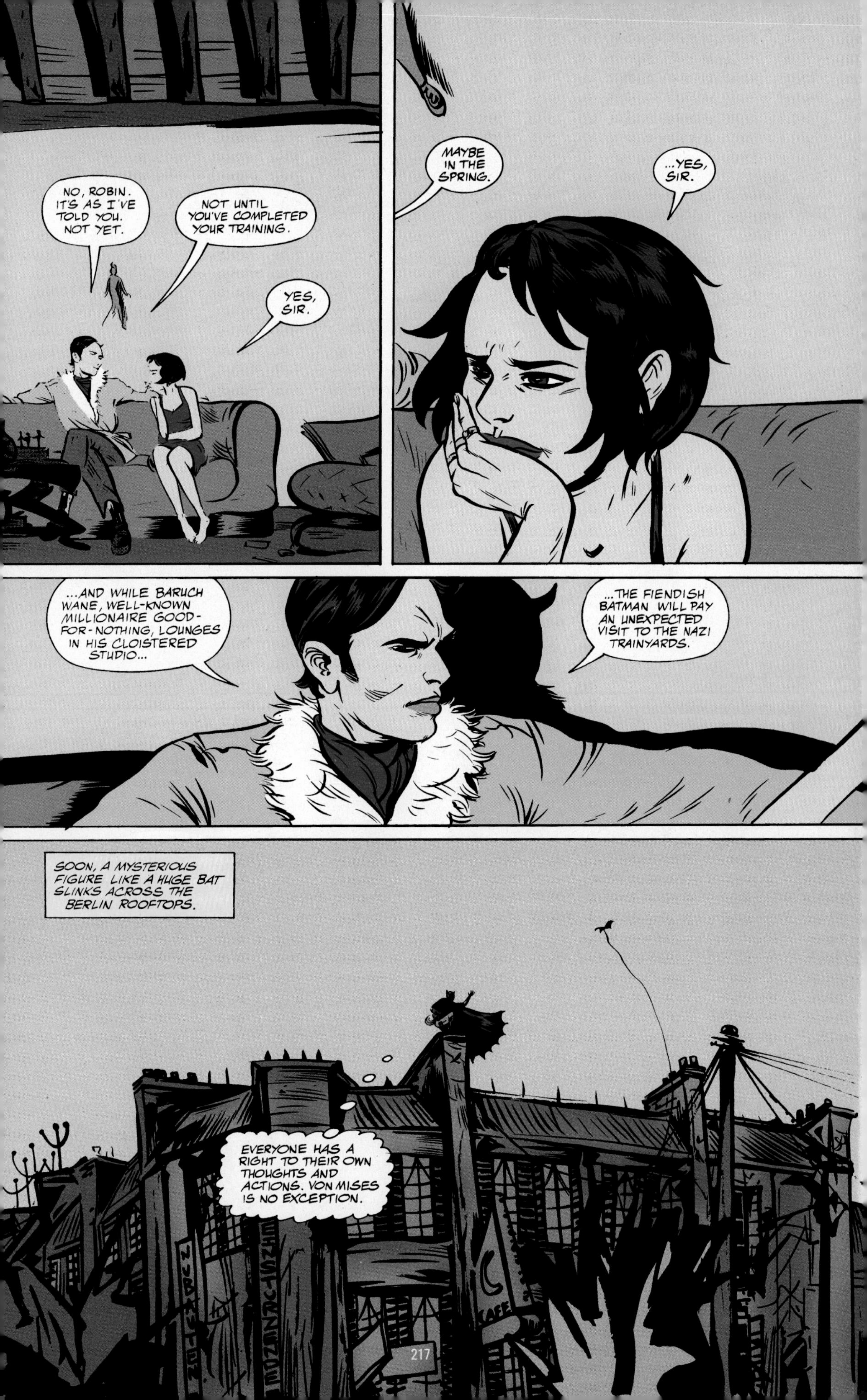

NO, ROBIN. IT'S AS I'VE TOLD YOU. NOT YET.
NOT UNTIL YOU'VE COMPLETED YOUR TRAINING.
YES, SIR.
MAYBE IN THE SPRING.
...YES, SIR.
...AND WHILE BARUCH WANE, WELL-KNOWN MILLIONAIRE GOOD-FOR-NOTHING, LOUNGES IN HIS CLOISTERED STUDIO...
...THE FIENDISH BATMAN WILL PAY AN UNEXPECTED VISIT TO THE NAZI TRAINYARDS.
SOON, A MYSTERIOUS FIGURE LIKE A HUGE BAT SLINKS ACROSS THE BERLIN ROOFTOPS.
EVERYONE HAS A RIGHT TO THEIR OWN THOUGHTS AND ACTIONS. VON MISES IS NO EXCEPTION.
KAFE

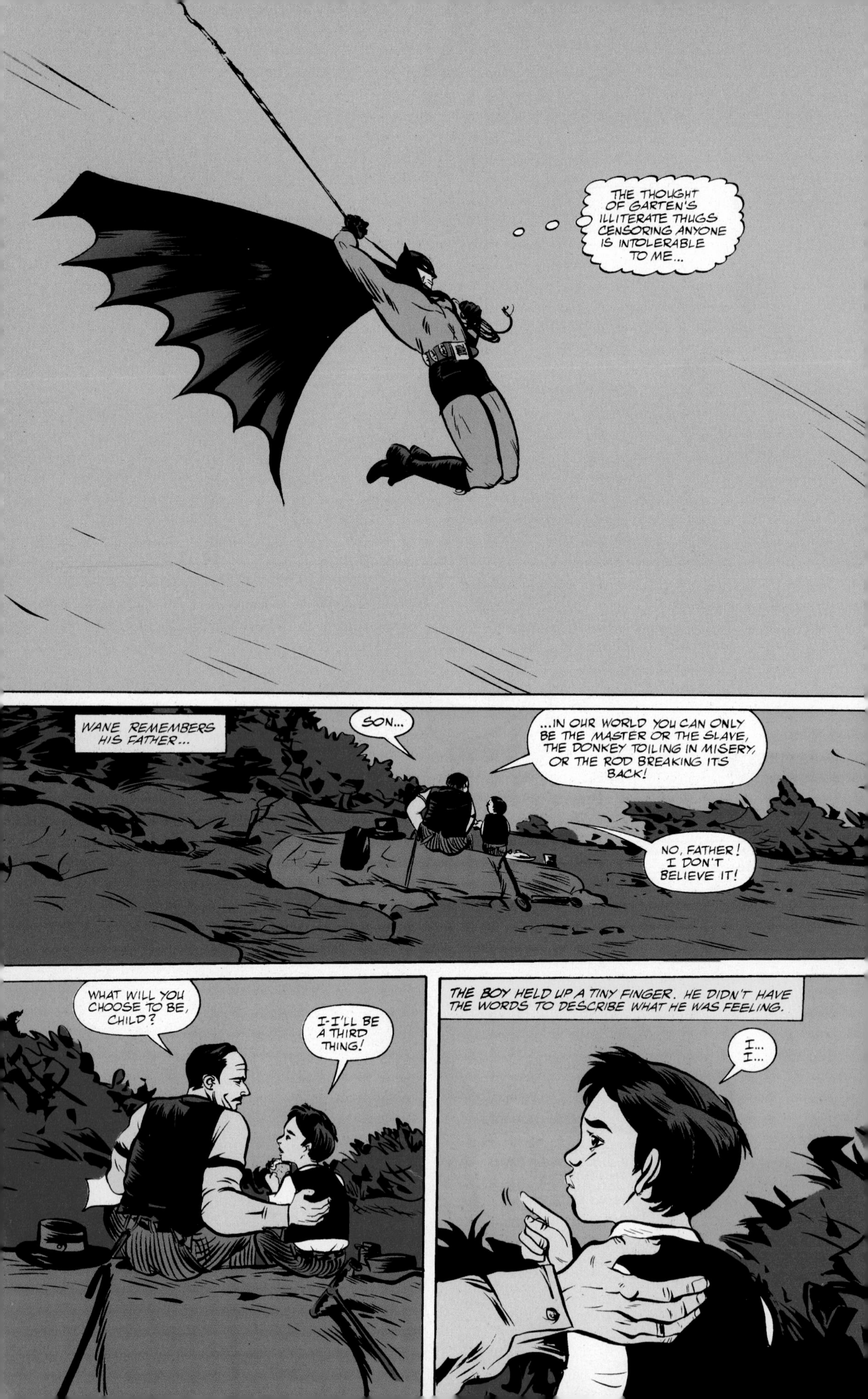
THE THOUGHT OF GARTEN'S ILLITERATE THUGS CENSORING ANYONE IS INTOLERABLE TO ME...
WANE REMEMBERS HIS FATHER...
SON...
...IN OUR WORLD YOU CAN ONLY BE THE MASTER OR THE SLAVE, THE DONKEY TOILING IN MISERY, OR THE ROD BREAKING ITS BACK!
NO, FATHER! I DON'T BELIEVE IT!
WHAT WILL YOU CHOOSE TO BE, CHILD?
I-I'LL BE A THIRD THING!
THE BOY HELD UP A TINY FINGER. HE DIDN'T HAVE THE WORDS TO DESCRIBE WHAT HE WAS FEELING.
I... I...

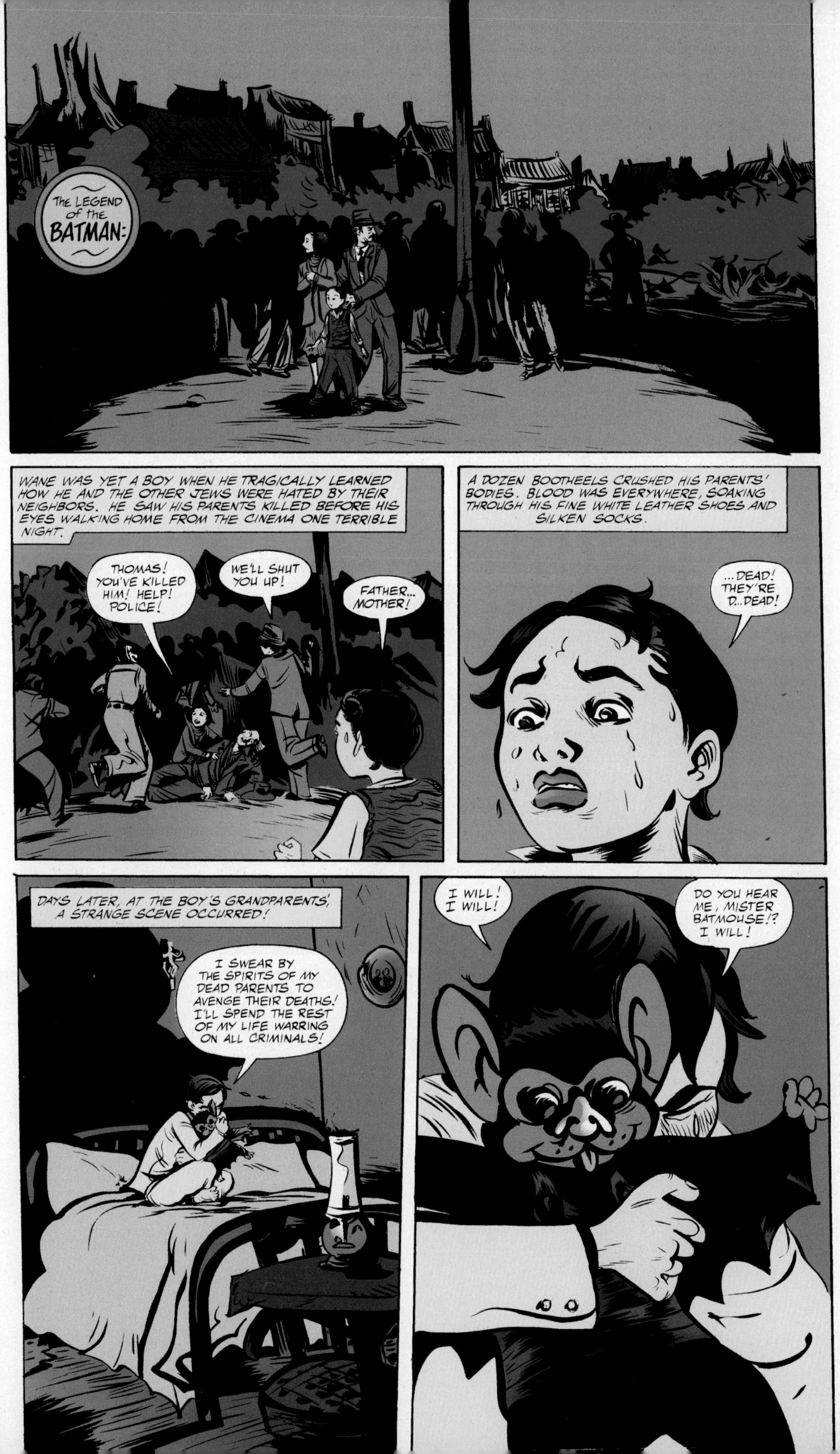
The LEGEND of the BATMAN:
WANE WAS YET A BOY WHEN HE TRAGICALLY LEARNED HOW HE AND THE OTHER JEWS WERE HATED BY THEIR NEIGHBORS. HE SAW HIS PARENTS KILLED BEFORE HIS EYES WALKING HOME FROM THE CINEMA ONE TERRIBLE NIGHT.
THOMAS! YOU'VE KILLED HIM! HELP! POLICE!
WE'LL SHUT YOU UP!
FATHER... MOTHER!
A DOZEN BOOTHEELS CRUSHED HIS PARENTS' BODIES. BLOOD WAS EVERYWHERE, SOAKING THROUGH HIS FINE WHITE LEATHER SHOES AND SILKEN SOCKS.
...DEAD! THEY'RE D...DEAD!
DAYS LATER, AT THE BOY'S GRANDPARENTS', A STRANGE SCENE OCCURRED!
I SWEAR BY THE SPIRITS OF MY DEAD PARENTS TO AVENGE THEIR DEATHS! I'LL SPEND THE REST OF MY LIFE WARRING ON ALL CRIMINALS!
I WILL! I WILL!
DO YOU HEAR ME, MISTER BATMOUSE!? I WILL!

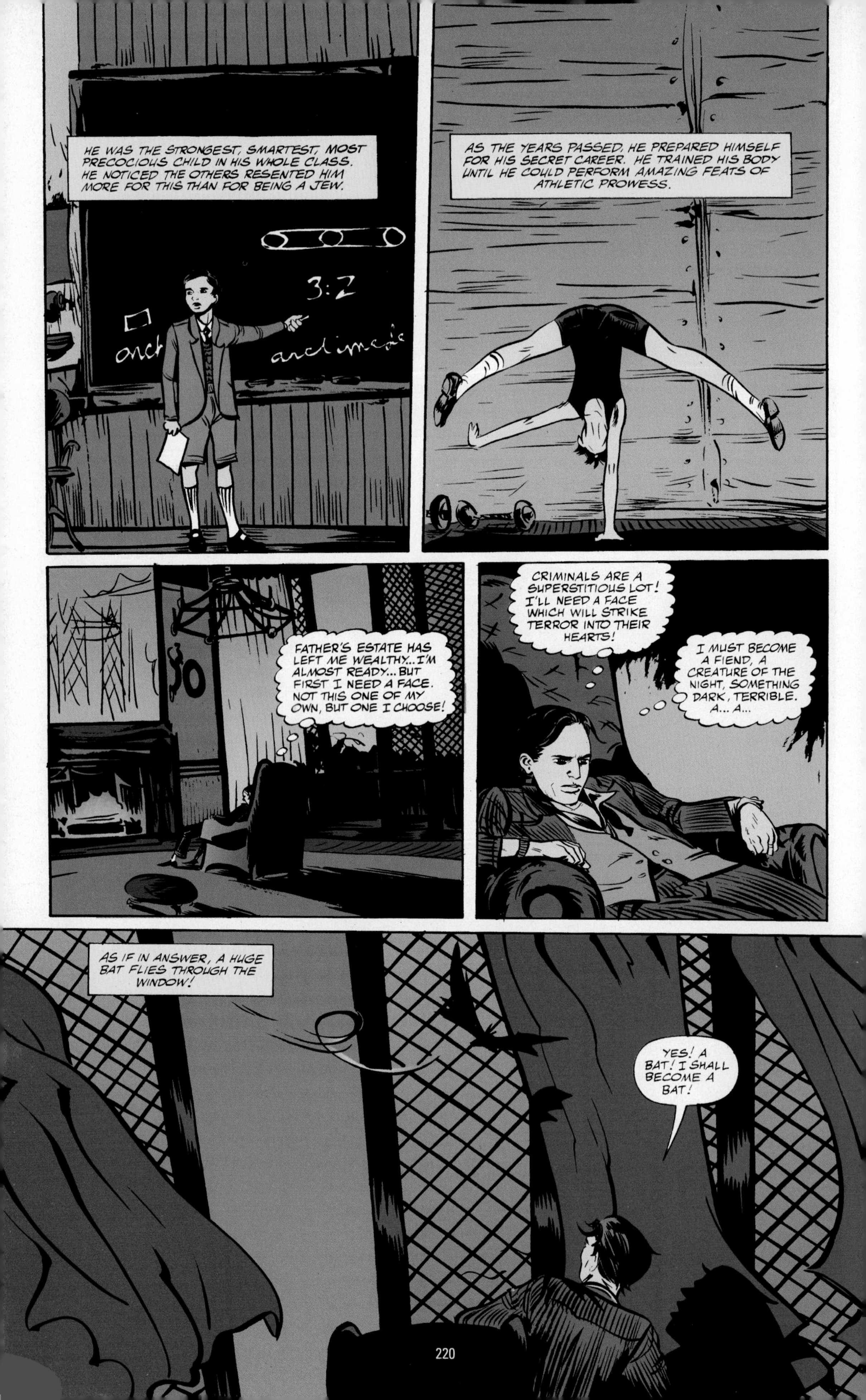
HE WAS THE STRONGEST, SMARTEST, MOST PRECOCIOUS CHILD IN HIS WHOLE CLASS. HE NOTICED THE OTHERS RESENTED HIM MORE FOR THIS THAN FOR BEING A JEW.
3:2
AS THE YEARS PASSED, HE PREPARED HIMSELF FOR HIS SECRET CAREER. HE TRAINED HIS BODY UNTIL HE COULD PERFORM AMAZING FEATS OF ATHLETIC PROWESS.
FATHER'S ESTATE HAS LEFT ME WEALTHY... I'M ALMOST READY... BUT FIRST I NEED A FACE. NOT THIS ONE OF MY OWN, BUT ONE I CHOOSE!
CRIMINALS ARE A SUPERSTITIOUS LOT! I'LL NEED A FACE WHICH WILL STRIKE TERROR INTO THEIR HEARTS!
I MUST BECOME A FIEND, A CREATURE OF THE NIGHT, SOMETHING DARK, TERRIBLE. A... A...
AS IF IN ANSWER, A HUGE BAT FLIES THROUGH THE WINDOW!
YES! A BAT! I SHALL BECOME A BAT!

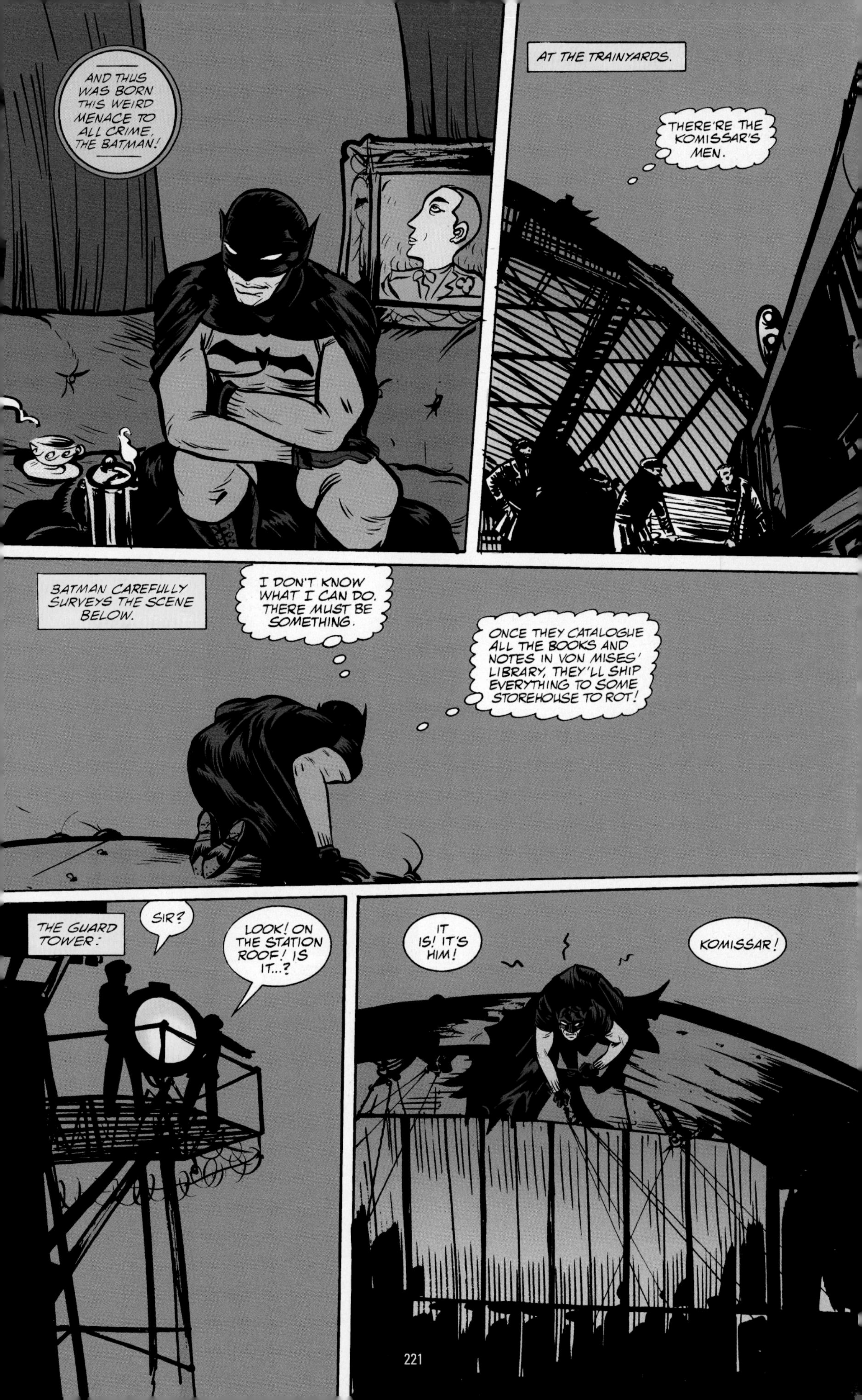
AND THUS WAS BORN THIS WEIRD MENACE TO ALL CRIME, THE BATMAN!
AT THE TRAINYARDS.
THERE'RE THE KOMISSAR'S MEN.
BATMAN CAREFULLY SURVEYS THE SCENE BELOW.
I DON'T KNOW WHAT I CAN DO. THERE MUST BE SOMETHING.
ONCE THEY CATALOGUE ALL THE BOOKS AND NOTES IN VON MISES' LIBRARY, THEY'LL SHIP EVERYTHING TO SOME STOREHOUSE TO ROT!
THE GUARD TOWER:
SIR?
LOOK! ON THE STATION ROOF! IS IT...?
IT IS! IT'S HIM!
KOMISSAR!

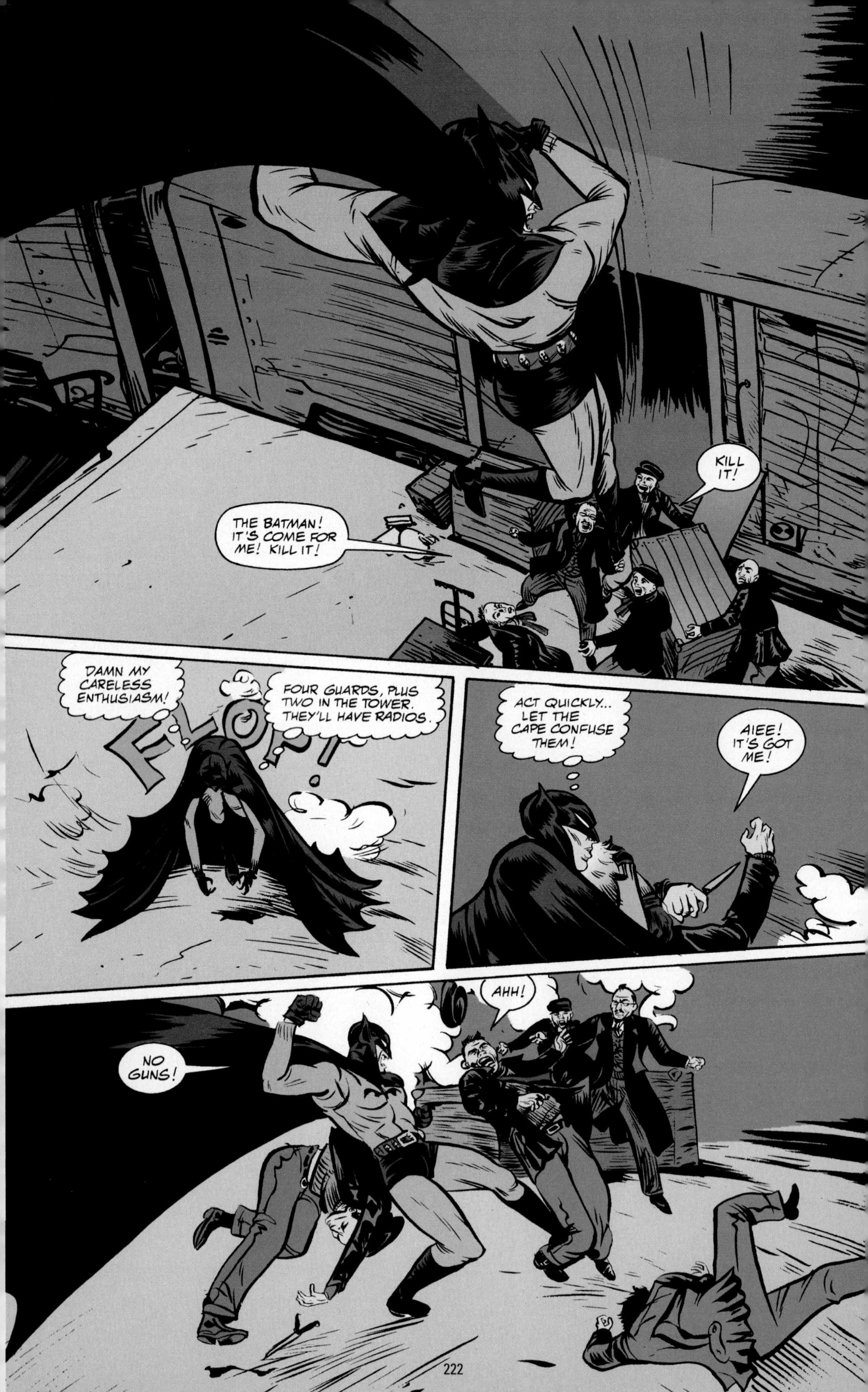
KILL IT!
THE BATMAN! IT'S COME FOR ME! KILL IT!
DAMN MY CARELESS ENTHUSIASM!
FOUR GUARDS, PLUS TWO IN THE TOWER. THEY'LL HAVE RADIOS.
FLOP!
ACT QUICKLY... LET THE CAPE CONFUSE THEM!
AIEE! IT'S GOT ME!
AHH!
NO GUNS!

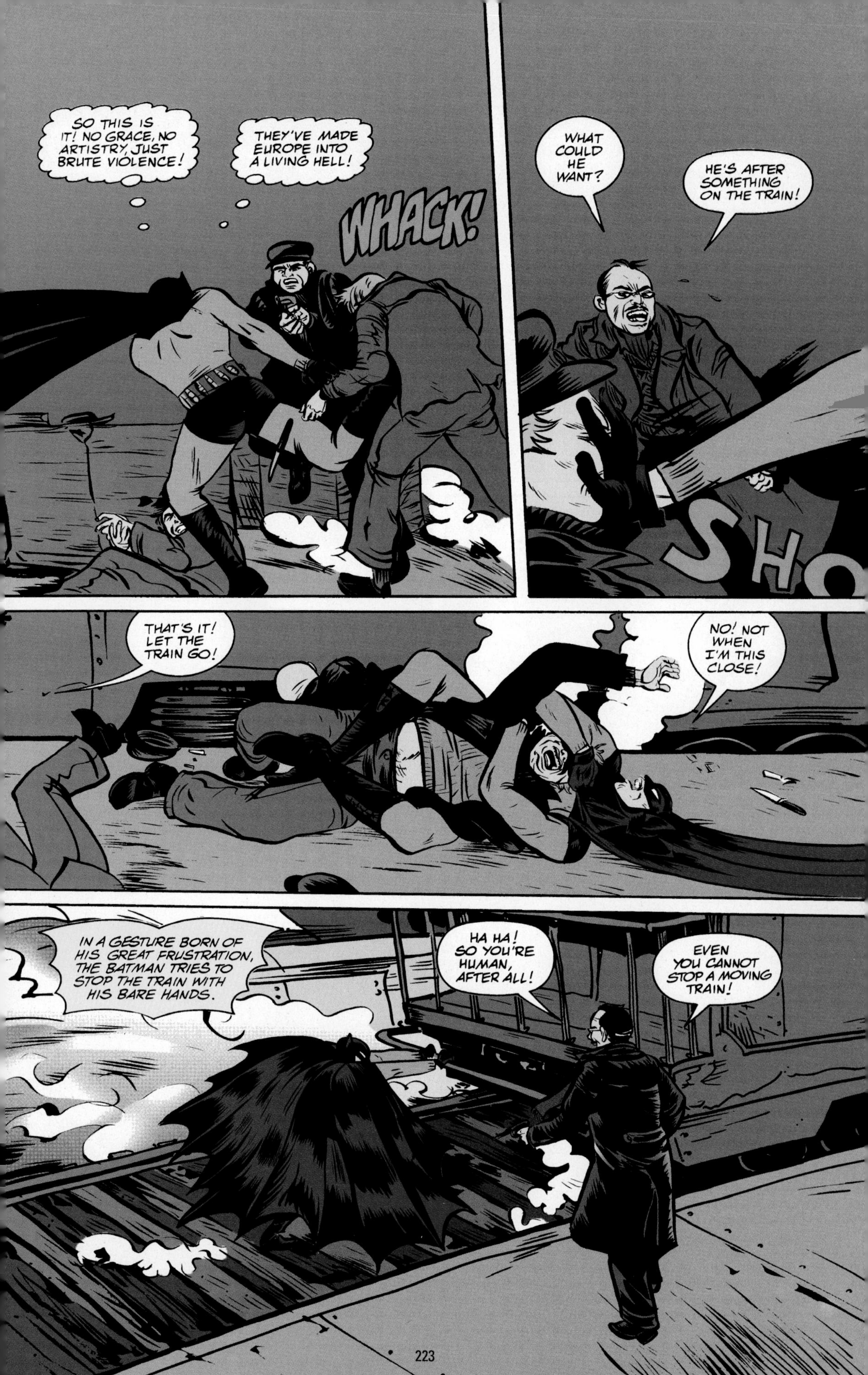
SO THIS IS IT! NO GRACE, NO ARTISTRY, JUST BRUTE VIOLENCE!
THEY'VE MADE EUROPE INTO A LIVING HELL!
WHACK!
WHAT COULD HE WANT?
HE'S AFTER SOMETHING ON THE TRAIN!
SHO
THAT'S IT! LET THE TRAIN GO!
NO! NOT WHEN I'M THIS CLOSE!
IN A GESTURE BORN OF HIS GREAT FRUSTRATION, THE BATMAN TRIES TO STOP THE TRAIN WITH HIS BARE HANDS.
HA HA! SO YOU'RE HUMAN, AFTER ALL!
EVEN YOU CANNOT STOP A MOVING TRAIN!

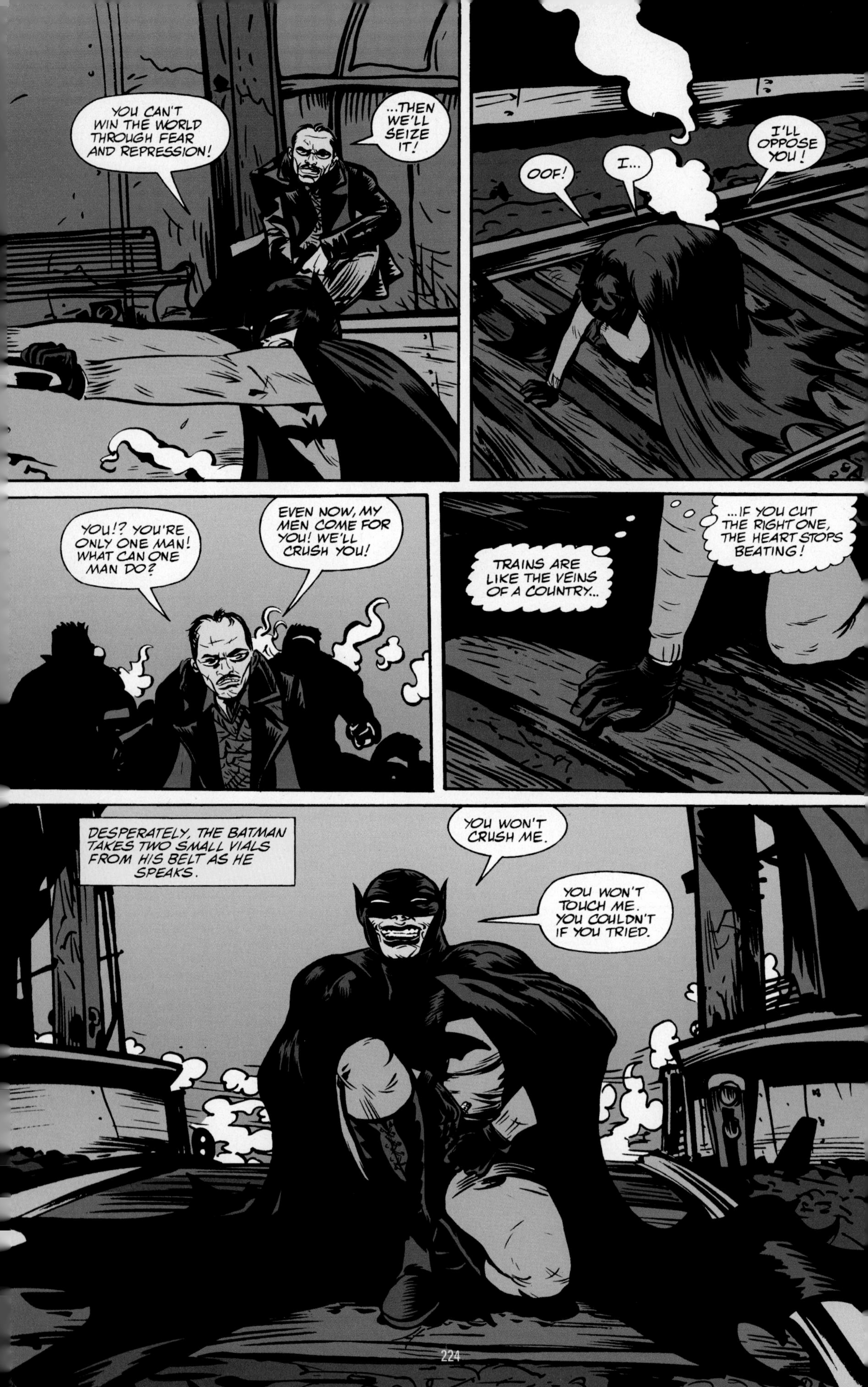
YOU CAN'T WIN THE WORLD THROUGH FEAR AND REPRESSION!
...THEN WE'LL SEIZE IT!
OOF!
I...
I'LL OPPOSE YOU!
YOU!? YOU'RE ONLY ONE MAN! WHAT CAN ONE MAN DO?
EVEN NOW, MY MEN COME FOR YOU! WE'LL CRUSH YOU!
TRAINS ARE LIKE THE VEINS OF A COUNTRY...
...IF YOU CUT THE RIGHT ONE, THE HEART STOPS BEATING!
DESPERATELY, THE BATMAN TAKES TWO SMALL VIALS FROM HIS BELT AS HE SPEAKS.
YOU WON'T CRUSH ME.
YOU WON'T TOUCH ME. YOU COULDN'T IF YOU TRIED.

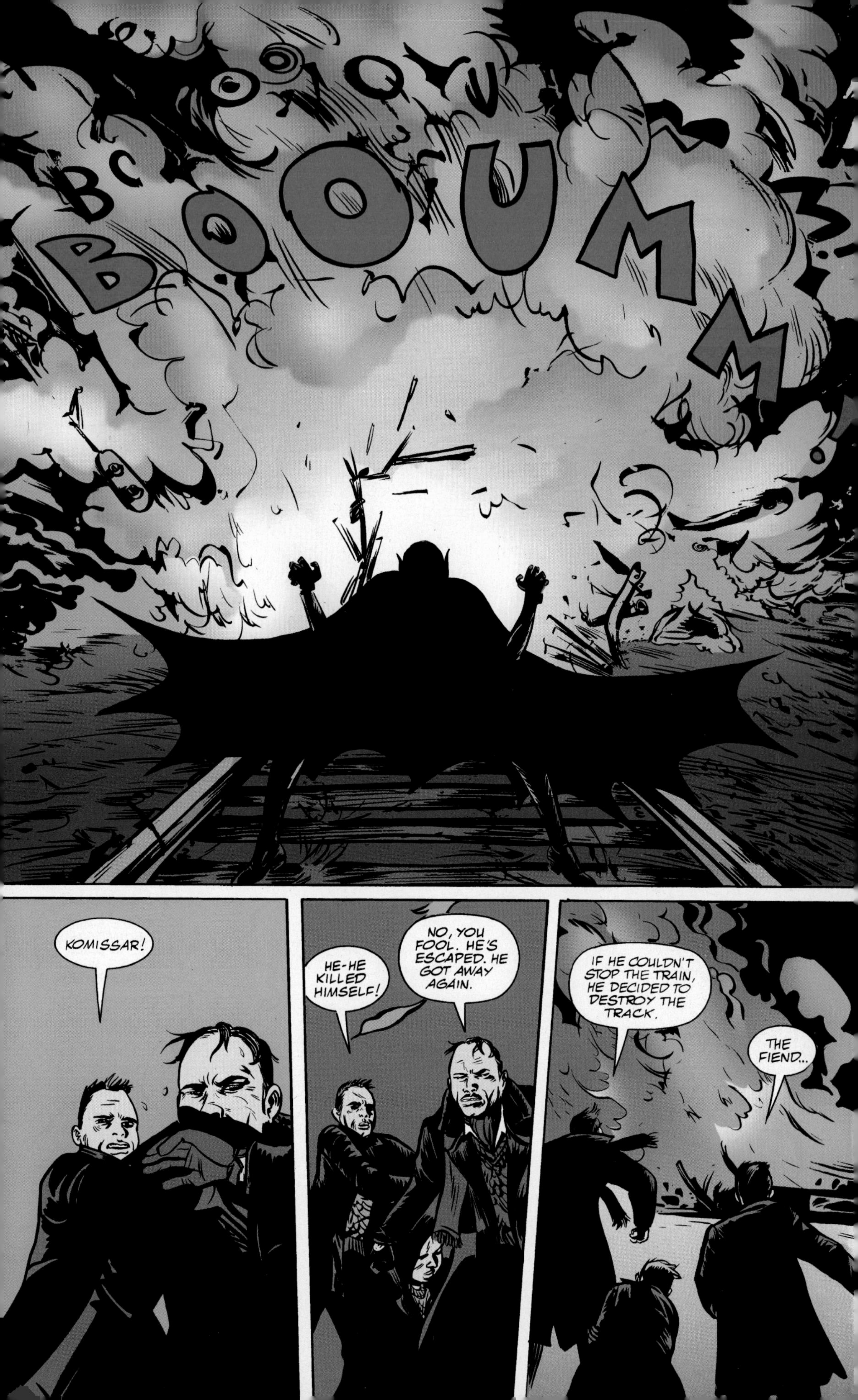
BOOOUMM
KOMISSAR!
HE-HE KILLED HIMSELF!
NO, YOU FOOL. HE'S ESCAPED. HE GOT AWAY AGAIN.
IF HE COULDN'T STOP THE TRAIN, HE DECIDED TO DESTROY THE TRACK.
THE FIEND...

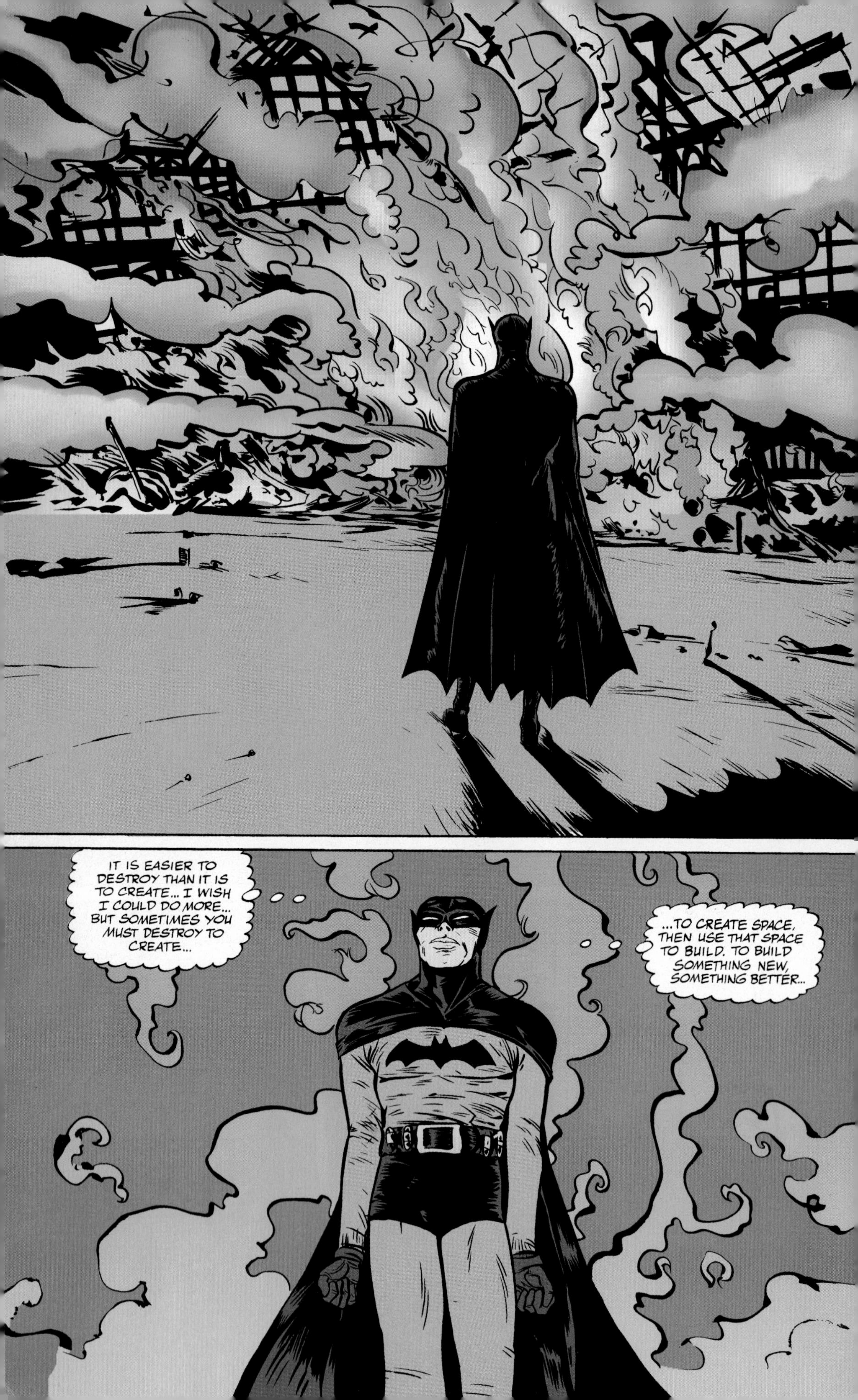
IT IS EASIER TO DESTROY THAN IT IS TO CREATE... I WISH I COULD DO MORE... BUT SOMETIMES YOU MUST DESTROY TO CREATE...
...TO CREATE SPACE, THEN USE THAT SPACE TO BUILD. TO BUILD SOMETHING NEW, SOMETHING BETTER...

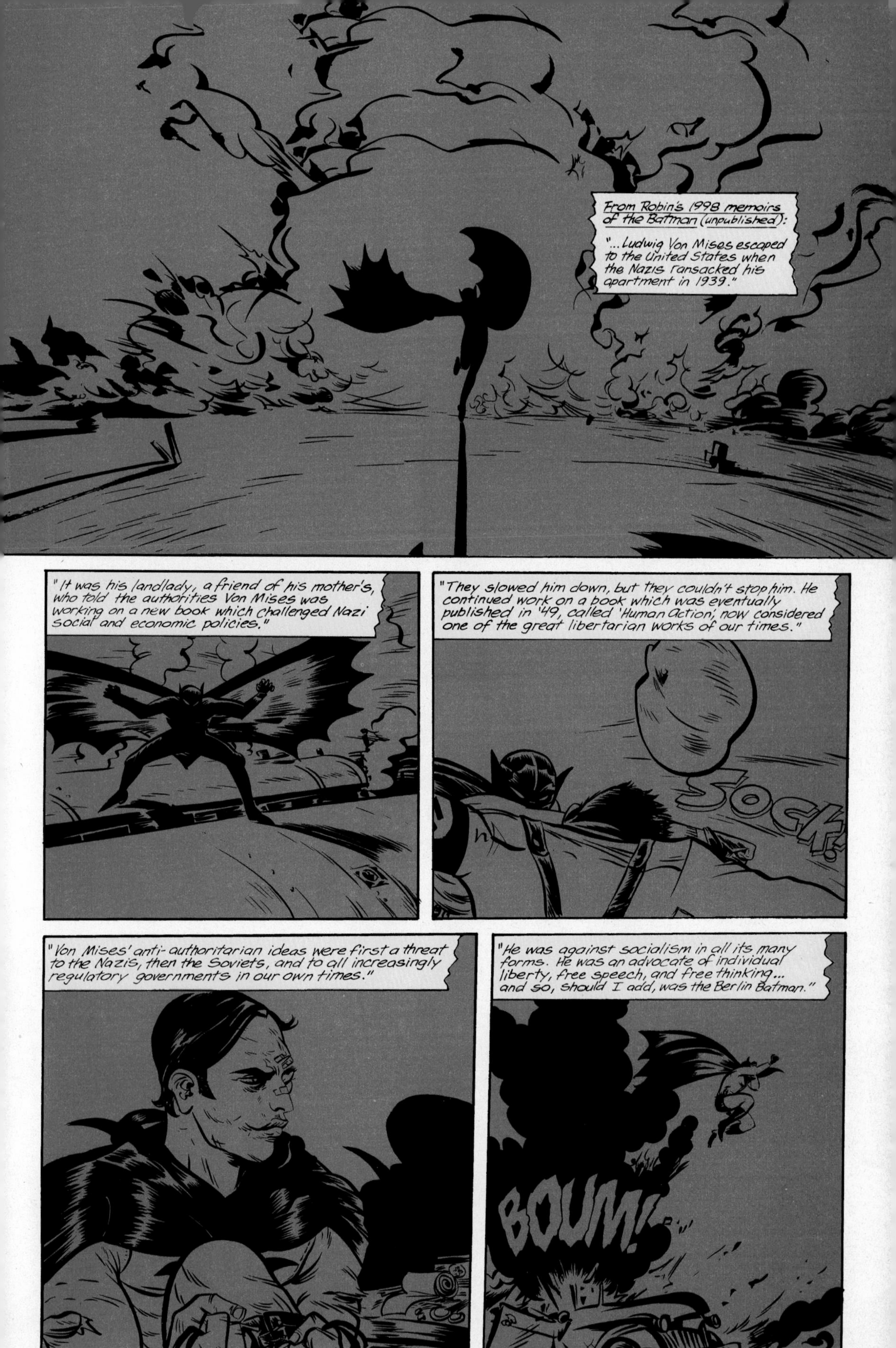
From Robin's 1998 memoirs of the Batman (unpublished):
"...Ludwig Von Mises escaped to the United States when the Nazis ransacked his apartment in 1939."
"It was his landlady, a friend of his mother's, who told the authorities Von Mises was working on a new book which challenged Nazi social and economic policies."
"They slowed him down, but they couldn't stop him. He continued work on a book which was eventually published in '49, called 'Human Action', now considered one of the great libertarian works of our times."
SOCK!
"Von Mises' anti-authoritarian ideas were first a threat to the Nazis, then the Soviets, and to all increasingly regulatory governments in our own times."
"He was against socialism in all its many forms. He was an advocate of individual liberty, free speech, and free thinking... and so, should I add, was the Berlin Batman."
BOUM!

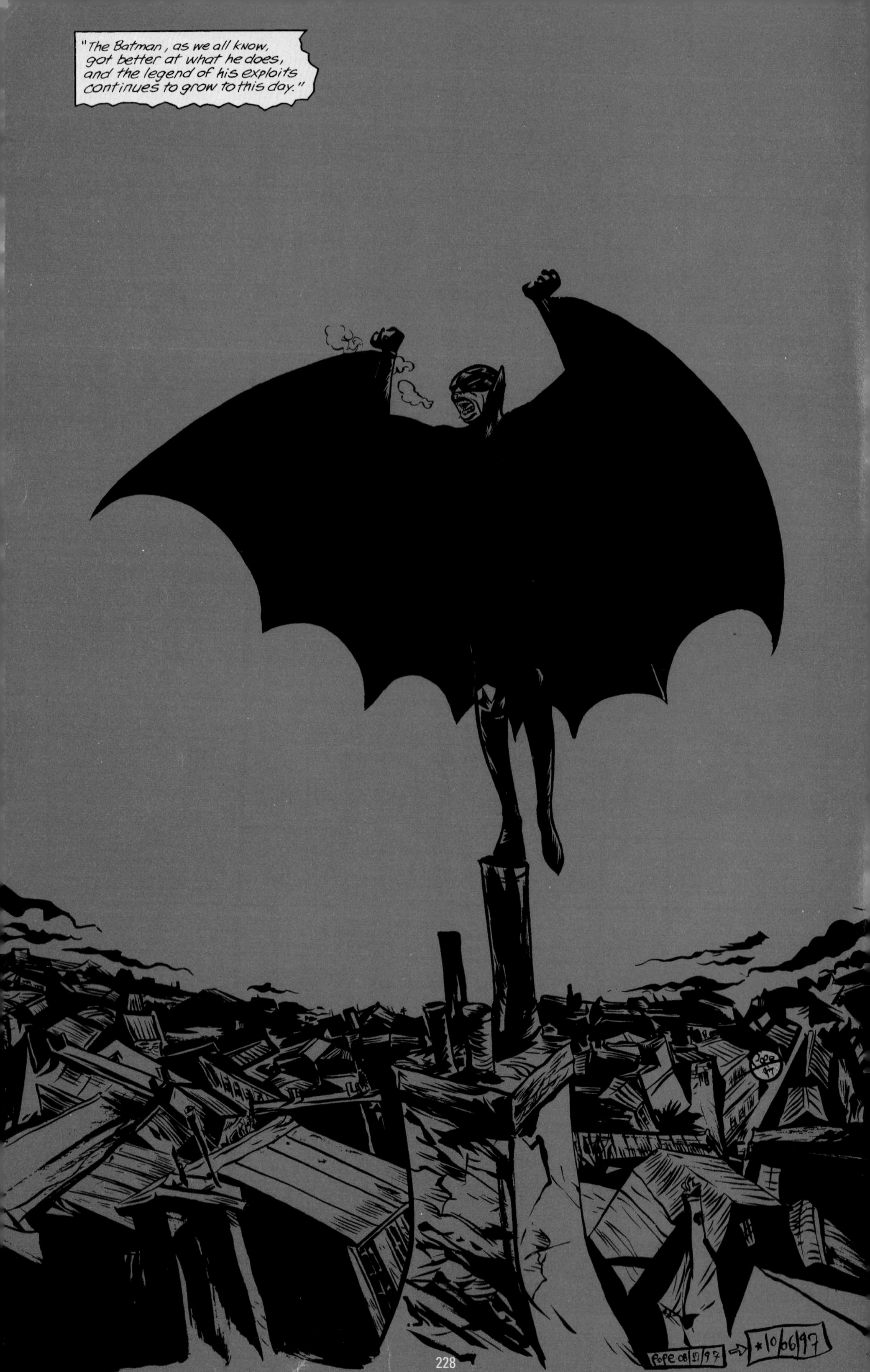
"The Batman, as we all know, got better at what he does, and the legend of his exploits continues to grow to this day."

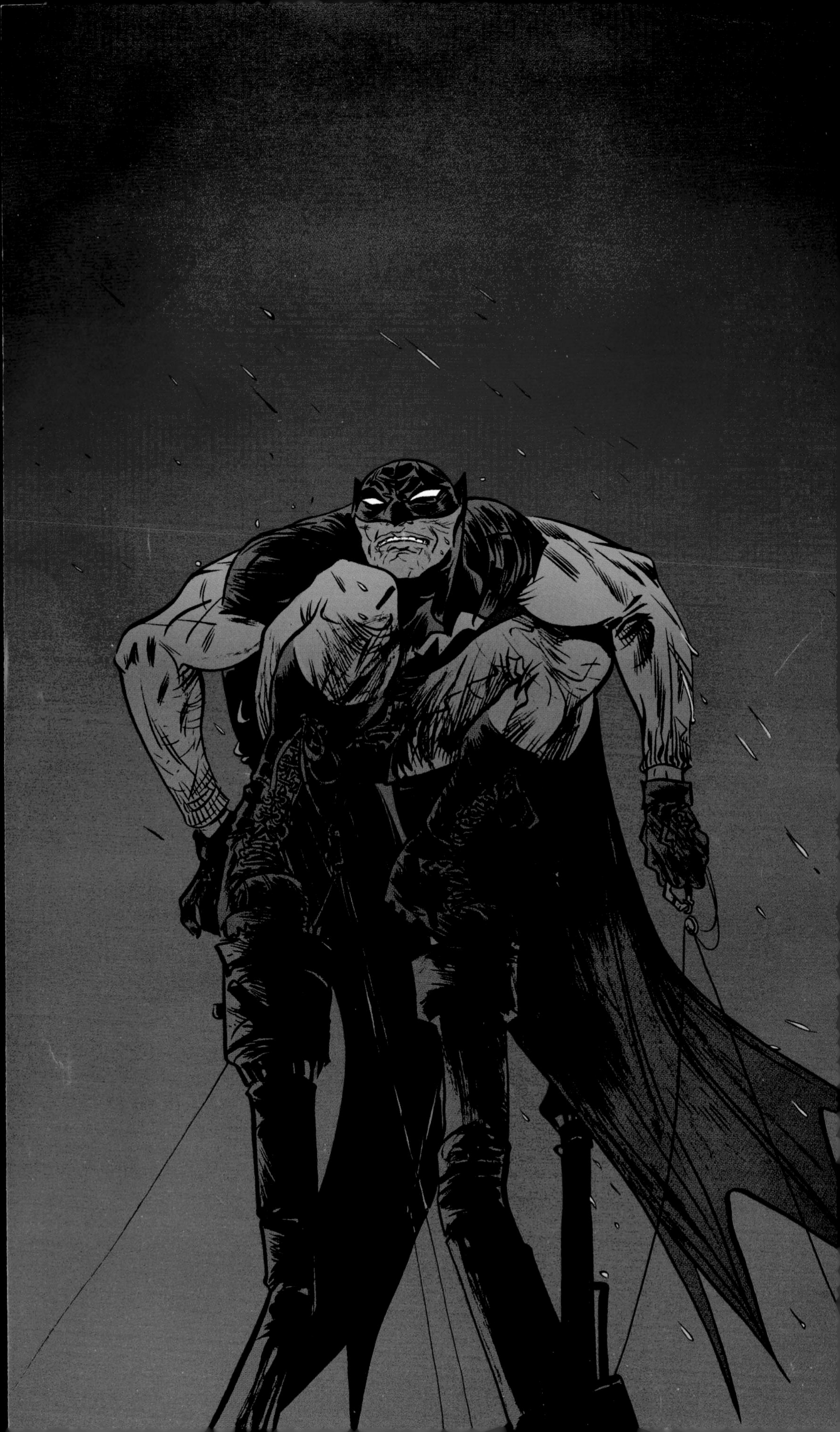

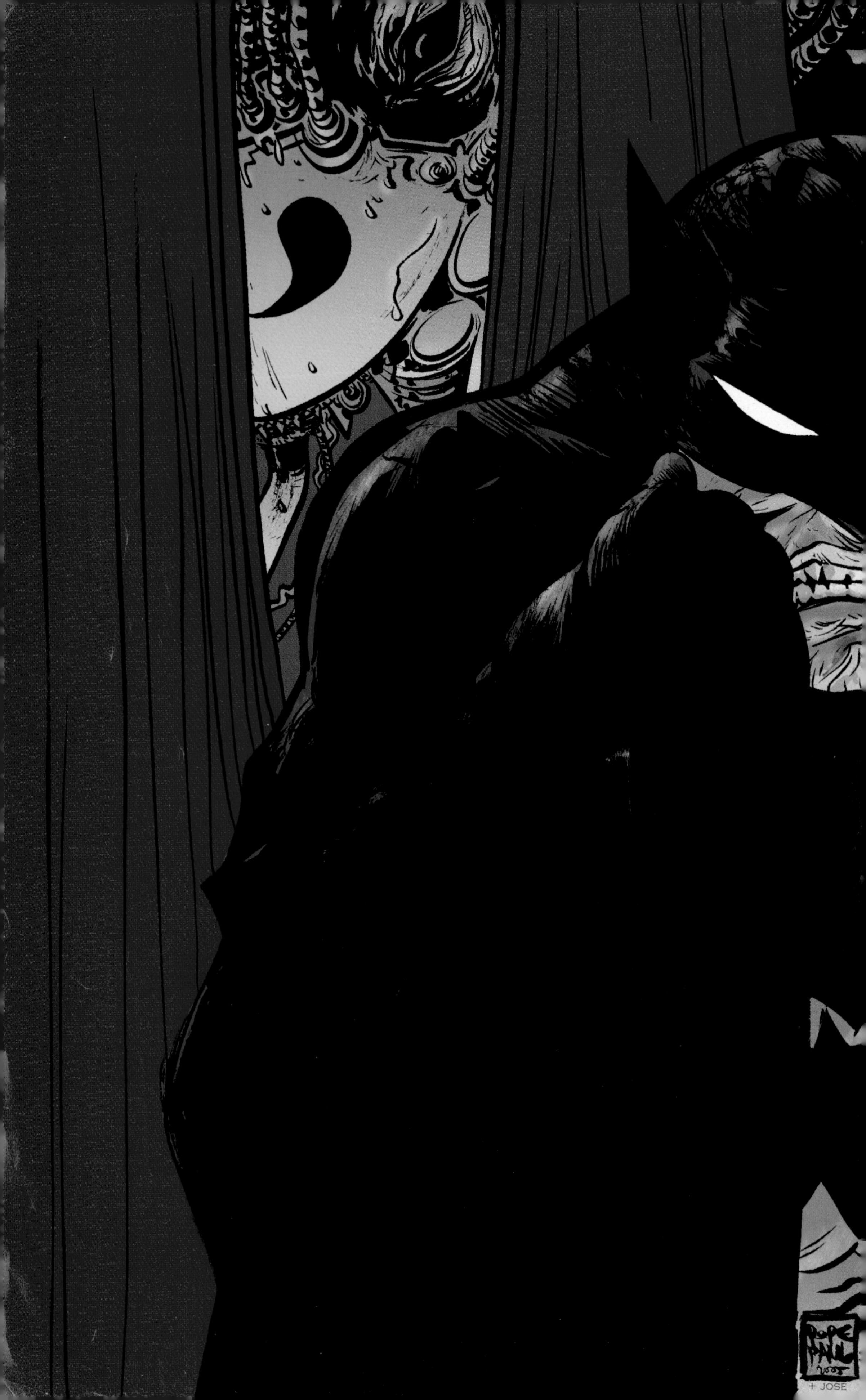
POPE PAUL
+ JOSE

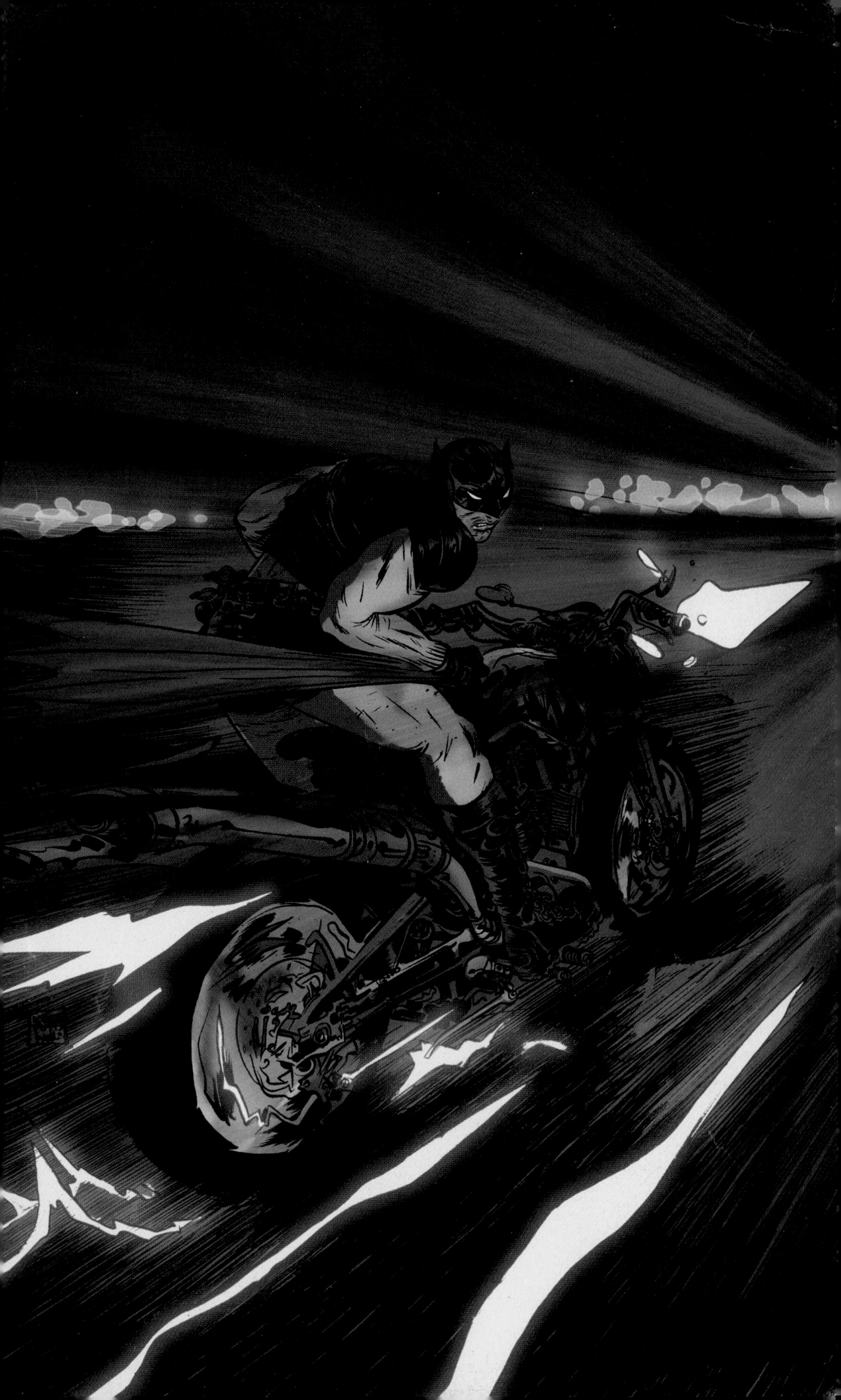

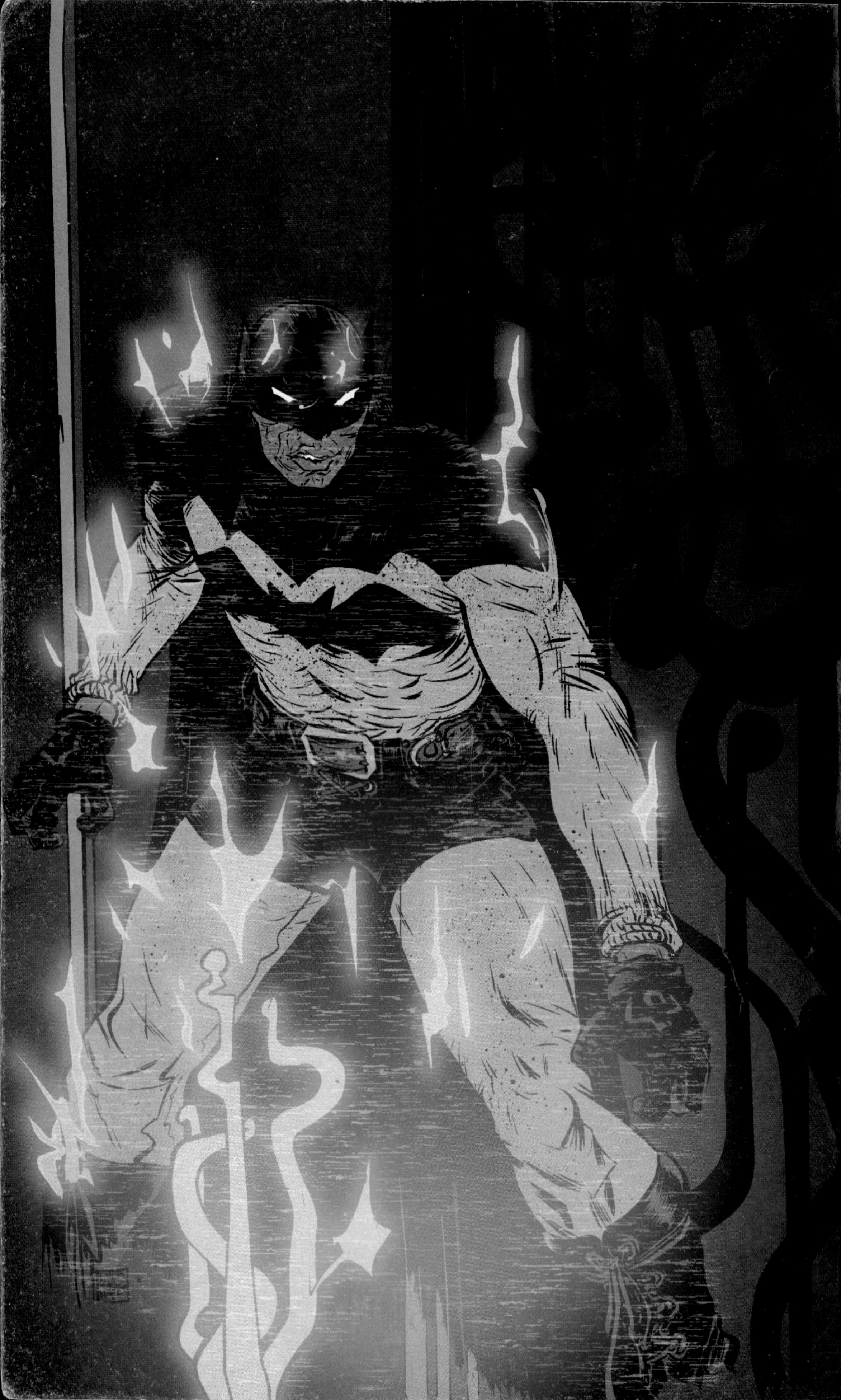